Philosophy of Law

Philosophy of Law: An Introduction provides an ideal starting point for students of philosophy and law. Setting it clearly against the historical background, Mark Tebbit quickly leads readers into the heart of the philosophical questions that dominate philosophy of law today. He provides an exceptionally wide-ranging overview of the contending theories that have sought to resolve these problems. He does so without assuming prior knowledge either of philosophy or law on the part of the reader.

The book is structured in three parts around the key issues and themes in philosophy of law:

- What is the law? – the major legal theories addressing the question of what we mean by law, including natural law, legal positivism and legal realism.
- The reach of the law – the various legal theories on the nature and extent of the law's authority, with regard to obligation and civil disobedience, rights, liberty and privacy.
- Criminal law – responsibility and *mens rea*, intention, recklessness and murder, legal defences, insanity and philosophies of punishment.

This new third edition has been thoroughly updated and extended again to include assessments of important developments in philosophy and law in the early years of the twenty-first century. Revisions include a more detailed analysis of natural law, new chapters on common law and the development of positivism, a reassessment of the Austin–Hart dispute in the light of recent criticism of Hart, a new chapter on the natural law–positivist controversy over Nazi law and legality, and new chapters on criminal law, extending the analysis of the dispute over the viability of the defences of necessity and duress.

Mark Tebbit is a Lecturer in Philosophy at the University of Reading. He is also Associate Professor and a Member of Faculty at the University of Notre Dame.

Philosophy of Law
An Introduction

Third edition

Mark Tebbit

 Routledge
Taylor & Francis Group

LONDON AND NEW YORK

Third edition published 2017
by Routledge
2 Park Square, Milton Park, Abingdon, Oxon OX14 4RN

and by Routledge
711 Third Avenue, New York, NY 10017

Routledge is an imprint of the Taylor & Francis Group, an informa business

© 2017 Mark Tebbit

First edition published by Routledge 2000
Second edition published by Routledge 2005

British Library Cataloguing in Publication Data
A catalogue record for this book is available from the British Library

Library of Congress Cataloging in Publication Data
Names: Tebbit, Mark, 1950- author.
Title: Philosophy of law : an introduction/ Mark Tebbit.
Description: Third edition. | Abingdon, Oxon [UK] ; New York : Routledge, 2017. | Includes bibliographical references and index.
Identifiers: LCCN 2016031115 | ISBN 9780415827454 (hardback : alk. paper) | ISBN 9780415827461 (pbk. : alk. paper) | ISBN 9781315281018 (ebook : alk. paper)
Subjects: LCSH: Law--Philosophy.
Classification: LCC K230.T43 A37 2017 | DDC 340/.1--dc23
LC record available at https://lccn.loc.gov/2016031115

ISBN: 978-0-415-82745-4 (hbk)
ISBN: 978-0-415-82746-1 (pbk)
ISBN: 978-1-315-28101-8 (ebk)

Typeset in Times New Roman
by Taylor & Francis Books

Contents

PART II
The reach of the law

Preface to third edition

There is much new material in this edition, along with extended treatment of many of the issues and themes raised in the first two editions in 2000 and 2005. Most of the changes aim to reflect the shift in focus of the discussion of philosophy of law and crime in the first decade and a half of this century. None of the existing material has been entirely removed, but much has been amended and expanded.

Part I on legal theory has been largely rewritten and restructured, opening with a more detailed commentary on traditional natural law and its critics. New separate chapters on legal realism, on Hart's concept of law and the recent criticisms of it, along with a more detailed chapter on the philosophical context of the rise and defeat of Nazism, are aimed at providing a more coherent account of the evolution of thinking about the nature of law from the early modern period to the twentieth century and beyond. In Part II on the 'Reach of the Law', which addresses three distinct problem areas that have shaped our contemporary world – obedience to law, human rights and the sexual revolution – there are some minor adjustments and additions to the chapters on the citizen's obligation to obey the law and on legal rights, for purposes of clarification and updating. Much of Part III on criminal law has been substantially revised, with longer discussions of the most striking cases. The chapter on responsibility has been replaced by separate chapters, one on recklessness and murder, and the other on the defences of necessity and duress, to reflect the closer attention these areas have been receiving in recent years.

The book is still presented in these three parts, and the three chapters in which postmodernism and other radical perspectives are explained and criticised, appear separately and unamended at the end of each part. Each of the chapters throughout the book is followed by a set of study questions and selections for suggested further reading on issues dealt with in that chapter. The main point of the study questions is to indicate typical questions that a student should be able to discuss at that stage of the course. They are also designed for use as essay titles and indicators of expected essay content. The suggestions for further reading draw attention to the most prominent contributions to the debates, and they have been selected on the principle of diversity of opinion within the tradition.

Acknowledgements

Above all, I want to thank Rosalind Dunning for her constant moral support and useful suggestions, especially on matters of law. I am also especially indebted to John Cottingham for his original encouragement to write these books, and for his critical readings of early drafts. In the Reading Philosophy Department, I have enjoyed the benefit of critical reactions from the Work-in-Progress Group over the years, especially from David Oderberg and Brad Hooker. Mention should also be made of the many anonymous Routledge readers, especially those from Malta and North America. I should also acknowledge some of the excellent reactions and contributions made by those students at Reading who took my Philosophy of Law and Philosophy of Crime modules since the 1990s. There are too many to cite all of them, but Daniel Whiting, John Evans and Jack Legon made memorable contributions, as did Isobel Aitken, Katy Fielding, Hannah Little, Chris Recaldin, George Fitzmaurice, Jo Morton and Melissa Hartley. In particular, I would like to thank Farbod Akhlaghi-Ghaffarokh for his exceptional insights into the central problems in criminal law, and for a constructive critical commentary on one of the chapters. Special praise should go to Sukh Thiara not only for her creative input, but also for her practical advice on countless problems and her unmatchable administrative skills, not to mention her infinite patience with dysfunctional members of staff. At the Notre Dame Faculty, I would like to thank Warren von Eschenbach for his occasional help with lectures when I was unable to give them, and his generally supportive response to my Philosophy of Law course. The Notre Dame students have been too numerous to give full acknowledgement to, but deserving of special mention for their insight and con-structive participation are Maureen Howard, Mary Clare McGregor and Nate Grams. The administrative efficiency of Alice Tyrell and Gemma Bencini has also been very helpful. I should not forget John Smallwood of Smallwood & Stewart for his invaluable legal advice during the preparation of the second edi-tion. I would like to thank again all the philosophy and law lecturers in the UK who responded so helpfully to my questionnaire in 1995, which made this project feasible. My thanks also go to the editors at Routledge, especially Tony Bruce and Rebecca Shillabeer, for their patience with deadlines. I am also indebted to James Thomas for his patient and thorough copy-editing of the final script. Finally, I really appreciate the e-mails I have received from around the world, especially from South America, since the appearance of the second edition.

Part I
What is the law?

1 Morality, justice and natural law

We all know what it means to break the law. It is perhaps the most fundamental fact governing our social behaviour that we understand the constraints and the pressures to stay within the law and the consequences of not doing so. The law is pervasive, controlling our lives in many more ways than we are usually aware; nevertheless, in most commonplace situations we have a fairly accurate knowledge of what the law requires and what it forbids. In those grey areas in which this is not clear, you might seek legal advice about your rights and obligations. In such situations, one thing you are unlikely to ask of a solicitor is where the law comes from, or, for that matter, why you should obey it; such questions would be quite inappropriate. These, however, are among the fundamental questions about the law. What exactly is the law? What does legal validity mean? What is a legal system? What is the 'rule of law'? These questions have been asked by legal philosophers since the first appearance of civilised legal systems, and the variation in answers has been of practical as well as theoretical significance. The purpose of this first chapter is to introduce the main points of disagreement on these questions and to explain some central strands of traditional approaches to an understanding of the meaning of law.

Morality and law at variance

The issue that stands behind nearly every controversy in contemporary legal theory is the problem of how law is to be understood in relation to moral values. A distinctively modern claim that any student of the subject will encounter almost immediately is the insistence that a systematic and rigorous analysis of the law requires 'the separation of law and morality'. This is frequently referred to as 'the separation thesis', and it is generally held to be the defining characteristic of legal positivism. Despite its apparent clarity, this thesis has been the source of much confusion and dispute. What does it mean to say that the law and morality are separate, that the law is one thing and morality is another? Before we proceed with the analysis of the various perspectives on law, it will be helpful to consider some ways in which law and morality appear to intersect and overlap, and other ways in which they clearly diverge.

Within the present-day common law jurisdictions, there is a general expectation that the written law and legal judgement will at least roughly approximate to prevailing moral values and moral judgements. A victim of a fraudulent contract or a libel, for example, seeks legal redress in the expectation that the court will adjudicate in the same manner as would any fair-minded individual independently of the legal context. In this respect, it seems that morality and the law have a common purpose. Similarly, the system of criminal justice is expected to reflect popular norms of approval and disapproval. The primary function of the criminal law is commonly taken to be the protection of people from those who threaten or violate the interests of others. The most characteristic criminal offences are those that are commonly regarded as morally wrong: assault, murder, theft, burglary, fraud, criminal damage and so on. In this respect also, it seems that the law is no more than the enforcement of a moral code, distinguishing right from wrong in much the same way. In short, if it is wrong, it must be illegal; if it is legal, it must be morally required or at least morally acceptable. To the extent that this is true, it can be said that there is a large area of overlap between morality and the law.

Closer examination, however, shows this to be a superficial assessment. There are in fact a number of distinct ways in which legal norms substantially diverge from moral norms. On the one hand, the law is in many respects *less* demanding than any serious moral code. The great majority of laws are prohibitions rather than positive commands, their main purpose being the negative one of establishing boundaries. The law generally does not require acts of charity or assistance that might be thought morally obligatory. In this sense, the law operates a minimal morality, based primarily on the need for restraint.

On the other hand, however, the law is in some senses *more* demanding than morality. In some relatively trivial respects, such as the requirements of bureaucracy or non-life-threatening traffic offences, it is arguable that one can break the law without doing anything morally wrong. What is often overlooked is that there are also more serious ways in which this can be the case. Legislation in the twentieth century has greatly extended the area of liability for harmful acts or omissions that are not directly intended and for which one would not normally be blamed. Whether or not this gradual extension of the 'duty of care' does actually reflect changing moral beliefs about responsibility is an issue about which more will be said in the course of the book. It is enough to say at this point that, on the face of it at least, the law has been ahead of popular perceptions of moral responsibility in this respect.

There is another distinct sense in which it can be seen that law and morality do not easily harmonise. Contemporary disagreement over such issues as the right to own firearms, the hunting of various kinds of animal, the stage of pregnancy at which abortions become unacceptable, the illegality of nearly every form of euthanasia, reveals an uneasy relationship between morality and the law. On such matters, the law cannot reflect the prevailing moral code, because there is no general agreement on the rights and wrongs at stake. In these contexts, the law must be out of step with morality, in the specific sense that it cannot match the prevailing moral beliefs of society as a whole.

The myth of the congruence between morality and law is also exposed by any reflection on the history of institutionalised injustice and the struggles for equality and human rights. Penal codes sanctioning excessively cruel or inappropriate punishment, the legal endorsement of slavery and the slave trade, the barring of religious and ethnic minorities from the professions, and the denial of civil rights to women have all been opposed primarily through pressure for legal reform. The Nazi Nuremberg laws, the laws establishing and upholding apartheid in South Africa, and the US racial segregation laws have all been taken as outstanding examples of manifest incongruence between morality and law.

Many of these, of course, have been in step with the prevailing local morality of the day, and hence there is no necessary antagonism between the state of the law and the demands of contemporary moral perceptions or sense of justice. It is only from the standpoint of moral objectivism that it can be argued that the demands of justice rise above any particular social belief system, and that such laws can be judged in absolute terms as right or wrong. Moral relativists tend to argue that what usually happens is that with the advance of civilisation, the law comes into conflict with evolving moral norms, as these practices are increasingly perceived to be wrong; and that the law continues to protect outdated moral beliefs until it is reformed. Either way – moral objectivist or relativist – these examples show that there is at least a permanent tension between morality and the law, and that moral values never rest easily with the state of the law at any given stage of its development.

The positivist separation thesis insists that the law is one thing and morality, or the moral evaluation of the law, is another. This means that the connection between law and morality is contingent; laws do not always coincide with moral values or moral codes. There is no necessary connection between morality and the law. A law does not have to conform with any moral standard to be counted legally valid. One thing the separation thesis does not mean, however, is that legislators and judges are concerned exclusively with legal matters and should be quite indifferent to the moral rights and wrongs of the law. This may in practice be true up to a point, if the administration of a specific law is concerned more with the protection of sectional interests than with promoting justice, or if a judge believes that he or she is obliged to apply the letter of the law even when it is morally counterintuitive. These, however, are mistaken interpretations of the meaning of the separation thesis, the function of which is primarily to develop an accurate description of the reality of law. This is a crucial point in legal theory, and it will be developed and clarified in the following chapters. To understand the prime target of the positivist separation thesis, we need first to focus on the concept of justice and the natural law theories that were built on an absolutist interpretation of this concept.

What is justice?

The concept of justice is not only the most prominent theoretical concept in the philosophy of law, equalled in importance only by that of 'law' itself, it is also so regular a feature of common discourse about public life that virtually everybody has an immediate intuitive understanding of it. It is one of those concepts – like 'being' or 'truth' – that is so readily understood, especially in the context of its negation, 'injustice', that any questioning of its meaning tends initially to cause consternation. We can all give examples of an injustice, but when faced with the direct abstract question of what exactly is the justice that is being denied, it is difficult to know where to start. One good starting point is to ask what kinds of thing the quality of justice can be ascribed to, and to confine our answer in the first place to common usage of words.

What rapidly becomes clear is that justice, as a fundamental moral concept, can only be ascribed in situations involving consciousness, rationality and a moral sense. The suffering caused by hurricanes, earthquakes or elephant stampedes is not in itself an injustice. What might be thought an injustice is the failure to relieve such suffering, or to help some at the expense of others. Justice is an issue only where there is conscious, purposive activity. Whether this is the activity of natural beings such as legal officials and emperors, or supernatural agencies such as angry or benevolent gods, the presence of conscious purpose is a necessary condition for speaking of justice.

The kinds of thing that can be described as just or unjust fall into three basic categories: agents, actions and states of affairs that are created by the actions of agents:

1   In traditional usage, the quality of justice is commonly attributed to individuals as such, a 'just God', 'a just monarch' or 'a just man'. Although this usage is still extant, it is more common today to speak of persons with a greater or lesser sense of justice. We also use the term collectively to describe governments, which can have a general reputation for justice or for tyranny.
2   It is also more common in contemporary discourse to ascribe justice to particular actions and decisions rather than to people as such. A just action or decision is one that is sensitive to the rights of all those affected by it. An unjust action or decision is one that violates these rights.
3   The institutions typically held to exhibit the qualities of justice or injustice in varying degrees are those of a human society, a rule of law and a legal system. A society can be just or unjust in different ways: it can be organised in such a way that its benefits or burdens are distributed unfairly, and 'an unjust society' can also be understood as one in which the discrimination against or persecution of minorities is commonplace. More specifically, a legal system – which is often assumed to be the very embodiment of the pursuit and protection of justice – can be just or unjust to a greater or lesser degree. Legal systems that fall into disrepute are those that, for

example, suspend *habeas corpus* or pervert the rules of evidence. Legal systems can be defective in other substantive ways, by failing to provide just and accessible remedies for civil wrongs, or by failing to develop an effective system of criminal justice. More specifically again, an unjust law is one that is perceived to perpetrate a formal or substantive injustice. For example, laws that are retrospective in their effect are widely regarded as unjust, because the subjects of the law are unable to decide whether or not to obey. In such cases, the form of the law is unjust. If there were a law, for example, preventing women from owning property, it would also be unjust in substance because there are no objective grounds for believing that they lack the ability to administer it.

The above threefold classification can be supplemented by Aristotle's pioneering analysis, which remains a classical point of reference for legal theory. Aristotle (384–322 BCE) divided justice into the distributive and the corrective (or 'emendatory'), the latter being subdivided into voluntary private transactions and involuntary transactions, the second distinction turning on the presence or absence of violence towards the victim of the injustice. This classification corresponds roughly to the distinction between social justice, civil justice and criminal justice.

Justice and equality

In the context of distributive justice, the problem of how the equality and inequality of status and entitlements between individuals are to be understood is paramount. Each political interpretation of what is to count as a fair distribution – whether rewards should be based on, for example, personal ancestry, individual worth and desert, effort or needs – has different implications for conclusions about political equality.

In sharp contrast, with both kinds of corrective legal justice, civil and criminal, the ideal of universal equality before the law is assumed. While it may often be true that legal practice falls short of the ideal, this equality in status between individuals who may be unequal in social standing or personal resources is one consequence of the first principle of formal justice, that 'like cases should be treated alike'. The relevant 'likeness' in this phrase lies in the actions and situations involved, rather than the types of people. This is not a timeless principle of formal justice, to be found in practice wherever there is a legal system; it is an ideal towards which civilised legal systems can generally be seen to be moving. It is a principle symbolised by the scales held by the statue of justice over the Old Bailey. The scales symbolise the essential aim of corrective justice as the restoration of a balance or equilibrium that has been tilted or broken. The scales also signify that all individual interests are weighed equally, while the symbol of justice blindfold signifies that all legal judgements will be made impartially, without favour or discrimination.

The development of formal justice

This aspiration to complete legal impartiality is one essential feature of what is known as the rule of law. If the justice in all kinds of human transactions is to be measured effectively, those transactions have to be governed by rules that are applied with as much consistency as it is possible to achieve. What this requires is the formalisation, and hence the depersonalisation, of justice. While the primitive human instinct for justice (for fair treatment, revenge, compensation) is inclined towards a holistic assessment of the merits of competing parties, or of the character of aggressors and victims, the development of legal justice must take the opposite direction. Moral principles and standards have to be formalised into unbending rules that then apply to the act, rather than the actor.

This formal conception of legal justice appears to many to run against the grain. It sometimes feels like an abandonment of real justice, which should surely take account of the full context and circumstances of a legal dispute or crime. The point of it, however, is that in the history of any legal system a stage is reached at which the influence of power and wealth on the administration of law is resisted and neutralised. When judicial independence is established, the ideal of impartiality – itself a precondition of equality before the law – can be developed. The outcome of such conflicts is a strong legal presumption in favour of the courts adhering to strict general rules, without which equality of treatment of parties would not materialise, leading to an arbitrary system of *ad hoc* decisions that would be no legal system at all.

The main purpose of corrective justice, then, in seeking to restore the equilibrium by penalising civil wrongs or criminal actions in proportion to the wrong or harm done, is to deliver this justice within the limits imposed by patterns of law that have already been established. This is one of the meanings of the phrase 'justice according to law'. Judges, it is generally held – especially in the light of the doctrine of binding precedent – are not free to arrive at what they in their conscience or individual wisdom believe to be the best decision; on the contrary, they are constrained to find the just decision *within the law*.

Justice, equity and the spirit of the law

Aristotle, who was writing both about the ideas of law and justice as such, and also about the realities of justice in the highly evolved legal system of ancient Athens, recognised the problems created by this systematisation of justice. While the strict application of general rules furthers the cause of judicial impartiality, its inflexibility does little for the adaptation of justice to individual cases that do not fall easily under such rules.

To counter the danger of justice becoming over-severe, Aristotle introduced the concept of equity (*epieikeia*), which he regarded as a quality intimately connected with, but distinct from and more precise than, justice. The equitable approach in law, for Aristotle, is aimed at the prevention of the unfortunate consequences of applying a general rule to a particular case that it does not, at a deep moral level, really cover. The feeling might be that while it is right in general that rule *X* should be applied, it does not really apply to this particular case *Y*, despite the formal requirements being fulfilled. For Aristotle, then, the function of the appeal to equity was to allow judges to temper the severity of legal justice, without departing from the constraints of law.

It is the *idea* of equity as a quality integral to law, rather than its place in the history of legal doctrine and practice, which is significant for disputes in the philosophy of law. The chequered history of its evolution, through Roman law and English common law, as the defining purpose of a higher court presided over by the Roman *praetor* or English Lord Chancellor, rendering 'equitable relief' to the victims of harsh justice in the lower courts, cannot be recounted here. What is of particular importance in this history is the role of conscience. The rationale behind the Chancellor's judicial intervention was to annul specific decisions, the outcome of which was unconscionable, or contrary to conscience.

If the spirit of equity is captured by the idea of an *ad hoc* overruling of the unconscionable, what does an 'equitable solution' mean? Does it imply that the equitable judge – for the specific purpose of this one case – casts aside the law in favour of a morally preferable standard? Or can this individualisation of justice be found within the ambit of law? This will ultimately depend, of course, on how we are to understand the concept of law. Does it exclusively consist of the explicit rules of 'black-letter law' as posited by a valid legal authority, or should it be taken in a wider sense to include the notoriously vague but irrepressible idea of 'the spirit of the law'? Those who are tempted to endorse the latter without further ceremony should bear in mind the conceptual problems here. 'Spirit' can be identified either with the justice with which the law is expected to be infused, or with the spirit of equity, which is to say that it can be contrasted either with a system of law that is indifferent to the requirements of justice, or with a rule-obsessed conception of justice that produces a repressively literalistic legal system. These are clearly two quite different senses in which 'the spirit of the law' can be interpreted.

Natural law theory and legal positivism

Despite these and other conceptual difficulties, the belief that justice is integral to law has been the guiding light of natural law theory since its inception. Firmly rooted in ancient philosophy and having undergone several significant revivals in the twentieth century, the evidence suggests that, despite its pre-scientific character and lingering religious connotations, the theory of natural law is not likely to disappear. In contemporary legal theory, however, legal positivism – the antithesis to natural law – is still in the ascendancy. It is the heart of this dispute that we need first to identify clearly.

The heart of the dispute with legal positivism

The exact nature of the conflict between natural law theory and legal positivism has always been, and remains, very difficult to pin down. While it is agreed on all sides that the dispute revolves around the question identified already, whether the concept of law must include the concept of justice, there is no general agreement as to the meaning of this conceptual inclusion. What does it mean to claim that justice is integral to law? There are two initial mistakes to be avoided here. The first common misconception is the drawing of a sharp practical contrast between a natural lawyer's concern with justice and human rights, and a positivist's supposed disregard of such matters. A further dimension of this mistake is the belief that positivists insist on obedience to the law, irrespective of how unjust it might be. The second, equally common, mistake is the assumption that the dispute is a purely theoretical one, with ultimately nothing substantive at stake at all. The truth of the matter is that there are substantive differences that cannot be resolved in a simplistic argument about which side values justice more highly.

The important point to note is that, given certain assumptions, each perspective appears to be wholly convincing. The two outlooks represent radically different ways of thinking, not only about the law, but also about the full range of ethical problems experienced in any kind of society. At the heart of the matter lies a conflict in intuition about the origin or source of law. Each confronts the question, 'What is law?' and each answers it in terms of where law comes from. Consider first the positivist answer to this question.

The legal positivist finds at the basis of law *a human convention*, something decided or stipulated at a determinate time, by flesh-and-blood individuals, for a particular purpose, with a specific function in mind. Law thus interpreted is an agreement in the sense that it is an outcome of decisions, rather than the issue of something beyond human control. The makers of these laws are people in a position of power sufficient to impose their will on the whole community, and the rules and sanctions thus put into effect might be implemented with or without consultation or consent. Either way, this is how laws are made; individual and collective decisions are the origin of law, and what law is can be explained in terms of what has been decided and laid down as law. These decisions or stipulations are essentially free creations. The laws thus created might reflect any interest or none, they may be steeped in wisdom and justice, or they might be widely regarded as tyrannical. Such considerations are irrelevant at the stage of the definition of law; the question as to how good or bad the laws are has no bearing on their status as laws. This is a 'conventionalist' view of law.

Consider now the natural law answer to the same question. 'What is law?' is again answered in terms of where it comes from. At the end of all analysis, the natural lawyer finds at the basis of law something beyond human control or arbitrary decision. It is something that binds human lawmakers quite irrespective of what any individual or group wishes or decides; it is a force we feel impressed upon us whether we like it or not. Law is the outcome, not of human agreement, but of first principles or natural foundations, the value of which runs deeper than the usefulness or expedience of conventions. This is a 'foundationalist' conception of law, according to which laws are discovered rather than made. The actual human makers of positive law are constrained by objective considerations relating to the intrinsic nature of the laws, considerations of justice that are external to the will of the legislators. If they ignore these constraints, they are not making law at all.

Although these are two incompatible answers to the same question, there is a certain discordance here, which suggests that the disagreement could be accounted for if it could be shown that they are in fact answering subtly different questions. While question and answer both follow the form of a definition, the first appears to be descriptive, the second stipulative. The first answer focuses on authority and the mechanisms of power, while the second focuses on authority and legitimacy. This might suggest that positivists are talking about the actual nature of the law, while natural lawyers are speaking of reasons for law being binding. This suggestion, however, leads to a serious misconstrual of the significance of the dispute; it implies that when the argument is clarified, the positivist and natural law approaches can be understood to complement one another, with the one concentrating on analysis of law as it actually exists, and the other addressing questions about the ideal standards to which law should aspire. This misses the heart of the dispute, because the leading exponents of each tradition are undoubtedly at odds over the definition of law as it actually exists. For natural lawyers, the legal principles revealed by a purely descriptive account of law are inherently moral; for positivists, the law in its actuality is the practical expression of a political decision, the moral content of which is quite irrelevant.

Traditional natural law theory

The main difficulty in forming a concrete assessment of the merits and contemporary relevance of natural law theory lies in the sheer magnitude of its historical scope. Spanning more than two millennia, the natural law idea has permeated many legal cultures in various societies which share little else in common with each other or the modern world we are familiar with. One of the defining beliefs of natural law is nevertheless the idea that there are fundamental moral truths that should hold in any human civilisation. The most significant natural law philosophers are all renowned at least as much for their wider theology and philosophy as for their jurisprudence. The four to be focused on here – the Greek philosopher Aristotle, the Roman statesman and philosopher Marcus Tullius Cicero (106–43 BCE), the theologian St Augustine (354–430 CE) and the Italian theologian and philosopher St Thomas Aquinas (1225–74) – are all major philosophers in their own right, who have had enormous influence upon philosophy up to the present day. Although this influence is highly diversified, there are a number of themes we can pick out as typically natural law.

Natural tendencies towards good and evil

First, we should ask why they use the word 'natural' regarding the true law. This has two meanings:

- 'Natural' is contrasted with 'civil', or the actual positive laws of the land.
- 'Natural' means that the law is rooted in human nature: all individuals are inclined by nature towards the good.

The most important question, then, is what humans are capable of in their natural state. The capacity for reason that all mature humans possess works against the evils that they are also capable of. We all know only too well how extensive these are, and that they range from ordinary selfishness and dishonesty to the terrible evils of violent crime and war. For natural law philosophers, the point or very purpose of all social institutions, especially the law, is to counteract these evils and promote and protect civilised values. The idea is that the natural inclination towards the good needs to be cultivated and refined. They are not suggesting that humanity is a race of angels – far from it – only that everyone is capable of acting rationally and contributing to the common good. This is what the law is there to facilitate.

We find a concise illustration of this stark opposition in Aristotle: 'Man, when he reaches the perfection of virtue is the best of all animals; but if he goes his way without law and justice he becomes the worst of all brutes' (Aristotle 1948: *Politics* 2). Aquinas in his commentary on Aristotle added this comment: 'For man, unlike other animals, has the weapon of reason with which to exploit his base desires and cruelty' (Aquinas 1948: *Summa theologiae* (ST) 1-2.95.1). The natural law idea is that evil and criminality are not to be explained by evil being an equally powerful instinct in individuals, but by the natural faculty of reason being distorted and leading people away from the common good.

The whole point of natural law, then, is to counter these worst characteristics of humanity. Genuinely 'human' acts are those based on reason rather than mere brute instinct. The purpose of human law is to instil in everyone the habit of following the natural law. So the first point to note is that nothing could be further from the truth than the popular caricature of natural law that sees it as naively believing in an ideal world in which everyone is naturally inclined only towards the good. Natural law philosophers do not believe this at all.

Why is natural law relevant today?

The main reason for the perennial appeal of natural law lies in the idea that the law is there to be found and as such can be seen as a rock upon which we can depend, as a reliable arbiter or point of reference in disputes and conflicts. It also implies that there are natural limitations on what can be enacted or enforced as positive law, and still properly be regarded as law. This idea has persisted through all natural law's permutations from its early origins in ancient Greece and Rome, through to the present day. It is expressed today in the not uncommon belief that legal officials, councils and governments cannot act in ways that are contrary to natural justice or reasonableness. This idea takes a stronger hold when it is realised that, when they do in fact act in such ways, it is within the power of judges in the higher courts to rule them illegal, or – for example in the USA – unconstitutional. On the face of it, then, there do appear to be natural constraints upon lawmakers.

Ancient natural law: Aristotle and Cicero

Elements of natural law theory were already well developed in the ancient world, most strikingly in the works of Aristotle and Cicero. The idea that all legislation and judicial decisions are constrained by natural limitations, which are discoverable by reason, found expression in their postulation of a timeless higher law governing all human affairs. What we have to ask is what sense can be made of this higher law, a law that is said to have greater authority than those that happen to be posited as the laws of the land at any given time. While the source was clearly religious, as the quoted passages will show, not all of ancient natural law philosophers did think that the natural law came from God – either directly or indirectly – but believed that there were nevertheless deeper sources or higher laws that could not be ignored. These are simply there, at a deeper level than that of our everyday awareness of the rights and wrongs going on around us. As we saw in the context of equitable modification of the law to avoid injustice, Aristotle pointed to the authority of equity as a more refined form of justice which could be applied to problems arising from the law. In a famous passage, in which he uses as an illustration Antigone's defiance of the tyrant Creon's decree that her brother just slain in battle shall remain without burial rites outside the city gates, Aristotle writes of the higher law as by definition one that does not change, in contrast to the decrees of positive law, which are constantly changing:

> If the written law tells against our case, clearly we must appeal to the universal law, and insist on its greater equity and justice ... we must urge that the principles of equity are permanent and changeless, and that the universal law does not change either, for it is the law of nature, whereas written laws often do change. This is the bearing of the lines in Sophocles' *Antigone*, where Antigone pleads that in burying her brother she had broken Creon's law, but not the unwritten law:

> Not of today or yesterday they are,
> But live eternal (none can date their birth)
> Nor would I fear the wrath of any man,
> And brave God's vengeance for defying them.

We shall argue that justice indeed is true and profitable, but that sham justice is not, and that consequently the written law is not, because it does not fulfil the true purpose of law.

(Aristotle 1924: *Rhetorica* 1.15)

The idea here is that there are some things that simply have to be done and other things that cannot be done – without a terrible violation of the natural law. This law continues through a succession of generations and civilised societies and survives any manifestation or denial of it. The edict at issue – the king prohibiting the burial rites for a dead brother – was one that excited a sharply focused abhorrence not only in the character Antigone, but in the audiences watching this play, who would have seen it as, in a peculiarly literal sense, an unnatural law. This seems to be why Aristotle chose it to dramatise the conflict between human law and natural law. Creon is deemed to have broken one of the natural limits that constrain the kind of laws that can be passed. It was of course within his power to use the law to enforce his will, but the point that natural law philosophers are always making is that a proclamation with all the trappings of legality, if it violates the natural law, has no authority whatsoever. It is precisely this higher law of nature that makes it legally void.

A similar line of thought was developed by Cicero a few centuries later. He echoed and developed the idea that properly constituted law does not guarantee its legality. For him, law is the highest product of the rational human mind when it is in tune with the elemental forces of nature. The validity of human law rests upon this attunement and harmonisation with these forces. It was this blending of reason and law with *nature* that showed that while it was possible for rulers to ignore the constraints of natural law, such actions ran against the grain of the natural order of things in a way that was unholy and blasphemous. In Cicero's uncompromising words:

Law is the highest reason, implanted in Nature, which commands what ought to be done and forbids the opposite. This reason, when firmly fixed and fully developed in the human mind, is Law. The origin of justice is to be found in Law, for Law is a natural force. True law is right reason in agreement with nature. To curtail this law is unholy, to amend it illicit, to repeal it impossible. One and the same law, eternal unchangeable, will bind all people and all ages. What of the many deadly, the many pestilential statutes which nations put in force? These no more deserve to be called laws than the rules a band of robbers might pass in their assembly. Law is the distinction between things just and unjust, made in agreement with that most primal and ancient of all things, Nature.

(Cicero 1928: *De Legibus* 1)

This passage had enormous influence upon later writings on natural law. Like Aristotle, it is pre-Christian but has shown itself to be compatible with either religious or secular world views. The idea of 'right reason' being in agreement with nature is particularly important. This means that reason is something that stands above any individual and simply has to be accepted as true. The idea that this reason is written into the very nature of things is the idea that it is not created or invented by human ingenuity, but is there to be found by those who want to find it. The other important feature of this passage arises from the 'pestilential statutes' which like Creon's edict have no more authority than those of brigands. This point, which of course links up with Aristotle before him, is also taken up and developed much later by the Christian natural law philosophers.

Christian natural law

In *The City of God*, St Augustine related a story of a pirate who defied the emperor Alexander the Great.

> In the absence of justice, what is sovereignty but organised brigandage? For, what are bands of brigands but petty kingdoms? They also are groups of men, under the rule of a leader, bound together by a common agreement, dividing their booty according to a settled principle. If this band of criminals, by recruiting more criminals, acquires enough power to occupy regions, to capture cities, and to subdue whole populations, then it can with fuller right assume the title of kingdom, which in the public estimation is conferred upon it, not by the renunciation of greed, but by the increase of impunity. The answer which a captured pirate gave to the celebrated Alexander the Great was perfectly accurate and correct. When that king asked the man what he meant by infesting the sea, he boldly replied 'What you mean by warring on the whole world. I do my fighting on a tiny ship, and they call me a pirate; you do yours with a large fleet, and they call you Commander.'
>
> (Augustine 1958: *City of God* 4.4, pp. 88–9)

The main point to note is that the first half of this quote is a very bold denunciation of those who through force have illicitly acquired the trappings of power and are enabled by their plundered wealth to conceal their criminal past. If this applied to the emperor Alexander, it was true also of many other rulers in subsequent world history. Augustine's second point, illustrated by the pirate story, is that the mere power of any emperor – no matter how great – does not in itself give him any more authority than that of a criminal or a pirate. It is only *the justice* of the laws of the emperor that gives them their authority and legitimacy. Hence it is at a fundamental level that law and morality cannot be separated.

St Thomas Aquinas

By far the most important of the medieval natural law philosophers was St Thomas Aquinas, who is widely regarded as the greatest of the Christian

theologians. It was Aquinas, a very learned scholar of Aristotle, who synthesised ancient natural law theory with Christian theology. At the heart of this
synthesis he laid down a fourfold distinction between different levels of law:

1   Eternal law: God's plan for the world, known only to Himself. 'The
    whole community of the universe is governed by divine reason. Thus the
    rational guidance of created things on the part of God, as the Prince of
    the universe, has the quality of law. This we can call the eternal law.'
2   Natural law: that part of God's law accessible to us through the use of
    Reason. 'The light of natural reason' is 'the impression of the divine light
    in us'. The 'participation in the eternal law by rational creatures is called
    the natural law'. As rational beings, we derive from God's reason 'a natural
    inclination to such actions and ends as are fitting'.
3   Human law: those laws declared by human authorities that are derived
    from, or are at least consistent with, natural law. Tyrannical law, which
    deviates from reason, 'is not law at all, in the true and strict sense, but is
    rather a perversion of law'.
4   Divine law: that part of God's law as made known to us through revelation.
    This is needed in addition to natural law and human law, because (a) we
    need guidance towards our salvation; (b) divinely given laws are infallible,
    whereas human reason is not; (c) enacted laws deal only with external
    activities; (d) the divine law punishes all manner of sin, not all of which is
    punishable by human law. (Aquinas 1948: ST 1-2.91.4–12)

There are a number of points that should be noted here. What makes
Aquinas a natural law thinker rather than a subscriber to any of the rival
theologies is the central place he accords to the faculty of Reason. It is through
this that the natural law is accessible to us. Most will acknowledge reason as a
distinctive human ability, but he sees the source of it as divine, and the
cosmos as an extension of the mind of God. Reason governs the universe as
created by the all-powerful God. We should not conclude from this, though, that
Aquinas saw the unconstrained will of a self-sufficient God as the sole moral
authority behind Christian natural law. It is through 'the light of natural
reason' – the unique gift from God that enables us to become moral agents –
that we as conscious reasoning beings are able to distinguish good from evil,
and free to choose one over the other. This means that we do not have to rely
solely on revelation (through the scriptures) to understand God's will. We
have the faculty of reason to discover it if we put our minds to it. This claim was
to have lasting importance for legal theory. It should be noted that under the
fourth level, Aquinas describes human reason as the kind of fallible mental
power we are all familiar with, in contrast to the perfect or ideal reason as it
is in itself, in the hands of God.

The way of thinking that emerges from Aquinas's theology is complex, but
what follows here are the essential points. The most fundamental precept of
morality and law is to do good and avoid evil. The good is defined in terms of

the promotion and defence of the basic goods, of human life, procreation, knowledge and sociability. All the non-basic precepts are derived from this fundamental precept relating to good and evil. As a general maxim, it might be objected, 'doing good' – and 'avoiding evil' for that matter – is highly abstract, and could be claimed by any government or ruling individual who first defines good and evil according to criteria convenient for their own purposes. This is why Aquinas links it to the concept of the common good, which is of central importance to natural law thinking. All law must be directed at the common good – the whole community, not a minority interest or even the majority. This is a communitarian philosophy, which long pre-dates the individualism of the modern epoch in the evolving liberal democracies, when the idea of the common good shifted from the community as a whole to the majority of society. So the first concern for Aquinas is the community taken as an unbroken whole. 'The correct definition of law ... is nothing else than a rational ordering of things which concern the common good; promulgated by whoever is charged with the care of the community' (ST 1-2.90.4). 'The law must have as its proper object the well-being of the whole community' (ST 1-2.90.2).

Aquinas's moral philosophy is a version of what is called intrinsicalism. What makes actions good or bad is their inherent character, rather than anything external to them, such as their consequences. Actions are good or bad in varying degrees in themselves. They are not good because God has commanded them; they are commanded because they are intrinsically good. They are not assessed in an instrumentalist manner according to what they are good for. An act of kindness or charity is seen as an intrinsic good, just as an act of gratuitous cruelty is held to be an intrinsic evil. What follows from this is one of the most famous features of natural law, its rejection of the kind of moral thinking that allows the calculation of good ends to justify the adoption of immoral means to achieve them. To put it bluntly, evil means can never be justified by the good ends that might come out of them. To be morally acceptable in the eyes of God, the means selected must be integrated with the outcomes intended or hoped for. At the same time, this is one of the most difficult of natural law principles, because it has never been easy to identify with any precision the kinds of means that must be excluded, or how bad they have to be. Aquinas nevertheless rejected this means–ends thinking as a general principle and in its place he promoted the alternative principle – which has become a 'doctrine' – of double effect. This applies throughout society to all practising Christians, who are told that one may not do evil that good may come out of it, but it is directed in particular at rulers to constrain the methods they use for the defence of the state and the community. The injunction is always to try to adhere to and promote the good, while accepting that there are sometimes unavoidable negative or evil side-effects – hence 'double effect' – of actions that have to be taken for the common good, such as the defence of the realm. The central constraint is that these side-effects can never be directly intended, or chosen as a means to a greater end. Achieving victory in a just war – the example in Aquinas's mind being the defence of Christendom – must

be constrained in its methods by this principle. This promotion of the doctrine of double effect is connected with the defence of absolute values, in the
sense that there are some evils that are completely prohibited. There are some
types of action that are wrong in all circumstances, especially the intentional
killing of the innocent, for whatever purpose. We will see in later chapters
how important this principle has become in more recent times.

One of the most controversial aspects of Aquinas's legal philosophy arises
from his definition given above of the third level of 'human law'. It is of course
clear why he lays it down that all laws that are human-made should be derived
from or at least consistent with the natural law that we are aware of through
our God-given reason. When he turns to 'tyrannical law', however – the law
which deviates from reason – he is more cautious in his response to it than
either Cicero or St Augustine, both of whom had equated such law with that
of plundering villains and criminals, who would command no respect at all.
Here one should note the careful language of Aquinas, describing perversions
of law as being not in the true and strict sense law. The important point is that
he was not here declaring such bad laws to be outright invalid, as others had
done, but rather suggesting that they fall short of the ideal and are thus
defective as law. Elsewhere, he expressed his condemnation more strongly:

> [The prince's] will, if it is to have the authority of law, must be regulated
> by reason when it commands. It is in this sense that we should under-
> stand the saying that the will of the prince has the power of law. In any
> other sense the will of the prince becomes an evil rather than law.
>
> (ST 1-2.90.3)

'An evil rather than law', if taken literally, would mean that it was no law at all,
rather than merely bad law. It is quite doubtful, however, that Aquinas intended
his comments on bad or perverted law to suggest that this negative quality
undermined it as law in the sense that it invalidates it, such that it can simply be
disregarded as law. On this issue, he made an important distinction. In most cases,
there are good pragmatic reasons to accept the authority of a law deemed to be
unjust, mainly for the avoidance of social disturbance. There are some cases,
however, when human statutes do lose their authority as law and it might even be
one's duty to disobey them. The example he gives is that of a law commanding
direct offences against God, for example blasphemy or the worship of false idols.
The ambivalence – or perhaps due caution – exercised by Aquinas on this issue
has persisted right through the history of natural law philosophy, and we will
see this controversy raised again and again, in the context of the obligation or
otherwise to obey laws or legal systems widely regarded as iniquitous.

Conclusion

The fortunes of natural law have fluctuated over time, especially in the
modern period, which in the West has seen a process of steady secularisation.

This process, as we shall see, does not spell the death of natural law philosophy, because its roots go deeper than a dependency on any set of religious beliefs. The conflict between natural law and its critics is not essentially a religious one, but is rather the expression of very different responses to the question of how we should understand the status of law as posited by authorised rulers. In the following chapters, we will see how alternative perspectives on the law and its relation to morality and justice have developed.

Study questions

General question: What are the main differences distinguishing natural law from positivist theories?

Further study questions: How does Aquinas use the concept of reason to construct his natural law philosophy? Think of ways in which law overlaps with morality. Explain the conflict between the natural law and positivist interpretations of such overlaps. What are the implications of the natural law insistence that the connection between law and morality is necessary, or conceptual? How would you explain the difference between these two theories in terms of justice and equity? Are either of them indispensable to the concept of law? Is the spirit of the law more important than the letter of the law? Is the pursuit of justice an essential feature of law?

Suggestions for further reading

For a general historical treatment of traditional theories of law, see J. Kelly (1992) and Lloyd (1964).

On the conceptual relation between law and morality generally, see Lloyd (1964: ch. 3), Lyons (1984) and Fletcher (1996: ch. 3). For general introductions to the natural law–positivist dispute, see Meyerson (2007: ch. 2), Golding and Edmundson (2005: ch. 1), Rommen (1947), D'Entreves (1951), Golding (1975: ch. 2), Lyons (1984: ch. 3), M. Davies (1994) and Harris (1997: ch. 2). For more advanced studies, see further reading in Chapter 6 below.

Aristotle's writings on justice and equity are mostly contained in the *Nicomachean Ethics* (Aristotle 1985) and *Politics* (Aristotle 1948). See also the articles by Burns (1998) and Schroeder (1981). The relevant writings of Cicero on law and justice can be found in the first book of *De Legibus* (Cicero 1928). Excellent commentaries include Baraz (2012), Powell and North (2001) and Zetzel (1999).

For Aquinas on natural law, see Aquinas (1948) and (1988a) or (1988b). Among the numerous books on Aquinas that stand out, Eleonore Stump (2003) and John Finnis (1980) are recommended. A good general book on justice is T. Campbell (1988). See also, Meyerson (2007: ch. 7).

2   From common law to modern positivism

Common law today

The common law model for the legal system is predominant in the English-speaking world today. It is followed by Great Britain and Ireland, the United States and Canada, Australia and New Zealand, and the great majority of other countries which were once part of the British Empire, and are now or have been among the fifty-three members of the Commonwealth, the largest of which is India. The main alternative types of legal system are generally known as civil law, which originates in Europe and is the ultimate source for many other systems. Also important are socialist law – including China, Cuba, North Vietnam and North Korea today, Russia and many East European countries until the early 1990s – and religious law, most commonly sharia (Islamic) law, which is predominant in the Middle East and North and West Africa. Others such as Israel, South Africa and Singapore are strongly influenced by common law, but are hybrid systems, mixing common law with other sources and types of law. It should be emphasised that many of these jurisdictions are in the early twenty-first century still in a state of transition. Each of these types of system have entirely different traditions and local customs behind them. English and American common law accounts for over half of the population of the world, and it is this type of legal system that is the main focus of Anglo-American legal theory.

Roots of common law and common law theory

Although the common law systems we know in the twenty-first century have changed enormously since their inception almost a thousand years ago, these origins in early medieval England are important for understanding what it has become and how it works today. The system evolved gradually in the centuries following the Norman Conquest in 1066, influenced by elements of both pre-Conquest Saxon law and the invading Normans. By the thirteenth century, it could be said that there was a distinctively English common law system. This was based on a recognition of the authority of precedent, such that previous judicial decisions, provided they were made by a court of equal or higher status, had to be followed for cases in which the facts were essentially the same. This was known as the doctrine of *stare decisis* (to stand by the decision), which was derived from Roman law, and was at least ostensibly for the sake of consistency and fairness to the defendants and litigants. It was also to ensure continuity and stability. The authority of statute, however, was eventually recognised as an essential part of the overall common law system, so that the law on particular issues could be changed by decree from above. The statute was then said to be superimposed on case law. The role of statutes began in earnest in the thirteenth century and developed steadily over the centuries that followed, though case law was still in the ascendancy.

Common law systems today recognise the authority of both statute law and case law, each of which plays an indispensable role. This has allowed that case law in any area of law continues to develop, with intermittent interventions by government statute. As we shall see, though, the idea that law develops strictly through precedent within the confines of case law seems to be at odds with the doctrine of *stare decisis*. If the judges are really standing by every past decision, it might be asked, how can the law develop or change at all? In particular, how could they adapt to new circumstances and changing moral beliefs and values in society? The idea most deeply associated with common law thinking – past and present – that the judges are obliged *to declare existing law* rather than to legislate from the bench, so to speak, was the product of the belief that interpreting past precedent was a matter of finding what was lawful and thereby right. The thought that these might be different was unthinkable. To many modern critics, this approach is seen as a pretence, concealing what is really a legislative role, and by others as an indicator of the strong conservative tendency of common law. This controversy continues today.

Traditional common law theory has often been assimilated to natural law, but as we shall see, it is not as simple as that. Medieval common law theory was dominated by the writings of Ranulf de Glanville and Henry de Bracton, in the twelfth and thirteenth centuries, both of them developing and expanding common law at the expense of its rivals, canon (church) law and local law. Their writings showed multiple influences, from English, European and Roman law. They were nevertheless quite strongly aligned with the traditional motifs of natural law – law as the embodiment of justice, the rootedness of law in reason, and so on. The important developments, however, came at the outset of the early modern period, with two chief justices, Sir Edward Coke (1552–1634) and later Matthew Hale (1609–76). Both were major figures in the law at a time of a revolutionary conflict that was to culminate in the 1688 settlement, which would transform the relationship between the monarch and the representative parliament.

The theories of common law articulated by Coke and Hale overlapped extensively, but their understanding of the nature of law diverged in significant ways. For both of them, law was the accumulation over many generations of judicial wisdom which commanded reverence. They both nevertheless believed judges to be the spokesmen for the values embedded in the community, rather than the law being imposed from above. However, for Coke, who was embroiled in constitutional conflicts with the monarch James I early in the century, the common law was the embodiment of eternal and unchanging principles of natural justice. For Hale, it was in a state of slow organic evolution. The social customs on which it supposedly depended, were as much subject to change and evolution as anything else. This gave them different views of the role of precedent. Coke notoriously cleaved to the opinion that the common law had not changed on matters of principle for a thousand years or more, since long before the Norman Conquest. Under the surface, he believed that all its principles remained intact and unchanged. All appearance of change he saw as degenerative or as deviations from the true law. This apparently eccentric view of it is partly explained by Coke's championing of the liberties of the English people against sovereign monarchs. Arguing that these were ancient liberties that had been acknowledged since time immemorial made a better case than appealing to abstract ideas of liberty. So there were reasonable ideas within this myth. It presupposed the complete independence of the law from the sovereign, who was as much subject to it as anyone else. This was a deeply ingrained natural law idea, that 'the law' stood above everyone, judges and sovereigns alike. While Hale largely agreed with such ideas, for other reasons, he took the more realistic view that the law of the land was indeed changing, sometimes slowly, sometimes more quickly – as in his own time – but there was still continuity if not identity with the past. Even through the changes, the law remains the same body of common law.

Coke's views on the kind of reason exercised in the courts brought him into conflict with the king because he thought of it as a specifically legal mode of reasoning, which could only be acquired by great learning of immensely complex details of common law – which of course the king did not have – hence the judges were uniquely qualified to declare what the law on any matter was. It also marks out his kind of common law thinking from traditional natural law approaches, which see natural reason as that which is available to all honest people of ordinary intelligence. For Coke, legal reasoning derived from devotion to such learning was by contrast *artificial*, which is to say that it does not come by nature, but by unnatural application to learning, leading to the conclusion that legal knowledge rests upon the wisdom of the best judicial minds through the ages, as handed down through the legal profession, and that this law is largely 'unwritten' – in the sense that its authority does not depend upon any particular written legal work – and that this handing down has been going on 'since time immemorial'. This doctrine appealed to judges, but antagonised everyone else, especially as the country moved towards a more democratic political system. In the centuries to come, the conflicts would be more with the elected parliamentary government than with the monarch. Philosophers and other commentators criticising the theory and practice of common law saw in such interpretations of law a kind of unwritten font of wisdom, accessible only to highly learned specialists, a licence for judges to throw up smokescreens around their decisions and to be answerable to nobody.

Early positivism: an age of philosophical transition

The reaction against classical common law thought was not developed overnight. The rise of the positivist perspective that would transform the idea of law was a long slow process which had its roots in an intellectual revolution that would shake the whole of European thought, not merely the realm of jurisprudence. As a distinctively modern school of legal thought, positivism was not established until well into the nineteenth century, primarily through the writings of Jeremy Bentham (1748–1832), the founder of modern utilitarianism. Legal positivism has evolved as a school of thought in its own right, but there is little doubt that it owed its origins, in substance as well as name, to positivist thinking as a whole, which grew out of the seventeenth-century revolution in philosophy and scientific method. Although 'positivism' as a general term is notoriously vague, it can be said to signify a body of doctrines associated with the belief that human knowledge is confined within the limits of what can be observed and recorded.

As a particularly rigorous form of empiricism, positivism was one of several directions that the new philosophy could have taken. Traces of it had always existed within the empiricist reaction to rationalistic interpretations of the world. In retrospect, many distinct features of positivism can be seen in ancient Greek and Roman philosophy, and more clearly in the medieval philosophy of William of Ockham. The spirit of positivism as exemplified by these forerunners and by those of the early modern period is best captured by Ockham's celebrated 'razor', a methodological principle according to which it is illegitimate, for the purposes of explanation, to appeal to entities not strictly required by the explanation. In all our investigations of the natural world, there must be a presumption against theories that postulate a complex of unseen entities when a more simple explanation is available. This was not merely a deliberate bias against the unobserved; simplicity and economy are themselves regarded as explanatory virtues. The positivist assumption is that the more simple and economic the explanation, the more likely it is to be true.

The first feature of the positivist approach in modern philosophy, common to all versions, is the guiding principle that, in the search for knowledge and truth, the evidence of the senses is paramount. Second, the doctrine of phenomenalism, which first appeared in Berkeley, stipulates that we are not entitled to assume the existence of anything beyond the appearances. With sound scientific method, there should be no distinction between appearance and essential reality. Third, there is a strong tendency towards nominalism in most positivist philosophers. This rests on the principle that takes the referents of a general term to consist exclusively in concrete individual instances of that term. Underlying these three features, we always find – at least implicitly – the normative principle that, in the absence of empirical evidence to the contrary, the simplest explanation is to be preferred.

The overall purpose behind this positivist enterprise was the exclusion of every trace of speculative metaphysics from investigations of natural phenomena, the understanding of which depended on the discovery of natural causes that were in principle observable. What was resisted was reference to any underlying essence or principle that was in its nature unobservable. This much is perhaps an obvious implication of the main features of the positivist programme. What is probably less obvious is that the same programme also implied, from the outset, a radical change in attitude to questions of human value. If all reference to things other than concrete, observable particulars were to be eliminated from science, and science is the only form of knowledge, then moral and aesthetic judgements about such qualities as 'worthwhile', 'elegant', 'commendable' and so on, have also to be removed from the realm of knowledge and truth. One of the enduring positivist assumptions is that the objects of such value judgements are not given in experience in the sense that they are separable from the bare factual existence of particular things, and are therefore inaccessible to scientific investigation. The full impact of this exclusion of value by the scientific revolution as interpreted by positivism was not felt until it was spelt out in detail by Hume.

Hume's influence

The exact nature of the influence of David Hume (1711–76) on European philosophy has always been controversial, but there is a hard core that is undisputed. Our concern here is limited to the themes that are relevant to legal theory, in particular the rise of positivism and the eclipse of natural law. Hume's fundamental purpose in his philosophical writing was twofold: to challenge the traditional framework of moral philosophy in such a way that morality and law would be humanised by becoming more relative to human interests; and to undermine the overblown pretensions to knowledge of the rationalist philosophers of the Enlightenment. In carrying out this purpose, Hume inadvertently did much to establish the conceptual framework within which the transformation of every discipline into a rigorous science would be undertaken.

Hume stipulated two conditions for speaking with good sense on any subject. The first – which is known as 'Hume's Fork' – is that all investigations should be confined to the reporting of experimental observation on the one hand ('matters of fact') and the rational elucidation of 'relations between ideas' (logical connections) on the other. The second condition is that such matters of fact should be understood in complete independence from any subjective evaluation of the factual subject matter (the much quoted 'separation of fact and value'). Reasoning that moves from matters of fact to matters of value results in confusion and nonsense. This is the philosophical source of the separation thesis in jurisprudence. The facts of the matter are one thing. Evaluations are another.

To these two claims, Hume added a third essential point concerning the nature of this reasoning. Contrary to the suppositions of his predecessors, Hume argued that the faculty of human reason is perfectly inert and morally neutral: 'It is not contrary to reason to prefer the destruction of the entire world to the scratching of one's little finger' (Hume 1972: 2.3.3, p. 157). The idea here is that reason has no bearing on human interests one way or the other. When this idea is applied to the first two conditions, the Humean implications for the human sciences become clear. If reason is morally neutral, the rational investigation of any kind of human behaviour or institution will make no reference beyond what is either empirically observable or logically demonstrable. The two cannot be combined. Second, the investigation will have nothing to reveal about the moral content of its subject matter. The moral worthiness of any human activity is not in itself open to rational analysis. Approval or condemnation may be felt by a subjective moral sense, but this is no more than the projection of an inner feeling onto an external object. The implications of Hume's austere proposals, when drawn out, would transform the very idea of law.

Bentham's utilitarianism and his attack on the common law tradition

The beginning of the decline of natural law theory can be dated quite precisely from the time of Bentham's scathing attack in his *Fragment on Government* in 1776 on William Blackstone's (1723–80) *Commentaries on the Laws of England*. With hindsight, this can be seen as the historical turning point, the successful launching of modern legal positivism. Bentham's attack on the common law tradition was based upon his utilitarian philosophy, according to which all actions and institutions (including legal systems and laws) are to be judged solely in terms of their utility. A specific law, for example, is good or bad to the extent that it produces on balance more happiness than unhappiness, which Bentham measured in terms of pleasure and the absence of pain. On this way of thinking, the role of reason changes. It cannot distinguish just from unjust dealings without reference to consequences in terms of human welfare. The role of reason is removed from the central place it holds in natural law theory and reduced to that of rationally calculating the external consequences of actions and laws in terms of the aggregate good that will come out of them.

Bentham had many specific complaints about common law theory and its practice, which was closely tied to, though not identical with, the traditional natural law theories. He regarded much of what happened in the English courts as 'dog-law': that is, as the practice of waiting for one's dog to do something wrong, then beating it. His low opinion of the doctrine and practice of judicial precedent was illustrated by his likening of it to a magic vessel from which red or white wine could be poured, according to taste. This 'double fountain effect', whereby the decisions of judges are seen as capricious selection of whichever precedent suits their prejudice, was regarded by

Bentham as the inevitable outcome of a legal system that is not controlled by principles of utility.

Bentham's overriding passion for legal reform required the kind of clarification that would mercilessly expose the shortcomings, the corruption and obfuscation which he found in the common law as it existed at the turn of the nineteenth century. This clarity, Bentham believed, could only be achieved with a rigorous separation of law and morality. As we have seen, the exact meaning of this 'separation thesis' has become deeply controversial. What Bentham himself meant by it was reasonably clear. If the law was to be subjected to systematic criticism in the cause of reform, it was essential that its workings should first be described in accurate detail. This was a matter of dispassionate factual reporting of the nature and workings of law, which he termed 'expository' jurisprudence. What he found obstructing this project of clarification was the blurring of the boundary between legal reality and value judgement.

This was precisely what Bentham accused traditional legal writers of doing. Blackstone, as one of the most eminent of these common law writers in the eighteenth century, was singled out by Bentham as a prime example of one who clothed moral preaching in the language of law. When law is analysed in such a way that each statute is represented as the embodiment of a Christian moral principle and a perfect expression of 'reason', the result is the kind of vagueness and indeterminacy that is inherently resistant to radical reform on the basis of the utility of the laws. When, by contrast, law is analysed according to Bentham's expository principles, the way is prepared for a clear-headed 'censorial' jurisprudence, subjecting the law to moral criticism, based on the principles of utility, principles that for Bentham were fundamental to legal reform, and were anathema to traditional natural law and common law thinking. Bentham's stated objective was to untangle the common law integration of law and morality which had evolved in such a way that the law, properly interpreted, was always seen as morally sound, when to observers like himself it clearly was not. More often than not, it needed to be measured against the standards of utility and changed, from above.

Austin's legal positivism

Bentham's disciple John Austin undertook a systematic investigation into what constitutes law, cutting through the mystifications of common law ideology and completely rejecting the precepts of natural law thinking. Austin developed his own distinctive version of utilitarianism for purposes of law reform, but as far as legal theory was concerned, he followed Bentham in keeping factual description and explanation clearly separate from moral evaluation. Indeed he made a point of emphasising this separation.

Austin did not follow Bentham's antipathy towards judge-made law (Austin 1995 [1832]: 163). On the contrary, he sees judges as those deputised by the supreme commanding sovereign precisely in order that they legislate and adjudicate well. What he objects to strongly, though, in statutory legislators as much as in judges, is the practice of obscuring the law with pronouncements on moral obligations, upon which the lawmakers or the judges can impose their own interpretation. When they do this, they can make the law mean whatever they want it to.

What exactly did it mean for Austin to keep law apart from morality? The famous passage relating to the question has often been misinterpreted. 'The existence of law is one thing', he says, 'its merits and demerits another. Whether it be or be not is one enquiry; whether it be or be not conformable to an assumed standard, is a different enquiry' (Austin 1995 [1832]: 157). While thus stated this is a simple and glaring truth, he argues, the history of common law is littered with instances of the forgetting of it. He cites Blackstone's wrapping up of common law in the language of natural law, as if any divergence from the latter will be denounced as invalid. If he were only speaking of *oughts*, comments Austin, urging law to maintain certain standards, he would have no objection; but it is clear that if Blackstone meant more than this, holding that the laws that conflict with the Divine law are not obligatory and binding, hence that they are not real laws, then he is talking 'stark nonsense'. If anyone disputes this, Austin argues, let them just try breaking one of these unjust laws. If the sovereign unjustly declares a harmless or beneficial act to be an offence subject to the death penalty and I perform it and argue against its unreasonableness, 'the Court of Justice will demonstrate the inconclusiveness of my reasoning by hanging me up, in pursuance of the law I have impugned the validity of' (Austin 1995 [1832]: 158). This is undoubtedly a good joke against the natural law position, which has been repeated many times, but how convincing is it ultimately as a statement about legal validity? There is certainly some truth in what Austin is saying here and elsewhere about legal validity and the determination of the moral status of laws, but as we will see later there are some serious problems with it. One obvious objection can be anticipated here: that these words and actions could just as easily have come from the self-appointed judge of a kangaroo court set up by vigilantes. It is a question of proper authority, not of the practical power to carry out sentence.

Law as coercion

Before we look in detail at Austin's command theory, we need to pay close attention to the concept of coercion, as it assumes a central place in his understanding of what the law essentially is. There is little doubt in the minds of those who suffer defeats at the hands of the law, whether civil or criminal, that they are being subjected to coercion. This is true whether it involves a criminal conviction and punishment or civil liability and enforced compensation. Such coercion is experienced as a plain fact, rather than as a reflective interpretation of what is happening. The serving of a prison sentence for a criminal offence – whatever else it might be – is not optional, it is the result of coercion. The same applies to the payment of compensation for breach of contract or inadvertent injury. Similarly, laws passed by the authorised governing bodies, legal statutes relating to all manner of human behaviour and interaction in the society concerned, are not conceived as gentle guidelines for the advice and benefit of citizens. On the contrary, they are laid down as directives to which those subject to the law must conform or pay the penalty.

In every modern society, there are many different agencies of coercion which will at least attempt to ensure this conformity, applying sanctions when necessary. Coercion can take many forms, as we will see later, some of them more subtle than others. Apart from the more obvious sanctions of law, under judicial direction families can be broken up, mental health patients detained or discharged, injunctions ordered for the restraint of antisocial individuals and so on. All of these legal directions undeniably involve the ultimate threat or use of direct physical force.

What is it that marks law out from other systems of norms or standards, such as those of morality or etiquette, or the rules applied to the playing of a game such as baseball or croquet? Do the various forms of coercion just cited give us the starting point for what is distinctive about law? The proposal that has been defended by many is that it is precisely such force, or coercion, that is the essential defining feature of law as a normative system. This is what legal systems have which those other normative systems do not. It is the coercive backup of sanctions that will actually compel people to do as they have been told, that makes a legal system what it is. With the other systems there will be voluntary compliance because they want to play the game. If they choose to flaunt the rules, nobody has official capacity to apply physical coercion. All the referee can do is blow the whistle.

If it were the case that coercion was in definitional terms the 'essence' of law, it would be true that where there was no coercion or threat of it, there would be no law. This, however, is clearly not the case. There are in fact many other features characteristic of law, some of which aim to avoid having to apply direct coercion. One such feature is that the law – working properly – provides information and warnings, so that people are aware of what is prohibited and what is not. In this sense, it simply delineates boundaries. Another is that it brings into being facilities that would not otherwise be available, facilities or institutions from which members of society benefit. Without the law to endorse them, marriage and inheritance would be more informal and less stable. Without it, contracts would be mere promises, difficult or even impossible to enforce privately. In short, the law performs a lot of different functions beyond the more obvious one of simple and direct coercion and punishment of people who will not conform with it.

Austin's command theory

Austin's command theory is a specific version of law understood as essentially coercive. What he set out to do in his 1830s lectures as the first Professor of Jurisprudence at University College London was to establish exactly what should be included in the domain of jurisprudence as proper and strict law. This was for the sake of developing the subject as a science to be taught to those in training for careers in the law. Austin proposed that anything that falls outside of the category of strict law should be excluded from the discipline. He singles out the concept of a command and aims to set it at the explanatory centre of law. He proposes that for a law to be really a law, thus worthy of study in the young science of jurisprudence, it must take the form of a command given by one person or persons to another person or persons of lower status. Furthermore, he stipulates that the command must be issued by a supreme commander – a sovereign individual or collective, such as a monarch or parliament – who is him/herself (or themselves) not in the habit of obedience to any higher sovereign. The chain of command must stop with the sovereign, and all those lower down the chain must be in a habit of obedience to the sovereign.

Such commands, which will always be backed up when necessary by threats or sanctions, constitute the law, properly and strictly speaking. Austin arrives at this conclusion through an analysis of the usage of the word law in everyday speech. One crucial stipulation is that a law in the relevant sense must be the expression of a personal will and it must incite the will of another to obey or disobey. Where there is no such will, there is no real law. One common usage is easily excluded in this way. We frequently speak of 'laws' of nature, but unless we adopt an eccentric philosophy of nature, there is no will to incite in the attractive force of gravitation or the orbit of the planets, apparently 'obeying' Newton's 'laws', or in the growth and decay of a flower. These Austin sees as laws only by remote metaphor, which seem to operate as laws by virtue of the observable regularity in their motions and development.

From the vantage point of a modern scientific understanding of nature, there is no suggestion here of commands and obedience. Within this category of improper law Austin also places non-legal systems of norms such as those represented by the fashion and etiquette of the day, informal rules of correct or polite behaviour. These he sees as law only by analogy with the real thing. These do have a will to incite and control, such that it sometimes looks 'as if' they were systems of real law. Although closer relatives than the laws by metaphor, these still have no status as real law, because they are lacking the crucial element, commands backed up by sanctions. Even in those cases where commands or orders are issued, there is no law unless it is ultimately commanded by the supreme sovereign. Controversially, he also includes international law under this heading, on the grounds that there is no structure of command coming down from a sovereign who is habitually obeyed.

What is more difficult for him to explain, in order to set up his command theory in the right way, as a comprehensive explanation of law, is his exclusion of God's moral law from the domain of jurisprudence. God, after all, had long been seen as the supreme commander, indeed the author of the Ten Commandments as the basis of revealed and human morality. For Austin, this morality is properly – but not strictly – speaking law. As a more or less orthodox Christian, he has to separate these divine commands from the commands that emanate from the earthly sovereign, because only the latter are recognised as actual, strict law within the legal system. What in fact becomes the proper and strict law of the land, as laid down by the political authorities, may well have been motivated or influenced by religion-inspired moral beliefs and values, but this has nothing to do with determining whether or not they actually constitute the law, or how they attain their authority as law. If one questioned the legality of an order, one would not be referred to the Ten Commandments or the Sermon on the Mount.

While for Austin God's commands are morally binding, because they are the expression of perfect utility, they have no legal standing at all. God applies only moral sanctions. The legal status of any command is determined exclusively by the chain of command stretching back to the ultimate lawgiver, the sovereign, at this time in Britain the monarch in conjunction with Parliament. The whole body of morality, the basis for everyday moral judgements of human acts, has no place in the assessment of the question of what it is that qualifies as law. This question can only be answered in terms of whether or not it has been commanded by the legitimate sovereign. This legitimacy is determined only by the sovereign's *de facto* power. It is not sufficient, however, for a sovereign power to be proclaimed. Austin's criteria for sovereignty stipulate that the sovereign must be determinate, such that one can say exactly who it is; it must be unlimited in power, such that there is no higher power to answer to; and – crucially – the majority of the populace must be in the habit of obeying the sovereign's commands. It is by these three criteria, and these alone, that a sovereign can lay claim to legitimacy.

Austin faced a lot of problems, many of which he recognised and attempted to answer, in making this theory of sovereign commands coherent and convincing. He was well aware that many laws did not seem to conform to his pattern, but it was in fact the whole point of his enterprise to show that despite appearances to the contrary, the stark reality of commands, obedience and sanctions gives us the real picture of law as this specific kind of coercion, underlying these appearances. Two examples will illustrate this.

Austin's tacit commands

First, Austin's concept of a *tacit* command was introduced to counter a number of potential criticisms. One of his first principles is that the sovereign must be a human individual or a number of individuals in an assembly such as Parliament or Congress. The commands must be personal, addressed to other persons. One consequence of this is that the authority of the sovereign would seem to depend on their own success in their own lifetime in commanding the obedience of the mass of the populace. Furthermore, given that there are many laws at any given time on the statute book that the present sovereign would not even be aware of, as they were drafted by civil servants, it is difficult to maintain that the present sovereign has personally commanded them. Even worse, the laws that previous sovereigns have proclaimed or commanded in the past, which remain on the statute book, cannot possibly have been commanded by the present sovereign, yet they retain their legitimacy. To compound the difficulty, how does a monarch who has just inherited have the authority to command, when the people have not yet had a chance to acquire the habit of obedience to this particular commander?

There are a number of possible responses to these interconnected problems. One is that the king or queen has been appointed by divine right, so there is no problem with the transition from one to the next. This, however, is obviously directly at odds with Austin's theory, which displaces God in favour of the earthly sovereign as the ultimate commander. Another response is the initially attractive argument that the obedience is to the institution represented by the sovereign, but this is not available to Austin, given his insistence that the sovereign is a determinate person or persons, actually issuing commands. The concept of a command, remember, is an inherently personal one. The argument that he favours is that most commands are not explicit, instead we should understand them as tacit or implicit commands. If the sovereign allows other officials of lower status to issues laws that s/he is unaware of, or does not repeal an old law, s/he has allowed them to stand, and in doing so has implicitly commanded them. Similarly, if the sovereign does not interfere in the creation of laws by the legislature, even if these are unknown to him/her, then it can be taken that these have been implicitly commanded as well.

This solution is not as bizarre as it might at first sound. Many have found the very concept of a tacit command to be inherently contradictory, but the idea that for a command theory of law to work, it must be shown that all commands are explicit, suggesting a children's picture-book image of a king or queen on the throne proclaiming laws to the nation which everyone hears and obeys, is itself rather implausible. The point that Austin quite reasonably wants to make and uphold is that there is an identifiable chain of unconditional command emanating from one point at the top of the legal hierarchy, putting laws in place which the bulk of the population are in the habit of obeying. The idea that many commands or orders are inevitably tacit rather than explicit, that by not interfering – whether through ignorance or disinclination – the sovereign allows them to be posited and enforced, while it is not ultimately convincing, is at least intelligible. So this objection is not necessarily fatal for the theory. Even if Austin's tacit command solution is accepted, however, the inheritance problem is not solved.

One of the most discussed criticisms of Austin revolves around the issue of what happens during a transitional period following the death of a personal sovereign. Taking as the paradigm the succession of monarchs with which Austin was familiar, what is it that makes a king or queen's orders lawful when he or she has just succeeded to the throne? As seen already, it cannot be the habit of obedience by the populace, because there has been no time for such a habit to take root. One might say that the habit is 'transferred' from the old sovereign to the new, but this is not compatible with Austin's insistence that it is the living sovereign who gives the commands and is obeyed. What really happens is that it is the authority, not the habit, that is transferred. Consider the case of James VI of Scotland inheriting the crown of England on the death of Elizabeth I in 1603.

En route to London to assume his throne, James ordered the immediate execution of an apprehended thief, who was promptly hanged. While some onlookers approved, this act also caused much consternation, because it was contrary to English common law to execute anyone without due legal procedure, and even the anointed sovereign was acting beyond his power in doing so. King James, who very soon was crowned as James I of England, nevertheless had the established powers of a sovereign as soon as he had been declared the rightful heir. On Austin's account of sovereignty, this is inexplicable. First, although the new king answered to no higher power – as Austin's theory requires – this power was not unlimited, as the shocked reaction to the hanging of the thief shows. His advisors made sure such an act did not happen again. Secondly, it shows that the regal powers were already there, by virtue of a constitutional rule that recognizes the right of certain persons to inherit the throne, not by virtue of the general habit of obedience to anyone. This was a widely accepted constitutional convention. What happened in this case was that the newly designated sovereign exceeded his constitutional powers. Austin's theory cannot account for either of these points.

Areas of law without commands

The second major problem arising from the theory of law as a structure of commands is that there are large areas of law that do not seem to have any-thing to do with commands or the application of sanctions or punishment for disobedience. This has proved to be one of the greatest stumbling blocks for the command theory. While it is allowed by critics that the theory enjoys some plausibility in criminal law, where there are countless prohibitions with punitive sanctions attached, there are many other areas of what must be genuine law in which there are neither commands nor sanctions. The greatest part of contract law, for example, lays down the conditions under which contracts will be valid or invalid, but nobody entering into a contract is commanded to do so by the sovereign, and there is no sanction for not doing so. Similarly, nobody is commanded to get married or to leave a will for their heirs. Laws relating to these institutions have an entirely different function from those of criminal law. They do not command and punish at all, because their function is of a different order. They are there to facilitate transactions and interactions between people in society, to change the legal relations between them and generally to raise the quality of life.

Austin was well aware of this problem and his response to it was to argue that there are indeed commands in these areas of law, which consist of the rules that must be followed if the participants wish these transactions to be fulfilled. Failure to comply with these rules will indeed be followed by negative sanctions, which will consist in the failure of the contract, the will, or the marriage to be legally validated. In his words, the 'nullity' of the transaction is the sanction. Nothing will have been achieved. Therefore, the command theory is correct. Coercion in the form of commands either explicit or tacit, backed up by sanctions, whether positive or negative, is indeed the essence of law, or is at the very least nearly pervasive.

Conclusion

There is no doubt that despite the apparent weaknesses of the theory, Austin changed the course of modern jurisprudence. Although the reception of his work after his death was mixed, it became a standard text in the teaching of the subject for over a century. It was regarded as an excellent starting point for the study of jurisprudence. While it was widely thought that the command theory captured insights that others had ignored or failed to see, and that it was an effective and largely accurate counter to natural law and pure common law theory, there were also growing doubts about its ability alone to present a comprehensive picture of law. These were expressed by many leading American legal philosophers, from Oliver Wendell Holmes to Roscoe Pound, based largely on the problems outlined above. It was not, however, until the mid-twentieth century that Austin's command theory was challenged by a major legal philosopher who had his own theory of law to present as an alternative version of positivism. This will be the subject of the next chapter.

Study questions

General question: How did positivism displace natural law as the dominant legal theory?

Further study questions: Why did Bentham reject the common law ideas of Coke, Hale and Blackstone? Do you find his critique convincing? What effects did philosophical positivism have on legal theory? Explain how and why Austin proposed to keep law apart from morality. Was he justified in doing so? Is it right to understand the law essentially as a form of coercion? Explain Austin's command theory and his theory of sovereignty. Can it be reconciled with the existence of laws that do not involve commands? Is this form of positivism preferable to natural law as an explanation of law? How do you think natural lawyers can come back at Austin?

Suggestions for further reading

There are numerous histories of English common law, including J. Baker (1990), Fleming (1994) and Harding (1966). On Coke and Hale, see M. Davies (1994: ch. 2). On Lord Mansfield, see Poser (2013).

On Hume and positivism in philosophy generally, see Kolakowski (1968). For Hume and the fact–value separation, read the relevant passage in Hume (1972: 3.1.1). A good concise commentary on this is found in Woolhouse (1988: ch. 8). On Bentham's legal positivism, the main text is Bentham (1970). For commentaries, read Hart's essay in Summers (1971) or Hart (1982 and 1983: ch. 2). Dinwiddy (1989: ch. 4) and Postema (1986) are also useful. Austin's primary text for the command theory is Austin (1995). There are useful commentaries in Harris (1997: ch. 3), Riddall (1999: ch. 2), Bix (2015: ch. 3) and M. Murphy (2007: ch. 1). See also Meyerson (2007: ch. 1) on law and force. For a more detailed comment on Bentham and Austin, see Cotterell (1989: ch. 3). The most important comprehensive recent work on Austin is Schauer (2015).

3 Hart's legal positivism

Hart's challenge to Austin

H.L.A. Hart (1907–92) began writing on the law in the 1950s, in a very different world from the one known to Austin. With his critique of the latter's command theory and his construction of a new theory of law to replace it without relinquishing the basic principles of legal positivism, we are moving into an entirely different approach to understanding the essential features of law. In his groundbreaking work, *The Concept of Law* (1961), Hart developed his own method of analysis in the atmosphere of post-war Oxford. He undertook the double task of 'demolishing' the command theory and finding the basis for 'a fresh start', from which a more accurate account of law as a social phenomenon could be developed. These two tasks should not be understood or interpreted separately. The second grew out of the first. The serious faults and shortcomings that he finds in a typical sovereign-command–sanction theory, in particular Austin's, are linked closely to the key concepts in Hart's own theory, which are explained in order to remedy these defects and to clarify what he sees as the essentials for understanding the law. It should be remembered that Hart was writing from within the legal positivist camp, and that it was his main purpose to rescue this approach from the distortions that he saw in the analysis of law developed by Bentham and Austin.

The law for Hart is much more than the expression of the coercion of the population by a powerful elite. One misconception should be set aside immediately. Hart does not doubt that the law through the ages, including our own legal system, relies heavily upon the threat or use of physical force. His intention was not to soften this picture of law, but rather to show that it does not capture what is really important about law, because it obscures distinctions that are absolutely crucial to understanding it. Writing a century after Austin, Hart incorporates all the criticisms made over the years by other critics, transforming them into one powerful critique. With each of the criticisms he aims to show that the command theory falls short as an explanation of the law and the authority behind it.

One general idea behind these criticisms is that there are many familiar rules in society which it would be highly eccentric to deny the title of legality to, which are simply not allowed by Austin's command model. These include those we have considered already in the last chapter, the laws in place when the sovereign comes to power, all the laws of precedent in a system of common law, the origin of which is often unknown, and above all the rules which confer powers on officials and ordinary people, rather than embodying any kind of command. Hart counters most of Austin's anticipations and responses to these criticisms, by portraying them as *ad hoc* defences designed to save the theory when it is really beyond rescue. We can summarise Hart's criticisms as follows:

1   Austin conceals the distinction between being obliged or forced to obey and being placed under an obligation to obey.
2   He fails to solve the problem of power-conferring rules: those that confer powers on officials to perform legal duties which do not involve commands at all, such as marriages, wills and contracts.
3   The sovereign-command–sanction picture does not reflect the ways in which many laws have actually arisen, originating as they do in ancient custom.
4   The problem of habitual obedience to the sovereign.
5   The problem of the unlimited power of the sovereign.

The most damning criticism is the first of these, which rests upon Hart's rejection of the central notion that the force brought into play by the sanction-backed commands of the sovereign brings with it an obligation upon those commanded to obey.

Legal and moral obligation

This is the central point of Hart's critique. Why do people have an obligation to obey the law? What is it and where does it come from? On Austin's account, this is explained solely by the force, the threats of sanctions. On Hart's account, this is not only simplistic, it is wholly wrong and gives rise to many misunderstandings of legal realities. Hart has frequently been criticised for drawing a distinction which does not match common usage, a distinction between being obliged and being under an obligation. He highlights the difference by representing the idea of 'being obliged' as meaning that force or the threat of force is brought to bear on the person thus obliged. Being under an obligation, in sharp contrast, is being in someone's debt and having a certain duty to perform.

The idea of 'being obliged' to someone actually has multiple uses in English. Think of the different ways in which the phrase 'I am obliged' can be taken. For example, it can indicate an expression of thanks, or more precisely it can suggest the free admission of being in someone's debt for a service, as in 'I am obliged to you'. Or it can have the quite different connotation of having no choice but to respond in some specific way, as in the case of being obliged to give way or to accept advice, as in 'I am obliged to do as you say'. Hart takes the typical meaning of 'obliged' to indicate a quite extreme instance of the latter. In his striking example, an armed robber 'obliges' his victim to hand over the money, whether he wants to or not. For Hart, then, 'obliged' simply means 'forced' or 'compelled'. The gunman obliges the bank clerk to obey his orders. It would be quite wrong, he says, to imagine that the clerk or any other victim has 'an obligation' to hand over the money. While they may feel compelled to, they know they are under no obligation to do anything of the sort. For one thing, a genuine obligation has an enduring quality. When the gunman's threat is removed – imagine that the gun is suddenly recognised as a water pistol – the reasons for obeying disappear with it. So this is not what we mean by obligation at all.

Hart's critics have argued that being obliged has a wider range of application than he allows, as he fixes on the one meaning just given. This criticism misses the point. The way in which Hart draws this distinction is indeed idiosyncratic, but he is still drawing a legitimate distinction which highlights Austin's elision of the crucial features of legal obligation, which involves acceptance of the authority behind the rules. This is what is absent from the gunman scenario. While it is impossible to be definitive about the usage of these terms, Hart's distinction is close enough to be serviceable.

Right from the outset, this is how he introduces the general problem of legal coercion. The point he wants to establish is that Austin's sovereign is in effect a larger version of the bank robber who points his gun at the cashier. If we are to believe Austin's account, then the sovereign is doing exactly the same thing on a greater scale as a common criminal or gangster. He gives orders backed by threats, and large numbers of people obey because they fear the consequence of disobedience. Austin's sovereign state, says Hart, must be seen as 'the gunman situation writ large'. As this is so implausible, we must find another way of explaining what the obligation is and where it comes from.

It is worth noting that with this gunman example of Hart's there is a probably unintended echo of St Augustine. 'I do it in a small craft and you call me a pirate. You do it with a mighty navy and they call you the emperor.' For pirate, read gunman. For emperor read sovereign. (See Chapter 1.) Hart, however, is not making the same point as the natural law philosopher. Augustine wants to say that if the emperors govern like large-scale pirates, their rule is not legitimate. Hart does not think this. What he wants to say is that there is more to law than exercising the coercion and force that might more aptly describe, on a smaller scale, the behaviour of a gangster with a gun. So we need to look for where the difference really lies.

Internalisation

What is absolutely crucial in Hart's defence of his new picture of law is his distinction and contrast between the external viewpoint of the outside observer and the internal viewpoint of those who are active within the legal system, either as officials or citizens subject to its jurisdiction. His rejection of Austin's habitual obedience to the sovereign as the criterion for the existence of a legal system is based on his contrast of habitual behaviour with rule-following behaviour in everyday social life. Anyone following habitual patterns of action, such as going to the cinema every Wednesday night, or eating toast for breakfast every day, is merely falling into a habit or routine. Such activities only possess what Hart describes as an external dimension, which can be observed by an outsider.

Other regular social activities, however, such as attending religious ceremonies on a certain day or at a certain hour, or selling flags for charity on another day, in addition to having an observable external aspect, also have an internal dimension. With such activities, they are not just habits, the participants are adopting or accepting it as a rule that they should do such things. In other words, they are internalising the rule, making it a rule for their own behaviour. This involves the crucial feature of acceptance of the rule, and it is accompanied by 'a critical reflective attitude' towards one's own activity. A failure to perform the expected or required actions will be felt as a lapse. This is not the case with a break in one's merely habitual behaviour. The famous example he gives to illustrate this distinction imagines a car slowing down and stopping at a red traffic light. From the external viewpoint, someone watching this repeatedly will see the light merely as a *sign* or an indicator that the car will stop, just as dark clouds signify impending rain. From the observation of such signs, predictions can be extrapolated. The previous ten cars stopped, so this one will. From the internal point of view, the driver sees the light as a *signal* to stop – quite different from a sign – hence as a rule to be followed. The driver has internalised the traffic rule that she must stop at red lights. The important point that Hart is making is that genuinely rule-governed behaviour can be observed from the outside, from the external point of view, without any recognition of this internalisation of the rules that are followed. From such a standpoint, an alien anthropologist from Mars would simply note the patterns of behaviour and draw no such distinction between habits and rules. This, Hart thinks, is precisely what Austin's analysis does. In focusing on the habitual obedience of citizens to sovereigns, he obscures a huge and crucial dimension of social life. This in turn obscures the most important ways in which the legal system works, and indeed what it actually means to have a legal system.

It is Hart's emphasis on linguistic concealment that is crucial in his critique of command theories such as Austin's. It is not merely that their models of coercive orders as representing the essence of law are wrong, falsely identifying the sovereign as the key to understanding the concepts relevant to jurisprudence, it is rather that Hart's criticism points to their active concealment and distortion of the real picture, which has several dimensions. The coercive theories have a strong tendency to reduce these dimensions to just one. In this way, a genuine legal obligation seems to be created by the sheer force of the state, which, Hart sees, simply has to be wrong. There may be compulsion and compliance or submission, but to speak of an *obligation* here is wholly inaccurate and inappropriate. It is not that this implies a lack of moral justification, as natural lawyers would contend, it is rather that it obscures the internalisation and acceptance of the rules by active participants in the behaviour of those aligning themselves with the rules and acting within their framework.

Conventions and obligations

Hart does not suggest, however, that every example of social rule-following is an instance of internalising an obligation. He also identifies forms of convergent behaviour which do have an internal aspect, but do not involve what anyone would call obligations, either moral or legal. This is a midway category that might be called that of convention. Hart has in mind sets of rules governing correct grammar and speech; the rules of fashion or etiquette; and such activities as ball games like football, or board games such as chess. These sets of rules are commonly meticulous and detailed, laying down conventional rules for correct modes of speech or 'legal' moves in a game of chess, and they often involve criticism and correction of one's own or others' behaviour, along with a certain kind of pressure to conform when the rules are broken, as when a chess player starts to move the pieces any way she likes, or a footballer ignores the offside rule, but it would simply be misleading to say that such conventions involve obligations or duties. These are just the rules of the game that have to be followed if they wish to continue playing.

It is only in areas of life where the social pressure to stay within the rules becomes greater or more insistent that we can begin to speak about obligations or duties. When the appeal to shame, remorse and guilt becomes prominent, says Hart, we can begin to identify a social morality and speak about obligations created by the rules. When this pressure to conform involves punitive sanctions, then we can identify these as primitive law, as legal obligations. This pressure is the primary indicator of an obligation, but there are also two others. First, the rules in question, deviation from which is being constrained by the rules, have to be thought of as necessary for the maintenance of social life, for example, rules barring the free use of violence. Secondly, obligations usually involve serious sacrifice or renunciation on the part of those controlled by them, because they are more likely to conflict with individual interests and desires. These three elements take us way beyond the character of conventional pressures to prevent deviation from the rules in games and are, for Hart, sufficient to distinguish obligations from these other conventional sets of rules.

Hart presents this analysis as the laying out of plain facts about the morality of any society. It is hardly controversial to argue that moral and legal obligation is distinguished by the use of punitive sanctions, but the point Hart is making against Austin is that obligations cannot flow from the mere use of such sanctions for deviation from the commands laid down by the sovereign. The sanctions are in place to prevent or deter and punish such deviations from the rules. As instruments for their enforcement they cannot be their off-spring. The obligations are already there when the sanctions are applied to enforce them.

Minimal natural law

The reason Hart's book made such an impact on modern jurisprudence is that he skilfully pitched his critique in several directions at once, projecting it well beyond the relatively narrow limits of an internal positivist dispute. What he believed was that the old debate with natural law had set up a sterile conflict between two mindsets that could never be reconciled, because each of them was coming from the wrong starting point. While the natural law insistence that justice and equity were integral to law, although at first sight intuitively plausible, concealed the real nature of law and legal systems, which in practice might as often be unjust as they are just, yet still be law, the command version of positivism was equally to blame for overemphasizing the role of state force and coercion, and – to many minds at least – expelling moral considerations from legal analysis completely, as though law and morality were wholly alien to one another. 'You are all blind', the natural law philosophers said to the positivists. 'You are all seeing ghosts', the positivists replied (Lacey 2004). Hart went to great lengths to disentangle this confusion and, by changing the starting point to show that law could be analysed more profitably by looking at it from a different angle. From this new vantage point, it would become clear that there was truth in both of the old theories, but also a great deal of distortion.

The right way to look at it, for Hart, was as a legal system in which the role of coercion was decentred. While it did play a very large part in many areas of law, the way to understand such concepts as legal authority, obligation and rights – and of course, law itself – was to set aside the pattern of command, sanction and obedience to threats, so that the patterns of rules in all their complexity, with many different functions, came into view. Among other things, understanding it in this way allowed insight into why natural law philosophers had always seen the law as rooted in human nature, such that they understood crucial aspects of justice and morality relating to the protection of the vulnerable and the recognition of human limitations as essential to the existence of law. Without such recognition, they believed, the law was not properly speaking law at all.

Where they went wrong, Hart argued, was in taking this law–morality connection to be necessary or conceptual, so that it was true by definition that real law must be the embodiment of morality and justice, when the truth was that the connection was based on contingent empirical facts about the human species as we happen to have evolved, facts such as our approximate equality in intelligence, height and strength, or the plain moral fact that most humans are neither angels nor devils, lying somewhere uneasily in between. These facts make law both possible and unavoidable whenever there is society on any significant scale. Hart called this a 'minimum content' of natural law theory, but one which must be combined with a positivist analysis of the legal concepts, keeping the factual description and conceptual analysis separate from any evaluation or moral assessment. With this kind of minimal recognition of the basic truths of natural law, it was possible to see clearly that there is no necessary connection between what is legal at any given time and what is morally sound or just, but also one can see that the hard-line command theory at the far end of the spectrum is very wide of the mark as well.

Primary and secondary rules

For Hart, the explanatory centre of the law is the union of and interaction between two kinds of rules, which he calls primary and secondary. The primary rules are those concerned with directly constraining people's behaviour – all the familiar rules of criminal and tort law, prescribing or prohibiting certain specified acts or kinds of behaviour – and the secondary rules are those whose only purpose is to control the operation of these primary rules. The principal difference from the Austinian picture is that these secondary rules are in place, not by the grace of a commanding sovereign, but by means of a complex network of rules that originate from many different sources in the evolution of the legal system.

Hart asks us to imagine a society at an early stage of development which has not yet set out a system of legal rules. Human nature is such that a society could not survive long without the articulation of at least some informal rules. Agreements that certain kinds of behaviour will not be tolerated or that various duties will be assumed would provide the basis for a number of primary rules, which would steadily grow over time. If the society tried to proceed with these rules alone, however, it would, says Hart, be afflicted by three defects. It would soon become uncertain what the rules were, they would be static and unchanging, as there would naturally be resistance to change, and the irregular and disorganised social pressure on deviant individuals to conform with the rules would make them increasingly inefficient. What would quickly emerge, Hart argues, would be a set of rules designed to counter these defects. Clear procedures would have to be put in place to establish which rules are to be recognised as valid. This would be the fundamental rule of recognition, an ultimate standard to be referred to. There would also be rules of change, to allow for the cancellation of unwanted rules or addition to their number. Rules of adjudication would develop, to set up authorities empowered to make definitive rulings on disputes over the breaking of the primary rules. Finally, there would have to be agreed ways in which to impose sanctions or punishment for the breaking of the rules. This is how Hart presents the essential features of a legal system.

The rule of recognition

The most fundamental of these secondary rules Hart calls 'the rule of recognition'. This is the rule to which the authority of all the primary rules is referred. It is a secondary rule that settles doubts and uncertainties, and provides the authority to resolve them. As such, it is the all-important source of legal validity, from which the legality of any law, minor by-law or legal document, or the legitimacy of any court of law and the proceedings therein, any action by a legal official, is ultimately derived.

This basic rule, Hart maintains, can appear in any number of forms or guises. It can be written or unwritten, spoken or unspoken. It might be the rule that 'whatever the sovereign says is law'. It might be the way in which the primary rules are uttered or enacted. It might be a formal document or a constitution. In the UK, it happens to be the rule that 'what the Queen in Parliament enacts is law'. Whatever form the rule of recognition takes, it is simply a socially accepted fact in any given legal system, every one of which must have one if it is to qualify as a legal system, rather than a prelegal assemblage of unvalidated primary rules.

For Hart, this fundamental rule of recognition plays the same role in theoretical terms as Austin's sovereign. Just as the latter validates any law by having commanded it, the fundamental rule of recognition stands at the apex of the legal system, conferring validity on any and every specific law in question. The moral or political quality of this rule does not come into play. All Hart is doing here is presenting what he takes to be a more accurate and realistic picture of the way in which the legal system is structured.

Positivist doubts about Hart's system of rules

With the publication of *The Concept of Law* in the 1960s, Hart's influence spread rapidly, especially in America. However, not everyone in the positivist camp has accepted that Hart emphatically won the argument against Austin. Apart from a range of criticisms relating to the logical consistency of his account of power-conferring rules, it has been argued, most recently by Frederick Schauer (Schauer 2015), that Hart's critique was at best only partly successful, because he underestimated the plausibility of Austin's coercion-centred theory of law, and was himself seriously at fault on empirical issues, especially on the question of obligation and the habit of obedience to law for its own sake, thus generally underestimating the actual role of coercion in law. Although Hart himself expressed doubts as to whether his analysis of obligation had been successful in distinguishing its legal and moral forms, we need to be careful in assessing the merits of the arguments against his general theory of law.

For Schauer, Hart's emphasis on the internalisation of legal obligations was based on an almost naive belief in the readiness of people to comply with the law just because it is the law, out of respect rather than fear. With his constant emphasis on 'acceptance' of the law as an essential feature of obligation, he argues, Hart exaggerates the extent of this voluntary compliance. As a matter of empirical fact, he thinks, Hart's position is highly dubious. Leaving aside core criminal offences, from which the typical citizen would recoil anyway, most people do in fact comply with the law as law on matters such as taxation and acceptance of civil liability, on drug laws and speeding limits, largely out of self-interest, rather than because it has an authority which is respectfully accepted. Most people know that if they ignore these laws they will be pursued. Hart himself had taken as an example the model of law proposed by the American realist Oliver Wendell Holmes in hard positivist mode, according to which the best way to understand the law and what it demands is to look at it through the eyes of 'a bad man', for whom conscience means nothing, and who only wants to know what the courts of Massachusetts or England will require of him and allow him to get away with, to stay out of prison and avoid paying fines (Holmes 1897).

This was part of Holmes' attempt to lay bare the difference between law and morality. His 'bad man' was a heuristic device for looking at the law from an angle that would reveal its real contours. If you look at it from this angle, Holmes was suggesting, you would get a much better view of what the law was really likely to deliver, than you would if you were idealising it as the embodiment of all things good. Hart confronted this model in *The Concept of Law* (Hart 2012 [1961]: 40) with what he believed to be a more realistic type of citizen. Thus he proposed 'the puzzled man' as an alternative to Holmes' somewhat cynical model, which sees the law only as an obstacle, whose coercive powers will come into play if you miscalculate. Hart's puzzled man is what he thinks is the more common type who is frequently unsure of what the law is and wants to find out so that he can comply with it and avoid its sanctions.

The dispute here is perhaps oversimplified. Schauer wrongly interprets Hart as implying that typical people in society are 'saintly law-abiding angels'. To bring more clarity into this dispute, we might consider another type – to switch to the more acceptable contemporary idiom – as 'the anxious person' who wants to know for prudential reasons how to avoid breaking the law, but whose motives cannot be said to be either purely respectful of the law, nor purely prudential, because she also sees it as the right thing to do. It is more plausible to argue against Schauer that this mixed type is one of the most common, and to the extent that this is true it will uphold the position of Hart and others who argue against Bentham's and Austin's versions of law as essentially coercive, because it supports Hart's insistence that coercion-free law-following, and an internalised sense of obligation to obey the law because it is the law, is indispensable to a full understanding of what the law actually is.

Schauer nevertheless correctly identifies a weak point in Hart's critique of Austin's sovereign and his own rule of recognition, with reference to his description of the sovereign as 'the gunman writ large' (Schauer 2015: 159–61). As Schauer points out, 'the sole gunman in the bank' scenario fits Hart's argument well enough. Austin's theory on his account implies that this is what the state comes down to – a gunman with menaces on a larger scale. If, however, we switch from this imaginary example to the real world of mafia-style organised crime, Schauer suggests, a different picture emerges. When a gang succeeds in imposing its protection racket on large areas in a city such as London or

Chicago, and it is structured in such a way that its 'employees' obey the orders of the mob boss, there are many features which resemble not only Austin's sovereign state but also Hart's system of rules.

Regarding the former, the boss will satisfy the criteria that he is a determinate person who answers to nobody else and the typical citizens along with his 'officials' are in the habit of obeying him. Regarding Hart's system, one might even, Schauer says, describe the rule of recognition as 'treat the general orders of the boss and no-one else as authoritative' (Schauer 2015: 160). There might also be a strong element of internalisation of the rules, rather than mere submission out of fear. So how is the law issued by the governments of the United Kingdom or the United States, or any other state that is recognised as legitimate by the United Nations, to be distinguished from the 'law' of these hierarchical networks of rules? Why is one set of commands or rules legitimate, the others not? It is easy enough to point to the political conventions on how we recognise legitimate authority, and there is little doubt about the illegitimacy of protection rackets, but the point is that Hart as much as Austin is ill-equipped by his theory of law to explain the difference.

Conclusion

Any assessment of the ongoing dispute between positivists and their natural law critics must take account of the ways in which these doctrines have evolved since the days of the classic theories of Bentham and Austin. The differences between the modern versions of positivism and those of their predecessors are almost as important as their arguments against natural law. It seems clear today that Hart's largely successful critique of Austin can indeed be questioned, not only in its details, but also on substantial matters. Ultimately, however, his critique and the theory that arose from it did crystallise the issues in a way that lifted positivist theory out of the stagnation into which it had fallen and opened up a new era of Anglo-American jurisprudence. Hart's new concept of law was significant for many reasons, which have only been touched upon here. Other important features of it will be covered in later chapters. The most important of these reasons was his conceptual liberation of legal positivism from the straitjacket of the command theory of law.

Study questions

General question: How successful was Hart's theory of law as an alternative to Austin's command theory?

Further study questions: Explain and evaluate the main features of Hart's critique of Austin. How convincing is Hart's distinction between being obliged and being obligated? Is he right in his rejection of coercion as the essence of law? Explain Hart's emphasis in his own theory on the internal point of view. How does it reveal the weaknesses of Austin's theory? Does

Hart's analysis of rules give us a convincing picture of the difference between moral and legal obligation? What part does the rule of recognition play? Explain and critically assess Hart's 'minimum content' theory. Does he succeed in finding the middle way between command positivism and natural law theory? How effective is Schauer's critique of Hart on the question of the place of coercion in law?

Suggestions for further reading

The basic texts for Hart's critique of the command theory are Austin's *Province of Jurisprudence Determined* (Austin 1995: lectures 1, 5 and 6) and Hart's *Concept of Law* (Hart 2012 [1961]: chs 1–6). Important critical reactions include those of Raz (1970: chs 1–2) and Dworkin (1977b: ch. 2). Significant short studies are found in M. Murphy (2007: ch. 1) and Bix (2015: ch.3). Useful short commentaries also include Davies (1994), Lyons (1984: ch. 2) and Riddall (1999: ch. 4). Earlier criticism of the command theory can be found in J.C. Gray (1921: 85–8).

Hart's classic work (Hart 2012 [1961]) is fundamental to his theory of law. Among the numerous studies and commentaries on Hart, those that stand out are Lacey's biography (Lacey 2004), MacCormick (1981), Gavison (1987) and the essays collected in Hacker and Raz (1977), and Summers (1971).

The most important critique of Hart's interpretation of Austin is Schauer (2015). See also Cotterell (1989) and Morrison (1997: ch. 13).

4 Legal theory and the Nazi legality problem

The military defeat and occupation of Nazi Germany in 1945 was a watershed in twentieth-century world history. The long-term effects included the heightened awareness in the Western world of the need to protect individual human rights in the future. On the immediate agenda, the problems were twofold. First, the need to reconstruct a large industrial nation at the heart of Europe, a major power that had been all but destroyed. Secondly, the practical problems arising from the termination of the Nazi legal system were almost incalculable. Bringing to justice the Nazi leaders and other perpetrators of some of the worst crimes seen in modern times was regarded by the Allied governments as a priority. The International Military Tribunal set up in the German town of Nuremberg in October 1945, presided over by judges from each of the leading Allied nations, charged twenty-four defendants with crimes against peace (launching a war of aggression), numerous war crimes and crimes against humanity. The last relatively new charge was defined as 'murder, extermination, enslavement, deportation ... or persecutions on political, racial, or religious grounds' (Adams 1992: 4).

There was a very keen awareness that the Tribunal's proceedings should have the authority of law, and that the rulings and verdicts had to be based on sound legal arguments. This was difficult because many saw their authority to sit in judgement at all as at best paper-thin, at worst non-existent, flowing as it did from military victory. It was also a question of whose law was being applied. The rules governing the procedures of the trials were a careful combination of Anglo-American common law and European-style judicial principles, but this was seen by critics as makeshift window-dressing. The Nuremberg trials faced many criticisms from various legal quarters, but the crucial point for our purposes was that the judges and prosecutors on this tribunal, like those of the West German courts that followed in the late 1940s, found themselves compelled to refer to what sounded very much like natural law to justify the prosecutions of people who had committed their offences under a jurisdiction that had sanctioned or even ordered their actions. In the legal academic world, this prompted a long renewed debate on the respective merits of legal positivism and its natural law critics. The main thing we need to look at carefully here is the natural law charge that positivism was at least partly responsible for the rise of Nazism, and that the whole experience of this tyranny exposed the theoretical shortcomings of positivism as a legal theory. In other words, it was not just a practical failure to encourage resistance from the legal profession or the population at large, but primarily a philosophical failure to grasp the real meaning of 'law'.

Hans Kelsen's pure theory of law

As we have seen, the pedigree of legal positivism was a long and respected one not only in the European but probably even more so in the English-speaking world, and these difficulties were not likely to bring about its instant demise. Many deplored the effects of the positivist outlook in Germany, as it supposedly encouraged a passive attitude to the law, even when it is manifestly wrong. Others, however, including Hart, insisted that these matters had no real bearing on the claims of positivists to have developed the most accurate analysis of law and legal systems. He also vigorously disputed the natural law claim that 'law', properly speaking, had ceased to exist in Germany during the Nazi period. Terrible law it might have been, but nevertheless law. Whether citizens had a duty to obey it – for Hart, as for natural lawyers, they clearly did not – was an entirely separate matter. One of the principal examples of this kind of analysis is provided by the jurisprudence of another prominent mid-century positivist, whose reputation rested on his determination to keep what he saw as the autonomous science of law completely pure and value-free.

Hans Kelsen (1881–1973) was Hart's chief rival for the title of leading positivist of his day. An Austrian by birth, he left his homeland to escape the Nazis in 1940 and settled in the USA, where he continued a distinguished academic career. Kelsen had been a jurist and philosopher of international standing since much earlier in the century. His most fully developed work, *Pure Theory of Law*, was first published in 1934, and this was eventually followed up by an expanded version in 1960. Of all the leading contributions to the history of legal positivism, Kelsen's stands out as the most uncompromising. Thoroughly conventionalist in his assumption that all laws are human artefacts, Kelsen refined a 'pure theory of law' with its subject matter quite purposefully sealed off from outside influence. Although he opposed the reduction of law to 'science' in the normal sense, he was himself interested in developing a rigorous science of purely legal norms. This was intended to be a science based on norms in contrast to the more typical empiricist conception of natural and social science resting on the observation of causally related facts. So it was in underlying legal norms or 'oughts' rather than observed facts that Kelsen situated the reality of law. His jurisprudence, then, was a 'science' in his own distinctive sense.

Taking his cue from Hume, and for some time working in parallel with the positivist Vienna school with which he was loosely associated in the 1930s, Kelsen applied the is–ought dichotomy to law in a way that was clear and radical. Keeping facts separate from values was the overriding imperative. In his quite separate moral philosophy, Kelsen subscribed to the emotivist theory, which in his version led to the view of moral ideals – especially ideals of justice – as being essentially subjective expressions of feeling, grounded in irrational emotion rather than in rational reflection, and hence entirely unsuitable for any kind of legal analysis. For emotivists, there is no such thing as objective moral truth. This moral theory had a decisive impact upon his jurisprudence, the main object of which was for Kelsen the uncovering of the strictly logical form behind the confusion of empirical appearances and subjective moral judgements. He conceived this discovery of logical form as a project of rational reconstruction of the law as a unified whole. As an autonomous and distinctive science the object of study was held to be law as such, rather than any particular legal system; what he was seeking was the purely formal structures of any possible legal system. In this enterprise Kelsen was implacably opposed to any version of natural law theory; justice and the higher law had no place in his kind of scientific jurisprudence. In short, he was attempting to push the positivism of Bentham and Austin to its logical conclusion, to his own pure theory of law, while detaching it from its empiricism and objective utilitarian moral basis, and in so doing also to root out the hidden presence of natural law assumptions in modern legal theory.

Kelsen's 'pure' theory of law is pure in two senses:

- *The purification of subject matter.* In order to establish law as an independent science, it is necessary to strip it down to what is distinctively legal. To focus on the purely legal dimension of law – specifically legal validity – all the moral, political, sociological and psychological dimensions must not just be bracketed out but also displaced from the science. The ideal sought here is a distilled conception of the *object* of legal science, decontaminated or purged, so to speak, of all subjective elements.
- *The purification of the investigation.* In order to undertake this scientific investigation effectively, the investigation itself must be value-free. The science of law is 'pure' in the sense that the investigation is free of ideology. In pure theory, there is no approval or disapproval, either implicit or explicit. The ideal sought here is a distilled conception of the investigating *subject*, the legal scientist, understood as a purely formal rational mind.

Taken in combination, these two conceptually interlocked senses of purification – of law itself and of its methodology – led to a focus on the pure form of laws and the legal system. In this sense, Kelsen's theory is what we call formalist. It involves the bracketing out and suspension of the concrete content of the laws that link up into a legal system, to concentrate on their pure form. The concrete content – the social function, the political purpose, the supposed justice or injustice of the laws – is irrelevant to the investigation of the formal structure of this system.

So what is Kelsen's image of law? How does he understand the formal legal reality laid bare by this positivist method? When purified of all extraneous elements, what comes into view – in any legal system – is one rationally con-nected structure of norms, in the shape of a pyramid. These 'norms' have to be understood as specifically legal 'oughts', which are distinct from either moral oughts or legal rules. 'Ought' is meant strictly in the legal, not moral, sense. Legal rules as rules are not logically linked with one another. Legal norms are oughts of which legal rules are the visible manifestation. The 'formal logical' connections that give the legal system its unity apply to norms rather than rules, and it is these connections that the formal analysis reveals.

Thus it is in these logical connections between legal norms that Kelsen locates legal validity. To this effect, the language of law is formalised by recasting every rule in terms of a legal ought, each of which is expressed as an 'imputational connective' ('if X conditions obtain, then Y sanctions ought to be applied'). This is the inner structure of any possible law. The directive to apply specified sanctions, whenever given conditions obtain, is addressed to a line of legal officials enforcing any kind of law along the full length of the legal process. Each norm can only be validated by referring it to a higher norm (in the hierarchical pyramid), 'higher' in the sense of being more general. Thus each norm is validated logically by being a more specific instance of another norm. The formal connection, hence the validity, abstracts from the concrete content of the norm. Any statement containing a legal norm can be validated or invalidated in this way. Thus, for example, a norm which requires that anyone who insults the government should be executed would be validated by a more general norm according to which all enemies of the state should be executed. Such a norm would clearly be intrinsically abhorrent. The point is that for Kelsen legal validity has nothing at all to do with any kind of moral or political judgment of the norms.

Kelsen's basic norm

If the formal validation of any particular legal norm must always lie in the identification of another legal norm, it clearly faces a problem of infinite regress. This takes us into the central and most controversial feature of Kelsen's pure theory. If norms are always referred to other norms, what is the ultimate source of their legal validity? It is not sufficient to say that validity is derived from the fabric of the normative order, that this order is purely formal and that content is irrelevant. The continued reference to norms further up the hierarchical structure inevitably raises the question of what stands at the top of the structure, the apex of the pyramid, the most general norm. What is it that gives the legal system its rational unity? Kelsen's answer is that the existence of any legal system must assume or presuppose a basic norm (*Grundnorm*). This norm he describes as 'hypothetical', in the sense that we can only hypothesise its existence.

The basic norm, then, is the most general norm hypothesised as the norm behind the final authority to which all particular valid norms can be traced back. This is the only norm that cannot itself be questioned or validated. It is in this sense that its validity is presupposed or tacitly assumed in any legal activity – for example, the relevant actions of a court official, a police officer, a solicitor, a gaoler – which acknowledges the validity of particular norms. It should be noticed especially that the basic norm is not the actual constitution – of the USA, the UK, Germany or wherever – which would be the empirical object of *political* science. It is what Kelsen terms the *logical* constitution that takes the form of an ought-statement that the constitution 'ought to be obeyed'. It is this norm that is presupposed as the basic one underpinning or tying the entire structure of the legal system. Another sense in which it is presupposed is that by its very nature it has never actually been posited or laid down as an act of will. In this sense, Kelsen insists, the basic norm can only be an act of *thinking*, and as such cannot be regarded as a norm of positive law.

Criticisms of Kelsen's pure theory of law come from every angle. For traditional defenders of the higher law of natural justice, the theory is seen as the high tide of dehumanising positivism. Also, as an expression of relentless formalism, seeking out the most abstract patterns in the law and deliberately excluding all sociological factors, the pure theory is clearly at the far end of the spectrum from American legal realism (see Chapter 7). It has also been attacked from within the positivist camp for its supposed ambivalence about the value-free nature of the normative science it proposes, and accused of sliding back towards the very natural law theory that it is supposed to be rooting out.

Does Kelsen equivocate between a specifically legal concept of the validity of norms and a morally evaluative analysis of validity? Many critics believe that he does. Much of the confusion, however, is due to the normative language he is using. It often sounds as though Kelsen is describing a moral obligation when he is not. 'One ought to behave as the constitution prescribes' (Kelsen 1970: 201) is typical. When he distinguishes a state execution of a criminal from murder, by tracing the norm requiring it back to the authority of the constitution and the basic norm that this should be obeyed, it sounds as though he is justifying it. But in fact this is a purely logical account of why the execution is legally valid, while other acts of killing would be counted as murder. Kelsen is at least explicit in his declared *intention* to separate legal validity from any moral connotations: 'The science of law does not prescribe that one ought to obey the commands of the creator of the constitution' (ibid.: 204). Also, he insists that

> the contents of a (specific) constitution and the national legal order created according to it is irrelevant – it may be a just or unjust order; it may or may not guarantee a relative condition of peace. The presupposition of the basic norm does not approve any value transcending positive law.
>
> (ibid.: 201)

In short, Kelsen is wholly committed to legal positivism, to the strict separation of law and morality in the relevant senses, and indications to the contrary are misleading. This was the assumption made by his natural law critics, who linked up this separation thesis directly with what they saw as the positivist failure to confront Nazi law.

Kelsen and Hart

There are of course clear parallels between Kelsen's basic norm and Hart's rule of recognition as the source of legal validity. They both perform the same vital function in giving the legal system its systemic character, by presenting it as a unified whole. The basic norm, like the rule of recognition, is the linchpin that gives the system unity, and every other norm must be linked with it. The differences, however, are as great as the similarities. Hart's basic rule of recognition is a (secondary) rule of law that can be empirically verified, not a Kelsen-style norm, or 'ought-statement'. As such, it is a social fact to be investigated, rather than a hypothetical norm that is presupposed by all legal activity. As a social fact and a rule of law, it is itself a part of the legal system, whereas the Kelsenian basic norm lies outside of the system. There is also a different reason for its validity being unchallengeable. For Kelsen the basic norm must be assumed but can never be demonstrated. For Hart it is a mere statement of social fact that there is a rule of recognition, and 'no such question can arise as to the validity of the very rule of recognition which provides the criteria; it can be neither valid nor invalid but is simply accepted as appropriate for use in this way' (Hart 2012 [1961]: 109).

Radbruch against Kelsen

There has been no shortage of critics of Kelsen, arguing that as the strongest exponent of the positivist separation thesis, he – or his work – must carry a lot of responsibility for the success of Nazism. In fact, it should not be surprising to hear that nothing could have been further from his intentions than that any such political disaster should follow from the theory. The whole point of his theoretical enterprise of purification was to prevent or discourage the politicisation of the law, whether from the left or the right. His intention was the opposite – to protect the law from political control and corruption. The criticisms, however, are directed at the actual implications of his strong version of the separation thesis, rather than on anything that he in fact intended. If law and the moral questions about justice have absolutely nothing to do with one another, as Kelsen seems to be saying, then at least on the face of it, there does seem to be some truth in the criticism of his work that at the very least it did nothing to develop the kind of legal culture that might have been less congenial to the success of Nazism. In the post-war years, the worry was that the continuation of the dominance of Kelsen's positivist thought would present an obstacle to the development of a legal theory which would have been more conducive to an engaged and critical response to whatever dangers lay ahead.

There could be no greater contrast than that between the jurisprudence of Kelsen and Gustav Radbruch (1878–1949). As a liberal with leftist leanings, who had been a Minister of Justice in the government of the Weimar Republic, Radbruch had been removed from his professorship in law at Heidelberg as soon as the Nazis came to power in 1933, and had subsequently survived internal exile until his reinstatement to the same post in 1945. The following year, Radbruch published a famous article (Radbruch 2006 [1946]) in Germany, in which he announced his conversion from the positivism he had accepted in the 1930s to a natural law position. He argued for this in two ways. First, he explained the 'intolerability' thesis:

> Preference is given to the positive law, … , unless its conflict with justice reaches so intolerable a level that the statute becomes, in effect, *Unrichtiges Recht* (false law) and must therefore yield to justice.
>
> (Mertens 2005: 286)

This formulation has had an attractive appeal for post-war legal theory, but Radbruch was not the first to have proposed something like this. At the height of the early twentieth-century formalist period in the USA, similar accounts of the natural law perspective are to be found. The idea is that judges should follow the law to the letter, formalist style, in the normal run of things, but in cases where there is a really glaring injustice they are entitled to intervene with an appeal to the higher law, to overrule it. When Radbruch calls such injustices 'false law', or translated more literally, unrighteous law, he means that it is *prima facie* law, but that it can be overridden in the name of natural justice by authorised judges. The idea is that there is a threshold or 'ceiling of injustice', and any law that breaks through it becomes intolerable. What this formula amounts to is an attenuated version of natural law, as compared with the full-blown Thomistic versions at the time Radbruch was writing, such as that of the French Catholic Jacques Maritain, one of the moving spirits behind the United Nations Declaration of Human Rights in 1948. It is nevertheless a strong anti-positivist statement insisting that when the law does go through this ceiling, it can legitimately be overridden. This idea does have considerable appeal, but as a general proposal it has been criticised as arbitrary, *ad hoc* and overdependent on an individual judge's moral intuitions, especially on the question of when this ceiling is reached. With hindsight it is easy enough to apply it to Nazi statutes, but in a wider context it is not so easy to defend, because of the uncertainty at the time about whether this limit has been breached. This does not mean it is false. It was attacked by Hart and at least implicitly by Kelsen, both of whom thought that it was better to be open and honest about recognising the legal validity of the Nazi statutes, then deal with the problem by adopting the lesser evil of retrospective legislation in order to secure justice for the victims. On the other hand, many have argued against this positivist stance in defence of Radbruch's position, on the grounds that the evil of these statutes must be the main focus when deciding on their inherent legality.

The second way in which Radbruch argued for natural law was through a 'betrayal' thesis:

> Where there is not even an attempt at justice, where equality, the core of justice, is deliberately betrayed in the issuance of positive law, then the statute is not merely *Unrichtiges Recht*, it lacks completely the very nature of law.
>
> (Mertens 2005: 286)

This quite clearly goes beyond the intolerability thesis. 'To lack completely the very nature of law' is a very striking phrase. This is not a mere injustice or breach of conventional morality, but a completely contemptuous disregard for justice in its basic meaning, as displayed by the Nazi statutes. These, of course, were what the thesis was specifically aimed at. Radbruch's position here is in alignment with the strongest interpretations of the classic natural lawyers from Cicero to Aquinas when they declared the 'laws' of tyrants to be classed with those of brigands, and to be regarded as 'no law at all.' In the face of such injustice under the Nazis, Radbruch argued, positivists in Germany had let everyone down by accepting the legality of their statutes, while quietly deploring their immorality, because 'with its credo "a law is a law" [positivism] has in fact rendered the German legal profession defenceless against laws of arbitrary and criminal content' (Radbruch 2006 [1946]: 6). This undoubtedly commendable legal thesis faces a number of problems. The first is how to distinguish it from the intolerability thesis. When does the intolerable become something even worse, a fundamental betrayal of everything the law is supposed to stand for? Secondly, what are the practical consequences of this second thesis that go beyond the first thesis, according to which 'false law' must yield to justice? Either thesis would seem to deliver the same desired result, the retrospective invalidation of the Nazi statute in question. A third problem is how to set the limits to how widely this can be applied to abuses of the law around the world since 1945. The deliberate betrayal – or at least denial – of *equality* can be interpreted in any number of ways, and is certainly not confined to the Nazis' stripping Jews and other minorities of their fundamental human rights. This is a problem that has not been resolved by contemporary jurisprudence.

Fuller's secular version of natural law

Lon L. Fuller (1902–78) played a central role in these debates in the 1950s. As a distinguished Professor of Law at Harvard from 1939 to 1972, Fuller contributed more than any other individual to the revival of natural law in the post-war years. This is principally because he was engaged in the dispute about Nazi legality, and developed a line on it not dissimilar to that of Radbruch. Inspired by a deep antipathy to the positivist concept of law, but equally unimpressed by what he saw as the dead weight of the traditional natural law approach, he developed an original humanistic perspective based on the idea that law itself, as a human institution, naturally generates a specifically legal morality that is the proper starting point for the solution to the problems of legal theory. Fuller's early criticism was directed at classical positivism, but from the 1950s on it was increasingly aimed at his contemporaries Kelsen and Hart. With the latter, he was engaged in an extended controversy over the basic question of the nature of law. How and why Fuller regarded his own position as a modern version of natural law theory is the main question we will need to consider here.

Natural law and secularism

The idea that natural law can be detached from religious ethics, that it can flourish without an ultimate authority in the will of God, has never been entirely absent from natural law theory. What has always been uppermost is the place in the theory occupied by the natural faculty of reason. In Aquinas's natural law theology, the role of reason is pivotal as the source of legal validity. It was ventured as early as the fourteenth century by the Ockhamist Gregory of Rimini that offences against reason would still be sinful, even if God did not exist. The famous declaration by Grotius in the seventeenth century, that 'even if that which cannot be conceived without the greatest iniquity, that God did not exist, were true, natural law would still have binding force', echoed and reinforced this idea, and paved the way for the secularisation that came with the Enlightenment. Many legal thinkers of the eighteenth century, while detaching themselves from Christian orthodoxy, were still committed to the foundational ethical principle of natural law.

Nevertheless, the survival of natural law theory into the twentieth century, against the tide of scientific positivism, owed a great deal to the tradition of Aquinas and the influence of the Roman Catholic Church. The idea that human behaviour is and should be controlled by objective ethical standards derived from a higher law, ultimately sanctioned by the will of God, was still dominant in early twentieth-century natural law thinking.

Fuller's attraction to natural law theory was a purely rationalistic one, which owed nothing to the 'higher law' of the traditional theory. Along with his insistence on putting God out of play, he rejected the idea of law itself, in Holmes's famous aphorism, as 'a brooding omnipresence in the sky', a pre-existing moral order to which lawmakers have to submit. In contrast to this 'higher law' analysis, Fuller saw law as an entirely natural skill, but one that was subject to the same kind of deeper 'natural laws' as other human crafts, such as carpentry or engineering. Just as there are unskilled methods by which tables or window frames cannot be crafted, there are ways in which laws and legal systems cannot be constructed. This 'good carpentry' metaphor was central to Fuller's entirely secularised version of natural law. The sense in which these laws are discovered, rather than made or freely invented, is the sense that aligns Fuller's theory with the basic natural law idea, the foundationalist idea that laws are drawn from natural sources, rather than being the product of pure will.

The procedural shift and the rule of law

With Fuller's complete secularisation comes the most controversial of his adjustments to natural law theory: the shift of focus from the substantive to the procedural. What this means is that the validity of individual laws or the legality of the legal system does not depend in any way on an assessment of the justice or other moral qualities of individual laws or the legal system. Without God's higher law, there is no absolute standpoint from which to make such assessments. Fuller's strategy is to avoid the problem of the variability of moral codes and conceptions of justice by denying the need to engage natural law theory in this kind of argument. The shift to the procedural is a change of focus to what Fuller regards as crucial: the inner morality of law. What he means is that moral values are written into the very idea of law, in such a way that laws and legal systems can be assessed according to the extent to which they satisfy criteria that are specifically legal and procedural.

What Fuller means by the procedural is that, in all legal systems deserving of the title, the creation and implementation of legal rules are guided and constrained by principles relating to the purpose of these rules. These 'qualities of excellence' include generality and efficiency, clarity and intelligibility. Also, they must be well publicised as guides to action. Laws that are internally inconsistent, applied retrospectively or impossible to comply with are excluded. Taken as a complete set, general fidelity to these principles constitutes observance of the rule of law, which means more than effective coercion authorised by a sovereign power. The rule of law means that the exercise of legal powers is constrained by the requirements of procedural correctness.

Several features of this set of criteria should be emphasised and borne in mind. First, as qualities of legal excellence, they were conceived by Fuller as perfections that legal practice aspires to but rarely attains completely. Second, this implies that fidelity to each of these principles or to the whole set is nearly always going to be a matter of degree. Third, as these principles are conditions for the existence of a legal system, law as such is taken to be inherently moral, in the sense that 'where there is truly law, there is procedural excellence'.

Fuller's rejection of the separation thesis

It should be plain why these procedural criteria indicate a clear-cut rejection of the morality–law separation thesis. If the very existence of a legal system requires the satisfaction of moral criteria, then it is impossible to say what the law is in fact without reference to the way it ought to be. The credibility of Fuller's challenge to positivism hinges on clarifying this claim that the separation thesis is not only undesirable but also actually false, and that – contra Kelsen – law may not have any content, that what law is actually includes its positive qualities. Its qualities and defects are not extraneous to the question of whether or not it is law. This, for Fuller, is what the necessary connection between law and morality means. He maintained that the attempt to separate law from morality breaks down with the recognition of law as essentially purposive. Law as a whole – a legal system – has a purpose that makes it what it is. The purpose is to provide a framework of guidance by which people can regulate their own behaviour. Within this framework, each individual law has an essential purpose, for example, to discourage fraud and avoid its harmful consequences. All laws are means to specific ends. The general purpose of law can only be implemented by the acknowledgement and observance of the eight rule-of-law principles, without which it would be ineffective in promoting its essential purpose and would fail as law.

It should be understood that Fuller – as an advocate of a distinctly secular version of natural law – was not trying to reinstate the traditional outlook that Bentham and Austin had broken down. As we saw in previous chapters, the integrity of law and morality for common law thinkers like Blackstone was exposed by Bentham as Christian moral sermonising about the virtues of existing law. The necessary connection between law and morality in this context in effect meant that 'if it is law, it must be justified'. The assault on this kind of confusion of law and morality was inspired by the need for clarity, in order to expose and denounce bad laws by the standards of utility, and to campaign for legal reform. The crucial Benthamite point here is that there can be and often are bad laws; their mere legality is not an argument for their moral worth.

Over the course of the following century, this interpretation of the separation thesis was upheld by Holmes, Gray, Kelsen, Hart and the Scandinavian realists, all of whom insisted that individual laws are only contingently related to morality, in the sense that they can range from the most enlightened to the most reactionary, prejudiced and unjust. The stamp of legal validity guarantees nothing about their moral status. All of these thinkers were opposing what they took to be the natural law idea, whether explicit or residual, that legality means justice. The reason for this lay in their restricted attention to the essentially Blackstonian version, which encourages the doctrine that all genuine law is good law. These critics saw it as inherently resistant to progressive legal reform, with a tendency to consecrate the existing legal order, by conceptually excluding criticism of it. At the same time, however, it was also generally recognised that the natural law slogans inherited from Cicero and St Augustine to the effect that an unjust law is no law at all, appeared to have the opposite implication. On this interpretation, only good laws are legal. Manifestly bad 'laws' do not even enjoy the status of legality, regardless of their authoritative source. In this way, the 'necessary connection between law and morality' can mean that legal systems and laws must satisfy a 'minimum morality test'. For positivist critics such as Alf Ross and Kelsen, this only compounded the confusion that natural law brings to legal theory.

Fuller's adoption of the natural law standpoint as the best vehicle for his theory of procedural justice led him to a conclusion distinct from either of these interpretations. On the one hand, he rejects outright the notion that mere legality confers moral legitimacy, and denies that natural law implies this. On the other hand, he does not argue that substantive injustice in the content of a law invalidates it as law. What he does argue, in opposition to positivism, is that the violation of or disregard for the basic procedural principles demanded by secular natural law reduces the validity of a legal system in proportion to the extent of these violations. Among other things, this had the desired result of completely invalidating the Nazi statutes as law.

At the same time, Fuller attempts to turn the tables on positivism by accusing it of degenerating into the kind of formalism that assumes that the law is the law and is there to be obeyed, whatever one may feel about it. This, he argues, is implicit in the separation thesis. The positivist attempt to study law in a coldly factual, scientific manner leads to the acceptance of the authority of law, no matter how unjust. What he is arguing is that the identification of law according to strictly factual criteria – as opposed to his own 'inner morality' criteria – has the effect of endorsing it as law in such a way that it will, in practice, command moral authority, with politically disastrous consequences. On these grounds, Fuller follows Rommen, Radbruch and others in holding legal positivism partly responsible for the success of Nazism and allowing Nazi statutes to assume an aura of legal authority that should not have been contemplated.

Fuller also questions the central positivist claim to greater analytic clarity. He denies that the separation thesis, which might have originally been directed against the mystification created by common law moral verbiage, does in fact lead to greater clarity about the nature of law. What it does lead to, he argues, is the command theory, which even the positivist Hart can accept does not reflect the reality of law. Real clarity, he maintains, will only be attained by relinquishing the separation thesis along with the command theory. Hart, he believed, had wrongly thought that the former could be rescued while ditching the latter.

What Fuller thinks the obsession with trying to describe the law in its pure facticity obscures is the crucial dimension of law, namely, its purposiveness. In eliminating value, the scientific approach is eliminating what is at the centre of law. Stripped of its general and specific purposes, a law or a legal system is not fully intelligible. If the legal analyst deliberately puts these purposes out of play for the sake of scientific accuracy, the picture created will not be one of law the way it actually is, but of the way it would be if legal systems and laws had no essential purpose. This approach treats law as if it were an inert, natural object. For Fuller, it is the result of the inappropriate transfer of positivist methodologies of natural science to the science of law. If a scientific method devised to root out and exclude all traces of purpose or teleology is applied to law, the result will be a 'factual' account of legal behaviour that bears little resemblance to the reality of law. Law is essentially a human creation and must be treated as such.

The problem of Nazi legality

The case of Nazi Germany and its legal system moved to centre stage in this dispute partly because of the meticulous attention that the Nazi leaders paid to legality. The special attention is merited because this particular modern tyranny was in a class of its own in terms of its abuse of the law, which amounted to a violation on a grand scale of so many principles of natural justice. Their statutes and court rulings laid down and enforced laws that would be regarded as deeply unconscionable in any civilised country. As we have seen, it was this legal dimension of Nazism that initiated the fresh collision between natural law and positivist jurisprudence, with each of these schools of thought responding differently.

Let us return to these questions. Was Nazi law genuine law? The problem was that despite the horrors it had perpetrated, their laws had every appearance of belonging to a genuine legal system and there were numerous lawyers of high rank close to the centre of government. In Austinian terms, there was a clearly identifiable determinate sovereign in the person of Hitler, who answered to nobody else of higher status, and to whom the officials and the majority of the populace were very soon in the habit of at least showing outward signs of obedience. In Kelsen's terms, there was a basic norm at the apex of a logically connected system of coercive norms which legally speaking were binding. To anticipate Hart (who had yet to develop his own empiricist theory of law), the system did indeed constitute a network of primary and secondary rules, and one could easily interpret the fundamental rule of recognition – as Hart said himself – as something like the rule that the Führer's word was final. It should be stressed that this was a morally neutral description of the facts of the matter. As Hart was to say, the positivists at this time thought nothing was to be gained by distorting these facts and denying that there was real law in Germany at the time. It was indeed real law, but too wicked for any person of conscience to obey.

The second question that this runs straight into is that of authority and obligation. Were any of the officials or soldiers carrying out the commands of their superiors under an obligation to obey them, and if so, what kind of obligation? Were citizens acting in a way that would be seen as grossly wrong under another jurisdiction protected by the law that sanctioned their actions, or by the defence that they were only following official orders or merely that they were acting in accordance with the law of the day? In other words, how guilty were they?

The reasoning by the Nuremberg judges and later by the federal courts was complex. The essential point is that, although there was no explicit reference to the higher law of natural law theory, the authority of standards of conscience independent of existing positive law at the time was seen as indispensable. At the Court of Appeal in 1949, one defendant was found guilty of an offence because the (Nazi) statute that sanctioned it was deemed 'contrary to the sound conscience and sense of justice of all decent human beings'. Making such reference to independent standards seemed to be the only way in which either the 'following orders' defence could plausibly be rejected, or those who took private advantage of the Nazi statutes for their own vindictive ends, denouncing 'enemies of the state' to the authorities, could be prosecuted for these acts, which were protected by Nazi law.

We have seen how Radbruch argued from a natural law position that the kind of extreme injustice suffered at the hands of the law under such a regime should not be regarded as law at all. Lawyers were duty-bound to take a stand against it, to give the lead to citizens who might thus be more inclined to disobey. Many other natural law philosophers after the war followed Radbruch's line and developed the argument. It is often thought that the practices of these post-war courts in West Germany, tacitly conceding that the content of rules and orders was – contra the positivist view – in some sense and to some extent relevant to legal validity, were a significant concession to the natural law world view. The belief was growing, especially in Germany but also elsewhere, that positivism had been discredited on the grounds that there are laws, the content of which is so foreign to any concept of justice that they do in fact lose their status as law. The Austinian precept, that the law is one thing, its merits and demerits another, was believed to be confounded by this unprecedented departure from the ideal of the rule of law in the Nazi legal system, the 'demerits' of which had become central to assessing the regime's claims to validity.

This line of argument against positivism, however, has never become universal; it has been seen more as a worry than as a decisive argument that would allow natural law standards to assume a central place in the contemporary understanding of law. For one thing, the systematic abuse of power on this scale is seen as a special case, and it is argued that only in such extreme cases can the natural law perspective be seen as convincing. This response is unsatisfactory. Serious institutional injustice sponsored or sanctioned by various legal systems is a matter of degree, and there are few if any jurisdictions in the world that have been or are completely free of them. The second, more significant positivist response is the basic one that the argument confuses legal validity with justification. The stamp of legal validity, according to Hart and others, does nothing to confer moral legitimacy on a legal system, a particular rule of law or an order, a commercial transaction or anything else. Legal validity concerns only the identification of formal criteria, and as such is morally neutral.

Conclusion

The dispute over the legality of Nazi statutes and courts has continued until the present day, and there is no consensus on its outcome. While some see it as more of a verbal than a substantive dispute, the responses to arguments laid out in this chapter should show that it is a very real one, not only because of its political importance, but because of its implications for the more central disputes in contemporary jurisprudence about the meaning of law and the question of how it relates to morality and justice.

Study questions

General question: To what extent, if any, was the positivist separation of law from morality to blame for the success of the Nazi movement?

Further study questions: Is Hart's separation of legal from moral obligation and individual conscience a sufficient reply to the criticism? Can Kelsen's pure theory of law be defended against the natural law criticisms? Explain the difference between Radbruch's intolerability thesis and his betrayal thesis. Do either of these solve the problems raised by the Nazi abuse of law? Does Fuller's secularization of natural law provide the basis for a solution to the problem of legal validity? Or is Hart right to insist that legal validity has nothing to do with moral justification?

Suggestions for further reading

On the basic materials for Nazism and Nuremberg, see the collection in Adams (1992), which contains R.H. Jackson's opening address for the United States at Nuremberg, Stanley Paulson on 'Classical Legal Positivism at Nuremberg', and Lon Fuller on the problem of the Grudge Informer.

Essential to the debate are Radbruch's article in 1946, 'Statutory Lawlessness and Supra-statutory Law' (Radbruch 2006 [1946]), and Hart's criticism in *Concept of Law* (Hart 2012 [1961]), ch. 9, 'Laws and Morals', 206–12. Bix (2011) provides an important assessment of this debate. See also Fogelson (1990) on the Nuremberg legacy, Thomas Mertens (2005) and Yang (2012).

On Kelsen's pure theory, the main text is Kelsen's own *Pure Theory of Law* (Kelsen 1970), first published in 1934. Some radically different perspectives on Kelsen are available in the collections of Tur and Twining (1986), and in Summers (1971). Useful short commentaries include Bix (2015: ch. 4), Harris (1997: ch. 6), Riddall (1999: ch. 11) and Dias (1985: ch. 17).

On Fuller and his dispute with Hart, see Fuller's own *Morality of Law* (Fuller 1969 [1964]). Summers (1984) is the best full-length study of Fuller. See also Summers's 'Professor Fuller on Morality and Law', in Summers (1971), and Lyons (1993: ch. 1). For details on the Hart–Fuller debate and the rule of law, see Lyons (1984: 74–87), Harris (1997: ch. 11), Riddall (1999: ch. 7) and Bix (2015: ch. 6).

5   Legal realism

Pragmatism and legal realism

Legal realism was a movement of thought among lawyers and academics that originated in the US law schools in the late 1890s and early 1900s. Although it was closer in spirit to positivism than to natural law, the new realist movement, which reached the height of its influence in the 1920s and 1930s, spreading through every level of the profession, offered a perspective that was reducible to neither tradition. There was no single outlook shared by all the realists, and there was no conscious attempt to formulate a technically precise concept of law. What nevertheless informed most of their writings was a broad conception of legal theory and practice that scandalised existing legal opinion at the time. Despite the great variety of theoretical perspectives among the realists, it is possible to identify the prominent themes that taken together represent a third point of view, a pragmatic conception of law that threatened to undermine the plausibility of orthodox legal positivism as much as the traditional natural law outlook.

Who were the realists?

The initiators of realism in law were Oliver Wendell Holmes Jr (1841–1935) and John Chipman Gray (1839–1915). Its first phase can be dated from 1897 to 1917. As the name suggests, realism was guided by the perception that legal theories and doctrines as they were taught did not reflect the reality of the law as it was practised in the courts. So realism reflected a growing distrust of the official jurisprudence of the time. To put it bluntly, the realists thought the teaching of law as it was currently practised, was not fit for purpose. They saw some of it as antiquated, all of it as excessively formalised. What Holmes – in his seminal article 'The Path of the Law' (Holmes 1897) – and Gray, in his influential lectures of 1908 (J.C. Gray 1921 [1909]), were proposing was a radical revision of the basis of legal theory to bring it into line with the actual realities of the legal process. As dissatisfaction with the legal theory of the law schools grew over these years, numerous legal writers followed in this new realist vein.

While some see Holmes and Gray as forerunners, as proto-realists at most, exercising a strong influence upon the emergence of realism proper, others see them as early realists, as the leaders of the first wave of a new movement of thought. It should be borne in mind that the highly charismatic Holmes in particular was by 1897 already acquiring the status of legal authority in his own right, and was in the course of time to become the longest-standing Justice (1902–32) – eventually and briefly Chief Justice – of the Supreme Court. Radical and famous for his dissenting opinions, and for his liberal views on labour disputes and on freedom of speech, it was nevertheless no surprise that, from this position, Holmes later kept his distance from the full-blown realism of the 1920s. His hand in the birth of it, however, was never forgotten.

The second phase of legal realism can be dated from approximately 1919 to 1941, between the First World War and the US entry into the Second World War. In the post-war years, realism did not reappear, as much of its work was perceived to have been done, and simply because legal theory had moved on. The two leading lights of this second phase of realism proper were Karl Llewellyn (1893–1962) and Jerome Frank (1889–1957). In 1931, a decade of turbulence in the legal profession culminated in a polemic between Llewellyn and an eminent critic of realism – who nevertheless had his own radical agenda – Roscoe Pound (1870–1964), another giant of early twentieth-century legal theory. The stand taken by the academic Llewellyn was fairly representative of the sceptical temper of the movement as a whole. Llewellyn's book, *The Bramble Bush* (Llewellyn 1930), was one of the most read legal books of this era. Jerome Frank, a judge who was ultimately to be appointed by F.D. Roosevelt to the Supreme Court at the time of the New Deal, represented the more radical wing of realism. In his best-selling book *Law and the Modern Mind* Frank launched a frontal assault on what he saw as a systematic web of illusion and deception in the legal profession about the nature of law. Although many others are worthy of note, one in particular stands out. 'The Judgment Intuitive', an article written by Justice Joseph Hutcheson, was a highly influential account of the realities of judicial reasoning, developing the ideas of Wendell Holmes on this subject, and scandalising the legal establishment both with his emphasis upon the informality and creativity of the thought processes of the best judges, and with his confrontational approach to leading figures of his day.

Legal theory and judicial practice

One popular misconception of realism should be dispelled immediately. The belief that legal realists were hostile to legal theory, that they attempted to undermine it by shifting the focus to the realities of the courtroom, was not well-informed. On the contrary, the realists wanted to increase and widen the scope of legal theory enormously. Even the most radical and apparently extreme of the legal realists were interested, not in overthrowing theory, but rather in transforming it from a fixed body of dogmatic doctrines, rooted in tradition, into a more useful and dynamic approach to real legal problems in an age of rapid social and legal change in the USA, and in order to do this they were stressing the need to open legal theory up to the rising disciplines of economics and sociology.

The origin of this misconception that they were anti-intellectual was that the realist theories were indeed much concerned with what happened in the courts, with the law in action, and they were more interested in what judges actually said and did than in what the textbooks told them they should say and do. What they were arguing here, however, was that the actual reasoning and practical justice handed down by real judges was the appropriate starting point for theory, and that this was to be preferred to the *a priori* deduction of the meaning of law and what reason tells us it must be. This practical reorientation in jurisprudence is analogous to the argument in the philosophy of science that theoretical speculation on the nature or spirit of the scientific enterprise should be grounded in the actual practice of working scientists. This does not mean that the lawyers or the scientists take over from the philosophers; it means only that philosophy that ignores these real practices is likely to remain barren.

The implications of the realist focus on actual legal cases, however, went much further than a reminder that theory should keep both feet on the ground. What it also implied, in a number of different ways, was an understanding of the nature of law which was quite foreign to traditional ways of thinking. For John Chipman Gray, for example, the decisions of judges and nothing else constitute the reality of the law. All else – the rules and principles of common law, the enacted statutes, the maxims of morality and equity, the dictates of custom, even the body of judicial precedent – is relegated to the status of *sources* of law, sources upon which the judges laying down the law can draw, if they so choose. For Gray, this was a strictly realistic assessment of how the law develops historically. Behind the rhetoric of a higher law, the will of the community or the command of the sovereign, what actually counts as law is the ruling of the judge, because this is what will be enforced. Gray's distinction between the law and the sources of law may seem arbitrary and implausible; it is difficult to accept the claim that a legal statute is not actually a part of the law until it has been tested in the courts. Gray did, however, make a persuasive case for his contention that much of the confusion in legal thinking stems from its failure to observe the distinction between law and its sources, and his emphasis on the need for interpretation of laws before they acquire the status of law was soon developed by many others.

An equally spartan conception of law had been suggested by Holmes's famous maxim expressed in 'The Path of the Law' that 'the prophecies of what the judges will do in fact, and nothing more pretentious, are what I mean by the law' (Adams 1992: 92). If this is taken literally, it means that for all practical purposes the law on any given issue actually consists only in the best predictions that well-informed lawyers can make about the way in which a case will be decided. Even the decisions themselves are not hard and fast law, because they will rapidly become no more than the basis for future predictions. Also prominent in this article was what was to become his notorious idea that when trying to determine the way the law stood on any matter, it was better to adopt the viewpoint of 'the bad man', who is only interested in finding out how he can stay out of jail and avoid fines, rather than that of the honest man, for whom conscience is paramount, and will tend to see the law optimistically as guaranteeing fairness and justice, a viewpoint which is often unwarranted. The bad man has the more accurate picture, because he has an eye only for the probable sanctions in force. The reality of the law is reflected essentially by that which people are made to conform with. This bad-man 'theory' of Holmes has often been disparaged as an excessively cynical take on the workings of the law, but it should be read more as a colourful expression of the positivist separation thesis. What he was saying was that one should not confuse the actual law with one's own moral expectations of it, and that the tendency to do this is very widespread. The shrewd practitioner of jurisprudence will always suspend such expectations.

None of these pronouncements became dogma for the subsequent realist thinkers, probably because they could see their defects, but the hard-headed, unpretentious approach to legal analysis that they embodied did become the guiding spirit of the realism expounded by Llewellyn, Frank and many others. Holmes and Gray were both motivated by a desire to deflate what they saw as a persistent idealisation of law, the inevitable consequence of removing it from its actual practice. Many years later Llewellyn's realist programme made central the need to recognise the fluidity of law and society, and therefore the futility of trusting established legal doctrines and fixed-rule formulations. In place of such reverence for the past, Llewellyn proposed a shift of emphasis to the actual effects of judicial decisions.

The pragmatist attack on certainty

The realist critique of conventional jurisprudence at this time needs to be set against the background of philosophical developments at the turn of the century. The leading light Holmes was a close friend of C.S. Peirce, who was the first of a succession of American pragmatist philosophers to challenge the epistemological tradition in European philosophy head on. The point upon which this enterprise hinged was the question of whether human knowledge can ever aspire to complete certainty about anything. Peirce – and following him, William James and John Dewey – was famous for defending the idea that certainty was an elusive ideal which could never be attained, hence we should relinquish the attempt to construct such an epistemology. For over two centuries, most philosophers – rationalist and empiricist alike – had followed Descartes' attempt to show how certain knowledge could be attained.

According to the dominant strain of thinking in the late nineteenth century – the strain of thought against which Peirce and Holmes were reacting – natural science was a raging success story, a steadily expanding accumulation of fully established unrevisable truths. For some supreme optimists it was only a matter of time before the human sciences – especially sociology, psychology, economics – would be elevated to the same level. Even for those who were more reflective about the foundations for this supposedly unrevisable knowledge, certainty was an ideal that was largely unquestioned. After all, how could one claim to know anything if one could not attain certainty? The main input of philosophy into scientific method was the attempt to place the sciences on a sound footing, showing how we could build knowledge from secure foundations of which we were certain. Peirce's rejection of certainty as the guiding ideal of science, a rejection that was soon to be vindicated by the upheaval and crisis in the mainstream sciences in the first quarter of the twentieth century, was echoed by the legal realists. From Holmes to Frank, the reaction against the pursuit of the ideal of law as a certain science, requiring systematic rigour that would leave no room for error or indeterminacy, was the central feature of legal realism.

The rejection of certainty in epistemology was anti-foundationalist. The number of issues this challenge raises is even today in the early twenty-first century nowhere near resolution, but the point to note here is that the denial of the need for certain foundations upon which to ground knowledge, allows such knowledge to be provisional. Traditional philosophy has held that the first condition of knowledge is that what is believed must be true. Without truth, there is no knowledge. If a belief turns out to be false, then what was thought to be known was not known at all. This seems self-evident. And what also seemed self-evident was that for knowledge to be knowledge, the possibility of error must be eliminated completely: hence the importance of the quest for certainty.

What Peirce and later pragmatists were arguing for was the initially counter-intuitive claim that knowledge does not require the elimination of every possibility of error. What we 'know' now may later turn out to have been mistaken, but this does not mean that we do not know it now. For many philosophers such reflections lead straight into scepticism, the denial that any of our claims to knowledge are sound. For the pragmatists, and others influenced by them, it leads to a far-reaching revision of our understanding of the character of knowledge and – notoriously – a redefinition of truth. For Peirce, the true opinion is the one destined to be believed by an ideal community of future scientists. For William James, the true opinion is the one that it is to our best advantage to believe. Although neither of these pragmatic concepts of truth, which seem to involve too radical a departure from conventional usage, have gathered much of a following, the pragmatist rejection of certainty has nevertheless been widely endorsed by the entire movement of anti-foundationalism in epistemology.

The movement against certainty in legal theory runs along parallel lines. Legal absolutism in the 1890s was as unconvincing to radical thinkers as the uncritical scientific positivism of this period was to philosophers who saw the weakness of its foundations. Holmes – very much in the spirit of

Peirce – regarded the almost universal belief that the law could be determined and applied with scientific precision as explicable only in terms of 'the longing for certainty and repose', a natural impulse found in every area of thought. Much of his writing was directed at breaking down this illusion and its damaging consequences for the law. The illusion of certainty that he and subsequent realists assailed was the comforting official belief that 'the law' was a fully formed pre-existing reality, a coherent body of rules ready to be applied by judges trained and sufficiently skilled in syllogistic reason to deduce the correct answer to any legal problem that might arise, with complete certainty. For Holmes, the law thus understood became an imaginary 'brooding omnipresence in the skies', a reified power that guaranteed a spurious certainty and determinacy. The hard reality of law was for Holmes, as for many other radical thinkers, inherently indeterminate and uncertain, a more gritty affair involving the unpredictable outcome of the collisions between multiple principles, policies and unspoken assumptions.

Jerome Frank's attack on the basic myth of certainty was more polemical and uncompromising. In Frank's writing, it becomes forthright and explicit that legal certainty is as undesirable as it is unattainable. This is a much debated point, even today. For the realist Frank, the absence of certainty is no cause for regret, and the indeterminacy of how the law stands at any given point on any given issue is to be welcomed rather than deplored. We will see in a later chapter how important this dispute became much later in the century. The point Frank was making was that the widespread pretence that law can be made fixed and unwavering was so pervasive in his time that it stifled any understanding of the real nature of law. What he and his fellow realists were struck by was not merely the gap between theory and practice, but what he depicted as an astounding self-deception at large in the interpretation of law as a fixed body of determinate rules when it was plain for all to see that the opposite was the case, with rules adapted, changed and invented every day throughout the numerous jurisdictions of the USA. Although these were all rooted in common law, it was increasingly the individual states' own version of common law, and there was no denying that any particular decision was highly unpredictable.

Why was this belief in legal certainty so strong? For Holmes, this required no more explanation than that the craving for certainty, and the belief in it against so much evidence, was a natural impulse. Uncertainty leads to deep unease, which the human animal finds very difficult to live with; it craves the right answer so much that it will accept any rather than none. Frank looked elsewhere for the explanation. Using Freudian psychoanalysis, he explained it in terms of the unconscious yearning for the lost security of childhood, provided by the omniscient father figure. Frank believed that this almost universal creation of a chimerical certainty infected every aspect of legal theory in particular, because the law with its judges and judgements was peculiarly qualified to stand in for the father figure. Belief in 'the law' as a fundamental certainty fulfils a vital psychological need. The realist attack on this belief was inspired by the desire to uncover the reality of the workings of the law that had been obscured by this myth of certainty.

The realist revolt against formalism

The pragmatist-inspired rejection of the idea of certainty in law goes hand in hand with the hostility to the legal formalism that, in the perception of the leading realists, lay at the heart of modern legal analysis. 'Formalism' is a term with several distinct meanings and connotations in philosophy, mathematics and legal theory. What is relevant here is the realist interpretation of legal formalism as a tendency that has a damaging effect on both our understanding of law and the practical administration of justice. The criticisms of formalism intensified as the realist movement developed.

Formalism was defended and keenly advocated by leading influences on legal education at the turn of the century, especially by the dominant figure of Christopher Columbus Langdell, who as Dean of the Harvard Law School in the late nineteenth century was famous for pioneering 'the case method', an early book on which was – curiously enough – warmly praised by Holmes in a review (P. Kelley 2002: 4). Langdell's passionate belief was that the study of the law could be put on a firm scientific footing with the case method. The point to register here is that formalism – which has acquired a negative image over the years – is not self-evidently wrong. The idea behind the case method was that legal erudition was to be accrued less by listening to lectures and more by the study of a vast number of ideal cases, each of which was to represent a legal principle, such that any real case that came before the courts was to be dealt with by the deductive application of the principle to the case in hand, which would go hand in hand with the scientific method of induction. In such a way, the law is steadily improved as an instrument of consistent justice.

The criticisms developed by the realists were essentially that the formalist case method leads inevitably to a preoccupation with the outward forms of the law as it is written, at the expense of the inner content or substance of the law. This exaggerated emphasis on the formal was expressed by the realist critics in a number of ways. The central point is that law is interpreted as a formally closed system, governed by strict rules of inference and demonstrative proof. This has two main implications: (1) as the narrowing down of legal reasoning to the form of the deductive syllogism, a formalistic approach is one that is guided by the belief that all legal problems can be solved by framing them in syllogistic form, whereby major and minor premises yield a demonstrable conclusion; and (2) law is closed off to outside influences, so its interpretation becomes a purely internal matter, to which other social, political and economic factors are irrelevant.

The essential criticism is that the formalist approach makes the mistaken assumption that the law can be completely understood by studying and applying deductive formal logic to principles and cases. With syllogistic reason placed at the centre of law as a formally closed system, it becomes possible to resolve every problem in such a way that it leaves no room for doubt. Holmes described this in 'The Path of the Law' (Holmes 1897) as 'the fallacy of logical form', the error in which lay in the refusal to recognise the non-logical forces at work in the determination of the content and growth of the law. The structure of the legal syllogism is such that the truth of the conclusion does not depend to any degree on the substantial content of any of the premises.

What follows from this essential criticism is a general picture of the formalist approach as 'a mechanical jurisprudence', according to which all problems of interpretation can be definitively resolved by meticulous attention to logical detail. It is called mechanical because a calculating machine could do it: one could feed the question in at one end and wait for the answer at the other. The chief danger, as Holmes saw it, lay in the modelling of the system of law on mathematics, imagining that the whole system can be deduced from general axioms, so that a judicial mistake can be seen as 'not doing one's sums right'. What this obsession with certainty leads to is a strong tendency towards literalism, focusing on the letter at the expense of the spirit of the law. It leads to a tendency to follow rules for their own sake; the natural consequence of this is the elimination of equity in the assessment of individual cases. The peculiar features of each unique case are to be found in the substantiality of the concrete circumstances of the case, not in the formal rules that can be made to fit the case. A mechanical jurisprudence – so the realist argument runs – trains the legal mind to abstract from these circumstances, to find the applicable rule that will provide the correct answer.

What were the realists urging against, or in place of, this mechanised jurisprudence? What would a non-formal, un-mechanised jurisprudence look like? For Holmes, 'the root and nerve of the whole proceeding' is the judgement – often inarticulate and unconscious – that lies behind the logical form. What he is referring to here is not the judicial pronouncement on the case, but the individual act of judgement that precedes it, the judgement of the relative worth of competing claims, a judgement that comes before its rationalisation in logical form. What Holmes was arguing was that the real factors influencing these pre-logical judgements – in particular, matters of social policy – are nearly always camouflaged by syllogistic reason. Holmes' 'realism' consists in his advocacy of making conscious and explicit what was damagingly left half-conscious and concealed by the logical rationalisations surrounding these judgements. It was the nature of this judgement, then, and the influences forming it, which needed to be brought into the light as the basis of a realist jurisprudence.

Realists of the later phase of the movement broadened the scope of these 'real factors' enormously and focused on the nature of this judgement. Jerome Frank's provocative itemisation of the types of conscious and unconscious personal preference and prejudice at work in the judicial proceedings, attempting to explode the myth of judicial impartiality and objectivity, was seen by traditionalists as an attack on the integrity of the profession. While it is true that Frank was sometimes gratuitously offensive in his attacks on individuals, behind the polemic there was a serious and sustained assault on mechanical jurisprudence.

Abductive inference to the best explanation

This was nowhere more visible than in the realists' scrutiny of the manner in which judges formed their judgements and arrived at their own conclusions. Justice Hutcheson's account of 'the judgment intuitive' literally reversed the established assumptions about this thought process (Adams 1992). Hutcheson confronted the security of the legal formalist mind, and its systematic application of general rules to yield a certain result, with the real human mind of the judge, in which the prominence of the faculty of imagination allows the natural process of *backward* reasoning to be given full rein. In this, Hutcheson, like so many other realists, was strongly influenced by Peirce, who had developed the logic of abduction in philosophy as a challenge to the dominance of deduction and induction. This was a highly significant development in the history of modern philosophy, the implications of which have only gradually been worked through over the course of the following century. Today, this abductive reasoning is more commonly known as 'inference to the best explanation', and is much more widely accepted. Peirce understood this to be a logic of creativity and discovery, both scientific and philosophical. The reasoning is described as abductive or retroductive because it involves a backward move or leap in the mind from a puzzling problem or mystery to its potential solution, to the hypothesis which if true would dissolve the problem. Peirce saw this not only as essential to the reasoning mind but as the most important of our intellectual faculties, and argued that it had been systematically suppressed because it was wrongly dismissed as unreliable intuition or guesswork, rather than being worthy of any study as a mode of reasoning with a distinct logical form.

So in sharp contrast with the formalist belief that judges must move carefully forward from premises to conclusion, reaching their judgement through a painstaking rational process, Hutcheson paints a vivid picture of the judge assembling all the relevant data and withdrawing to introspect and 'brood over the chaos', waiting for 'the flash of understanding which makes the jump-spark connection between question and decision' (Adams 1992: 201). The phrase of Hutcheson's that was to become highly influential was that of 'the hunching out' of a solution. What he maintained was that the inspired hunch, the sudden flash of understanding – it might be called today 'the eureka moment' – lay at the very heart of the process of discovery, and that it was precisely the role of this hunch which was suppressed by formalistic reason. For the realists, this hunching out can by its very nature never be performed by a machine; it is entirely the product of the human imagination. In fact it was this freeing up of thought that the legal formalists were very keen to eliminate, to keep the judges' eyes on what logic and case law dictates. On Hutcheson's account, the judgement is reached first, the rationalisation follows. The public or official reasoning of the judge as declared and published is an elaborate justification of the decision already reached by other means.

It is essential to note that Hutcheson's analysis was not intended as an attack on the judiciary, of which he was himself an eminent member. What he was criticising was the failure of many judges, under the influence of a formalistic training, to make full use of the human intellect in the way that the best judges did. It should also be made clear that he was not proposing the casting away of careful deductive and inductive logic in favour of the creative logic of abduction, which would indeed have been reckless. What he was proposing was the use of all three modes of thought, each in their proper place, in one connected logical process. A 'hunched out' solution does not stand alone; it has to be checked and corroborated against the facts before it is reached as a considered judgement. Furthermore, any number of abductive hypotheses might be thrown up before they hit on the right one. The point is that it is the deliberate exclusion of this faculty that has the effect of imprisoning the inquiring mind, so that it does not even throw up the relevant possible solutions.

This aspect of the attack on formalism and mechanism in law was taken up with alacrity by Jerome Frank. Reinforcing Hutcheson's assessment of the nature of creative legal reasoning, he argued that it was more important for lawyers to catch the creative scientific spirit than to imitate scientific logic. He insisted that the judgement in a court of law was no different in principle from judgements in any other context; that what it essentially involved was the working backwards from a vaguely formed conclusion to find the premises to substantiate it, the search continuing until the right conclusion is found. Referring to this feature of judicial reasoning as 'the dominance of the conclusion', he maintained that what was clearly evident in the practice of a legal advocate who is openly partisan for a conclusion favouring his or her client, was less evident but equally operative in the case of the impartial judge. The fault, for Frank, lies not in the backward reasoning of the judge, but in the concealment of this reality by the myth of certainty and the pretence that the conclusion is the outcome of formal reason. What he advocates is a shift in focus from the study of legal logic to the study of the explicit and unconscious factors – political, social, economic and personal – which have the real influence on the judge's selection of the conclusion.

Realism and rule-scepticism

The rule-scepticism to which numerous realists subscribed in the 1920s and 1930s has been misrepresented and distorted more than any other feature of legal realism. Treated by many as a fantasy that flies in the face of the facts about legal rules and such doctrines as *stare decisis* – an official doctrine of precedent that is quite clearly adhered to – dismissed by others as an eccentric exaggeration of the idiosyncrasies of unconventional judges, the genuine insights of the realist rule-sceptics have more recently been acknowledged once again.

The contemporary reaction to the realist scepticism towards rules, however, was hardly surprising. The sceptical questioning of the status and role of legal rules in the judicial process was the most potentially damaging of the realist criticisms of traditional formalism and mechanical jurisprudence. Emerging as it did from the realist attack on legal certainty, this scepticism threatened to bring down not only the entire edifice of legal theory but also the credibility of law as a respected institution, a basic premise of both theory and practice being the idea of law as a coherent set of authoritative rules governing human transactions. What we need to be clear about, then, is what exactly this scepticism amounted to. What exactly was it the rule-sceptics were denying? Did their analysis really threaten to undermine the law? Or was it – as Llewellyn insisted – proposing a viable alternative to law as understood and practised?

What does it mean to be sceptical about legal rules? First, can we as a matter of fact say that there actually are any legal rules? If sceptics are doubting their very existence – in other words, expressing an ontological doubt – this can surely be dismissed as eccentric. The rules are there for everyone to see the application and effects of. If scepticism means this, it can easily be rejected. This ontological doubt has nevertheless been attributed to the extreme legal realists and dubbed 'rule nihilism', analogous to the claim that, for example, there literally are no rights. We have to ask whether such extreme propositions even make sense. To say, for example, that there actually are no rules on inheritance or the validity of contracts, would be manifestly absurd. Moreover, as Hart later pointed out, the very existence of the court of law presupposes the existence of secondary rules conferring legitimacy on the court. Once one accepts this, one can establish one set of rules after another and refute this form of scepticism (Hart 2012 [1961]: 136–7).

It is doubtful, however, that any of the prominent realists took this position seriously. Frank – widely regarded as an extremist – explicitly repudiated it, arguing that this literal nihilism was the product of the formalist critics' inability to see any other alternative to their own absolutism. With this false alternative, either rules operate without exception, or there are no rules at all. As we shall see, the realist exposure of the mythical status of legal rules does not entail this nihilism at all. The basic argument is not that legal rules do not exist, but that the rules do not play the kind of role that formalists believe they do. They do not determine the outcome of cases, but in reality should be seen as only one factor among many governing court procedures and decisions.

The second question, then, concerns the role of legal rules. Given that there are numerous rules of law, what part do they play in the administration of law? Does the activity of judges consist in the careful application of the rules to the case in hand, as the formalist case method would have it, or do the rules play a more subordinate role than this? To answer these questions, we need to draw a contrast between various strengths of rule-scepticism, from minimum to maximum.

A minimal form of scepticism makes the claim that judges do in reality –
irrespective of official doctrine – have at least some discretion in at least some
areas of law, to make decisions without reference to any pre-existing rules. In
other words, they can and do quite frequently break out of the framework of
the rules and apply their own best judgement. In so doing, judges can be seen
as themselves making new rules. Advocates of this thesis believe that complete
codification and predictability are neither possible nor desirable. What is
needed in some areas of law is flexibility and adjustment to circumstance.
This is minimal rule-scepticism in as far as it doubts the value of complete
codification and understands the virtues of judicial flexibility. As such, it is a
rather limited critique of formalism.

The maximum thesis is that judges do in reality – irrespective of official
doctrine – have full discretion, in every area of law, to make decisions without
any reference to pre-existing rules. They might allow the rules to constrain
them for the sake of appearance, but the underlying truth is that there is
nothing to stop them in effect legislating from the bench continuously. In so
doing, judges are not making new rules, they are simply deciding one unique
case after another according to their own predilections. Their apparent
obeisance to rules is mere camouflage. So advocates of this thesis believe that
the existence of rules exercises virtually no practical constraint on judicial
discretion. The elaborate legal doctrine of precedent, of the binding nature of
authoritative judicial decisions, is a pretence that conceals the truth of arbitrary
creativity. This is uninhibited rule-scepticism, which constitutes a complete
rejection of formalism.

Two initial points about these theses should be noted. First, the minimum
thesis is only minimally sceptical of the prominent role played by rules.
Supporting this thesis is quite insufficient for being counted among the
realists. They do accept that the regulatory framework is broadly accepted
and that this is as it should be. They include those who were at the most on
the periphery of the realist movement, such as Pound and Cardozo, and soft
positivists such as Hart. Essentially, what it involves is no more than a rejection of
the extremes of formalism and mechanical jurisprudence. This is what it means to
allow that there exists and should exist a certain amount of free discretion on
the part of the judges to derogate from the rules from time to time.

Secondly, the maximum thesis should not be confused – as it so very often
has been – with the ontological nihilism already referred to, the view that
legal rules are a complete mirage. However, advocates of this strong position
regard the rules as little more than a front or facade, the purpose of which is
to cover the tracks of judicial innovation. One striking feature of this position
is that it seems to flatly contradict the original purpose behind the critique of
formalism, the idea that judges trained in this manner should be criticised for
their obeisance to rules and their unimaginative approach to the logical solution
of problems, rather than using their own abductive reasoning powers. This is a
source of deep confusion running right through the realist movement, which
is only partly explained by the diversity of this loose-knit school of thought.

Some of its advocates often did not seem to be able to decide whether they are accusing typical formalist judges of being dull and unimaginative servants of the system, or cunning manipulators of the system for their own purposes.

The versions of rule-scepticism promoted by most of the realists fell somewhere between these two positions, stronger than the minimal, weaker than the maximal. According to the moderate thesis, the role of rules in every area of law is radically suspect. Sometimes the rules are fully operative, sometimes they are not. All decisions, its supporters think, although not haphazard and arbitrary, are inherently unpredictable. The theory and practice of applying general rules, of using these rules to reason to a conclusion, and in so doing following precedent, do have some force, but nowhere near as great as imagined by formalist theory. In reality, the moderate sceptics think, judges at every level are able to select or disregard precedent to suit the conclusion already arrived at. On the moderate thesis, the idea that judges are helplessly bound by the rules is indeed a myth.

It was in the spirit of this moderate thesis that Llewellyn (assisted by Frank, who put his name to it) drafted a list – a realist 'manifesto' – of what he regarded as the shared points of departure of twenty of the leading realists in the early 1930s. These included tendencies towards '*distrust* of traditional legal rules and concepts which purport to describe what courts or people are actually doing', and – crucially – towards 'distrust of the theory that traditional rule-formulations are THE operative factor in producing court decisions' (Twining 1973: 79–80). It was the limited extent and the uneven application of the rules that Llewellyn was highlighting. Rule-formulations were regarded as one operative factor among others, which may or may not be applied in any given instance. What he and others were resisting with this emphasis on distrust was the assumption that rules were necessarily, or by definition, the decisive factor influencing judicial decisions. The adoption of this moderate position, then, did not mean that all rules were to be regarded as bogus; what it meant was that a critical scepticism toward their actual authority should be maintained. Llewellyn was also careful to avoid endorsing the positivist separation thesis. According to a prominent point in his manifesto, *is* and *ought* are to be 'divorced' for purposes of the study of what the courts are doing, so that one refrains from moral judgements of what they ought to be doing. He was not saying that 'law is one thing, morality is another', only that it should be studied as if it had no moral implications, in order to focus on what it was actually saying. He was distinguishing this from an endorsement of the substantial separation thesis, because of his well-known sympathies for natural law.

Jerome Frank acknowledged the realist direction of those who advocated the minimum thesis, but criticised their half-heartedness in this respect, arguing that they were still caught in the spell of the myth of certainty, and urging them to adopt a more thoroughgoing scepticism. His own position as a rule-sceptic was more ambiguous, seeming to oscillate between the moderate and the maximum thesis as described above, between Llewellyn's critical scepticism and an outright denial of the efficacy of rules. Much of his writing is in the spirit of the later, of uninhibited rule-scepticism, according to which rules are no more than aids for testing conclusions already reached, influences towards wise or unwise decisions, formal clothes in which to dress these decisions. In short, 'rules' of law in truth are guidelines rather than rules.

What is instructive here is Frank's understanding of the *status* of rules. He sees every rule as a formalised description of the past, as a useful abbreviated general description of the way previous courts have reacted and decided various cases. On his account, rules are not *established* by precedent, they are themselves merely compressed accounts of precedent in the abstract. They are informative of law, not constitutive of it. The determination of any actual concrete case adds another notch of authority to the traditional legal thinking on any given subject, but it is itself a part of the creative tradition. Every judge can either ignore this and fall against the tradition, thus reinforcing the formalist approach, or recognise it and contribute constructively to the continuing vitality of legal thinking.

Frank was also responsible for an extension of this rule-scepticism into the area of legal facts. The notorious fact-scepticism he promoted was what often attracted the attention and wrath of his critics. Emphasising the personal behavioural quirks of judges and jury members, he argued that the tendency to manipulate the facts of each case, as well as the rules applied, undermines certainty in the prediction of its outcome completely. All lawyers, he claimed, made a pretence of 'having considered all the facts ...', but this was mere rhetoric, designed to cover their tracks. The rulings of judges often depended on their moods and what they had eaten for breakfast. He also insisted that juries never found the facts in accordance with the evidence, but rather that they distorted the facts and found them in such a manner that they were able to confirm their already formed prejudices, such that the 'facts' were found in order to reach the result. What has to be said against Frank on these issues is that such criticisms of the judicial process are easy to make if one looks relentlessly with a cynical eye at such proceedings. There is always inevitably some truth in criticisms such as these, but it is another question whether they can be represented as being typical characteristics of judges and jury members. It also raises the question of what realists could propose to replace such a system with, or even improve the existing one, given that it is highlighting the inevitable weaknesses of human nature.

The pragmatics of justice

While it would certainly be an exaggeration to say that the realists were concerned entirely with the individualisation of justice, it is also true that their guiding purpose in opposing the formalist approach was the development of a perspective that would assist, rather than hinder, the ability of judges to arrive at just solutions to difficult cases. Behind this purpose lay the conviction that the attempt to operate the law as a closed logical system had a stultifying effect on the very idea of legal justice.

The formalist approach to justice was traditionally justified by the need to discover and maintain rules and principles that could be applied impersonally, without fear or favour, on the basis of the principle of equality before the law, that 'like cases should be treated alike'. The subjection of all to the rule of law, and the reluctance to make any exceptions, was believed – not unreasonably – to be indispensable to the development of a just legal system. This was felt to express the inner meaning of justice, that the same rules be applied to everyone.

It was against this picture of formalised justice that the realist rule-scepticism reacted. The realists had a pragmatic attitude to justice in as far as they regarded this picture as an unattainable idealisation of law. In the real life of the law, there is no certainty, no guarantee that the legal process will deliver just solutions to every problem. This absence of certainty is due, not primarily to the human fallibility of judges and juries, but the fact that any real legal system will always contain indeterminacies. What the realists were trying to expose and dissolve was the illusion that a sophisticated modern legal system, perfectly formalised and idealised, is the perfect vehicle for legal justice. What Frank saw in this was the elimination of the human factor, specifically the marginalisation of the spirit of equity. If justice is to be real, it has to be individualised and adjusted to the circumstances of each concrete case. As we saw in an earlier chapter, the idea of equity as the necessary correction to justice delivered too literally, originates in Aristotle. Frank argued that the tradition emanating from Aristotle's account of equity distorts it by removing it from the ambit of law, by representing it as an unfortunate necessity disrupting the regular procedure of law, in the interests of a wider sense of justice than is allowed by law. Frank's challenge to this interpretation, which has been very influential, reverses its assumptions. The spirit of equity, he argues, is not an expedient to be wheeled in for the odd occasion, it is inseparable from the rest of what we call the law. Furthermore, as the superior aspect of justice, it is found at the very heart of the law (which, for Frank, it should be remembered, is what actually happens in its main arena, the courts) because 'as against Aristotle and Pound it would be wiser to go to the other extreme and to say that the law is at its best when the judges are wisely and consciously exercising their discretion, their power to individualise cases' (Frank 1949: 141).

With the abandonment of the quest for certainty, the problem of the objectivity of justice also diminishes. Hutcheson's model judge, the realist waiting for the flash of inspiration and 'hunching out' solutions intuitively, rather than applying the deductive syllogism, has 'a roving commission to find the just solution' (Adams 1992: 203). In contrast to the lawyers, who are partisan for their clients, the judge is partisan for justice. This is what Hutcheson argues against those who see the model judge as the one who dispassionately applies the rules to find the correct solution. The justice of the pragmatic decision is relative to the moral judgement of a real individual, who depends primarily on understanding and experience, using formal reason only to check and reinforce the decision. The justice rendered by the strict application of pre-existing rules is an abstract justice that makes no real contact with the interests of the competing parties in the legal dispute.

A final point about the pragmatic nature of justice concerns the opening up of the deliberations of the judge to outside influence. The idea that the intrusion of non-logical, extralegal considerations of social policy should be made explicit and legitimate, for the sake of the continuing vitality of the law and its interaction with a changing society was first made forcefully by Holmes. This idea has influenced the whole of modern jurisprudence, not just the legal realists. Its general character is essentially forward-looking. For the realists, it meant an instrumentalist focus on probable outcomes of legal rulings, rather than a backward-looking reverence for past decisions. What they were advocating was a future-directed honesty about the social objectives of the judiciary, reflecting contemporary views of morality and justice in a changing world.

Hart's criticism

It should be clear from the foregoing that legal realism had many strengths and weaknesses. Its main strength is visible in the apparent success of its main enterprise, in loosening the grip of the formalist theory it was attacking. By the post-war years, it was widely regarded as having served its purpose in this respect. Mechanical jurisprudence was no longer popular. The attention the leading realists had drawn to the question of how to guide judicial reasoning along more sophisticated lines than the legal profession had been familiar with, was of great value. At the same time, however, we have also seen that many of their criticisms were not well directed, and the realists often seemed to be unsure of what they were proposing in place of the theories they were attacking. Writing in the 1950s with the benefit of hindsight, Hart engaged with the more moderate versions in a constructive criticism in *The Concept of Law* (Hart 2012 [1961]: 136–54). In developing his own positivist theory, he was simultaneously rejecting rival versions of positivism along with traditional natural law theories, but also saw it as important to expose what he saw as the central mistakes of realism. While he approved of their critique of mechanical jurisprudence and formalism, he focused his criticism on their rule-scepticism.

The criticism of Hart's cited already, that if they are denying the very existence of primary and secondary rules they are talking nonsense, is well made, but it applies to very few of the realists. More importantly he rejects Gray's notion that there is really nothing but legal sources, rather than hard and fast law in the written rules. These sources are still there, says Hart, and they have real effects. On the more pervasive idea that law is what the courts say it is, and that the best one can do is predict their next finding, he argues that this is ultimately unintelligible. He draws an analogy with an imaginary game of cricket which he calls 'scorer's game', according to which 'the score is what the scorer says it is'. Quite an amusing game this would be, he says, but it is complete nonsense, because it would mean that the scorer could never make a mistake. There is an independent standard: the actual score. The same applies to law. If the rule-sceptics are right, the judges could never make a mistake in law, which they quite clearly can, as the successful appeals show.

Frank had argued that it was a false alternative imagined by the formalists that we had to accept either their absolutism or a nihilistic picture of no rules at all. Hart turns this against Frank and the other rule-sceptics by arguing that this is just what they set up, a false alternative between accepting that for a rule to be a rule it must have no exceptions, and declaring that there is no rule at all. He concludes that the extreme realists are disappointed formalists, highly sceptical of the rules whenever they see any exceptions made. He was perhaps overstating his case here, as it was only the most extreme of the realists who veered into maximum rule-scepticism. Whether or not this is true, the argument here leads into Hart's own critique of formalism and his theory of open texture, which will be taken up in the next chapter.

Hart's criticism of Hutcheson's 'judgment intuitive' is that it may well be possible that some judges bypass rules to reach the desired conclusion via hunches, then find a rule to match it, but the more common case is the judge who does abide by a rule antecedently recognised, or if intuition is indeed used, makes the greatest effort to justify it with such rules. This does seem to miss the point of Hutcheson's argument, which is precisely that such abductive 'hunches' do always have to be corroborated by more conventional reasoning. What he objects to is the way in which abductive reasoning is eliminated completely by formalism.

Hart's overall verdict on legal realism, then, was mixed. He did not deny its value in exposing the narrow-mindedness of many of the ideas about law that dominated the establishment at the time that realism was rising, but he offered serious criticism of its central theories. From our vantage point, we can also see that in this area Hart was sometimes hitting his target accurately, sometimes not.

Conclusion

As a movement spanning several decades at a time of rapid change and upheaval in American society, legal realism had an enormous impact on jurisprudence around the world, both short-term and permanent. One of the reasons it did not continue in the post-war years was that so many of the realist insights had been accepted. Formalism was no longer the force it had been in the early twentieth century. Another reason was that other theories were coming to occupy centre stage. In retrospect, we can see legal realism as brilliant but flawed. Even when they were wrong, though, its leading adherents addressed questions and problems in the law of their day with such acuity that they could not be ignored.

Study questions

General question: How realistic was American legal realism?

Further study questions: Explain and critically examine the realist revolt against legal formalism. Consider Hart's criticisms and make the best case you can in defence of realism. How far does it stand up to the positivist criticisms? Does Holmes' bad-man theory of law help to illuminate the real processes of law? Read the section on abductive reasoning carefully, then apply it to one of the cases with which you are familiar. Is the realist model of judicial reasoning convincing? Which version of rule-scepticism, if any, do you find the most convincing? How might one defend natural law theory against legal realism?

Suggestions for further reading

The most important primary sources for the early phase of American legal realism are Holmes' 1897 article, 'The Path of the Law' (Holmes 1897) and Gray's lectures *The Nature and Sources of the Law* (Gray 1921 [1909]). The full-blown realism of the inter-war years is best represented by Llewellyn's *Bramble Bush* (Llewellyn 1930), Frank's *Law and the Modern Mind* (Frank 1949 [1930]) and Hutcheson's 'Judgment Intuitive' (Hutcheson 1929).

Full studies of this movement include Rumble (1968) and Twining (1973). Novick (1989) is an interesting biography of Holmes. Kelley (2002) and Kellogg (2007) are important studies of the original emergence of realism. Other significant commentaries include Bix (2015: ch. 17), Golding and Edmundson (2005: ch. 3), M. Davies (1994), Friedmann (1944: ch. 25), Dias (1985: ch. 21) and Cotterell (1989: ch. 7). The most influential criticism of realism and rule-scepticism comes from Hart (2012 [1961]: 136–47). For a useful collection of the American pragmatist writings that influenced the legal realists, see Thayer (1982).

6   Competing images of law in contemporary jurisprudence

The publication of Hart's *Concept of Law* in 1961 changed the face of modern jurisprudence. In the years that followed, Hart's position was the one to develop or dispute. His critique of Austin's long-standing version of command positivism and his replacement of it with his own rule positivism, succeeded in revitalising the fortunes of this legal philosophy. It was not long, however, before he was faced with a rival theory developed by Ronald Dworkin (1931–2013), an old student of Hart's who became his most influential critic. Deeply opposed to all forms of positivism, Dworkin styled his own theory 'law as integrity', in which, while showing some affinity with natural law and some of the realists, he kept a critical distance from these perspectives and developed an independent theory of law, which was to become a major force in contemporary jurisprudence. Over a long career, spanning the late twentieth and early twenty-first centuries, Dworkin's theory steadily evolved to higher levels of sophistication, but remained essentially the same on the issues that divided him from Hart and other positivists. In one of his last books in 2011 (R. Dworkin 2011), he described himself as a 'hedgehog'. Compared with 'the fox', who has many tricks, the hedgehog has one big idea, but it is a good one. This one big idea was what he called the unity of value. What he meant by this was that at the deepest level all the things we value, the best ways to live, the ethical and the moral, the values of democracy, liberty, equality, dignity and so on, are mutually interdependent. Some should not be bought at the expense of others. This was the idea that Dworkin sought to articulate and defend right through his career. What I will be concerned with in this chapter is the content of his early works in the 1970s to 1980s, because these were at the centre of his dispute with Hart.

Austin and Hart on hard cases

What is of particular importance to contemporary theory is the nature of judicial reasoning and the problem of hard cases, which has become the testing ground for the competing theories of law. It is in this context that the disputes between the positivist models of rules and their critics become most explicit. The problem revolves around the issue of what judges are entitled or obliged to do when faced with a case for which there is no clear judicial precedent, or upon which there appears to be no definite and unambiguous statutory guidance.

Although Austin had little to say about hard cases, he said enough to launch a tradition of positivist interpretation. It was clear to him that in practice the sovereign could not allow for every peculiarity in the cases that come before the courts. For such purposes the sovereign delegates powers of discretion to its judges, powers that are only to be used when there are no appropriate general rules to apply when the law runs out. These 'temporary commanders', however, hold their authority only by virtue of appointment by the ultimate commander.

Austin believed that the inevitability of unforeseeable cases arising was due to the inherent vagueness or lack of perfect precision in the wording of the law. The delegation of powers of discretion was unavoidable because laws had what he called 'furry edges'. Therefore, one of the most important functions of a judge is to act as a subordinate deputy legislator to create new law by clarifying these furry edges.

Hart's approach was more developed and philosophically sophisticated than Austin's, upon which he built. On Hart's conception, the nature of law is such that some degree of discretion is unavoidable, because no matter how well drafted the legislation and how wide-ranging existing precedent in case law, the established rules cannot cover every eventuality. Nearly all rules lack certainty in their range of reference.

On Hart's theory there is usually in hard cases what he calls a 'penumbra of uncertainty' surrounding the application of a rule. This penumbral quality of a rule is explained by the language in which any kind of rules – legal or otherwise – are invariably expressed. Sometimes it is possible to express a rule so precisely as to avoid any ambiguity or vagueness; however, this is often impossible because of the open texture of language.

Hart's standard example is of the use of the word 'vehicle' in a by-law banning vehicles from a public park. There is an undisputed core meaning of the word: it clearly applies to cars and motorcycles; but less clearly to such things as bicycles, pedal cars, roller skates, skateboards or even prams. Unless they are specified by the rule, these cases are left to judicial discretion as to what is to *count* as a vehicle. On Hart's conception, then, while there are penumbral areas in which the law is not settled, it still has a core of settled meaning. There are 'rules which are determinate enough at the centre to supply standards of correct judicial decision' (Hart 2012 [1961]: 145).

In contrast to legal realists, Hart argues against the idea that the best a lawyer can ever do is to use his or her knowledge of past legal decisions to guess how a judge will decide a particular case. This, however, is exactly what Hart does accept when the rules become blurred by the vagueness of their language; that is to say, in hard cases. 'When the area of open texture is reached,' he asserts, 'very often all we can profitably offer in answer to the question "What is the law on this matter?", is a guarded prediction of what the courts will do' (ibid.: 147).

This, for Hart, is why it is not always easy or even possible to apply existing law. The indeterminacy of rules makes it inevitable that a certain amount of strong discretionary judgement has to be made in court. It is also, according to Hart, desirable. Without some degree of discretion, it would be a repressively rigid legal system. But while Hart sees this situation as acceptable, Dworkin and others regard it as a gesture of despair in the face of the complexity of the law. Instead of repressive rigidity, they see justice and consistency in complete determinacy.

Between the nightmare and the noble dream: Hartian discretion

In 1977, Hart published an essay in which he responded to Dworkin's growing influence in jurisprudence, reinforcing his own original interpretation of hard cases. In this essay, he depicted Dworkin's defence of complete determinacy and unique right answers as an overreaction to the extreme rule-scepticism of the American legal realists, with Hart's own positivistic account of judicial discretion as the genuinely realistic middle ground. Reviewing the last century of American legal theory, he points to the two extremes of regarding the law either as wildly arbitrary and unpredictable, or as a fully explicable, wholly determinate and certain process.

On the one hand, he maintains, we can see the American 'nightmare view that, in spite of pretensions to the contrary, judges make the law they apply to litigants and are not impartial, objective declarers of existing law' (Hart 1983: 127). In contrast to this surface appearance of impartiality, the judge is in reality a legislator, indistinguishable from a politician. Why is this a nightmare? If it is true, it means that the image of judicial impartiality is a complete fraud. Litigants or defendants are entitled to expect judges to apply the existing law even-handedly, rather than to have new law made for every occasion.

At the other extreme, argues Hart, we find the utopian noble dream, according to which judges never make new law, that despite superficial appearances to the contrary, judges never determine what the law *shall* be. Judges are confined to saying what they believe the law consisted in before their decision, which is the mere application of it. Dworkin he describes as the latest in the line of these 'noble dreamers', denying, in the face of all the evidence, the reality of judicial discretion. What we need to consider now is whether Dworkin's defence of complete determinacy really does imply this kind of utopian idealisation of the legal process.

Dworkin's theory of law as integrity

The comprehensive theory unfolded by Ronald Dworkin over the last four decades owes much to the analysis developed by both Fuller and Hart. Dworkin took over and developed many of Fuller's natural law themes, but the importance of his writings to mainstream Anglo-American legal theory rests largely on the claim that they represent a sophisticated and plausible alternative to Hart's version of legal positivism, succeeding where Fuller fell short in providing a concrete exposition of the unity of law and morality, thus undermining the key thesis of legal positivism. He regarded all versions of positivism, from Bentham to Kelsen and Hart, as fatally flawed in their assumptions about legal validity. There is nevertheless a degree of convergence and dialogue between Dworkin and Hartian positivists that had not been possible in the stark confrontation between classical natural law and its positivist enemies.

This is partly because Dworkin's own theory can – as he said himself – only loosely be called a theory of natural law. Although it inclines in this direction, he is concerned more with the merits and faults of a historically specific legal system than with general or timeless concepts of law. What does link Dworkin with natural law, however, is his rootedness in the common law tradition and the central claim that the principles of justice that have evolved within this tradition are an essential ingredient of law. This is closely connected with his 'rights thesis', that judges are obliged to recognise and protect pre-existing individual rights. It will also become clear from this account of Dworkin's theory of law that, while it is indebted to many of the insights of philosophical pragmatism and legal realism, especially in its court-centredness and focus on controversial judicial rulings, it rejects the most characteristic of the realist tenets. The result is a strikingly original and independent theory of constructive interpretation or 'law as integrity'.

Rules, principles and policy

The centrepiece of Dworkin's rejection of the positivist concept of law is his distinction between what he identifies as legal rules and legal standards. The assumption he makes explicit from the outset is that the model of law as an elaborate set of rules, whether Austinian or Hartian, expresses only one limited dimension of the law, and this limitation obscures the wider reality of law as a whole. This inclusion of 'standards' of law, in addition to rules, is the keystone of Dworkin's theory because what it amounts to is an attempt to refute, on the grounds of actual legal practice as well as philosophical argument, the defining positivist thesis that law and morality are separate. For Dworkin, as for Fuller, law and morality are inseparably intertwined. Whereas for Fuller, however, the 'inner morality' of law is primarily procedural, for Dworkin, the moral dimension of law is wider and more substantive than this. Law is more than the factual matter of predicting and applying 'black-letter' rules as laid down in the past by legislatures and courts; it also comprises intrinsically moral legal standards such as principles of justice, rights and perceptions of good social policy.

Considerations of policy, however, are regarded by Dworkin as subordinate to the principles of justice and the recognition of rights. It is the distinction between rules and *principles* that is crucial to his critique of positivism. The essential point is that a legal rule is something that is either applicable to a given case or it is not. It is an all-or-nothing concept. Principles of justice and fairness, by contrast, have what Dworkin calls the dimension of 'weight'. If a valid rule of law exists, it is normal procedure to apply it automatically. If a legal principle is acknowledged, its weight or seriousness has to be taken into account, possibly to be balanced against other principles, before it is allowed to affect the judicial decision.

Legal validity and interpretation

The purpose behind these distinctions is to show that the positivist theories of legal validity are unrealistic and ultimately incoherent. Although his arguments are aimed equally at past and present versions of positivism, Dworkin concentrates his fire on Hart's account of legal validity in relation to the rule of recognition. What he sees as mistaken in this account is the continued positivist assumption that there must be a single master test for distinguishing legally valid from invalid rules. On Hart's account, the valid rules of law are those that can be traced back to the original rule that authorises the entire structure of law. What Dworkin rejects, then, is the pyramid structure of law that is common to all the leading positivists, whether this originates in the power of the Austinian sovereign, the Kelsenian basic norm or Hart's rule of recognition. What Dworkin is himself asserting is that this image of legal validity does not in fact match the ways in which laws are actually validated in advanced legal systems.

In order to get this match, we have to look in detail at the complexity of arguments that support judicial decisions in controversial cases. The general point, however, is that on Dworkin's alternative to the positivist account of legal validity, judges are under a legal obligation that is imposed, not by hard and fast rules underpinned by a basic norm or rule of recognition, but by 'a constellation of principles' (R. Dworkin 1977b: 44) as well as rules. This is an obligation to come up with the right answer to the case under consideration, no matter how difficult or controversial. The source of the obligation lies in the past, in the body of judicial and legislative rules, decisions and unwritten principles of the common law. With these raw legal materials to hand, the role of the judge is to aspire to a completely coherent theory of law that will yield a judgement which (1) will provide the best 'fit' with existing legal materials, i.e. with previous rulings and legislation; and (2) will reveal the law in its best possible light, in terms of moral and political soundness, as exemplified by the liberal values of justice, fairness, equality, due process and individual rights. These two aspects of interpretation Dworkin describes as the dimensions of 'best fit' and of 'best light'.

The most illuminating analogy that Dworkin uses to justify this approach is a comparison of legal with literary interpretation. As the mouthpiece of the law, the judge is in the position of a creative writer asked to continue an unfinished novel in the vein of the original. 'The complexity of this task models the complexity of deciding a hard case under law as integrity'

(R. Dworkin 1986: 229). The completion of the analogy requires that we imagine a chain of authors each expected to write another chapter. Using the plot of Charles Dickens' *Christmas Carol* as a model, he argues that law is like an ongoing literary narrative, the only difference being that it is open-ended. Each author in this situation would have to interpret what had gone before; the new chapter would have to fit the materials already written. At the same time, however, the author would have to make the novel the best it could be as a novel, integrating plot, image and setting, using substantive aesthetic judgement to accept one interpretation and reject others. The assumption is that there would only be one best way to continue it, rather than several equally good ways. Similarly, the judge has to fit his or her interpretation of previous law to the existing materials, while at the same time making the narrative of law the best it can be in terms of political morality.

Right answers to questions of law

Must there always be 'right answers' to questions of law? This question, made prominent by Dworkin, is another way of asking about the nature of the discretion exercised by a judge in a hard case. When a case arises, with every appearance of being incompletely covered by existing law, one's instinct is to assume that there must be several options left open, more than one way of solving the difficulty. If there were only one way, how could it qualify as a hard case?

One of Dworkin's main endeavours is to show that this is mistaken, and that, contrary to appearances, there must in principle always be one and only one right answer to any hard case, and that this is 'right' both morally and legally. The allowance of alternatives or a range of possible acceptable answers is regarded by Dworkin as the result of a failure to recognise the duty imposed upon the judge to reach a decision that reflects the objective balance of rights in the case. The question here, then, is whether there is one determinate answer to every difficult case in which legal rules or principles or rights are in conflict, seemingly pointing to different but equally persuasive conclusions.

If there were no single decision required by law, then the judge could not decide the case 'according to law'. If more than one outcome is legally possible, then it seems that there are gaps in the law, gaps that must be filled by the judge, whose judicial function is then that of a creative legislator. He or she determines what the 'right' answer in this case 'ought' to be. It would seem that judges are then supplementing their legal knowledge and expertise with their own moral perceptions, that they have a free hand to refer to their own instincts for justice and equity, and so on. It is the freedom or judicial caprice seemingly sanctioned by this view of hard cases that Dworkin is opposing as contrary to the spirit of common law, which requires a degree of principled consistency in its succession of decisions.

Hercules and moral objectivism

Dworkin's advancement of the 'one right answer' thesis is an integral part of his wider defence of moral objectivism against moral scepticism and relativism. This moral objectivism is presupposed by the one right answer thesis and by the rights thesis. The claim that answers to moral problems or conflicts can be 'right' or 'correct', and the related claim that some rights prevail over others, is objectivist in the sense that the standards of morality or justice are taken to be independent of human decision or convention.

It is to illustrate this principle of moral objectivity as a model for legal reasoning that Dworkin introduces the mythical judge Hercules. This is the name he gives to an imaginary judge of unlimited intellectual power, for whom the failings of memory and the pressure of time would be no problem. Without any such impediments, Hercules would find the unique correct answer to every hard legal case, because he would have all the relevant information about the entire history of the rules and principles of the common law, and about the facts and competing claims in the case before him. With these superhuman powers he would not simply follow precedent; he would reason his way to the correct solution by constructing a complete theory of law and what it required for the case in hand. His interpretive reasoning would be guided by the requirement of 'best fit' with all relevant legal precedent, and at the same time by the criterion of 'best light', finding the interpretation that provides the best political reading of past law. Both criteria presuppose moral objectivism, the assumption being that there can only be one morally sound interpretation of precedent. Hercules symbolises legal reasoning at its best because, with maximum knowledge of the law, he can justify his decision by legal precedent and balance the relative weight of the relevant principles and act accordingly, endorsing the rights that are entitled, on the balance of arguments, to prevail. Above all, Hercules will see that he has no discretion to act otherwise.

Dworkin's hard cases

From the many morally controversial cases in English and US law cited by Dworkin, the one he has made pivotal to his argument is the relatively minor one of *Riggs* v. *Palmer* (New York, 1889). The relevant facts of the case were as follows. Elmer Palmer was a sixteen-year-old who successfully prevented his grandfather from changing his will, of which he himself was the main beneficiary, by murdering him. After serving a very lenient prison sentence, there appeared to be no legal obstacle to prevent Palmer from claiming his inheritance. This was challenged in court by relatives (who were minor beneficiaries), but the judge upheld Palmer's claims because the formalities of law in relation to the will had been satisfied. This decision was overturned by a majority decision in the Court of Appeal, depriving Palmer of his inheritance, on the grounds that no one should profit from their own wrongdoing.

It is not difficult to see why Dworkin regarded this case as a striking illustration of his concept of law as a complex of rules, principles and policies. The central conflict in the case was between the black-letter legal *rules* of probate relating to the validity of wills and legal inheritance, and the unwritten *principles* of the common law. The case also provides an excellent illustration of the practical implications of the competing theories of law. A number of points should be noted before we examine these.

First, it seems intuitively obvious, given the prevailing moral views on such cases, that anyone who murders for profit thereby forfeits their right to the proceeds. Nobody would suggest that a man convicted for armed robbery should keep the money he had hidden before serving his sentence. The difference with Palmer, of course, is that he appeared to be legally, if not morally, entitled to it. Second, it should be remembered that two judges did not find it intuitively obvious that he should forfeit the right to inherit, or at least not obvious enough to find against Palmer. One dissenting judge declared that it would be bad social policy to punish someone twice for the same crime. There had also been earlier cases similar enough to *Riggs* v. *Palmer* to be cited as precedent, in which apparently shocking judgements had not been appealed. In *Owens* v. *Owens* (Adams 1992: 138), for example, a widow convicted of being accessory before the fact to the murder of her husband was nevertheless granted entitlement to the legally specified portion of his estate.

Third, many still believe that unworthy claims like these have to be upheld for the sake of legal consistency. If the current state of the law points in an unwelcome direction, it can always be amended for future cases. This might be unfortunate, so the argument goes, but it is necessary for maintaining the credibility of the institution of legal inheritance. Consider now how the advocates of the main theoretical positions might react to and deal with a case such as *Riggs* v. *Palmer*.

Christian natural law. It seems unlikely, given their standpoint on the necessary connection between law and morality, that any traditional natural lawyer adhering to the higher law of reason would countenance such a manifest injustice. Good law is derived from the moral precepts of Christianity, rather than a literalistic reading of the law. A decision for Palmer would be contrary to the requirements of right reason. This is not to say that the ruling would be invalid, only that a natural law judge would have been more inclined to apply principles of natural justice.

Black-letter positivism. It was probably only those who advocated following the rules of law to the letter who supported the decision in Palmer's favour. This is the narrowest possible interpretation of positivism, according to which judges should apply the rules exactly as they find them, no more and no less, regardless of the consequences. The dissenting judge Gray justified his rejection of the appeal with the opinion that:

> the matter does not lie within the domain of conscience. We are bound by the rigid rules of law, which have been established by the legislature

[which] has by its enactments prescribed exactly when and how wills may be made, altered, and revoked, and apparently, as it seems to me, when they have been fully complied with, has left no room for the exercise of an equitable jurisdiction by courts over such matters.

(Adams 1992: 138)

Although this severely literalist approach has a strong following in the courts, it should not be assumed that all positivists accept it.

Austinian positivism. According to Austin's command theory, judges apply the orders or rules authorised by the sovereign, and in situations that require clarification they act as delegated 'temporary commanders' to resolve ambiguity or vagueness. On the face of it, this seems straightforward; judges stand in for and legislate on behalf of the sovereign when hard cases arise. Austin's own recognition of the problem of cases unanticipated by the drafters of statutes is limited, as we have seen, to the observation that some rules have blurred edges. In a case like *Riggs* v. *Palmer*, however, the rules have run out; there is no relevant rule to apply. This, though, is only the beginning of the problem. Do the 'temporary commanders' make the ruling as they see fit, following their own inclinations, or do they rule in such a way that they believe the sovereign legislature (Parliament, Congress or whatever) would have done with this case in mind? The latter course – which is called 'equitable construction' – was in fact taken by Judge Earl, who found against Palmer, stating that:

it was the intention of the lawmakers that the donees in a will should have the property given to them. But it could never have been their intention that a donee who murdered the testator to make the will operative should have any benefit under it.

(Adams 1992: 136)

His reasoning proceeds to justify the reconstruction of the intentions of the lawmaker by imaginary interrogation. This doctrine certainly goes beyond Austinian positivism, but could easily be accommodated by it.

Hartian positivism. In substance, Hart's approach is essentially the same as Austin's. Does the idea of a judge's discretion to bring clarity into the area of the penumbra, where the meaning of the law is indeterminate, provide an answer to a case in which the rules have simply run out? In fact, Hart's response is that it is in cases like these that judges have genuinely free discretion to formulate an appropriate rule and create new law. According to Hart, the 'noble dream' of complete determinacy breaks down in cases like this, leaving judges to their own best devices. What this means is that the discretion they exercise is a freedom to apply their own moral beliefs or values, rather than merely a discretion to interpret the law in their own way. In a case like *Riggs* v. *Palmer*, there is no legal guidance on how to proceed.

Realism and rule-scepticism. As we have seen, there is no easily identifiable 'realist' position, and there are many degrees of rule-scepticism. On Hart's account of the rule-sceptic 'nightmare', they see nothing but perpetual *ad hoc* creativity and unreliability in the law. This kind of rule-sceptic would undoubtedly see *Riggs* v. *Palmer* as a dramatic confirmation of the sceptical image of law as a chaos of personal bias and prejudice, in which judges, when backed into a tight corner, do just as they please. The case would indeed have been seen by Hutcheson or Frank as corroboration of their criticism of the false certainties of mechanical jurisprudence. Even these 'extreme' realists, however, were not as one-sided as this. They might also have seen the outcome of this particular case as a vindication of their belief in the ability of the best judges to reason their way intuitively to the just and equitable solution to the most difficult of hard cases. Hutcheson in particular described judges as waiting for the creative flash of inspiration, seeking out the solution from their knowledge of written and unwritten rules and principles of common law.

The important point here is that this kind of solution does not require the 'equitable construction' of the intentions of the original lawmaker. The Aristotelian 'equity', the ability to individualise general principles of justice to a particular case, is in the hands of the judges, not the legislators. Why, after all, should a court appeal to what a legislator or drafter of a constitution, perhaps as long as two or three centuries ago, might or might not have intended in the wording of a statute? Realist reflections such as these in the 1920s and 1930s were an important source of Dworkin's theory of hard cases.

Dworkin's theory. Dworkin's treatment of *Riggs* v. *Palmer* as a paradigm case differs radically from all of these interpretations. He took this case as a paradigm because he believed that it brought into sharp focus the shortcomings of every version of positivism. The central point is that, for Dworkin, the rules may have run out but the law has not. Dworkin's argument is that the decision finally reached by the majority of judges in the Court of Appeal was the right one, not only allowed by but also required by law. In other words, the judges were under a duty – in this as in all cases – to find a particular decision in accordance with the objective rights of the parties involved. There was a real solution to be discovered, rather than a workable decision to be taken.

The decisive principle of common law in this case was, as we saw at the outset, the principle that no one should profit from their own wrongdoing. This is why the relevant rules did not prevail. The manner in which this was cited by Judge Earl was, however, more complex than this. The wider context was that:

> all laws, as well as contracts, may be controlled in their operation and effect by general, fundamental maxims of the common law. No one shall be permitted to profit by his own fraud, or to take advantage of his own wrong, or to found any claim upon his own iniquity, or to acquire property by his own crime.
>
> (Adams 1992: 137)

This judge was in no doubt that he could detect the operation of this principle in countless previous rulings in every area of common law. It was to be taken as paramount in this case because he perceived it to be authentically legal, not because it was a worthy moral principle. On the other hand, of course, he believed that unless it were morally sound, it could not have become an embedded feature of the common law. It is this general outlook, binding the moral with the legal, as well as this particular decision that Dworkin is endorsing as an exemplification of the most justified legal practices.

Dworkin, however, does not maintain that such principles drawn from the common law tradition should be treated as absolute. On the contrary, the decision reached in this case was legally sound because it took account of the relevant rules, principles and social policies. As we saw earlier, the status of principles is logically different from that of rules, which either apply or they do not. Principles, by contrast, have the dimension of weight, which means that if they are in conflict with established rules, other principles or good social policy, they have to be balanced against them. Also, the source of their validity is different. Whereas the 'pedigree' of rules is traced back to their enactment, thereby confirming their validity, principles such as 'nobody should profit from their own wrongdoing' have never been enacted or otherwise laid down; they are inferred as the best explanation for existing legal practices.

How far does the outcome of *Riggs* v. *Palmer* support Dworkin's theory of law as integrity? In the first place, it does seem to confirm the proposition that common law moral principles, distinct from legal rules, are themselves an integral part of the law. This in itself, however, is insufficient to support the further claim that a holistic assessment of the case would provide a unique correct answer, according to the lights of political morality. On Dworkin's reading, the judgement of Earl did discover that answer, by applying the criteria of best fit and best light. One of his key comments in this respect was his observation that Gray seemed to have agreed with Earl that the law would be better if it blocked Palmer's inheritance, but did not agree that the law therefore did deny it to him (R. Dworkin 1986: 36). Faced with conflicting precedents, Earl was looking for the best fit with the past and reading the law in its best possible light, making the best moral sense of it, thereby finding a deeper consistency and making the law speak with one coherent voice.

Others, however, have rejected this interpretation and have even denied that this was the right decision according to law, or that the judges had the legal right to innovate in this manner. On this view, the proper legal procedure was to apply the rules and leave the matter to the legislature. If true, this would imply that Dworkin's criterion of best light is a misconceived intrusion of moral and political values into law and legal reasoning.

Criticisms of Dworkin

The rule–principle distinction

It is central to Dworkin's case against positivism – especially in its Hartian version – that the law is a moral–legal complex of rules and principles. This is the fundamental challenge to the separation thesis. If it is true, there is no morally neutral procedure of legal validation, because it is not possible to abstract the purely factual rules from this complex and identify those that are binding in the sense that they will always prevail in a hard case. The determination of legality always involves the recognition of moral principles. Given this wider and more flexible concept of law, it is possible for Dworkin to argue that while the rules may run out, the law need never do so, that it will always have the principled resources to deal with any question which arises.

There are several plausible responses to the rule–principle distinction. The first is to question the intelligibility of ascribing different logical status to a principle, which according to Dworkin has weight rather than an all-or-nothing quality. What does it mean to say that whereas a rule is either applicable or it is not, a principle can be 'weighed' against another one? In the end, it also either applies or it does not. In the *Riggs* v. *Palmer* example, the principle prohibiting profit from wrongdoing is applied, while in other cases it is not. Indeed, what is the difference between a rule and a principle? It is not a matter of particularity and generality; there can be particular or general expressions of either. It cannot be that a principle can be unwritten or 'understood'; so can a rule. This problem, which has never been satisfactorily clarified by Dworkin, is in the end, though, only a matter for clarification. The implications of the distinction for legal validity are undeniable.

Given that the distinction is accepted as meaningful, one uncompromising line of criticism is to insist that only hard and fast rules laid down by legislation or judicial ruling are genuinely legal, and that the cases which Dworkin highlights, bringing common law principles into play, are examples of dubious legal practice, allowing judicial decisions to be politicised. This has also been said about the case of *Henningsen* v. *Bloomfield Motors Inc.* (1960), in which substantial damages were awarded against a motor company standing on a valid contract, and about more famous cases deployed by Dworkin, such as *Brown* v. *Board of Education* (1954), declaring racial segregation in schools to be unconstitutional. With this formalistic approach, saving the predictability and determinacy of existing law at the expense of admitting serious gaps in the law – to be filled by subsequent legislation – judges have to operate within the rules, applying law as they find it. No element of moral or political assessment is required or permitted. On this line of argument, the separation thesis stands intact: the law as we find it (or the sum of the rules as we find them) is one thing, our moral judgement of its merits and defects is another.

Most positivists today, however, accept that something like Dworkin's principles do play a prominent and legitimate part in legal reasoning, while denying that this has the implications Dworkin argues for. It has been argued, for example, that in Hart's account of positivism he understands 'rules' in the wider sense that includes principles, thus bringing them into the system of validation whereby they are traceable back to a rule of recognition.

Alternatively, it can be conceded that Hart's account is defective in this respect, that it needs supplementing with principles, but that the resultant legal–moral complex can be subjected to a positivist master test. On this 'inclusive' account, principles as well as rules have ultimately to be validated by the original rule of recognition.

If this much is conceded, however, it might seem that positivism has fatally compromised its position by abandoning the separation thesis, allowing that moral principles are an integral part of the law. What is required, according to 'inclusive' positivists, is a closer examination and re-articulation of the separation thesis, of what is separable from what. According to Neil MacCormick, for example, Dworkin scored a palpable hit in his critique of Hartian positivism's exaggerated attention to rules to the exclusion of principles, but failed to show that the essential tenets of positivism were thereby discredited. MacCormick accepts that law is never value-free; on the contrary – he agrees – in both its rules and principles it *embodies* values, and is always already infused with values. He claims that Dworkin is right to argue that the law cannot be 'hermetically sealed from morals and politics' (MacCormick 1978: 236), but wrong to conclude from this that the law cannot be described in a positivistic manner, independently of evaluative appraisal, or that the rule of recognition criterion for determining the legality of rules should be abandoned.

The real meaning of the separation thesis, for MacCormick, is that one could describe, expound or explain, for example, the South African system of apartheid – rules, principles and all – without thereby morally endorsing or condemning it. The separation thesis, properly understood, requires only the descriptive–normative distinction. This is what moral neutrality means: judgement is suspended for purposes of analysis and description. The laws of England or the USA on sex or race discrimination cannot be explained without reference to moral and political principles, but they can be fully described without moral judgement one way or the other. This, MacCormick argues, is the defensible form of the separation thesis, rather than the claim that the law is intrinsically value-free.

As a modified version of Hart's model of rules, extending it to include Dworkinian principles, this is a plausible alternative to Dworkin's theory of constructive interpretation. MacCormick's further insistence, however, that no positivist has seriously entertained the 'intrinsic' interpretation of the separation thesis, and that this suspension of judgement was what they had in mind all along, is unconvincing. The least that can be said is that the leading defenders of the separation thesis (Bentham, Austin, Holmes, Kelsen) equivocated between the two versions as described by MacCormick. What he implies is that they did not see the issue clearly, and that his explanation is a clarification of what they really meant. There is little doubt, however, that they were proposing more than a method of objective detachment, of refraining from evaluation. The underlying reality of law described from this position – law as an object of legal science – was indeed understood to be 'value-free', a bare pyramid structure of commands, rules or Kelsenian norms, stripped of the moral language of rights and duties. It was this image of law that Dworkin, following Fuller, was rightly challenging.

To use MacCormick's own example (MacCormick 1978: 200–4), the Rent Restriction Act of 1920 would not have been understood by the classical positivists to have no moral implications for the interests of landlords and tenants, but their separation of law and morals would have required not only that they look dispassionately at the content and operation of the Act, but also that they disregard the moral or political principles of fairness, justice and rights governing the introduction of the rules. What they were looking for was the underlying structure of validation of these legal rules, in terms of the authority of the sovereign, the basic norm or whatever. This 'science of law' requires the expulsion of these principles from the domain of law; they are regarded as extraneous factors. Dworkin's response was to argue for their inherent legality, not by virtue of their sources or points of origin, but by virtue of their mere presence in the common law. MacCormick's acceptance of these principles as authentically legal, by virtue of their function in relation to rules, thus indirectly validated by the rule of recognition, aligns him with a developed Hartian positivism against Dworkin while at the same time distinguishing his own position from that of classical positivism.

While Dworkin's assault on the model of rules and his emphasis on the role of principles have received a generally favourable response, and have stimulated refinements and adjustments to the positivist position, it is his own alternative to these models that has attracted the most fundamental criticism.

Dworkin's moral objectivism

Much of the criticism of his theory as a whole is an extension of the wider philosophical disputes about the moral objectivism upon which Dworkin's legal theory rests. If it were true that all moral judgement had an inescapably subjective element (Mackie 1977a), then it would be clear that the one right answer thesis would have to be rejected. Given that Dworkin's concept of law includes moral standards, we would have to conclude that with questions of law there is either more than one possible 'right' answer, or that the very idea of correctness as applied to law is inappropriate. Those critics of Dworkin who do emphatically reject any form of moral objectivism tend to focus their criticism accordingly on the figure of the ideal judge Hercules, who symbolises the possibility of objective judgement. If Hercules can be exposed as a fraud, it is believed, the idea that every hard case has a unique correct answer, and that this answer will be based on the recognition of objective rights, will go down with him.

Arguments from disagreement

The most common criticism of Hercules is that, as a mythical figure embodying the possibility of objectivity about legal problems with a moral dimension, he is inappropriate because the supposition that such a judge is possible in principle presupposes what Dworkin is trying to prove. Sceptical feelings about the role of Hercules are reinforced by the suspicion that the objectivity claimed on his behalf is just another substitute for God as the absolute and omniscient authority and ultimate arbiter of human disagreement. On this reading, 'law as integrity' is no more than a recycling of a discredited legal formalism, declaring that fallible human judges can shed their subjectivity and use the law 'as a whole' to cut through intractable moral problems and conflicts between rights to find the elusive right answer, which in fact does not exist. Those more sympathetic to Dworkin's approach, however, regard this as an exaggeration of the problem of objectivity and a misrepresentation of what it requires. Dworkin himself, it should be remembered, sees objectivity in the assessment of conflicting rights in accordance with existing law not only as a logical possibility, but also as a practical reality, as law working at its best. Hercules – with his unlimited vision – is only the perfected ideal of what is often actually achieved in the courts. They do often get things right.

The important criticisms, however, are more specific than this. One of the main types of criticism is that there is too much fundamental disagreement between people, and especially between judges presiding over hard cases, for Dworkin's thesis to be plausible. If there were right answers to moral questions, one would expect more convergence of opinion, at least between rational individuals who have reflected long and hard on the matter. All the more so might we expect such convergence in legal decisions, when the adjudicators are professionals; yet one case after another is inherently controversial, dividing judicial opinion at every level in the system. Surely this is an indication that there cannot be one objective answer?

In this form, the argument from disagreement should not be taken too seriously. The first point is that 'objectivity' does not *mean* convergence of opinion (either of universal or of well-informed opinion); such convergence or consensus is no more than a symptom, and certainly no guarantee of objectivity. Objectivity here means *mind independence*, that the answer is right or wrong independently of any opinion. There is nothing inherently implausible about serious disagreement on difficult moral matters leading the best-informed opinion astray, any more than there is in disputes in the natural sciences in contexts where the point at issue is subject to demonstrable truth. Disagreement in itself, no matter how extensive, proves nothing against a truth-claim. Being right does not mean having the ability to command universal assent. The second point is that the majority is not necessarily right. Two judges on a bench of five can be right, the other three wrong, about the state of the law and what it requires in the instant case. Dissenting judges are often vindicated by a higher court. The frequency of dissent is no indication either way on the question of whether or not there is a right answer to be found.

If the argument from mere disagreement is ineffective, however, others directed more specifically at the nature of judicial reason and at Dworkin's version of objectivism are potentially more damaging. Brian Bix, for example, has argued that there are reasons why it is inevitable – rather than just a matter of fact – that judges would give different judgements if they were to apply Dworkin's criteria. When it is all a matter of interpretation, the criterion of moral soundness ('best light') will vary from one judge to another according to variations in their political and moral beliefs, as will the criterion of best fit with the relevant legal materials. Furthermore, there is too much flexibility in the application of these two criteria, such that judges are not sufficiently constrained by the requirement of 'best fit'. If applied, Dworkin's theory, supposedly objective, would generate more disagreement than already exists. Dworkin's only defence, he argues, is that his theory is an interpretation of actual judicial practice in its best possible light, but in this case he is prescribing and cannot present the theory as a description of actual practices (Bix 1993: 106–11).

It is doubtful, however, that this criticism does undermine the right answer thesis, or even establish the claim that Dworkin's theory would have this unsettling effect. Dworkin's own understanding of the points at issue here is that he is advocating the interpretive approach to steer it between the undesired alternatives of mechanical jurisprudence and free discretion. The best judicial practices, he believes, adhere to neither of these options. Judges are indeed bound by the constraints of best fit with existing precedent, hence they are not free creators of law; however, at the same time – by virtue of the criterion of best light – they are more free than those who believe that they are mechanically finding law (R. Dworkin 1986: 234). The question here is whether Dworkin's recommendations, if universally adopted, with every judge constructing a complete theory of law, would be likely to generate more disagreement than exists at present. This question persists through all the significant criticisms of the Dworkinian theory.

MacCormick, who as we saw above accepted the value of Dworkin's critique of Hart's model of rules, develops the argument from disagreement to attack the rights thesis and the one right answer thesis. His argument is that there are no right answers because of the *kind* of disagreement involved in hard cases. Citing Thomas Reid's argument against Hume's subjectivism – that the very presence of genuine disagreement proves that there is always in principle a correct answer to moral questions – MacCormick argues that Reid's mistake here lies in the conflation of two kinds of disagreement, the speculative and the practical. With speculative disagreement, the differences can in principle be resolved because they are wrangles over what is or is not actually the case. With practical disagreement, what it always comes down to is a decision about how best to lead our lives, or how society should be organised. What rights and principles of justice, in the end, do we want to acknowledge?

MacCormick's illustration of this distinction is the principle established in the historic case of *Donoghue* v. *Stevenson* (1932) (C. Baker 1991: 90), which changed the course of English law on negligence. The salient facts of the case were that a customer in an ice cream parlour had bought her friend Mrs Donoghue a bottle of ginger beer, the contents of which she had partially consumed before discovering the remains of a decomposed snail. On account of the distress and subsequent illness suffered, she sued the manufacturer Stevenson for compensation. Her first action in Scotland failed, because the manufacturer was only legally liable to the person with whom he had a contract, the one who had actually purchased it. This rested on the principle of privity of contract. When the appeal was heard by the House of Lords, however, the decision went in her favour, by a majority of three to two. The important point established here was that there existed in law 'a general duty of care'. This was expressed by the 'neighbour principle' expounded in Lord Atkin's ruling, according to which every person has a legal duty of care towards his or her neighbour, who is defined as anyone who it might reasonably be foreseen will be affected by that person's acts or omissions, not merely as those with whom one has a contract. This majority ruling was disputed by two judges, whose main arguments rested on privity of contract and the prediction of disastrous implications for the manufacturing industry, which turned out to be unfounded.

One question here is whether this neighbour principle was already present in English law. Was the prevailing opinion a new departure, or was it a recognition of what was implicitly there? While for most positivists, such landmark rulings quite clearly signal new departures, a Dworkinian interpretation is that positive law on this matter did indeed change in 1932, but that this change was superficial compared with the deeper continuity in terms of its emergence from earlier principles and rulings from which the neighbour principle was inferred. The decision that the Lords reached on this occasion was, legally and morally speaking, the right answer, rather than a deduction from a principle snatched out of thin air. If they had decided any other way, they would have been *wrong*. MacCormick, however, uses this case to undermine the one right answer thesis. The legal disputes in such cases he sees as distinguishable into both kinds of disagreement, speculative and practical. He concedes to Dworkin that the principle recognised in *Donoghue* may well have been implicit in the law before 1932, by virtue of earlier decisions, and that disputes of this nature do admit of an objectively right answer. Against Dworkin, however, he argues that once such speculative disagreement has been settled, 'we find ourselves beyond that which can be reasoned out'; we are confronted with a choice between what are often equally plausible alternatives. When all speculative disagreement is resolved, the practical question remains: which right do the courts, speaking for society, prefer to support? In the practical sense, there was no one right answer to which of the equally tenable rights (of the manufacturer's right of contract, or the customer's right to compensation) should be upheld. In the event, a narrow majority endorsed the neighbour principle and significantly changed our way of life. The matter was resolved by mixed considerations of public interest, corrective justice and common sense. The overall point here is that on this interpretation, while it might be true that there is in principle a right answer to the question about fitting precedent, the same cannot be said about the moral soundness of the adjudication between competing rights. Hercules can cope with the first question, but not with the second (MacCormick 1978: 108–15, 251–8).

The best Dworkinian reply to this is not, as MacCormick suggests, the argument that all legal disputes are speculative. The best way is to question MacCormick's Humean premises, which include the supposition that competing conceptions of justice are essentially subjective, in the sense that they must, in the end, simply be a matter of preference. It is not true that, in cases like this, judges can only reach out beyond reason and decide which social policies to endorse. Is it really true that the competing rights here were 'equally tenable'? What was actually happening was that one principle-based right (to compensation) was outweighing the principle behind a rule-based right (of contract). The manufacturer was found to be liable because the outweighed principle was objectively weaker than the one that prevailed. Such claims are not 'objective' in the sense of being value-free. Questions of justice are imbued with value, but they can still be resolved objectively.

Arguments from incommensurability

Two things are said to be commensurable when there is a common standard by which to measure them. Any two trees are commensurable in terms of height. It is meaningful and true to say that a 3-yard line is longer than one of 8 feet, and a 2-mile road is longer than one of 3 kilometres, because in either case there is a determinate method of conversion from one scale to the other. When two things are incommensurable, lacking a common standard, the one cannot be measured against the other. Only like can be compared with like. The quality of two pieces of music can be compared, but they cannot be compared with the quality of a scientific treatise.

The problem of incommensurability has been raised against Dworkin by a number of critics, including Mackie (1977b), Finnis (in George 1992), MacCormick (1978) and Bix (1996). The general thrust of this criticism is that opposing rights cannot be weighed against each other, because there is no common standard by which to measure the respective value of, say, the rights based on contract and the right to compensation. It is a problem of finding a neutral standpoint from which to judge the competing claims. If the situation is such that one of the rights has to give way, then it is a matter of public policy for judge, legislature or society to decide which of the rights is to be preferred. Hard cases cannot be resolved by declaring which right 'scores' higher than another.

Mackie's criticism is that with his rights thesis, Dworkin presupposes a single scale upon which opposing rights-claims can be measured against each other, with one right outweighing another. The idea that a unique right answer can objectively emerge from 'too simple a metric of commensurability on a linear scale' is rejected by Mackie on the grounds that the merits of opposing claims cannot be measured in this manner.

Dworkin's reply to this criticism – that we make such 'best decision all things considered' arbitrations all the time – has generally been regarded as unsatisfactory. It is difficult to see what distinguishes this from a Hartian positivist interpretation. It is not the best decision Dworkin is looking for; it is the right answer. A better reply here would follow the same course as the reply to the arguments from disagreement. In the same way that there is no need to argue that all legal disputes are speculative, there is no need to argue that all rights are commensurable in the sense of being quantifiable. Rights can have objectively discernible relative weight in terms of principles of justice, without this relative weight being expressible in numerical terms.

Finnis' criticism is quite different. As a natural lawyer, his quarrel is not with Dworkin's moral objectivism. Dismissing the arguments from disagreement and the subjectivist scepticism about correct moral judgements, Finnis argues that Dworkin's mistake is that he has failed to understand the real complexity of the tension between the technical requirements of law for providing the means for unequivocal dispute resolution, and its character as an instrument of justice. This failure, he argues, is reflected in Dworkin's theory of the relation between the dimensions of best fit and best light, which he assumes to be commensurable. According to Finnis, commitment to moral objectivism does not entail the one right answer thesis in law, because looking for one right answer to a hard case is like looking for the single English novel that is both 'the funniest' and 'the best'. Similarly, one answer might provide the best fit, but another answer the soundest morally speaking. In other words, the scales of moral soundness and of fit are incommensurable, a fact that is obscured by Dworkin's assumption that the right answer can always be found on each scale, with Hercules interpreting law in its best light by selecting the morally soundest from the range of those that fit the best. This argument was never resolved.

Conclusion

Within the theoretical framework established by Hart and Dworkin, the most influential interpretations of law in recent years are still essentially rooted in the traditional antagonisms between conflicting perspectives in moral philosophy and radically opposed understandings of the relation between law and morality. In many ways, the contemporary disputes are still seen by some as continuations of the long-standing conflicts between common law thinking and its critics. What has changed, however, is the level of sophistication in the opposed theories and the degree of convergence between them. The exchanges between Dworkin and his Hartian and natural law critics, in particular, are no longer marked by the mutual incomprehension displayed in earlier episodes of these disputes.

Study questions

General question: When judges decide hard cases, should they be understood as applying existing law or as making new law?

Further study questions: Is there always one and only one right answer to questions of law? Explain and critically evaluate either Hart's or Dworkin's theory of hard cases. Critically assess Dworkin's theory of law as integrity. Does Dworkin's criticism of the positivist models of rules succeed in undermining the positivist understanding of law? Which theory of law do the cases of *Riggs* v. *Palmer* and *Donoghue* v. *Stevenson* support? Are there morally neutral and legally objective answers to these cases? Is MacCormick's revision of the separation thesis more convincing than the traditional version?

Suggestions for further reading

Recommended general reading on contemporary legal theory, representing a range of views and approaches, are Gavison (1987), George (1996), Raz (1975), Finnis (1980), Lyons (1993) and Posner (1990).

From the extensive literature on hard cases, Hart (2012 [1961]: ch. 7.l; 1983: ch. 4) and R. Dworkin (1977b: chaps 1–4) are essential. The second revised edition of Hart (1994 [1961]) contains a postscript in which he replies to Dworkin's criticisms. Useful and important general commentaries include MacCormick (1978: ch. 8), Bix (1993), Cotterell (1989: ch. 6) and Lyons (1984: 87–104).

On Dworkin's theory of law as a whole, the most sympathetic is Guest (1992). An anthology of critical essays (Cohen 1984) includes replies from Dworkin. Discussions of Dworkin can also be found in Mackie (1977b), MacCormick (1982: ch. 7), Posner (1990: ch. 6) and Simmonds (1986: ch. 6). On contemporary natural law theory, there are valuable collections by Finnis (1991: vols 1 and 2) and George (1992). Other significant works include Finnis (1980), Beyleveld and Brownsword (1986) and Weinreb (1987). On contemporary positivism and the analysis of rules, the main works to read are Raz (1975), Twining and Miers (1976) and George (1996).

For further details and conflicting interpretations of the significance of the case of *Donoghue* v. *Stevenson*, see C. Baker (1991: 90–5), Halpin (1997: ch. 6), MacCormick (1978) and Fleming (1994: 158–64).

On Dworkin's later work, see his *Sovereign Virtue* (R. Dworkin 2000), *Justice in Robes* (R. Dworkin 2006) and *Justice for Hedgehogs* (R. Dworkin 2011). For a comprehensive study of his work by a number of leading philosophers, see Waluchow and Sciaraffa (2016).

7   Radical challenges to mainstream theory

In this chapter we will be looking at some key aspects of the conflict between traditional legal theory and its more radical critics in recent decades. These disputes originate in the wider world of philosophical, cultural and political controversies that flared up in the last quarter of the twentieth century, and can only be understood against that backdrop. Unlike those dealt with in earlier chapters, the most representative and influential of the new theories are deeply confrontational in the sense that their explicit aim is to destabilise and overthrow a traditional approach to legal thinking in its entirety, rather than propose modifications of prevailing images of law. At the same time, they seek to refocus legal studies on addressing fundamental questions of social justice. Despite this apparent breach with the established traditions, however, it is still the perennial question of justice, what it means and how it relates to law, that stands at the centre of these controversies. Socialist, feminist and race theory critics of law, for example, are concerned with the injustice towards subordinate social classes, repressed women and ethnic minorities, injustices that are argued to be perpetuated by legal institutions and reinforced by legal theory. At the same time, however, much of the criticism aims to undermine the very notion of justice, to expose it as an ideological facade, the function of which is to conceal the essentially oppressive nature of law. This tension – between the urge to broaden the basis of justice and at the same time to denounce justice as a fraud – runs right through the arguments for and against the new criticism.

The roots of modernity and the Enlightenment

To understand this, we have to look at the roots of what is now often disparagingly known as *modernity*. This is a concept with multiple layers of meaning that has become so pervasive today that it is almost impossible to pin down. In cultural terms, 'being modern' can mean anything from being tuned in to all the latest fashions to a naive enthusiasm for the most advanced technology. In a philosophical context its meaning is disputed – as are the related terms 'modern' and 'modernism' – but the sense most relevant here is modernity as a body of thought (ideas, beliefs, values) or way of thinking that took root at the beginning of our 'modern' age, with the changes in mentality that brought about the scientific revolution of the seventeenth century and the political revolutions of the 1780s. Crucial to the contemporary debates is the period of Enlightenment that emerged from and consolidated the age of reason in science, philosophy and politics over the course of the eighteenth century. Much of the philosophy in Europe over the last century has been preoccupied with critically examining the heritage of this period of Enlightenment.

The imagery of light and enlightenment has permeated modern thought so thoroughly, especially with the idea of enlightened thinkers or politicians being the most civilised and morally advanced of their day, that one needs to be constantly aware that the Enlightenment as an intellectual achievement was only established as the result of an immensely complex struggle against ignorance and tyranny, and that it was itself by no means a homogeneous movement, with its leading advocates deeply divided over fundamental issues. It was less the agreement on any particular doctrine than a consensus on more abstract commitments that defined the Enlightenment, such as the belief in the power of the individual human mind to think rationally and arrive at objectively true and reliable conclusions without the assistance of traditional authority. Thus, the mark of enlightenment was described memorably by Immanuel Kant (1724–1804), one of its leading exponents, as humanity emerging from its childhood, as a process of reaching maturity, or the ability to reason independently. This was envisaged less as the abrupt casting away of tradition, more as a process of reaching the kind of maturity that would systematically subject all traditions hitherto received uncritically to the criticism of reason. It was not an enlightened age, declared Kant, but it was an age of enlightenment. Humanity was growing up. The autonomous individual became one of the principal symbols of the age.

Liberal individualism

What was taking shape throughout this period was the philosophy of liberal individualism, with growing demands for freedom of speech and freedom from the arbitrary acts of unjust despots. Universal values, true for every human society, were confidently proclaimed. Truth and reason were presented as the natural enemies of the abuse of sovereign power, an abuse that thrives on lies and irrationality. Above all, reason dictated that a society of free and equal individual citizens be subject to the rule of law, with everyone protected in their individual rights, rather than to the rule of an unchecked sovereign. This revolution in political awareness would not have been possible without the equally dramatic shifts in consciousness that had initiated the scientific revolution in the previous century. At the heart of this enterprise also lay the search for an elusive method to guarantee objective truth. In combination with the dispassionate study of empirical details, the light of reason would eventually illuminate the entire world of nature, society and political morality. With the rapid advances in scientific knowledge, it was natural to believe that the trust in reason would ensure unstoppable progress in every field of inquiry.

Critics of the Enlightenment

These were the main features of the Enlightenment that made it so plausible and attractive to many of the leading philosophers of the day. The prospect was one of complete human emancipation from self-inflicted ignorance and suffering. In recent years it has become fashionable to echo its early critics and caricature it as an age of arrogant certainty coupled with a naive belief in progress and a quasi-religious worship of Reason as the answer to every problem, ignoring the dark and irrational side of human nature. Many critics have seen it as the beginning of a long hubristic venture, leading ultimately and inevitably to the environmental disasters and dehumanisation associated with advanced technology and globalisation.

Marx and Nietzsche

The two most radical thinkers of the nineteenth century, Karl Marx (1818–83) and Friedrich Nietzsche (1844–1900), were diametrically opposed in their responses to modernity. If Marx represented the internal challenge from the radical wing of the Enlightenment, confronting liberalism with its failure to deliver on its promises of universal emancipation and equality, Nietzsche developed a comprehensive critique of its philosophical underpinnings, aiming to destroy what he saw as the democratisation and decadence of European culture. Both were concerned with exposing ideals as lies and masks for forms of social domination and oppression, but while Marx denounced liberal or bourgeois morality as the hypocritical expression of the interests of a particular social group, Nietzsche represented almost the entire history of morality as a long tale of pitiful self-deception, transforming the experience of human suffering into a magnificent edifice of objective moral values, the truth of which was imagined to be independent of their creators. Whereas it is plausible to interpret Marx and his communist followers as genuine heirs to the Enlightenment, seeking to take it to a higher level, Nietzsche saw in its central ideas, the 'enlightened' philosophers' belief in the universality of values, nothing but the projection of these philosophers' own cultures. Whereas Nietzsche regarded this belief in the objectivity of created values as the pinnacle of human folly, the Marxists never relinquished their belief in objectivity.

Overall, the influence of Marx on the twentieth century's political conflicts has been more visible, but Nietzsche's influence on Western thought and culture as a whole has been more profound and far-reaching. His diagnosis of the nihilistic 'sickness' of modern European civilisation and his prophesy of the crisis that would engulf it in the following century had a formative influence on a number of crucial movements and figures of that century, notably Freud's theory of the unconscious, the development of abstract art and the philosophies of

Martin Heidegger (1889–1976) and Michel Foucault (1926–84). The nature of this crisis lies at the centre of all the discussions of the *post*modernist rejection of modernity and Enlightenment.

Nietzsche's perspectivism

The single idea for which Nietzsche has been most celebrated by postmodernists and others is contained in his perspectivism. This should be understood as the opposite pole to the seductive Enlightenment dream of attaining a standpoint from which all truths – metaphysical, scientific and moral – would be visible at a glance. Nietzsche's perspectivism, at first sight, not only rejects this as impossible, but also swings to the other extreme, to the denial of all truths whatsoever. This kind of 'global' scepticism was not new to philosophy – it has always been present as an epistemological overreaction against claims to certain knowledge and can be traced back to the ancient Greeks – but Nietzsche's perspectivist version gave it a novel twist. All truth-claims, whether they relate to everyday perception, scientific theories or moral judgements, are held to be wholly dependent upon the position or perspective of the observer. When they are represented as more than a particular opinion, as representing the 'objective' truth of the matter, they are aspiring to a standpoint that it is logically impossible to occupy. There simply is no outside point of view. One can only look through one's own eyes. Accordingly, no point of view is closer to or further from the object it seeks to represent than any other. All our concepts and elaborate theories of the structure of matter or the requirements of justice are nothing but more or less elaborate and ingenious perspectives provided by interpreters of a world that is not graspable in itself. Every point of view is as good or as 'valid' as any other. In short, there are no truths, only interpretations.

There has always been a tendency to respond to such claims with exasperation, not only because they collide with so many of our intuitions about obvious truths and falsehoods, but also because they are so difficult to refute. There is a standard 'quick' refutation of global scepticism, which involves demonstrating that it involves an immediate contradiction. If there are no truths, then it is not true that there are no truths. Any statement asserting the complete absence of truth is thus self-refuting, because at least one statement must be true. By its own standards, perspectivism is itself only one perspective. Nietzsche's perspectivism, however, has retained its influence over modern philosophy, because those who can see its allure regard such refutations as verbal trickery. Also, it should be noted that on closer analysis Nietzsche's own position was not as extreme as this. He did not in fact reject truth as such, but he has been interpreted by many of his postmodernist followers as having done so. Nevertheless, however one interprets it, it is Nietzsche's perspectivism that marks him out as the key source of the postmodernist attacks on the central pillars of Enlightenment rationalism.

The death of God and the will to power

Two prominent themes closely related to Nietzsche's perspectivism are 'the death of God' and 'the will to power'. The impending crisis of values was for Nietzsche the threat of cultural nihilism implicit in what he saw as the illusory rise of reason, science and democracy in Europe, creating a surface impression of progress towards ever higher levels of prosperity and social justice. This was an illusion because when reason turns its own critical light upon itself, it finds itself unsupported. Despite the steadily declining religious belief in an increasingly secular age, people were continuing to think and act as though God were still there as the basis of reason and thus the absolute source of all metaphysical and moral truth. It was only a matter of time before the moral values that were entirely dependent upon the history of Christianity would be seen as empty. According to Nietzsche's alternative to traditional metaphysics, all human life is driven by the fundamental urge that he calls the will to power, not only in the struggle for survival and dominance of nature, or in the explicit power relations between people, but also in its highest social ideals and cultural aspirations and creations, all of which are masks for the will to power. Taken together, these ideas about truth, power and the self-destruction of reason have had an immeasurable impact on contemporary philosophy.

The postmodernist attack on modernity

Postmodernism, as it emerged in 1960s French philosophy, was in large part a reaction against its post-war domination by Sartrean existentialism and Marxism, both of which were regarded as essentially modernist in their basic assumptions. The reinterpretation of Nietzsche that became the norm at this time was aimed at putting together a style of analysis capable of breaking the grip of Enlightenment modernity on philosophy, in order to initiate a way of thinking that was in turn as radically new as modernity itself had been at its inception. Every aspect of this old consensus came under scrutiny, and on all the key values postmodernist philosophy was asserting the opposite. Almost the defining characteristic of postmodernism is that it aims at constant disintegration, not in the sense of shattering or dispersing, but in the sense of dis-integrating apparently seamless unities. The objective was to take apart the systems and totalities of modernist philosophies and show how they are constructed, not out of naturally cohering elements but from either dissonant heterogeneous elements or from arbitrarily selected elements to the exclusion of anything that does not cohere. The circle either closes too quickly or it does not close at all. What they were drawing attention to was the propensity of the knowledge-seeking mind, in its quest for the safety of certainty, to close the general and specific circles of knowledge in such a way that they become impregnable. This is what they mean by the 'closure' inherent in modernity. Hence their main concern was with the breaking up of smooth surfaces, the disruption of false patterns and above all the particularisation of universals. In real life, we experience multiple fragments and loose ends of stories leading nowhere in particular, and to make sense of this experience we impose constructed unities upon these fragments, not least upon our understanding of our own selves. Modernity, according to its critics, does something similar at every theoretical level.

This theme of closure as the principal target of postmodernism opens out into all the other prominent themes. In Jean-François Lyotard's (1924–98) famous formulation, postmodernism is defined as 'an incredulity towards metanarratives' (Lyotard 1984: xxiv), which is to say that it is quite unbelievable that anyone today should have any lingering faith in the greatest of the myths of modernity, the grand-narrative Enlightenment story of humanity's steady progress towards perfection, either in its liberal democratic or communist versions. All grand overarching narratives are regarded with suspicion by postmodernists, and even the micro-narratives by which we live are seen as constantly revisable useful fictions. The closure of the systems of modernity is also seen as being purchased at great cost for those whose histories and experiences are excluded from the closed circle. One of the defining projects of postmodernism is the attempted exposure of the marginalisation and exclusion of those who do not conform with the modernist picture of reason, rationality and justice. Critical attention is thus focused upon what lies beneath the calm surfaces of the false integrities that are subjected to the postmodernist dis-integrative techniques.

Foucault on power and knowledge

Foucault's original and distinctive contribution to postmodernist thought lies in the use he made of Nietzsche's philosophy to undermine the legitimacy of modernity. The most influential dimension of his critique is found in his treatment of power, knowledge and truth. There are several key points to be made about power. The first concerns its location. Foucault regards power as decentred and scattered throughout society. There is no centre point from which it emanates downwards; there is only a multiplicity of lateral power or force relations right across the social spectrum. This metaphor contrasts sharply with both the liberal and the Marxist 'modern' views of the location of sovereign power in the state, the central question for them being the legitimacy of this power. The second point about power at first sight contradicts this, because it suggests a central organisation behind the diffusion of power, in that Foucault asserts that power is intrinsically linked with knowledge in such a way that the latter can only be understood as a manifestation of power, which would seem to suggest a central point behind the multiplicity of power–knowledge matrices. All claims to genuine knowledge at any stage in human history are said to be fraudulent, because they are simply the product of the political regime of the day. Thus the claims to objective and universal truths by Enlightenment liberalism are no more than masks for the political power that has successfully replaced the previous power. These two points do not in fact necessarily contradict one another, if one understands it in the sense that it is through the masking of power that it is diffused throughout society.

Taken together with Foucault's application of the perspectivist denial of truth, this creates the basis for a complete disruption of rational modernist thinking. Science and technology are reduced to power–knowledge complexes, uprooted from any relation to truth or reality. There is no disinterested knowledge, because the very idea of neutral and unbiased scholarship is merely a mask for power, all the more insidious because it represents itself as its opposite.

Derrida and deconstructionism

Jacques Derrida (1930–2004) above all is thought crucial to the emergence of postmodernist critical legal thinking. At the height of his influence in France in the late 1960s he played a central role in taking what was then seen as a philosophical language revolution a stage further. He is most famously associated with the philosophical method of deconstruction, a technique for analysing texts of any sort by taking them apart and revealing the deep instability of meaning in the words in which they are written. Although deconstruction in its very nature is said to resist definition – given the instability of all meaning – it is not intended to extend to any kind of negative critical analysis. It is a specific technique developed and refined by Derrida and his followers for specific purposes. The main purpose is to undo the apparently perfect stability and equilibrium of the concepts and conceptual schemes at the heart of modernity, by 'de-structuring' them and exposing these unnatural constructs as constituting an essentially repressive way of thinking, as an elaborate deception and self-deception on a grand scale. Derrida's central concept to illustrate endemic conceptual instability he calls *différance* (in deliberate contrast to *différence*), which has the double meaning of differing and deferring. This is supposed to indicate the impossibility of assigning a fixed meaning to any concept whatsoever. The differences that are found everywhere in a system of linguistic signs, the dissimilarities and oppositions between concepts understood as bearers of fixed meanings, are deficient compared with the *différance* that lies behind them. The concept of *différence* artificially narrows down and freezes the meaning of terms that are inherently unstable into a fixed core that does violence to their real nature, making the term represent something independent of language. The wider concept of *différance* points to the differences in relation to their incessant insecurity and impermanence, which makes them subject to the endless deferrals of meaning implicit in the words and concepts that they differ from.

Derrida's deconstruction of law and justice

In a famous lecture entitled 'Force of Law: The Mystical Foundations of Authority' (Cornell *et al.* 1992), Derrida's 'deconstructive interrogation' of law and justice was addressed to the perennial tension between established positive law and the timeless standards of justice as exhibited in the debate between legal positivists and natural lawyers. In a highly tendentious and arresting style, Derrida put forward in this lecture a number of reflections on the relation between legitimate authority, enforcement and violence in the law. He proposes a critique of modern legal ideology that involves a desedimentation of the superstructures of law that simultaneously conceal and reveal the interests of the dominant forces in society.

In the course of these reflections, he makes two distinct claims. First, in what he calls 'the ultimate founding moment or origin of law' there is only a *coup de force* that is neither just nor unjust, which cannot be validated by any preceding law. Second, there is no justice in contemporary law without the experience of 'aporia', a sense of paradox or impossible contradiction. The first claim involves the logic of justifying the authority of law. We obey the law, he says, not because it is just but because it has authority. If in our search for justification of this authority, we trace it back to the founding moment of law, 'the discourse comes up against its limit', in which 'a silence is walled up in the violent structure of the founding act'. This is the first sense in which he uses the term 'mystical'.

In the second sense, he discusses the experience of justice as compared to law. In this sense, the experience of justice is so alien to the legal order that it is equivalent to the sensation of a miraculous breach in the order of things, a rending of the fabric of time. What he means is that the deconstructive reading of law reveals the absolute irreconcilability of the smooth running of legal justice and its application of statutes and rules that exhibit the stable and calculable rationality typical of modernity, with the infinite incalculability and other-directedness of genuine justice. This paradox or impossible contradiction lies at the heart of the tension between justice and the law, generating further paradoxes in the experience of the judgement when the judge is aware that the law has to be both conserved and reinvented for each unique case. The judge is also aware that justice always 'cuts and divides', and with genuine justice must undergo an existential ordeal of 'giving oneself up to the impossible decision'. Without this ordeal, the decision can be legal in that it follows the rules, but can never be just.

How plausible is this analysis of justice and the law? The essential points in his argument for the mystical origins of law, on the impossibility of justice existing before or above the founding moment, are similar in structure to the positivist accounts of the origins of law. The standard critical discussions of Kelsen's basic norm and Hart's rule of recognition – to which Derrida briefly refers – have been addressing the same question, some would say with greater acuity. Derrida's description of the founding moment as 'a silence walled up in the violent structure of the founding act' adds little of any substance to Hart's comment on the logical impossibility of validating the fundamental rule of recognition in terms of itself.

In presenting law and justice as necessary antagonists, on the grounds that law in its very nature closes up and congeals the reality of justice into the general rules, norms and values of legality, Derrida contrasts the letter and spirit of the law. In doing so, he highlights the contrast and tension that he claims is buried by judicial language, that is to say the opposition between the general rules and norms of precedent, on the one hand, and the unique particularity of individual cases and decisions by judges, on the other. The aim of deconstruction (real justice) is to recognise and wrest this particularity away from the generality under which the legal cases subsume it.

The internal inconsistencies in this critique are numerous, the most obvious one being the equivocation on the meaning of justice. There are nevertheless features of it that appeal to anyone who has witnessed or experienced the sporadic unpredictability or unfairness of the law. The apparent ease with which the singularity of hard cases can be elided by the application of universal rules is one of the legitimate causes of discontent and disillusion with legal justice. The problems with Derrida's account, however, are numerous. The main problem is that its plausibility is gained by its caricature of 'law and legality' as a justice-dispensing machine, mechanically applying rules and algorithms in the manner rightly criticised by the legal realists in the 1920s. Derrida's assumption is that this mechanical jurisprudence is dictated by the reason and rationality of 'the modern', but this mechanistic approach that he lampoons represents only one narrow line of modern legal thinking. Derrida projects this formalist image of the law onto the entire judiciary, in such a way that his mystical representation of justice as the recognition of the singularity of the individual case gains credibility too easily. Overall, his account must be seen as either too close to the mainstream discussions of the relation between justice and equity in hard cases to constitute a distinctly radical challenge, or as too eccentric to be taken seriously.

Critical legal studies

The emergence of critical legal studies (CLS) as a loose-knit movement in the USA and Britain in the late 1970s owed as much to the earlier legal realists as it did to these critical developments in postmodernist philosophy. In large part, it was a conscious and deliberate revival and adaptation of the realist themes of rule-scepticism and indeterminacy to changing social relations and perceptions of justice in the late twentieth century, particularly on questions of sexual and racial equality and justice. The new legal radicalism tended to be more explicitly socialist than the predominantly liberal realists of the 1930s, but most of them had broken clear of the closed dogmas of orthodox Marxism, while still displaying traces of the less orthodox lines of Marxist thought. The critical legal scholars were also well in tune with the assault on modernity, bringing some of the postmodernist methods to bear upon what they saw as the dogmas of mainstream legal theory.

The rule of law

One of the principal virtues of a liberal democracy is widely assumed to be its commitment to the idea of the rule of law. Within the scope of liberalism, there have been several competing versions or models of the rule of law, but what it basically means, in accordance with the long-standing doctrine of the separation of powers, is that politics is kept out of law, so that the legal process resists the political interference of government. It is adherence to the rule of law that is supposed to be the mark that distinguishes contemporary liberal democracies from totalitarian states. It is not merely judicial independence from overt political pressure, however, that constitutes the rule of law. Law is also expected to be independent in the sense that it rises above the special interests of the parties involved in civil or criminal proceedings and makes rulings and adjudications with neutrality and impartiality. That is the hard core of the rule of law, but in addition there are various models relating to the question of how this impartial legal justice should be delivered. There are different views – as we saw in earlier chapters – on the importance of the consistent application of legal rules and the principle of treating like cases alike, on the predictability and reliability of the law, and on the acceptability of judicial discretion. The general point, however, of adhering to one model or another of the rule of law, concerns the issue of legitimation. If the law is systematically haphazard and unfair, it is widely agreed, the state loses its democratic legitimacy.

This essentially political question lies at the heart of the disputes between the critical scholars and mainstream jurisprudence. According to the most radical arguments, the legal process does not have this kind of independence from politics at all. The claims to neutrality, impartiality and objectivity are, in the view of most of the critical scholars, deeply suspect on philosophical as well as political grounds. That is to say, they are conceptually incoherent as well as being empirically implausible. The empirical disputes over this question are essentially trivial. While there are those who will insist that every individual judge always displays these qualities and rises majestically above all trace of interest and bias, there are others who will insist upon the opposite. It seems clear that in most advanced legal systems most judges at least aspire to neutrality and thus to the setting aside of personal preferences – and it is equally clear that not all of them succeed. The more serious question is whether or not, as the radical critics claim, this general appearance of the fairness and neutrality of the law – even when it seems to be operating at its best – is a veil or mask for the kind of partiality that, if established, would completely undermine the claim that judges draw exclusively upon purely legal resources to guide their actions, decisions and rulings. If this claim cannot be upheld, so it is argued, the rule of law is exposed as a pretence, and political legitimacy as little more than a confidence trick.

The critical legal scholars take up a more radical stance than their realist predecessors, whose rule-scepticism was directed in the first place at the early twentieth-century American formalists. Although the new critics have developed the old realist attempts to broaden the awareness of extralegal factors influencing judicial decisions, these are not seen as sufficiently radical, because they allow for a core of legitimate legal determinacy. More importantly, the realist position on the question of the very possibility of neutrality and objectivity was never consistent or clear, because realism remained within the framework of modernity and liberalism. By contrast, the orthodox Marxist answer to this question was relatively clear. Their explanation is that the judges – trapped within the legal superstructure, which is determined by the base of economic class interest – are either willing or unwitting mouthpieces for the ideology of the ruling class. This approach – however rigid and mechanistic it might have been – did not question the very possibility of reaching objective and just decisions. What was probably decisive for the critical legal scholars' attack on liberal legal determinacy and the rule of law was the Nietzschean postmodernist stance on all problems relating to truth and objectivity. For perspectivism, as we have seen, there simply is no outside standpoint from which to make true and accurate judgements. The values associated with the ideal of the rule of law – neutrality, impartiality, objectivity – are the supposedly naive and discredited ideals of modernity. From Foucault's perspective, there is no such thing as a disinterested search for truth, or indeed an independent truth standard at all, and all these claims to detachment and a desire for justice can be seen as integral parts of the power–knowledge networks permeating society.

The radical indeterminacy thesis

The critical scholars' arguments for the radical indeterminacy of law stand at the centre of the critical attacks on mainstream legal theory. The precise meaning of this 'radical' indeterminacy is one of the contested issues in this debate. In one sense it is merely an extension of the philosophical controversies in both analytic and postmodern philosophy of language into the area of legal theory. In contemporary philosophy it is generally recognised that a certain degree of indeterminacy is an inescapable feature of any natural language. Vagueness and ambiguity surround any concept, the meaning of which is open to more than one interpretation. Indeterminacy becomes radical when linguistic analysis seems to show that the meaning of virtually any concept or text can be interpreted in a multiplicity of ways. It becomes extreme when it is argued that there are no objective facts about meaning at all, that all meanings are conferred arbitrarily and that any word, sentence or text can be invested with any meaning the interpreter prefers, and no interpretation is superior to any other.

Applied to the language of law, it is easy to see how disruptive the implications of radical indeterminacy would be. If it were true of language as such, all the more so would it be true of the legal language in which statutes are laid down, and the judicial opinions, rulings and decisions declared and written. Any interpretation of what the law requires would be as good as any other. Judges could interpret precedent in any way that suited their personal or political agenda. Critics who support radical indeterminacy in law argue that this is the alarming reality concealed by the rhetoric surrounding the ideal of the rule of law.

One distinction that should be drawn clearly, but is often confused in the CLS writings, is the distinction between indeterminacy and underdetermination. If a judge's decision is *over*determined, it means that there is an excess of reasons or causes for the decision; that there are more legal resources than strictly required. If it is *under*determined, it means that existing law allows for a range of possible outcomes, rather than one or none. The disputes within the mainstream between positivists and Dworkinians over hard cases are focused on the question of whether or not this represents a threat to the authority of law. The point here, though, is that such gaps in the law indicated by underdetermination fall far short of what the critics mean by radical indeterminacy. On this radical view, existing law does not determine any outcome at all. Judicial discretion is total. We can see how extreme and implausible this is by comparing it with the positions defended by the legal realists and by Hart. For the realists Frank and Llewellyn, legal rules were always deeply suspect, but not because they were inherently indeterminate in their meaning. As we saw in an earlier chapter, their scepticism towards rules was moderate rather than nihilistic, in as far as they asserted that the boundaries between judicial discretion and the application of rules were blurred in nearly every area of law, and that they were always open to influence by extralegal factors. The rules, they were arguing, were usually less than decisive. Hart's 'open texture' argument was more concerned with the meaning of the legal concepts and much more cautiously or 'minimally' sceptical, in that he saw indeterminacy of meaning only at the periphery or penumbra of the core area in which the meanings of the concepts were thoroughly determinate. In their paradigmatic usage, the meanings were entirely fixed. The function of the judge in hard cases was to intervene and authoritatively fix the meaning of any contested terms. In sharp contrast to both of these theories, the radical indeterminacy thesis simply sweeps away this core belief in the fixity of meaning.

The contradictions in liberalism

The point of departure for all the leading CLS critics was the belief that legal and political liberalism had to be confronted and criticised root and branch, rather than in a piecemeal reformist manner, however radical the reforms. Although there was initial uncertainty and disagreement over what they were trying to achieve, a purpose common to many of them was that they should conduct conceptual and historical examinations of prominent legal doctrines, in order to expose the political and social assumptions upon which they were based, to show how these were concealed by liberal ideology, and to reveal their origins as socially specific rather than natural and inevitable. Their main tactic to this effect was to locate and explain what they took to be inconsistencies and contradictions in legal doctrines, contradictions that lay at the heart of liberal modernity and its way of thinking as a whole.

One of the most influential early writings of this nature was Duncan Kennedy's historical analysis of the doctrines underlying legal adjudication (Kennedy 1976). Focusing mainly upon contract law, the analysis was intended to show that beneath the appearance of a coherent ideology rooted in Enlightenment modernity, liberalism is torn apart by inconsistencies and contradictory values and beliefs in such a way that they are always working against each other and preventing the settlement of a genuinely determinate body of law. For Kennedy, this inconsistency is exhibited primarily by the two principal modes in which legal reasoning is expressed: rules and standards. The contrast that he draws out between the clarity and rigidity of rules and the vagueness and flexibility of standards is similar in structure to Dworkin's rule–principle distinction, but while Dworkin was – at around the same time – using this distinction to demonstrate the underlying determinacy of law as the embodiment of both rules and equitable principles and standards, Kennedy was drawing the opposite conclusion, arguing that the difference between rules and standards is expressive of an ineradicable tension driving the law in different directions at once, thus making it radically unstable and stripping it of any unity of purpose or determinacy.

The success of this argument depends partly upon Kennedy's controversial linking of the rule–standard contrast with the wider political and social opposition between individualism and altruism, which he describes as irreconcilable visions of humanity and radically different aspirations for our moral future. The kind of linkage he has in mind is not conceptual but rather a *de facto* historical link, in as far as the legal-rule form is congenial to furthering individualist aims, while the looser and vaguer standard is more suitable for communal or altruistic purposes. The advantages of clear-cut rules for the encouragement of business and commerce make it obvious why rules are naturally associated with individualism. Their presence restrains official arbitrariness and provides a degree of certainty. At the same time, however, their predictability makes it easier for the unscrupulous to 'walk the line' of illegality in commercial transactions. Counteracting equitable principles such as 'due care', 'good faith' and 'unconscionability', on the other hand, are standards that are also demanded by the altruistic or communal side of liberal modernity. The main historical change that Kennedy identifies in this analysis is the shift in the balance between the two terms of this opposition. With the passing of the classical individualism of the nineteenth century, US law (in parallel with other common law systems) saw the steady expansion of the range and quantum of obligation and liability to such an extent that it could be called 'the socialisation of our theory of contract'. With the gradual erosion of formalism in law as a whole, the two poles in the conflict (individualism and altruism) have faced each other on increasingly equal terms, creating more awareness of the fundamental contradiction in the law.

This contradiction Kennedy regards as fatal to the coherence of liberal theory, because the way that it has evolved has created wide-open discretion for judges who are increasingly aware that 'the presence of elements from both conceptual poles in nearly any real fact situation' undermines any attempt to determine the outcome of the case according to what is required by law. It usually goes unnoticed, he maintains, that this deep tension creates almost universal discretion behind the facade of judicial predictability and determinacy. The reality is an internal struggle between conflicting imperatives to apply rules in the true spirit of individualism or to appeal to standards in the communal spirit of equity, both ostensibly within the frame of liberal individualism. Accordingly, most areas of law in the liberal era should be understood in these terms.

Criticisms of Kennedy and CLS

Kennedy's arguments stimulated a long-running debate that raised many questions central to the dispute between CLS and mainstream legal theory. They drew out criticisms from other CLS writers, from positivists, natural lawyers and Dworkinians, too numerous to cover here. The most obvious one concerns the correlation of rules with individualism, and standards with altruism. If this is shown to be suspect, by producing counterexamples (that there are rigid rules, for example, protecting consumer interests), the argument clearly collapses. It was widely and wrongly assumed, however, that Kennedy intended this linkage as a conceptual one, rather than a contingent one of 'general tendency'. As such, it remains plausible, for the reasons initially given in his contrasts between the functions of rules and standards.

There are, however, more fundamental criticisms. Even if these modes of legal argument are that closely linked to the heart of the modern political struggle between individualist and communalist values, why should this lead to radical indeterminacy? Is it, to put it bluntly, such a bad thing that these values are in perpetual collision within the operation of the legal justice system? One can concede the plausibility of the deconstruction of the myth of judicial unanimity on such issues, without accepting the claim that this leads to complete incoherence in the liberal understanding of legality. One of the strongest positivist criticisms developed by Coleman and Leiter (Marmor 1997: 203–79) challenges Kennedy's assertion that the oppositions he has described are typical of a liberal legal system rather than an inevitable feature of the human condition as such, and therefore of any conceivable legal system. According to this criticism, there is a balance to be struck between the pressures of individualism and altruism, the protection of privacy and the interests of the public, selfishness and sacrifice, and so on, and that it is the ability to strike this balance that makes us human. Furthermore, Kennedy traces the history of the evolving values of liberalism and modernity, which as a history of pragmatic compromise and moral progress is of the very essence of liberalism, rather than fatal to its coherence, as he maintains. Finally, many critics reject the use made by Kennedy and CLS generally of the term 'contradiction' to capture this idea of the tension between conceptual polar opposites. The term is used to suggest and heighten the sense of logical absurdity and literal incoherence, but it is only properly employed in logic to indicate a formal contradiction. It is only a contradiction in the formal sense to assert a proposition while at the same time denying it.

A more general criticism of all the leading CLS writings is that they set up too easy a target in order to demolish it more effectively. Too many of them take as the paradigm of liberal law the rule-fetishism that had been effectively demolished by their legal realist forebears, and to which very few contemporary mainstream theories subscribe. Even with the acknowledgement of the operation of standards in conflict with rules, the assumption is that there is no general awareness in mainstream theory of the complexity of the problems relating to the application of rules, when the truth of the matter is that these have been discussed extensively in the context of justice versus equity throughout the modern period. In particular, many of the early CLS writings ignored Dworkin's critique of rule-based positivism. Dworkin, however, soon became one of the main targets of their criticism.

CLS criticisms of Dworkin

Most of the CLS evaluations of Dworkin take the view that he was to be commended for pushing legal theory in a radically egalitarian direction, but criticised for the ultimately contradictory nature of this enterprise, which failed because he had a defective understanding of the sense in which law is thoroughly political. Although Dworkin is usually criticised from the right for his allegedly dangerous politicisation of the law, these critics from the left take issue with his conception of the rule of law as being set up to ensure that power remains within the hands of a political and judicial elite, to the exclusion of more democratic political participation.

There are two important lines of criticism of Dworkin. The first, argued by Hunt and Hutchinson (A. Hunt 1992), applies postmodernist critiques, especially those of Foucault, to Dworkin's overcentralised conception of power. His rights thesis is said to presuppose a legitimately all-powerful liberal state legislating and adjudicating competing rights, creating and protecting sovereign individuals within supposedly power-free zones, as if the state were the only source of power. In the light of Foucault's analysis of the diffusion and decentralisation of power, the reality of the situation is that these 'free' zones are shot through with relations of oppressive power, in the family, the workplace and society at large. Dworkin is said to ignore corporate economic power, male–female power relations and other forms of oppression, because he is preoccupied with the kind of legal rights to which they are impervious. This is an important line of criticism, but it should be noted that these criticisms have a tendency to downplay or interpret negatively the progressive side of liberal legislation protecting tenants, the rights in employment and property for women, the introduction of a national minimum wage, and so on, all of which Dworkin, among other liberals, strongly approves of.

The second line of criticism by Altman (A. Hunt 1992) is addressed directly to Dworkin's theory of law as integrity as a more expansive version of the traditional liberal conception of the rule of law. The main charge is that Dworkin's conception of the rule of law, as judicial adherence to the law conceptualised as a whole, is a naive distortion of real legal practices in the modern world. According to Altman, the real situation is that the courts enforce settled law that is in fact the outcome of a political power struggle beyond the courts, and that this does not match Dworkin's ideal of a political community thrashing out competing principles and conceptions of fairness and justice. It is also said to be dubious as an ideal to which law and politics should aspire, because Dworkin's 'law as integrity' would be completely undermined by his own political pluralism. Either ideal realised consistently would destroy the other.

There are two problems with this critique. First, it seems clear that contemporary democratic politics displays both features as described by Altman: on the one hand, a complex of sectarian-interest power struggles, on the other, campaigns for the recognition of genuine rights both within mainstream politics and from pressure groups. In fact, it is difficult to see how there could be one without the other. Second, the criticism follows the usual CLS pattern of demanding the kind of perfect consistency in a liberal theory that it does not adhere to itself, expecting an unequivocal commitment to one of the poles in a conceptual opposition, rather than a recognition of the inevitable ongoing tension between them.

Justice modern and postmodern

If the case for radical indeterminacy as argued by the critical legal scholars and others were established beyond doubt, it would certainly add strength to the argument that the courts are the agents of systematic injustice. If determinacy requires observance of the rule of law in the sense that it reaches a certain minimum level of predictability and reliability, that it is accessible and its content well advertised, that like cases are treated alike, then its failure to attain this standard in itself constitutes structural injustice and facilitates the judicial operation of personal prejudice and political bias. This minimum standard was the main point of Fuller's natural law criteria for the existence of a just legal system. It has never been clear, however, that the radical critics' case should rest upon the argument for raging indeterminacy. It is also entirely plausible that the body of law as a whole in any given system at a particular phase of its development can operate with discrimination and bias, and effect the same kind of marginalisation and oppression, without appearing to violate any of these procedural principles. This is indeed one line of radical feminist criticism – that under the liberal rule of law, many individual laws, such as those governing marriage and divorce, ownership of property, rape and other offences against the person, may be substantively unjust without any hint of indeterminacy, and with the current state of the law plausibly represented as 'natural', so that determinate outcomes of legal decisions will only reinforce the injustice that reflects the male-dominated moral consensus of the day.

This ambivalence about the value of determinacy raises an important question about the relation of the new radicalism to traditional natural law theory. Given the justice-centred tradition of natural law, why do the new critics not simply merge with this tradition, confronting the specific injustices embodied in positive law with the independent standards of universal justice? One answer, of course, is that some of them do. Belief in natural human rights has had a continuing impact on critical race theory in particular, since the civil rights movement of the 1960s, and on campaigns for specific legal rights by liberal feminists. Others, however, are more sceptical of the idea of universal justice. Despite its premodern origins in Aristotle and Aquinas, natural law today is too closely tied up with modernity and liberalism, and with the natural rights proclaimed by the Enlightenment. The concepts of nature and reason as the foundational source of justice are thoroughly suspect to anyone influenced by postmodernism, and the idea that there is a standard of justice that transcends particular societies and cultures is seen as hopelessly abstract and non-situated. The last issue that we need to consider at this point, then, is the overall credibility of the relativist and perspectivist thinking that has brought about this scepticism towards the idea of universal justice.

Conclusion: perspectivism and truth

The relativisation of all absolutes implicit in Nietzsche's perspectivism took hold of the philosophical imagination in Europe in the latter half of the twentieth century. Its main attraction in legal studies as elsewhere lies in its potential for the kind of critical analysis that exposes as fraudulent various theories and doctrines which do actually disguise specific vested interests as a natural and inevitable way of seeing things. First encounters with this mode of criticism (and the deconstructive techniques that it engendered) are often experienced as a liberation. It has to be acknowledged, though, that perspectivism is a double-edged sword, not merely because its criticism can be turned upon the critic, exposing his or her own nefarious hidden agendas, but also because it levels down every angle or viewpoint to the same standing. Applied to the interpretation of history, for example, it serves the creditable purpose of undermining the false official histories of political powers that seek to manipulate the past in order to control the present. At the same time, however, it has the unwelcome implication that if there is no historical truth, only a multiplicity of perspectives masking various ideologies, it levels out all interpretations and raises problems relating to notorious 'histories' such as

Holocaust-denial, which are elevated to the same status as the meticulously documented demonstrations of the real extent of the Holocaust, which are subject to methodological constraints and the systematic weighing of evidence. Deconstructionism in particular has been extensively criticised on these grounds.

Within the arguments for universal perspectivism there is nearly always an illicit move from the discovery that many claims to objectivity and justice are false, to the conclusion that all perspectives must be false and that there can be no objectivity and hence no impartiality or disinterested pursuit of justice. It always has to be remembered that this conclusion does not follow. Critical examination of the premises of Aristotle's defence of slavery as natural, or the modern pseudo-scientific theories of natural female and racial inferiority, exposes these theories as false; it does not show that there can be no objective truth on these matters. Assumptions such as these may well be built into the Western way of thinking, but this should prompt relentless rational criticism, aimed at revealing the true picture, rather than a nihilistic assault on the concept of truth. It is insufficient to deconstruct these theories and unmask the will to power behind them, showing how they are rooted in specific social circumstances, and it is misleading to direct this criticism indiscriminately at every theory of law and justice.

Universal perspectivism has often been criticised as self-defeating. On this reasoning, in order to show that some views lay false claim to objectivity, one already assumes that one view is truly objective. Without this assumption, the charge of falsity would not make sense. It has to be said that this criticism has never convinced universal perspectivists. Atheists might argue that there is nothing but an array of false images of God, but it would not count as a valid argument for the existence of God to assert that atheists thereby commit themselves to a true image of God. It is the same with the denial of all absolutes or all truths. Other criticisms highlight the excessive use of optical and spatial imagery in Nietzsche's often inconsistent accounts of perspectivism, and argue that the case is made only by illicitly reducing all forms of knowledge and understanding to inexplicable switches of perception and literal changes of standpoint. It has to be accepted that there are no conclusive refutations of universal perspectivism, but it can be rendered less persuasive by focusing on the contrasts between concrete instances of justice and injustice.

Study questions

General question: What difference has postmodernism made to legal theory?

  Further study questions: What is the significance of the Enlightenment for critical theories of law? Do the arguments for radical indeterminacy undermine the entire range of liberal theories of law? Compare the rule-scepticism of the legal realists with the radical indeterminacy of the critical legal scholars. How does Foucault's concept of power affect our understanding of law? Compare Derrida's concepts of justice and equity with those of Dworkin and the legal realists. Critically assess Kennedy's critique of the contradictions in liberalism. Can perspectivism be applied usefully and consistently to legal theory?

Suggestions for further reading

Recommended general reading on the critical theories are Morrison (1997) and M. Davies (1994). The best introductory books on postmodernism generally are the selections in Bertens and Natoli (2002) and the articles in the Cahoone anthology (Cahoone 1996). One of the most influential texts is Lyotard (1984). For the relevance of postmodernism to legal theory, see Stacy (2001) and the article by Douzinas in Connor (2004).

From the numerous commentaries on Foucault, Gabardi (2001) and Owen (1994) are recommended. Gutting's (1994) *The Cambridge Companion to Foucault* is also very useful. On Derrida's philosophy, see Royle (2003), M. Davies (1994: ch. 7.3), Murdoch (1992: ch. 7) and Culler's article in Sturrock (1979). Derrida's article on justice is included in Cornell *et al.* (1992), which also contains discussions by others of Derrida on deconstructionism and justice.

The best general books on CLS (critical legal studies) include Fitzpatrick and Hunt (1987) and Kelman (1987). Important general articles include Kennedy (1976), reprinted in Patterson (2003); and Altman (1986), reprinted in Adams (1992). A. Hunt (1992) is a collection of critical essays on Dworkin. For critical discussions of the radical indeterminacy thesis, see the essays in Marmor (1997) by Coleman and Leiter. For discussions of impartiality and the rule of law, see the essays in Dyzenhaus (1999) and Montefiore (1975).

On Nietzsche, truth and perspectivism, see Clark (1990), D. Robinson (1999), L. Hunt (1991) and Owen (1994). For an excellent overview of truth and perspectivism in general, see J. Campbell (2001). The best short introductions to 'continental philosophy' are Critchley (2001) and Solomon (1988). On the meaning of the Enlightenment, see the selections from Kant *et al.* in Schmidt (1996), and for defences of the values of the Enlightenment against postmodernism, see Wolin (2004), Porter (2000) and Porter (2003).

Part II
The reach of the law

8 Obedience and disobedience

In a civilised and mature democratic country today, it is widely considered reasonable to assume that the state is both entitled and duty-bound to lay down the law in all its aspects, for the purpose of promoting the common good, in the expectation that every citizen will recognise their obligation to obey the law, even when they do not like it. The mere fact that a law genuinely has the force of law is usually seen as sufficient for this recognition. At the same time, it is also widely believed that the reach of the law is not unlimited, that there are legal and moral constraints upon the ways in which the law can be used, if it runs up against individual or civil rights. In the face of clear and extreme injustice, it is thought, the initial or *prima facie* obligation to obey the law can be challenged.

Questions about this general obligation will be the focus of this chapter. On the assumption that there are sound moral reasons for not breaking contracts or committing frauds or acts of violence, does the unlawfulness of wrongful acts provide an additional reason independent of these moral reasons to conform? That is the question. If sound moral judgement were a sufficient guide to action in society, legal obligation would be no more than a reinforcement of moral obligations. The law would merely be a system of coercion to prevent or discourage people from acting badly. As we saw in the opening chapters, the law has to be seen as more than this.

Should we respect the law as law?

One obvious reason in addition to moral obligation can be found in the instinct of self-preservation, hence the fear of sanctions. In other words, we should obey the law – no matter what we think of any particular instance of it – because it makes good sense to do so. Otherwise we run the risk of incurring the penalties or punishments that we know are attached to them. Something like this might certainly be part of the message from government to populace, but such prudential arguments do not amount to much, because the same might all the more so be said of a truly iniquitous law under a tyranny, that it is in everyone's best interests, for the sake of their own safety, to submit to them. While this might be true, it hardly suggests the existence of an obligation. The conclusion one must reach here is that the existence or non-existence of the obligation precedes the question of whether or not it is wise to obey it, so this argument simply bypasses the main question under consideration. The question that remains is whether the fact of legality as such creates an obligation to obey. Should we respect the law as law?

There is a standard, almost official answer to this question. In a democratic country today, in which we as the electorate are supposed to be ultimately responsible for the state of the law as passed by elected representatives, there is a very strong presumption in favour of obeying whatever the rules of law require, regardless of their content, simply and solely because they are properly authorised rules of law. On this view, it is not for us as citizens to question it in such a way as to claim entitlement to weigh up the positives and negatives and decide for ourselves whether the law on any given occasion ought to be obeyed. From such a perspective, to say 'I know this is the law, but I am under no obligation to obey it', is a contradiction in terms.

Natural law and positivist responses

It is vital to understand that there is no simple correspondence between the major theories of law and these theories of obligation. It is a common mistake to divide natural lawyers from positivists by imagining that while the former urge us to disobey unjust law, the latter insist that a bad law is still a law that has to be obeyed. In fact, the problem is much more complex than this. The mere statement or exposition of what the law actually expects and demands in no way begins to answer the question about the duties of citizens with respect to this law. The fact that there are sanctions to enforce it does not create an obligation; it means only that the citizens can be compelled to conform.

We have already seen some indication of the natural law response to the question about obedience to the state and its laws. Traditional natural law was never entirely clear on the question of obligation. It is one thing to denounce the law as unjust, and to declare it to be 'no law at all', it is another thing – and more far-reaching – to say that bad law has no legal standing at all and is no more than an unprincipled order which individuals can or even should disobey. There has always been a tension within the natural law camp on this issue. Aquinas sometimes seemed to follow St Augustine and others in declaring seriously unjust laws to be invalid, but at the same time urged caution in how one should respond to this. Some laws, he said, were so bad that one might even be regarded as being under an obligation to disobey them. More commonplace lesser lapses in moral standards by the law, however, should be endured for the common good. This is because he wants to make it clear that the state is not above criticism or control by the church, but at the same time does not want to urge unrest or rebellion at times of social discontent. This response is partly prudential, partly principled. So traditional natural law left an ambivalent heritage.

In the modern era, natural law thinking on this issue has been equally ambivalent. While the mainstream interpretation has been to accept the authority of the secular rulers, the justification of disobedience in the cause of racial equality was taken up enthusiastically by church leaders of civil disobedience movements in the 1950s–60s. Martin Luther King Jr (1929–68) – the American civil rights leader – frequently quoted St Augustine and Aquinas in his justification of confrontational disobedience, urging African-Americans to disobey the discriminatory laws of segregation on public transport and elsewhere because these laws 'are no law at all'. Other natural law philosophers have thought that this interpretation diverges from an authentic natural law position and have argued that the 'no law at all' maxim is supposed to be the basis of criticism of government and a guide to judges rather than addressed to the general population. We will return to these issues at a later stage in this chapter.

Legal positivists have also been internally divided on this question. They are all agreed that the law is one thing, its merits and demerits another. This does not mean, however, that they necessarily think that this means that the law as it stands has the authority to command unconditional obedience from everyone subject to it. Some of them, though, did seem to take as strong a line as this. Austin took the view that when a law was commanded by the sovereign, this not only made it legitimate law, but also automatically created an obligation to obey. Although he was freely critical of the law from a utilitarian standpoint, he certainly did not advocate disobedience. Bentham also had explicitly condemned such disobedience. 'Obey punctually, censure freely' was his famous maxim.

What these and many other positivists thought was that there was a great deal wrong with the law as it stood, many laws and common law procedures being irrational and unfair. They were fully aware that there was sometimes serious state oppression, issuing in discontent and riots. But this was exactly why positivists wanted to reform and codify the law, making it more subservient to the general good. The last thing they wanted was people taking the law into their own hands and deciding which laws to obey and which to ignore. This, they believed, would have led to anarchy and the collapse of the state, which would be to no one's benefit. In the twentieth century many positivists have reiterated this stance. In fact, it became the standard practice of positivists in the period leading up to the Second World War, which was why this line of thought attracted such criticism. Subservience to the law was not the best thing to advocate in Germany when the Nazis had taken over the legal system. Against this tendency, though, many others have followed H.L.A. Hart in his renowned comment that it is no contradiction to say: 'This law is legally valid; but it is too wicked to obey' (Hart 2012 [1961]: 208). We have already seen how the positivist Hart deals with obligation in his critique of Austin's analysis, and have seen the problems with his own approach to obligation, as highlighted by his critics. We need to take a wider view now, and look at the various competing theories of obligation.

H.D. Thoreau: conscience as the sole basis for obligation

Although there is a consensus among the majority of philosophers that there is a strong presumption in favour of a general obligation to obey the law, and that the real problem is to determine the exact extent to which this can be justified, there are a number of dissenters, who deny that there is any such obligation. This is not an unpopular attitude today. The reasoning is straightforward. One might, on reflection, think something like this: 'No, there is no general obligation to obey the law. I know what my moral obligations are anyway. It's not for a distant, impersonal state to tell me what I should and should not do.' You may think that most of what you count as right and wrong overlaps anyway with what the law tells you to do. The fact that you are not about to commit murder or theft or rape has nothing to do with their being against the law. And where it does not overlap – where your moral beliefs conflict with the law – that is because what the law demands offends your personal conscience.

The most striking example of a philosopher defending this position is that of the American writer Henry David Thoreau (1817–62). When it comes down to it, he said, conscience is all that matters. If the law tries to compel you to act against it, the law has no authority at all. This position still strikes a chord with many critics of the excessive power of the state in the twenty-first century. It certainly has a strong appeal, especially in the context of the issues over which Thoreau spent a night in jail for a principled refusal to pay his taxes, in protest against what he saw as a war of aggression against Mexico and the issue of slavery in the south at a time when north–south tension over this was escalating. This attitude, though, can be generalised beyond these specific issues. If the law tells you to do anything unconscionable, so the argument goes, you should self-evidently be morally entitled to resist it, to refuse to do it, for example, rather than just refusing to pay your taxes. One difficulty lies in the word 'unconscionable', which presupposes an objective concept of conscience.

What Thoreau is in effect arguing here is that there is no presumption at all in favour of obeying the law. One should only obey it when one is completely satisfied that the law is by one's own lights morally defensible. One real problem here is that this quite seriously raises the prospect of anarchy. While it is certainly an exaggeration to say that everyone's conscience is different, it is equally questionable that there is a universal conscience. Many of Thoreau's fellow taxpayers would have genuine conscientious objections to things quite different from the war against Mexico or slavery. One of the most important reasons for accepting a general obligation is to persuade people at least to some extent to compromise their own moral beliefs when they come into conflict with those of others. Should those others also have the right to break the law? If so, where does it stop? For real anarchists, of course, law lies at the very heart of state oppression, and the idea of a general obligation to obey is not even worth discussing. This is not Thoreau's position, because he nowhere suggests that just laws have no authority, or even that morally neutral laws can be disregarded, but at the same time he provides no arguments for why we should take them seriously and obey the law at all, rather than just following our own moral consciences. What he says about cultivating respect for the right, rather than the law, does of course find a lot of echoes, not only in natural law circles, but also in positivists like Hart, a century later. In the context in which Thoreau was speaking, of course, his preference for respect for what is right can hardly be denied. People should definitely not be encouraged to support laws which create or support widespread injustice, especially the institution of slavery or the subordination of women.

Those, however, are only one part of the law, and there is a danger of losing one's perspective if one falls into thinking that the law is to be primarily associated with the moral horrors of slavery and war. Surely we do have to cultivate respect for the law as such, on the whole, given that it is the condition for the development of civilised society? There is serious and deep disagreement on this issue. Even in the freest of societies, though, we do need arbiters and ultimate authorities to uphold civilised values. And of course we need the law to protect us from the aggression and dishonesty of others. Some will contest this, of course, but most of the philosophers engaged in this debate do think that at least a better balance has to be struck, that it is right to cultivate a critical respect for the law, as well as for the right.

Socrates' arguments in Plato's *Crito*

At one end of the spectrum, then, we find a very strong scepticism towards claims made on behalf of the law's authority, denying that there is even a *prima facie* general obligation to obey it. At the other extreme, we find what is probably the more common response to the same question, that there is indeed such an obligation and that it is virtually absolute or unconditional. The idea is that as soon as one allows exceptions, the authority of the law will break down. From this position one might concede that it is only 'virtually' thus, so as to forestall counter-examples of situations in which it would be madness to follow the law to the letter for its own sake, such as dutifully following legal regulations when lives are in immediate danger. What will be argued from this position is that for all practical purposes there is always an obligation to obey, and that failure to observe this will be criminal and punishable.

As we have seen, Austin and other classical positivists took this view of it. This position can also be traced back to early modern philosophers such as Thomas Hobbes who insisted that the sovereign's power and authority were near-absolute, allowing the citizen only the right of self-defence against deadly threats. The most important source for this position, however, was the ancient Greek Socrates, as reported by Plato in the dialogue *Crito*. The highly dramatic scene reported here was on the eve of Socrates' execution by the Athenian state, after a trial in which the philosopher had been convicted on a number of capital charges, including that of betraying the city to its Spartan enemies. Convinced of the injustice of the conviction and sentence of death, Socrates' friends were imploring him to accept their assistance to escape. In his relentless refusal to contemplate this, Socrates put forward a number of arguments, the reasoning behind which has been used by political and legal philosophers ever since. Overall, the thrust of Socrates' arguments is that he is under an obligation to accept and submit to every law of the city-state that has nurtured him, no matter how unjust he might perceive it to be, because it is the law.

This is the outcome of an imaginary dialogue with 'the laws' of Athens, in which Socrates admits that he would have no answer to their accusations if they saw him trying 'like a thief in the night' to escape the process of law. His reasoning can be broken down into six distinct arguments. The first and perhaps basic one is that unless there were general obedience to the law, there would be no state at all, hence complete anarchy, which would be a disaster for everyone. This is the first reason he must obey and accept the verdict. This is a common enough reason for general obedience. We should, however, question its applicability here. The idea that the creation or continuation of a state depends upon the absolute submission of its subjects, so that no defiance is to be contemplated, even when it seems that its system of justice has at least on this occasion failed, is certainly questionable.

Socrates' second argument has been repeated and disputed in every debate on this issue down to the present day. Each of us owes an immeasurable debt of gratitude, he argues, in the same way that we do to our parents, who gave us life. The state is like the collective parent of all its citizens, because none of us would even be alive outside of its protection. Even allowing the premise of this rather strained analogy, however, should we accept Socrates' implication that the gratitude should be slavish and unconditional, even to the point of accepting an unjust sentence of death? It seems almost contradictory to say that he is so grateful for the life he has been given that he will accept his own death with equanimity. Gratitude to parents does not extend that far, so the analogy is dubious. Should one continue to feel gratitude to a state that abused and tortured you? The gratitude argument does provide grounds for conditional obligation, but it is highly dubious whether it supports Socrates' defence of an unconditional version of the same.

His third argument has been enormously popular, and there are echoes of it in today's democracies. Anyone who does not like the laws, he says, could at any time have emigrated. He himself could have done so at any point in his long life. He was free to do so and he never chose to. He therefore has to accept the findings of the law. This runs into the fourth argument, in which Socrates continues to reject all his friends' replies and points out that he has accepted countless benefits from the state of Athens over his seventy-year life. This places him in a debt that he can never repay. He did not have to accept these benefits and in so doing, he argues, he has implicitly agreed to obey all the laws of Athens. As he had stayed and accepted all these benefits, he has no right now to try to run away from the law. How convincing are these last two arguments? They clearly have some force, especially against someone who has violently attacked the state or their fellow citizens, but again does it justify an absolute obligation, such as Socrates is offering, rather than a qualified one? One might also question the supposed freedom of the average citizen to emigrate – as Hume in his criticisms later emphasised – or one might insist that it depended on the nature and gravity of the injustice inflicted by the state.

In his next reply – his fifth argument – Socrates switches to another line of reasoning. This is the crucial one. It was never part of the agreement between himself and the state, he says, that all its laws would be just. So there is no justification for selectively disobeying unjust laws. This is the most influential of the arguments, because it foreshadowed the social contract theories in medieval and early modern Europe. The idea that there is an implicit agreement underpinning the obligation to obey the law is later developed into an elaborate social contract theory, a theory that in this dialogue is only hinted at. Again, we can allow the serious nature of this argument, but question the idea that it justifies the expectation of total acquiescence.

In the last (sixth) argument, Socrates contends with the idea that there are many bad laws, which should be subject to criticism. Yes, he says, we always have, or should have the right to criticise the laws and lobby for their change, but this does not give us the right to disobey while they are still in force. This is a more difficult point to deal with, because it depends upon the context in which it is set. It is closely analogous to the democratic arguments today, that everyone is obliged to accept the outcome of judicial and political decisions, after full opportunity has been allowed for free and fair debate. Socrates himself was renowned for his relentless critical questioning and fearlessness in the presence of the powerful. In recent times, this argument in the *Crito* has been amplified by advocates of civil disobedience who are anxious to demonstrate their respect for the law while criticising and resisting it in specific ways. It should not be thought, though, that this sixth argument offers any support to active civil disobedience, however restrained. Socrates was emphatically ruling this out.

Overall, then, the *Crito* is one of the most uncompromising defences of the unconditional obligation to obey the law ever written. It should be clear by now that what Plato was doing in presenting his account of Socrates' reflections on his own situation and his own options, was making use of this to generalise to the question about obligation as such. There are clearly many flaws in these arguments, but the important points to grasp here relate to the dispute between those who argue for unconditional submission and those who resist this position and argue for the placing of constraints upon the state's right to expect our allegiance and unconditional acceptance of its laws.

Broadly speaking, then, three types of argument emerge from a close study of the *Crito*. We can summarise these briefly as follows:

Conceptual arguments. Bluntly speaking, the duty to obey is built into the concept of law. The fact that people have to or are expected to obey the law is part of what that concept means. The obligation to obey is written into the very idea of legitimate authority, which is what 'the law' means. Disobedience is therefore wrong by definition and the sanctions of the law are automatically justified. These arguments support an unconditional duty to obey.

Consequentialist arguments. The duty to obey is justified by the overall beneficial effects of universal obedience and the negative disastrous effects of general disobedience. The focus here is always on future consequences of how we behave now. Bad consequences of disobedience can include social disturbance or the complete breakdown of society. Arguments of this nature can point to an unconditional duty to obey, as they do with Socrates, or they can open up the possibility of a conditional duty, which normally prevails but can sometimes be suspended.

Contractual arguments. The duty to obey rests upon agreement – either explicit or unspoken – already reached between the rulers and the ruled. This is an expression of what is already due, rather than for the sake of keeping the peace, or any other benefits. The state has the right to expect obedience, because consent has already been given. This type of argument can also be either unconditional – as it is with Socrates – or conditional, depending upon the terms of the contract.

Consequentialist arguments for conditional obedience

One prominent strength of consequentialist arguments is that its response to the issue of obedience to law appears to be rooted in common sense. If the refusal to acknowledge the authority of law or even to show minimal respect for it became practised far and wide, the consequences for everyone – including the lawbreakers – would be disastrous. It is a step further than the statement of this obvious truth, however, to argue that our obligation to obey the law must be grounded first and foremost in the calculation of the consequences of either course of action – to obey or not to obey.

According to J.S. Mill's utilitarian position (Mill 1972b [1861]), our knowledge of such consequences is acquired by experience over many generations. The reason that we adopt moral and ethical rules to guide us through life is that we believe they are the kind of rules that tend to produce the best overall consequences for those affected by them. This position was much later – in the 1950s – retrospectively called 'rule-utilitarian'. Later again – since the 1980s – it has been regarded as an example of a wider philosophy called 'rule-consequentialism' (RC). This is a general moral theory which is applied to every question and problem that arises. In the present context, the question of legal obligation, it points to the conclusion that the state's demand for obedience can be justified by reference to future consequences. This distinguishes it sharply from the conceptual or contractual theories already alluded to.

This version of consequentialism should be compared with the most prominent alternative within this school of thought, the so-called 'act-consequentialist' (AC) position, according to which an action is judged right or wrong in terms of the predicted outcomes of that particular action, independently of any rules. From this perspective, which at a personal level is a much more demanding one, genuinely moral behaviour is the kind that evaluates every serious decision and act independently, and it involves the assessment of the probable consequences of taking one course of action rather than another. When applied to the question of whether to obey or not on a specific occasion, they will urge the taking into account of every relevant factor, not merely one's general knowledge that breaking the law is in the main a bad thing to do. In this respect, the duty to obey the law has no special status. If it would in the agent's estimation do more harm than good, then they should ignore it and take the course of action that produces the most good.

These two versions of consequentialism (AC and RC) in some ways converge in their answers to the question about obligation; in other ways they diverge sharply. They are of course agreed on the basic standard of consequences, and they are also agreed on the value of the law and the virtue of respecting the law as law. They both reject the conceptualist argument that produces a fetishistic duty to obey the law for its own sake, simply because it is the law. Furthermore, they agree that previous contracts or promises are only of marginal relevance to a calculation of what it is best to do now. Where they diverge varies according to the versions of each doctrine, but the essential difference is that AC is much more likely to endorse individual acts of law-breaking than RC. All versions of RC have an exception clause, so that moral agents will be released from any specific duty if disaster is looming; hence much more harm than good will be done by adhering strictly to the usual rule. As soon as such exceptions are allowed, however, there is an immediate danger that the whole RC approach will collapse, if in any situation in which there is a preponderance of negative effects on the balance sheet of predicted outcomes, they are prepared to override the rule, such that it is no longer distinguishable from the AC version. So, to remain as a coherent and preferable alternative, along with the exception clause they have to add a strong presumption in favour of obeying the law, on the grounds that experience has shown that an erosion of the respect for law will have worse social consequences than the short-term advantage to be gained on this specific occasion. In direct contrast, AC will always say that there is no special reason to obey when the outcomes will be manifestly bad or unjust.

RC is thought by many to be more realistic than AC because staying within the framework of moral rules generally thought to have good effects is less demanding than requiring people to calculate the probable effects of all their acts or omissions. It is also thought to lead to more social stability, as it directs people towards the rules that have evolved and been found acceptable in society, rather than allowing and expecting people to make all their own moral judgements on the spot. Why should we worry about keeping promises and paying debts? For RC, it is because the practice of honouring commitments tends to have more good outcomes than bad. For AC, each promise or debt should be judged independently.

The conclusion we can reach here is that while each of these positions can be described as conditional theories of obligation, clearly at odds with the unconditional theories, RC has a much more pronounced tendency to uphold the law than AC does. Conversely, some have seen AC as having inherently anarchistic implications.

Classical contract theory

The great age of social contract theory in Europe was the socially and politically turbulent seventeenth century, the outcome of which had great significance for the shape of the contemporary world. For many centuries before this, medieval theologians had sought justifications in the idea of the original contract both for the political power of the day and for rebellion against it. The practical problem that inspired the development of the theory was that of justifying the removal of tyrants. In the course of the arguments to this effect, they also laid down the terms under which an acceptable and effective monarch does rule. The answer, briefly, was that monarchs rule by virtue of the consent of the subjects, who have voluntarily subordinated themselves to the ruler in return for the ruler observing certain constraints on the exercise of power.

The situation in the early modern period was such that the leading political thinkers were deeply affected by the constitutional conflicts that culminated in the revolution of 1688, establishing the settlement that brought more or less permanent political stability to England. This century as a whole saw the transition from the accession in 1603 of James I – himself an intellectual defender of the divine right of kings and critic of social contract theory – to the establishment in 1688 of a monarchy firmly subjected to democratic constraint. The interim saw a succession of civil wars, the execution of a king and a period of military dictatorship. The leading English contractarian thinkers, Thomas Hobbes (1588–1679) and John Locke (1632–1704), were both motivated primarily by urgent political purposes. Hobbes, forced temporarily into exile in Paris by the English Civil War, inclined towards strong government without too much concern for its political colour. Locke, on the other hand, also suffering exile as a result of the repressive government of James II, was more interested in limiting the power of government.

The versions of the social contract elaborated by Hobbes and Locke, each based on radically different premises, have been and remain enormously influential in the modern world. What they proposed – Hobbes in *Leviathan*, Locke in the *Second Treatise of Civil Government*, which was largely a reply to Hobbes – were diametrically opposed accounts of political obligation, based on conflicting views of human nature as it exists, or would exist without law or the other structures of civil society.

In both cases, their contract theories rest upon their understanding of *the state of nature*, which is the state presumed to have existed prior to the creation of any laws. For Hobbes, this was a state of permanent war of all against all, in which there are 'no arts, no letters, no society; and which is worst of all, continual fear and danger of violent death' (Hobbes 1962: 143). Locke had a more benign view of the state of nature, but still saw in it enough danger to bring about the existence of law, the main purpose of which was the peaceful settlement of disputes (Locke 1924: 2.3).

It was the manner of the transition from the state of nature to civil society with which the contract theories were concerned. For Hobbes, the source of our present obligation to obey the law is the agreement that first brought it into being, a contract that was made when the majority of people invested authority in a few people or one person powerful enough to suppress the warlike state of nature and keep the peace. This original contract involved a trade of their natural liberty for security and protection. For as long as those invested with the power can enforce the rule of law, the contract is binding.

Locke's interpretation of what the contract consisted in was a direct challenge to the absolutism of Hobbes. For the latter, the contract was valid even under extreme duress, rather in the manner that a military surrender is valid, despite the obvious duress. For Locke, it was a strictly conditional trade by those who voluntarily became subjects, granting the sovereign or sovereign body the right to rule on condition that he, she or they administer justice efficiently, as well as simply enforcing the peace. For Hobbes – the initiator in England of the command positivist tradition – the will of the sovereign is absolute. For Locke, the sovereign is constrained by the democratic rule of law. If the sovereign's side of this bargain is not kept, the contract is void and rebellion is justified.

Weaknesses and criticisms of contract theory

Hobbes and Locke, in common with all contract theorists up to their time, wrote as if the contract between sovereign and citizens had actually taken place at some definite point in the distant historical past. From their point of view, this was a reasonable assumption. Given their theories about the social and political hierarchies in which they found themselves, and their respective interpretations of the free and equal state of nature, it stood to reason that there must have been a point in time at which this freedom and equality of status were negotiated away, in order to escape from the dangers of the state of nature. It was a question of establishing what this negotiation, this original agreement at the point of transition to political society, must have involved. So the main assumption was that the contract was a real event, rather than some kind of metaphor or convenient myth to underwrite obligation.

Given that the contract was a real event, and that this was necessary for it to be binding, the next question that arises is how it continued to create an obligation for all the subsequent generations. If their forefathers had signed away their freedom and equality, why and how should this affect their own position? Was there still an obligation to obey the sovereign? The answers to this question have varied. For medieval thinkers, the obligation is renewed by the reaffirmation of the contract with the succession of every monarch. This was implausible, to say the least. It could hardly be argued that the formal endorsement of a *fait accompli* was a free agreement carrying such significance. Hobbes's answer was not clearly formulated, but suggested a continuing obligation by virtue of the same arguments that had been persuasive at the time of the original contract. Hobbes's contract, it should be remembered, did not require free consent. For Locke, on the other hand, such consent was central; his answer to the question of continuing obligation was based on the claim that contemporary consent is *tacit* as opposed to the actual consent given at the time of the original contract.

The nature of social contract theory changed substantially in the period leading up to the American and French Revolutions. David Hume accepted the contract as a real event accounting for the origin of obligation, but denied that it could continue to operate as such a justification in the present. In particular, he poured scorn upon Locke's defence of tacit consent, likening it to the plight of a press-ganged sailor expected to accept the authority of the ship's master. For Hume, contemporary obligation has to be justified on the basis of actual benefits to be derived from a state that is generally obeyed.

The important breakthrough came with Kant's relinquishment of the assumption that the social contract must be understood as an actual, literal, historical contract between sovereign and subjects. For Kant, the contract was indeed the source of obligation, but it was to be understood not as something that had happened in the past, but as 'an idea of reason' that exercised its influence in the present. The Kantian contract is hypothetical rather than real. It is what rational people *would agree to* if they found themselves in such circumstances as described by the traditional theory. For Kant, it is rational to assume that such a contract between subjects and sovereign does exist.

One major type of criticism that should be mentioned in conclusion here is the charge of logical incoherence. It has frequently been argued that the very idea of a social contract as a literal historical event, brought into being between free subjects and a designated sovereign, is self-contradictory. In order for such an agreement to be reached, it is argued, there must already have been in existence the kind of institutions, the recognition of which depends on a prior agreement to respect them. What this suggests is that the original contract would be trying to create an authority that is itself needed to create it. An extension of this criticism is that the concept of a contract is a legal one, which by definition cannot be applied in a prelegal situation. A further extension of it is the argument that in a genuinely presocial state of nature, the individuals seeking a sovereign would not even have the appropriate language for appointing one and formulating the agreement.

While these criticisms show that the traditional versions of contract theory were making simplistic assumptions about the origins of political power and legal systems, they are not entirely convincing. They seem to depend on the more modern belief that the idea of a presocial state is a myth; however, even if this is so, there is nothing mythical about the creation of political authority and law. It is not clear why the transition from a prelegal society to a legal one would require a contract in this very literal legalistic sense; or that it would not have the linguistic resources to innovate in this way.

Even if these criticisms are not as damaging as they sound, however, the fate of literal social contract theory was sealed largely by the rise of utilitarianism from the late eighteenth century. For utilitarians, the source of obligation was essentially forward-looking or consequentialist; the justification for general obedience is future-oriented rather than rooted in a past agreement. The idea of a binding contract was seen as an anachronism. It was not until the second half of the twentieth century that this largely discredited idea was seriously revived.

Rawls: the original position and the conditional duty to obey

With this historical background in mind, we can now return to the contemporary revival of contract theory by John Rawls. One of his main explicit purposes was to promote a coherent alternative to utilitarianism as a general moral theory as well as a theory of obligation. The overall aim was to construct a theory of substantive justice rooted in the contract tradition. Rawls maintains that his own contract theory leads to principles of justice that would not be endorsed by utilitarianism. Within the social contract tradition, this firm linking of the contract to principles of justice owes more to Locke and to Kant than to Hobbes.

On this new interpretation, the idea of a real historical contract is completely defunct. As we have seen, there were early hints that a hypothetical contract could operate as the ground of obligation, and that this only became explicit in Kant's philosophy. Even in Kant, however, the notion was rather sketchy, and Rawls's project was to develop a complete exposition of this theme.

With the proposal that the contract is hypothetical, it becomes irrelevant whether such an agreement had any historic reality. It is more appropriate to understand it in a 'let us imagine ...' sense. Imagine a scenario in which a number of people are called upon to make the kind of agreement necessary to escape from the state of nature and establish civil society. Assuming that they are rational individuals in the sense that they are all concerned with striking the best possible bargain for themselves, what would be the content of the contract they would freely consent to?

In this imaginary situation, which Rawls refers to as 'the original position' or 'the initial situation', the parties to the contract would be required to reflect on the principles of justice to be adopted by the society in which they subsequently have to live. The contract would then involve the endorsement, in advance, of these principles, to which they would subsequently be committed. The crucial feature of this imagined position is that when choosing the principles that would govern a just society, each subject would be 'veiled' from all knowledge of the place he or she is to occupy in that society. They would have no knowledge of their natural endowment of intelligence or practical ability; or of whether they would be male or female, black or white, rich or poor, healthy or disabled, intelligent or disadvantaged. What is concealed is anything that might give them a head start or a handicap. They would not even have foreknowledge of their own personality traits and inclinations, whether acquisitive or unambitious, adventurous or cautious. This is Rawls's 'veil of ignorance', one of the most famous metaphors in contemporary philosophy.

This original position, despite its intended similarity to the presocial 'state of nature' of classical contract theory, is quite different in as far as its subjects are not real reasoning people, deciding on the nature of the bargain to be struck with a sovereign. Rawls's 'parties' to the contract are theoretical constructs, individuals stripped of all knowledge of themselves. In important respects they are not presocial; they understand everything of the basic workings of society except their own nature and their own position in it. What they are deciding is what it would be rational to accept as a principle of justice if they did not know how they personally were going to be affected by it. As such, the veil of ignorance, and the original position that it qualifies, is essentially a device for the elimination of unconscious bias and prejudice.

Rawls describes his theory of justice as 'justice as fairness'. What this means is that given the 'blind' starting point from which the principles of justice would be agreed upon, that of the original position, no one has an unfair advantage through inside knowledge of how the arrangements chosen will affect them. Justice is fairness in the sense that it is chosen in the dark, so to speak.

What is actually chosen by the parties in the original position is a conception of justice, which embodies a set of principles of justice. These will determine the nature of the constitution and a legislature to enact laws, a legal system to administer it, and so on. The important point is the nature of the principles upon which all the other arrangements will rest. Rawls argues that the rationality of self-interest of those who do not know which way their luck is going to turn will inevitably guide them towards principles that safeguard the interests of everyone in society with as much equality as is practically realisable. This leads him to two basic principles of justice, whereby everyone would have the right to equal basic liberties and socioeconomic inequalities would be arranged for the benefit of the least advantaged, with 'all offices and positions open to all under conditions of fair equality and opportunity' (Rawls 1972: 302).

These principles are certainly not self-evident, and Rawls does not make any such claim for them. They are what rational self-interest, veiled by ignorance, would demand. The truth of the matter, of course, is that such principles would be rejected by many in the real world. What Rawls does claim is that in modern democracies they are already widely accepted, and that those who do not accept them can perhaps be persuaded by philosophical reflection. The important point is that the reasoning is not based on considerations of utility or a concern for the general welfare, but on straightforward self-interest in the original position.

Criticisms of these basic features of Rawls's theory of justice have come from many different angles. Some critics have regarded the veil of ignorance as an elaborate way of expressing the commonplace observation that justice is objective and neutral, or that it achieves the same result as other less complex devices for adopting the position of the disinterested observer, such as the imaginary visitor from Mars. Others regard all these visions of impartiality as a sham, and Rawls's version of it as merely a projection of his own sense of justice. Others again have argued that on Rawls's own terms, the impartiality of the veil and rational self-interest would not lead to these two principles of justice. The basic assumptions behind the 'maxi–min' idea – that it would be in the rational interests of all to arrange inequalities for the maximum benefit of the least advantaged – has been subjected to extensive analysis and criticism. Robert Nozick (1938–2002) in particular has argued (Nozick 1974) that Rawls's egalitarianism is not justice at all, that it is a sophisticated piece of trickery to justify excessive intervention by a non-legitimate state, for the redistribution of the wealth and property legitimately held by those who have acquired it rightfully to those who have no right to it. For Nozick, only a minimal 'nightwatchman' state, protecting negative rights and regulating legal transactions, is justified. The Rawlsian contract, from this point of view, justifies systematic injustice.

On balance, however, Rawls's theory of justice and later theories influenced by it still stand up well against many of these criticisms. Although Nozick's rival libertarian interpretation of justice and rights has been influential, it is widely regarded not only as too extreme in its anti-welfare implications, but also as being basically flawed in its uncritical assumptions about the rightfulness of the acquisition of property holdings.

Rawls on duty and obligation

Throughout Rawls's analysis of the duty to obey the law (Rawls 1972: ch. 6), his reference point is that of the parties in the original position, the arguments that would prevail, the conditions they would insist upon and the social arrangements they would reject. For example, when he argues that consenting to unjust arrangements amounts to an extorted promise that is void *ab initio*, and hence that such consent does not create a natural obligation, his justification for this argument is that the parties in the original position, rationally aware of their own interests, would insist on these conditions. The original position, then, is the contractual source of the obligation.

From this position, Rawls argues, it would be relatively easy to establish 'a natural duty of justice' to support institutions that are in fact demonstrably just, in that they show no favour or discrimination. If they are consistent with the two principles of justice – or if they come as close as possible to satisfying them as circumstances allow – the parties to the contract would agree to accepting the duty to obey, because each individually would expect to flourish under such arrangements. This natural duty, he argues, would be endorsed in preference to a principle of utility, because the latter is based not on rational self-interest, but on a calculation of what would be best for the aggregate welfare of all the citizens.

The more important question for Rawls is that of whether there can be a duty to comply with an unjust law, or with unjust social arrangements. From the outset, Rawls rejects the idea that the duty to obey can be restricted to perfectly just laws and institutions. This, he says, is as mistaken as regarding the legal validity of a law as a sufficient reason for obeying it. Clearly, in the case of an unjust law, the natural duty of justice does not apply. What the proper attitude depends on, according to Rawls, is the arguments that would be persuasive from behind the veil. He anticipates the objection that nobody in this initial position in which they are still 'free and equal' would contemplate endorsing a situation in which they will be expected to obey clearly unjust laws, an endorsement that would be contrary to their own interests.

It is this voluntary relinquishment of complete freedom from a duty to obey unjust laws that Rawls seeks to explain. In so doing, he argues that the parties to the original contract would reason, with the benefit of their knowledge of the way society works, that all social arrangements being fallible and imperfect, it is better to consent to one fallible procedure that is bound to produce some injustice than to make no agreement at all. The important distinction for Rawls in this context is between a 'nearly just' society and constitution and a clearly unjust society and constitution. The conclusion he is seeking is that there is a certain amount of injustice in the specific form of unjust laws that we have to put up with and recognise as binding, so long as the basic structure of society is reasonably just. His argument is that this conclusion is warranted by reference to the considerations that would be persuasive in the original position; the parties would recognise the inevitability of a certain amount of injustice. As fully rational agents, they would know that it would be in their own interests to curtail their expectations of perfect justice.

As Rawls realises, the real problem lies in distinguishing between circumstances in which we are bound to comply with unjust or unreasonable laws, and circumstances that involve a degree of injustice that is entirely unacceptable. His central argument is that the duty to obey depends on the degree of seriousness of the injustice. We are only obligated to regard unjust laws as binding within certain limits to what would be acceptable to the parties in the original position. It is in order to establish the nature of these limits that Rawls's analysis turns to the question of how and when civil disobedience can be justified.

Injustice and civil disobedience

The central question in any discussion of civil disobedience concerns the point at which it becomes morally permissible – or even obligatory – to resist the authority of unjust laws or institutions. It should be noted immediately that it is never a question of legal permissibility: civil disobedience is illegal by definition and only reaches the political agenda when it is widely held that certain laws are wrong.

Definition of civil disobedience

A provisional definition of civil disobedience is that it means 'deliberate principled lawbreaking'. This makes it clear why it cannot be a legal activity, such as a campaign of demonstration against laws perceived to be unjust; its very purpose is to challenge these laws with defiantly illegal actions. One of the difficulties in defining it more precisely lies in the fact that its meaning has evolved by convention. Henry David Thoreau is thought to have been the first to use the term – in 1848 – in an essay justifying his principled refusal to pay tax to finance the US war against Mexico. The same term has since been used in many different contexts, the most famous of which have been the strategy of passive resistance employed by Gandhi against British rule in India and the civil rights movement in the 1950s–60s in the USA.

In each of these cases, there is an emphasis on civil disobedience as essentially a non-violent strategy of resistance. So, in addition to the illegal activity being based on principle, it must also avoid violence. Non-violence is usually stipulated as part of the definition of civil disobedience in order to distinguish it from other forms of resistance to injustice, such as direct action, rebellion or revo-lution. This does not necessarily mean that violence is always wrong; what it does mean is that if the action is violent, it cannot count as civil disobedience. It should be noted, however, that this condition is not universally accepted (Bedau 1991: 130–44).

A number of other stipulations are conventionally associated with the defini-tion of civil disobedience. It must be used only in the last resort, when all other legal methods to change the law have been explored and exhausted. It must be undertaken openly, which is to say that it must be an act of open defiance with the intention of publicising the injustice, rather than quiet non-compliance. Furthermore, those engaged in it should be prepared to submit to prosecution and punishment, rather than attempting to evade the process of law. Finally, it is usually stipulated that principled disobedience to one unjust law should be accompanied by scrupulous obedience to the law as a whole.

The initial definition from which we started was that of civil disobedience as 'deliberate principled lawbreaking'. This 'principled' feature distinguishes it from (1) common criminal or civil lawbreaking for personal convenience or personal gain; and (2) opposing injustice to oneself for the sole purpose of asserting or defending one's own rights. In the sense intended, 'principled' means that it is motivated by a selfless concern with opposing injustice. It has often been objected that the exclusion of the second of these is an unfair condition. If an injustice is generalised, then those participating in organised disobedience are likely to be affected by it themselves. Principled activity and the defence of one's own rights should not be seen as inconsistent. A striking example would be the refusal to fight in what was widely held to be an unjust war. A second complication here, with the insistence on selfless motivation, is that the appeal to conscience on every issue of moral significance is thought by critics of civil disobedience to display another kind of self-centredness: a refusal to accept that the consciences of others must be respected and weighed against your own.

Justification of civil disobedience

On the question of the justification of civil disobedience, there are two polarised positions of unqualified approval and complete rejection.

First, those who argue that active disobedience to unjust laws is always a matter of personal moral decision according to conscience are arguing that conscience always overrides any general obligation to obey the law. This in effect means that there is no obligation at all, because it implies that, in the case of just laws, the obligation derived from conscience would be sufficient.

The most renowned advocate of this position was Thoreau, who had little time for the idea that the law is owed any respect:

> Must the citizen even for a moment, or in the least degree, resign his conscience to the legislator? Why has every man a conscience then? I think we should be men first, and subjects afterward. It is not desirable to cultivate a respect for the law, so much as for the right. The only obligation which I have the right to assume, is to do what at any time I think is right.
>
> (Thoreau 1983 [1849]: 387)

The appeal of this statement rests on the plausible assumption that one always has the right to resist outright injustice. Read more carefully, however, what it amounts to is a thoroughgoing individualism on all questions of moral seriousness, the implications of which are anarchic.

Second, those at the opposite end of the spectrum maintain that civil disobedience is never in any circumstances justified. From this point of view, the 'general' *prima facie* obligation to obey the law means general in the sense of 'universal' or 'exceptionless', rather than 'generally speaking' or 'in most circumstances'. This position includes Socrates' *Crito* position, allowing criticism and persuasion but completely outlawing principled disobedience. It also includes Bentham's famous dictum, urging legal reformers to 'obey punctually, censure freely'. The view that civil disobedience is always wrong is usually confined to the context of liberal democracies or other forms of government under which some freedom of expression and criticism is possible.

Between these two polarised positions, many philosophers, including Rawls and Dworkin, have sought to develop a qualified defence of civil disobedience in carefully defined circumstances. What they are defending is the moral legitimacy of a certain kind of principled lawbreaking, overriding the *prima facie* obligation to obey the law.

Rawls on civil disobedience

Rawls's approach to civil disobedience flows directly from his contractual theory of obligation. Bluntly speaking, when the state breaks its side of the hypothetical contract, the obligation to obey is abrogated. Civil disobedience is then justified in carefully specified circumstances. What this means for Rawls is that a situation exists whereby the parties in the original position would find it irrational to agree with the suppression of basic liberties or the equality of opportunity for any group in which they might find themselves when the veil of ignorance is lifted.

What Rawls explicitly assumes from the outset is that civil disobedience is only appropriate and feasible in a democratic society, a society that is – at least in principle – committed to the values of liberty and equality. In non-democratic societies, other forms of opposition and resistance are appropriate; however, this is not what Rawls is concerned with. Civil disobedience is taken up by citizens who regard the system as in the main a just one. A precondition for justifying it, he believes, is that those resorting to it accept that the system is a 'nearly just' one. Although it goes outside of the law to make its protest, civil disobedience stays within the limits of what Rawls calls 'fidelity to law, albeit at the outer limits of it'. That is to say, they accept the moral legitimacy of the law as a whole; this acceptance is evidenced by their willingness to accept the legal consequence of their actions.

Rawls is arguing, then, that there is a general duty of obedience and that civil disobedience can be justified in a contemporary democratic society. As we have seen, he argues not only that there is a natural duty to obey just laws, but also a duty to obey them – within certain limits – when they are unjust. If the society is 'well-ordered and nearly just', accepting the democratic principles of equality and mutual respect, there are many injustices that have to be accepted. It is only when an injustice becomes grave enough that civil disobedience is justified.

What he means is something like this. In any large society, there will inevitably be many grievances, real and imagined, about the distribution of wealth, undeserved privileges, miscarriages of justice or the state of the law on many different issues. Some examples of these will be serious, while some will be relatively minor injustices. Most of them are more appropriately dealt with within the channels of the democratic political process. Relatively few of them justify civil disobedience.

In some cases, though, he accepts civil disobedience to be justified. How then does Rawls define it?

> I shall begin by defining civil disobedience as a public, non-violent, conscientious yet political act contrary to law usually done with the aim of

bringing about a change in the law or policies of the government. By acting in this way, one addresses the sense of justice of the majority of the community and declares that in one's considered opinion the principles of social co-operation among free and equal men are not being respected.

(Rawls 1972: 364)

Rawls is conscious of the restricted nature of this definition, which excludes many other types of principled disobedience. He adds that he does 'not at all mean to say that only this form of dissent is ever justified in a democratic state'. What he seeks to emphasise is the distinctiveness of this form of dissent, as opposed to, say, conscientious refusal.

What he means by calling it a political act is that (1) it is addressed to 'the majority that holds political power'; and (2) that it is an act 'guided and justified by political principles, that is, by the principles of justice' (ibid.: 365). What it always involves is an appeal by this dramatically public action to the commonly shared conception of justice in the society. When it is justified, Rawls sees civil disobedience as playing an important part in the democratic process, by highlighting the failure of society to live up to its own principles. So by its very nature, he argues, civil disobedience is a public act rather than a covert or secretive one. It is a form of public speech, and as such it needs a public forum. And for the same reason it is non-violent: as a form of speech, it is principally a form of communication. As violence, it negates itself as communication.

There are three presumptions that, according to Rawls, circumscribe the limits of justifiable civil disobedience. The first of these is the most important, identifying those types of injustice that are the appropriate objects for this kind of protest. What he argues here is that 'it seems reasonable, other things being equal', to limit it to instances of 'substantial and clear injustice' (ibid.: 372). For this reason, he says, civil disobedience should be restricted to protesting against serious infringements of (1) the principle of liberty; and (2) the principle of fair equality of opportunity. Both of these he describes as guaranteeing the basic liberties: the rights to vote, to hold office, to own property, and so on. Having included these clearly identifiable injustices in the category of wrongs that are rightfully opposed by civil disobedience, he proceeds to exclude socioeconomic injustices as suitable cases for civil disobedience on the grounds that they are much more difficult to ascertain. There is so much conflict of rational opinion as to whether and to what extent the existence of socioeconomic inequalities constitutes an injustice, that civil disobedience would become too difficult to justify. Thus, apparently unfair tax laws, he says, unless they are clearly designed to attack a basic equal liberty (for example, a tax on a religious group or an ethnic minority) are best left to the political process.

Rawls's second presumption is that, for civil disobedience to be justified, legal means of redress have to have been tried, to no avail. Attempts to have discriminatory laws repealed have to have failed, so civil disobedience should normally only be taken up in the last resort. He accepts that this is not always the case and that sometimes the matter is too urgent to spend years on legal campaigns.

The third and last condition is more confused than the first two. The natural duty of justice, he says, may require a certain restraint. If one minority is justified in disobedience, then any other minority in relevantly similar circumstances is likewise justified. So many groups with an equally sound case might take up civil disobedience and cause a complete breakdown of the law. There is an upper limit on the public forum to handle all these complaints. It does seem odd that Rawls can contemplate such a scenario, with so many minorities being deprived of basic rights, and still call it a nearly just, well-ordered society.

Criticisms of Rawls

Criticisms of Rawls's general approach to obligation and civil disobedience have come from every direction. Clearly, those who reject contract theory based on rational self-interest will also reject these implications of it. A standard consequentialist justification of principled lawbreaking in pursuit of civil rights will be based, not on an appeal to an implicit rational contract, but to a comparison with the consequences of continued acquiescence. What releases them from the general duty of obedience is an outweighing of the consequences of submitting to unjust laws by the positive consequences of defying them.

Criticism also comes from those who reject the justification of civil disobedience unconditionally, on the grounds that the obligation is universal in a democracy, where it is possible to change unjust laws through more conventional political channels. On this kind of conceptual argument, 'principled lawbreaking' is a contradiction in terms if the law is by definition morally authoritative, even in its unjust manifestations. The implausibility of this criticism is highlighted by any consideration of the claim to have established an automatic link between the existence of a proper legal authority and the obligation to obey. It is quite clear that we can accept the democratic authority of a government without submitting to such an unconditional obligation. People can and do recognise the political legitimacy of governments, while quietly disregarding not only the laws that do not suit them, but also the ones they think irrational or unfair.

Others have criticised Rawls on his own terms, suggesting that there is something arbitrary about his narrow confinement of legitimate civil disobedience to the special case of the civil rights of minorities. It seems obvious to many critics that there are other serious moral issues that might equally merit principled lawbreaking – issues relating to environmental dangers, unjust wars or unjust taxes – which are held to be wrongs or injustices that would not be countenanced in the original position. There is also felt to be something excessive about his justification of unjust laws that fall short of the threshold at which they create systematic structural inequality, on the assumption that rational agents – veiled from knowledge of whether they would be the victims – would regard such a high threshold of toleration of such injustices as 'the best possible world'. The objection here is either that this is not what we would agree to from behind the veil, any more than we would agree to extreme inequalities; or if it does imply this, then there is something radically wrong with the veil as a metaphor for justice.

If this last criticism is justified, however, it means in effect that there is no general *prima facie* obligation to obey the law, beyond the moral obligation that is there already. If at the first sign of injustice or unfairness the duty to obey disappears, it means that there is no special reason to respect the authority of the law. Another interpretation is that 'respect for the law' is just one reason to weigh against other reasons, enjoying no special status.

Conclusion

In contemporary legal theory, the relation between the idea of law and the meaning of its authority is still very unclear. As we saw at the outset of this chapter, any serious examination of the link between a valid authorised law and the duty of obedience leads into a conceptual quagmire. One thing that Rawls and his critics have done in recent years is to bring more structure into the debate on the origins of obligation and the conditions under which it might be suspended. One point upon which a degree of consensus is perhaps emerging is the recognition that there are limits to the authority of the law, and that the obligation to obey is not unconditional.

Study questions

General question: Do you agree that there is a general duty to obey the law? If so, what is its source?

Further study questions: What are the problems with the traditional social contract theories? Explain and critically evaluate Rawls's 'hypothetical contract' theory. Does it solve all the traditional problems of contract theory? Does he show that there is a natural duty of obligation to obey the law? Is a consequentialist justification to be preferred? What is civil disobedience? Is it compatible with the general obligation to obey? What problems does Thoreau's defence of it face? Does Rawls's 'original position' provide a sound basis for determining the justifiability of civil disobedience? If not, is there a better justification for it?

Suggestions for further reading

Among the general books and chapters on political and legal obligation, the most noteworthy are Greenawalt (1987), Horton (1992), Pateman (1979), Beran (1987), Smith (1976) and Flathman (1973).

Important chapters and articles to consult include Raz (1979: 266–75; 1986: ch. 4), Lacey (1988: chs 4 and 6), Soper's article and the subsequent discussion in Gavison (1987). Useful shorter comments can also be found in Bix (2015: ch. 16), Lyons (1984: ch. 7), and Harris (1997: ch. 16).

For Aquinas's writings on obligation, see Aquinas (1948). On the history of contract theory, see in particular Hampton (1986; 1997: ch. 2). There is also an excellent anthology by Lessnoff (1990), containing key selections from Hobbes, Locke, Kant, Rawls and others. The essential passages on contract theory can be found in Hobbes (1962: chs 6, 11–21) and Locke (1924: §§1–6, 47–55, 123–41). Abridgements of these and of Hume's criticism of contract theory are reprinted in Cottingham (1996: pt 9).

The essential reading from Rawls's *Theory of Justice* (Rawls 1972) is chapter 6. Important critical discussions of Rawls's theory as a whole include Nozick (1974: ch. 7) and Barry (1973). Daniels (1975) is a collection of critical essays.

On civil disobedience, the most valuable collections are both edited by Bedau (1969, 1991), including Plato's *Crito* and influential essays by Thoreau, Martin Luther King, Rawls and Raz. See also Singer (1973), Greenawalt (1987: chs 3–4), Leiser (1973: ch. 12) and Kipnis (1977: §4). There are useful shorter comments by Riddall (1999: ch. 22) and Singer (1993: ch. 11).

9   Legal and moral rights

Rights we take for granted in liberal democracies today include a maze of political, civil, legal and human rights so complex and deep-rooted that the idea of rights being indispensable to moral and legal discourse seems to be part of the fabric of social life. We have rights in property and rights created by contract. Everyone has the right to a fair trial and access to civil and criminal justice. We have rights as citizens and as consumers. The basic rights to 'life, liberty and security' are protected by the European Convention and the 1998 Human Rights Act (HRA) in the UK. At a more mundane level, everyone has the right to voice an opinion and to express dissent. We regularly claim the right to know or the right to reply. Controversy on these matters usually relates to the genuineness of each of these rights, or the extent to which they should be allowed, rather than to whether or not we should have them at all. Nevertheless, in the debates that have raged around the subject of rights in recent years, there is one particular issue that, logically speaking, precedes all the others. This is the question of whether we can meaningfully say that there actually are any rights at all, human or otherwise. While the rights theories of Dworkin, Rawls and Nozick begin from the assumption that there are indeed rights to theorise about, others are more sceptical.

So do rights really exist or are they phantoms? Sceptics argue that all our talk of rights is nothing but rhetoric and bluster, designed to draw public attention to specific moral claims. There are two extremes here. At the rights-realist end of the spectrum, we find writers such as Norberto Bobbio declaring that the problems about rights are not philosophical at all, that the real problem is 'to find the surest method for guaranteeing rights and preventing their continuing violation' (Bobbio 1990: 12). From this eminently practical point of view, the existence of rights and meaningfulness of rights-claims is presupposed. At the sceptical end of the spectrum, we hear Alasdair MacIntyre comparing belief in rights with belief in witches and unicorns, claiming that 'every attempt to give good reasons for believing that there *are* such rights has failed' (MacIntyre 1981: 67). From this standpoint, there are no rights to be guaranteed. What we will be examining in this chapter is the philosophical support for each of these positions, and for those which lie somewhere between these two extremes.

A more cautious scepticism than the outright denial of rights as such is expressed by those who regard it as meaningful only to talk of legal rights.

On this view, the background to any right properly so-called must be that of legal definition and sanction. Without this background, the language of rights as used to explain moral relations between people is at best metaphorical, and at worst meaningless. This denial of the intelligibility of moral rights is of course contested vigorously by those who regard legal rights as merely the official endorsement of pre-existing human rights, which some philosophers describe as natural. As we shall see, this dispute is not easily resolved.

An equally prominent theme here is the most general consequence of taking a realist view of rights. If there are indeed rights to be recognised, the bearing this has on the matter of the law's authority is immediate and problematic. To what extent is the state compelled to accept individual or collective rights as an effective constraint on the implementation of public policy through the criminal and civil law? What limiting effects do they have on the reach of the law? This will be taken up in the next chapter in the specific context of personal privacy, but the problem here is more general. It is a question, philosophically speaking, about how rights stand in relation to utility. What are we committed to when we accept that there really are rights? Does it mean merely that they should always be respected in the sense of being taken into account in every calculation of the common good? Or does it mean more than this, that rights can on no account be overridden by utility?

This points to the closely related problem of identifying 'basic' rights, those supposed to be guaranteed as a bare minimum. Are these the ones that should be defended unconditionally against utility or convenience? If so, which among the vast numbers of rights claimed today should qualify as basic? Does being basic mean that they are to be regarded as absolute, in the sense that there are no imaginable circumstances in which they might reasonably be suspended or overridden? The problem at the heart of the rights–utility conflict is that of determining the extent to which legislators have a free hand in deciding what is to be included, allowing in pragmatic concerns about resources and practicability; and the sense in which these choices are pressed upon them by the intrinsic nature of the rights in question.

Overall, the question of how rights and legality are to be understood is the paramount one. A great deal of the rights analysis in twentieth-century legal theory has focused exclusively on legal rights, independently of the question of how they relate to rights in general. The most important single influence on this development was the analysis initiated by Wesley Hohfeld (1880–1919), who was inspired by the closely connected aims of legal realism and analytical jurisprudence. What Hohfeld sought was an analysis that would clarify the real structure of legal relations between people, expressed in terms of rights and duties as they actually exist and are recognised and applied in the courts. The twin objectives were conceptual clarity and a faithful reflection of legal reality. To this purpose, Hohfeld stipulated a deliberately rigid eight-term structure, consisting of four pairs of conceptual opposites and correlatives,

Table 9.1 Hohfeld's analysis of the structure of legal relations between people

Jural Opposites	{right	privilege	power	immunity
	{no-right	duty	disability	liability
Jural Correlatives	{right	privilege	power	immunity
	{duty	no-right	liability	disability

Source: Hohfeld (1919: 36)

through which all rights-related legal phenomena should be viewed. This structure has been revised and reworded in various ways by others, but Table 9.1 shows how Hohfeld originally presented it.

The main purpose of this method was to dispel the confusion created by indiscriminate use of the word 'right' when something else (a privilege, a power, an immunity) was meant. Each word commonly used to designate a right is given its real meaning in terms of what it is not and what it implies as a correlative. Thus, a right, as opposed to a 'no-right', held by X, always corresponds to a duty in Y, instead of the privilege that would be had if X had no-right. X's privilege in doing something, as opposed to a duty, implies that Y merely has no-right against X, rather than the duty that would be created by X's right. If X has a legal power, as opposed to a disability, Y has a liability instead of the immunity that would be had if X was legally disabled. If X has a legal immunity, as opposed to a liability, then Y has a disability against X, rather than a power.

The general point of Hohfeld's analysis was that it is wrong to talk about rights when what we are seeking to indicate is a different kind of legal relation, with very different practical implications. It is only correct to speak of a right in the strict sense when there is a correlative duty. This is known as the correlativity thesis. There are several points to be grasped for present purposes. First, this schema was only intended to apply to the classification of legal rights. It has no direct implications for non-legal rights. Second, it does not imply that there are only legal rights. Third, Hohfeld did not mean that there are no rights at all, either legal or moral. The purpose was only to sharpen up talk about legal rights, to lay the foundations for more accurate and useful analysis. Hohfeld's main thesis was that the only legal rights in the full sense of the word are those with correlative duties. The Hohfeldian terminology will not be used in this chapter, but the reader should bear in mind the restriction of the use of the term 'right' to indicate a claim to which there must be a correlative duty.

Rights and rights-scepticism

In everyday language, most people have little doubt about what a right is. It is something about which they are entitled to protest if they are deprived of it, or it is withheld without justification. Consider now exactly what it means to assert, for example, that you have the right to the repayment of a loan. Clearly you would like it repaid, but is this all? Beyond the expression of a desire, there is an insistence with all rights-claims that you 'ought' to have certain things or be free to perform certain actions.

A right is usually understood to mean more than a standard moral claim, but when we move beyond this, the interpretation becomes controversial. If the right to the repayment of the loan is a genuine one, it may be argued, it is not merely a morally reasonable or worthy claim, the merits of which are to be evaluated against others, such as the use of the money for other purposes; it is something that you can demand as an entitlement, something to which you can lay claim. What you are laying claim to is in a sense already yours; it is not something that you merely ought to have. If you do have the right, you are in possession of a distinctive moral force or power to insist upon receiving it.

This is one popular interpretation of what a right means. It is a particular kind of strong moral claim. There is another interpretation, however, of how rights go beyond standard moral claims, which is inconsistent with it. According to this line of thought, rights are not held by people as a kind of natural property; they are granted or ascribed to people with a guarantee of protection. One does not merely have a moral case for the right to recover a loan; the right can, if necessary, be enforced. What we are talking about here is actual force rather than moral force. This is what makes a right a right; it can be insisted upon with the backing of the sanctions of law. What this means in effect is that for rights to be more than standard moral claims – which is to say, to exist as distinctive rights at all – they must be legal rights. This in turn implies that there are only legal rights.

A historical point of some significance is that the idea of a singular right ('a' right, rather than 'right' or 'the' right) held by individuals dates only from the early seventeenth century. The concept of an individual right as something held against other individuals or against the world was virtually unknown to the Greeks or Romans, or to medieval Europe (Finnis 1980: 205–10). Second, the idea of the reality of such a right was steadily eroded over the period between the French and American Revolutions and the Second World War.

A central philosophical problem, then, concerns the ontological status of a right. If it is taken to be an 'entity' of some sort, can we give a coherent account of what kind of entity is involved when we speak of someone having a right, for example, to compensation for an injury? It is clearly not an entity in the sense of an ascertainable object such as a physical attribute like weight, or a mental faculty like memory. The mere existence of either of these can be demonstrated. How does one demonstrate the existence of a right? If it is anything, it would seem, it is not a natural, observable phenomenon.

On the face of it, the most promising interpretation is that it is a moral power. Leaving aside for a moment the question of legal enforcement, which may or may not be available, the belief of an injured person that he has a right to compensation is a belief that he has a power that other people do not, a power to insist upon it. This would be a power that could be used to exert pressure on the party or parties alleged to owe compensation. This kind of analysis of rights as moral powers has been the target of a prominent strain of thought in European philosophy since Bentham, i.e. rights-scepticism. From the standpoint of this scepticism, a right is not seen as a natural entity of any kind, nor does it exist in another mysterious moral domain. It simply has no existence, and beliefs to the contrary are explained in various ways, ranging from dishonourable political motives to belief in the supernatural.

Bentham's attack on rights

Bentham was in the forefront of the attack on the theories of natural law and the social contract, both of which were associated with the idea of natural rights as natural powers. His own writings displayed a general unfriendliness to the idea that rights could pre-exist their legal codification. There were two reasons for this, one political, the other philosophical. Bentham was developing the doctrine of utility at the same time as the revolutionary movements in America and France were asserting the rights of man, under the influence of the doctrine of natural rights, especially as expressed by Locke and Rousseau. It is against the background of the Jacobin Terror in France that Bentham's intemperate and apparently eccentric outburst against the idea of 'the rights of man' should be understood. As far as Bentham was concerned, the only way in which it is appropriate to speak of rights is in acknowledgement of those codified in law. In short, there are only legal rights, no moral or natural rights, any talk of which is confusing and dangerous political rhetoric.

As a thoroughgoing empiricist, Bentham regarded all rights, including those codified in law, as at best 'fictitious entities' and at worst imaginary conjurings. *Legal* rights, then, along with the legal concepts of duty and obligation, and most of the language of the common law, he regarded as 'legal fictions'. These legal concepts, however, can be interpreted by Bentham's method of paraphrasis. A sentence containing the word 'right' can be rewritten and translated as a legal duty. Thus, '*X* has a property right' can be translated into a sentence of equivalent meaning: '*Y* has a duty to refrain from appropriating or trespassing on *X*'s property'. But a 'duty' is also a fictitious legal entity. This in turn can be translated into the language of coercion: 'If *Y* appropriates or trespasses on *X*'s land, then *Y* will be liable to a certain punishment'. Every legal term can be traced back in this manner to the pleasure–pain calculus of utilitarian social welfare. The threat of punishment is a perceptible and tangible, hard empirical reality. Bentham believed that all legal terms could be explicated by this method of paraphrasis.

The important contrast that Bentham draws is between these 'translatable' fictitious entities, which do have a meaning to be uncovered, and non-legal rights, which are not translatable at all. If they cannot be thus rendered into the language of coercion, we have to accept that they are literally unintelligible, or just plain nonsense. 'Natural rights is simple nonsense; natural and imprescriptible rights, rhetorical nonsense, nonsense upon stilts' (Bentham 1987: 53). Bentham regarded talk of natural and imprescriptible rights as 'terrorist language' and as so much 'bawling upon paper'. A natural right, which cannot be translated into a corresponding duty-sentence, is a self-contradiction. It is as nonsensical as the term 'cold heat'. There are no rights in nature. Natural rights are conjurings of the imagination. Talk of the 'Rights of Man' is 'a preposterous fraud', because it cannot be rendered into concrete meaningful terms.

Bentham's main substantial point which is of lasting importance is his argument that the legal rights which are actually recognised should be those that, having had their claims considered on their merits, are freely ascribed by government and are thereafter permanently on probation. If they turn out to be contrary to utility, it is self-evident that they should be suspended forthwith. It is worth noting at this point that while this may be self-evident to a utilitarian, if this is what legal rights amount to, then they are not rights in any deeper sense at all – *they are merely licences.*

Elimination of rights

As indicated earlier, there has been a general trend in modern jurisprudence towards the complete elimination or negation of the concept of a right; however, what exactly does it mean to 'eliminate' rights as a concept? Broadly speaking, it means that those who use the popular terminology of rights are labouring under the delusion that their language has objective reference, that there is something at some level of reality corresponding to the words they are using.

This ultimate conclusion applies as much to a legal right (and duty) as it does to a moral or natural right. It was expressed concisely by the Scandinavian realist Karl Olivecrona (Olivecrona 1971) in his assessment of the legal meaning of rights and duties. Rights are chimeras or imaginary entities 'interposed between the operative facts and their legal effects'. What this means is that in the situation in which we assume a right and a correlative duty to be created in law, such as the drawing up and signing of a contract, and the contract taking effect, the only reality is the complex of facts surrounding the contract and the actual consequences in law, all of which can be described in empirical terms. The idea that a right is created somewhere in this process is at best a metaphor or expressive abbreviation for a complex of facts. Between the two terms, the operative facts and the legal effects, which do have objects of reference, there is a universal tendency to conjure up the concepts of right and duty, which have no such objective reference. They are simply unreal figments of the imagination, as unreal as ghosts or hobgoblins. The same can be said, *a fortiori*, about the prelegal moral institution of promise-making.

The rooting out of the idea that the concept of a right has objective reference was rather like a process of exorcism. The ghostly object to be laid to rest was the moral power assumed by natural law theory. This was the power assumed to be held in the prelegal state of nature, the power to which the term natural 'right' refers. This concept continued to hold sway in theories such as the willpower theory of the early positivist Savigny (1779–1861), in which important features of natural law were retained, such as the continued recognition of an independent but accessible spiritual realm of reality in which rights existed. The denial of the existence of this spiritual realm was an essential theme in the working through of the philosophical recognition of the implications of the advance of the physical sciences.

The same sceptical line of thought was developed by Oliver Wendell Holmes:

> Nowhere is the confusion between legal and moral ideas more manifest than in the law of contract. Among other things, here again the so-called primary rights and duties are invested with a mystic significance beyond what can be assigned and explained. *The duty to keep a contract at common law means a prediction that you must pay damages if you do not keep it – and nothing else.*
>
> (Adams 1992: 93)

What Holmes recommends is that for heuristic purposes one take up the point of view of 'the bad man', who only wants to know what the courts will make him do. A legal duty means no more to a bad man than that 'if he does certain things he will be subjected to disagreeable consequences by way of imprisonment or compulsory payment of money' (Adams 1992: 93).

In Holmes' vivid metaphor, the legal analyst needs to follow the example of the bad man who applies 'cynical acid' to the legal concepts he encounters. In the case of legal rights and duties, the application of cynical acid strips down the ideas of such things to their real legal consequences. In reality, Holmes insists, all rights-claims come down to no more than prophecies of the ways in which the courts will decide concrete cases. If the courts ignore them, they are not in any meaningful sense 'rights'.

Responses to rights-scepticism

In the light of these sceptical arguments against the very existence of the rights that are dealt with as a matter of course in contemporary litigation, in the criminal courts and in the European Court of Human Rights, what should the proper response be? Most people today believe that they do have equal rights, that they have procedural and substantive legal rights, that typically rights are universal, and that it is often possible to enforce them in the courts. Should we conclude that all these people are deluded and that their belief in rights is analogous to, and no more justified than, belief in the supernatural?

Rights-sceptics may answer these questions in one of two ways. The first is that the denial of the reality of rights does not have any practical implications of this nature. Statutory 'rights' will continue to be claimed and enforced, regardless of what we call them, and in the struggles for civil rights campaigners against governments that practise genocide, torture or the suppression of civil liberties will no doubt continue to use the phrase 'human rights' without embarrassment. This type of answer suggests that the ontological issue is purely philosophical, that the denial of rights as 'entities' has no practical implications.

The second type of answer is quite different, and more fraught with ambiguity. On this kind of argument, rights-scepticism does affect the practical realities of the claims to legal and moral rights, but not in the sense of dispensing with rights altogether. The implication is that with this theoretical enlightenment, the status of 'rights' changes, that they are to be understood not as objective entities which are owned or held by every individual, which is precisely what has been disproved by the sceptical arguments, but rather as claims to our moral attention, claims that can have greater or less moral worth. None of these claims can be properly construed as an entitlement. This line of argument suggests a discriminating critique of any declarations of human rights that proceed on the assumption that they are merely declaring or endorsing rights that already exist. It is this assumption that the various versions of rights-scepticism are denying. The important point here is that this approach affects the content of any such declaration of rights. It is this second kind of interpretation of the implications of rights-scepticism to which the defence of the reality of rights must be addressed. First, however, we have to consider what is involved in the reassertion of this reality against the kinds of scepticism as outlined in the last section.

It is often asked how it can be true that there are human rights when they are routinely abused and almost universally ignored. This kind of scepticism is quite easily refuted. Widespread abuse or even universal neglect of rights does not count as an argument against their existence, any more than the failure to develop physics would have shown that there are no such things as electrons. Furthermore, just as the doctrine of natural law was only ever developed to counteract cultural relativism, it is only because people and their governments often act as if there were no human rights that the existence of such rights was ever asserted. The classical natural rights doctrines of the early modern period were developed mainly in resistance to the absolutist governments that almost completely ignored such rights. The later modern movements for women's rights and the rights of ethnic minorities started from a position of almost complete neglect.

More importantly, the insistence that rights are real must confront the reductivist and eliminativist arguments that deny their reality. The overall argument against reductivism – the claim that there are only legal rights – is that it is incoherent. If it is conceded that legal rights exist, then there must also be prelegal rights. Rights cannot suddenly spring into existence with the wave of a legal wand. Statutory recognition of a right only provides legal backing for what already exists; for example, a slave's right to be free. The legal emancipation does not suddenly create the right to be free, it merely acknowledges it and provides a sanction to prevent the continuation of slavery.

One reductivist reply to this is that it is merely one interest among others, with no special claim to our attention, which pre-exists the legal right. A law transforms an interest into a protected interest, which is all a legal right is. It exists in the sense that it is tangible, by virtue of its real effects. The realist argument, however, is stronger than this. If rights are suddenly created as legal entitlements, and this is on the grounds that there are interests that need to be given legal protection, then the legal rights are merely licences that can be revoked at the first sign of difficulty. On this conception, legal rights have no deep foundation. In other words, legal rights are not rights at all and reductivism is incoherent, because if prelegal rights are denied, then legal rights must also be denied. Reductivists can in turn reply that this would make all rights absolute or unconditional, which is absurd. They could never be overridden by other considerations or conflicting rights. We will see later how this objection can be countered.

The response to eliminative rights-scepticism – the claim that there are no rights of any kind, moral or legal – is more difficult. In what sense, we are asking, is the rights-theorist asserting or reasserting that rights do exist, when faced with the claim that there are no entities whatsoever corresponding to the concepts of legal and moral rights? Does it have to be reasserted that rights are things that exist in a 'spiritual' realm? Do they have to assume again that rights are magical or supernatural 'powers'? Are rights moral powers after all? Is a legal right a mysterious power held by the right-holder in addition to the observable facts about the legal process?

The argument against eliminative rights-scepticism that there are rights, both within the law and beyond it, would be implausible if it rested solely on the fact that it is widely believed that there are ways in which people should or should not be treated, solely by virtue of certain qualities they possess, such as reason or consciousness. The fact that it is widely believed that there are UFOs does not mean that UFOs have a certain kind of existence. The fact that in the nineteenth century virtually no one believed that women had the right to vote does not show that they had no such right. What the claim that there are rights means is that people who have rights have a stronger than standard moral claim, and that there is a *prima facie* case for their prevailing over moral claims that do not embody rights.

The irreducibility of rights

A central question, then, is whether there is any more to a right than that which can be expressed in moral or legal language that makes no reference to rights. Are rights reducible to needs, desert or utility, or does the entitlement implicit in a right give you a stronger claim than this? Consider again the case of *Donoghue* v. *Stevenson* (1932) (see Chapter 6), which established the general duty of care in English law. The question here relates to the nature of the claim made by the plaintiff who had suffered illness as a result of a defective product due to a manufacturer's negligence. Did she deserve or need compensation? Possibly. Is the right reducible to these deserts or needs? Did it enhance the overall utility of everyone concerned? This was not really the point. The Law Lords eventually determined that she did have a right to compensation, despite arguments that there was no clear precedent in English law and that the case would open a floodgate of litigation.

One argument against this decision – that it would make the manufacturer of a defective axle liable after a train crash – was a consequentialist argument against the recognition of this right. The claim to compensation that the plaintiff had was more than a standard moral argument based on desert, need or utility. Many people deserve compensation, but are not awarded it. Mrs Donoghue had brought the case and taken it to appeal because she believed that she was morally entitled and must be legally entitled, despite legal advice that she was not. What does this entitlement mean? Legally speaking, it might be simply that the law will back your claim. If you have a 'title' to it, the law *should* back your claim. Legally speaking, an entitlement is more than a desert or a need. The decision to recognise the right to recover for, say, emotional damages may originate in the recognition of desert or need, but it becomes more than this, and irreducible to it. A legal right to X means that you already have X; you are trying to claim what is already yours. If you merely deserve compensation, you are making out a case for being given what is not yet yours as of right.

Morally speaking, Mrs Donoghue's belief that she was entitled to compensation is also irreducible to the belief that she deserved it. It might include this belief, but it states something more. Once the moral right is recognised, there is no alternative but to hand it over. If it were merely desert, one might argue that there are more deserving claims. If it were merely need, it might be argued that there were others in greater need. Given that it is a right, she can demand it in a way that others cannot.

Absolute rights

It was declared in 2000 by the Lord Chief Justice, Lord Woolf, that the right not to be tortured is absolute under English law, which means that it will never be heard as a defence in an English court that the torture was justified by any other consideration. The debate over absolutes is a long-standing one. It is very commonly argued against rights-based moralities that, for a right to have any force at all, it must be regarded as absolute. Rights must be either subordinate to utility or they must be held to be completely inviolable. Either way, they are absolute and unyielding, or there is no way of stopping them dissolving into utility. Jonathan Glover, for example, argues that anything short of a defence of absolute rights, falling back on a theory of *prima facie* rights, is indistinguishable from his own utilitarian position (Glover 1977: 83–4).

There are essentially two rights-based alternatives to this stark choice. Either they take the middle course advocated in Dworkin's rights thesis, according to which rights that are less than absolute nevertheless have a quality which enables them to prevail more often than not over non-rights considerations (i.e. they can 'trump' them), which gives us a theory of *prima facie* rights; or they can take the line that absolute status means in practice that they can 'virtually never' be violated.

A standard argument to the effect that no rights, however apparently basic, can be absolute, proceeds from an imagined 'ticking bomb' scenario in which one is forced to choose between violating the rights of one individual and allowing the deaths of millions. If the only way to prevent a nuclear attack is to torture the person who knows the whereabouts of the bomb, in such a case it is said to be self-evident that nobody has the absolute right not to be tortured. If such a right is less than absolute, the argument continues, then all the more so are all the other 'basic' rights, for each of which possible exceptions can be imagined. The next step is to argue that if the ticking bomb scenario justifies torture on one occasion, then we must accept that there are many other less extreme situations in which it is justified, when the loss of utility seriously out-weighs the evil of the violation of the right. There are many faults with this argument, not least that it sets up an artificial scenario as its first premise, but the most relevant one for present purposes is that it highlights rather than detracts from the absolute status of these rights. The extremity of the examples required to undermine them only illustrates their intrinsically absolute status in normal circumstances, which in practice means virtually all circumstances.

This is what Finnis means (Finnis 1980: 223–6) when he defends absolute rights against utilitarians, for whom only utility is absolute. When we say that the right not to have one's life taken as a means to an end, or the right not to be condemned on false charges is absolute or exceptionless, what we mean is that even the violation of rights in these extreme circumstances is absolutely wrong. It may be a lesser evil, but it is still an evil. Anybody who commits it is not exonerated. The value of absolute rights-talk, for Finnis, is that it keeps the idea of justice in the foreground and undercuts the persuasiveness of pure consequentialism.

Rights versus utility – Bentham and J.S. Mill

The concept of a right is intimately connected with the concept of justice. If the modern natural lawyers are right to regard justice as a necessary feature of the law, the consequence of this is that the concept of a moral right is equally indispensable. On Dworkin's thesis, it is not optional for the courts to take rights into account in their deliberations; on his reading of the meaning of law, they are legally required to do so. The demand for justice relating to any particular situation is translatable into an insistence on the recognition of all the genuine and justifiable rights relevant to that situation. The point of identifying and defending any specific right is to raise an obstacle against arguments from utility, whether this means the general welfare or overall aggregate of benefit, or merely more effective government.

Bentham on utility and rights

For Benthamite utilitarianism, the above line of argument is complete nonsense. From Bentham's point of view, it was by definition false to argue that it was morally defensible to raise obstacles against social utility. A rational legal system as he imagined it would withhold or suspend the status of legal right from any interest that did obstruct the general welfare in this way. The common law system, with its entrenched principles protecting traditional privileges, was abhorred by Bentham precisely because it did not balance real interests in the cause of the general social good. In Bentham's rational legal system, any codified right that turned out to obstruct the general good would be revoked.

The important point to stress against Bentham, though, is that legal rights – properly understood – as much as moral rights, *must* operate to some extent as obstacles to utility. If there were no presumption at all in favour of rights prevailing over other interests, thus diminishing to some extent 'the general good', they would not in any effective sense be rights at all. They would merely be protected interests, protected only for as long as they do not become inconvenient. Rights only become important when they are likely to be denied, that is, precisely when they are inconvenient and unwelcome to the majority, especially when the majority in a democratic society is faced with the accusation that withholding minority rights constitutes an injustice. Defending them in these circumstances is one of the things Dworkin means by taking rights seriously.

John Stuart Mill on utility and rights

Although the Benthamite doctrine was highly influential, it did not prevail unchallenged. John Stuart Mill's (1806–73) discomfort with the utilitarian tradition was manifested in his rejection of Bentham's pleasure–pain calculus and his attempt to reintroduce the non-legal notion of a moral right. What he was attempting here was the modification and completion of the utilitarian doctrine by arguing that it was compatible with moral rights and justice. Mill's attitude to rights differed sharply from that of Bentham, but his ultimate conclusion was not entirely dissimilar. Mill was more aware than Bentham of the dangers inherent in unchecked majority rule. With some prescience, he saw the main source of injustice in modern industrial democracies in the growing suppression of the rights of individuals and minorities, for the sake of the greater good of the majority, rather than in the oppression of the masses by small governing circles. At the same time, however, he was defending his own version of utilitarianism. One of Mill's main theoretical objectives was to reconcile the requirements of utility with the demands of liberty, justice and rights, to demonstrate their deeper compatibility.

Mill's strategy to effect this reconciliation was not to argue directly against the anti-utilitarian theories of rights and justice, but to absorb them by representing them as distorted versions of the doctrine of utility. Kant, and

Kantian theories of rights in particular, were interpreted as justifications of individual rights ultimately rooted in instrumental conceptions of the social good. The central thrust of the Kantian approach was a *non*-instrumental attitude to human rights, which are recognised in Kant's famous maxim that individuals are always to be treated as ends in themselves, never solely as a means. From Mill's point of view, the only thing that can be treated as an end in itself is utility, or the general happiness. On his interpretation of Kant, which attempts to neutralise his influence on moral and legal theory, the justification of treating individuals as ends lies ultimately in the value of this kind of policy for society.

This is a projection of Mill's own solution to the problem of rights and utility, on to Kant and other respect-centred theories of rights derived from him. The justification in these theories really does end with the individual rights-holder, which is held to be the value in itself. Rights are respected for their own sake. Mill's solution, as outlined in his celebrated defence of liberty (Mill 1972a), was to argue that the cultivation of respect for individual rights and liberty, as exemplified by the right to freedom of speech, freedom of worship, the right to pursue one's own lifestyle and so on, has a strengthening rather than a weakening effect on the health of society, and the repression of individual difference and creativity has a devitalising effect that will ultimately lead to its destruction. What he is arguing is that legal and moral respect for individual rights and liberty is ultimately utilitarian, that such respect does serve the interests of society as a whole.

As a matter of historical fact, this claim may or may not be true. But can respect for individual rights be supported by this kind of appeal to utility? One reason this is not a popular theory of rights a century later is that it has become increasingly obvious that short-term utility is more persuasive than the long term. In the short term, the suppression of individual rights makes government more effective; the uncomfortable truth is that democratic freedoms do not always coincide with the interests of the majority, or with raising the aggregate welfare of society. It is much more conducive to efficiency to suppress dissent. The interests of utility, it seems, do conflict with a general respect for individual rights. Mill's is one of the more serious utilitarian attempts to accommodate a theory of rights, but ultimately, in making rights contingent upon utility, it does not essentially differ from Bentham's negative view of rights. With Mill's assumption that rights and utility are compatible and complementary, there is no room for the defence of rights for their own sake, in cases where they are contrary to the dictates of utility.

Dworkin's theory of rights

In modern thinking in philosophy of law, there is agreement between most utilitarians and their critics that there is no deep compatibility between the doctrine of utility and the concept of a right. From the utilitarian point of view, it seems that the unacceptable price of conceding reality to any kind of prelegal moral right is the acceptance of it as an absolute, as an unconditional barrier to social welfare or public policy.

Dworkin's rights thesis offers a perspective that avoids this dilemma. As we saw in an earlier chapter, Dworkin argues that the law consists of a combination of rules, principles and policies, all of which are and should be employed by judges in reaching decisions. They are all genuine components of the law, rather than external moral standards that can be made use of in an *ad hoc* manner to resolve particular hard cases. Along with the established rules of law and the principles or maxims of common law, then, we find an established practice of applying policies as determined by experience of the social consequences of various types of judicial decision. It is against this utilitarian background that Dworkin's defence of the rights thesis is unfolded.

The presence of rights that are both moral and legal in Dworkin's broad sense can, he insists, be deduced from the general sweep of judicial decisions on complex cases, the only explanation for which is often the supposition of the existence of various kinds of rights implicitly recognised by the law, and embodied in common law principles. Finding the right decision – the just and equitable one – is a matter of weighing these moral-legal principles against considerations of good social policy, neither of which automatically prevails against the other. It is in his metaphor of 'rights as trumps' that Dworkin's non-absolutist alternative to utilitarianism becomes apparent. A right, properly understood, is like a trump card that defeats competing considerations. 'Rights are best understood as trumps over some background justification for political decisions that states a goal for the community as a whole' (Dworkin 1977b). To say that such a goal is 'trumped' by a right does not mean that any right is absolute, that it can never be defeated. It will always be possible that there will be cards of a higher value to be played. A right can be outweighed by other rights, or by particularly pressing considerations of policy.

The right to free speech, for example, should in most circumstances be protected, even when it is not conducive to the general welfare. This does not make the right unconditional or absolute. It does not mean that the freedom of speech is unlimited. The basic condition is that, in order for a right to have any effect as a right, it must have some real power to override consideration of the goals of the community; it must have some power to cause inconvenience. As a trump card, this right can itself be defeated. It can be outweighed or overridden by another competing right. The right to free speech is sometimes opposed by the right to the protection of one's reputation, which is supported by the laws of libel and slander. But this competing right is itself a trump card to be played against the general good. When the general good is cited as a reason for overriding a right, it must be determined whether or not a competing right is involved. If the right to freedom of expression runs to making inflammatory speeches, the protection of the right is removed because it is trumped by the rights of the individuals or groups who are threatened by this abuse of free speech. What the rights thesis does mean is that there is a strong presumption in favour of the right prevailing. This, for Dworkin, is what it means to take rights seriously.

Criticisms of Dworkin's theory of rights are too numerous and diverse to explain here. The most obvious line of criticism comes from the utilitarian and openly rights-sceptical perspectives at which it is aimed. The most serious and persistent criticism, however, is that Dworkin's thinking is itself confined within the narrow space of utilitarian calculation, to such an extent that his 'rights' are no more real as obstacles to the tyranny of the collective than Bentham's equality of interests. The main thrust of this criticism is the suggestion that, in the first place, the mere presumption in favour of rights is not strong enough to establish the kind of firm protection needed, and, second, this failure is due to the lack of grounding of his rights in a source independent of utility. In short, it is just too close to utilitarianism for comfort. While there is certainly some truth in these criticisms, given that Dworkin's rights are always defended within the context of acceptable policy, against which they are weighed, it is quite false to claim that the only alternative to absolute rights is no rights at all. The problem of establishing the threshold at which pre-existing rights can be outweighed by arguments from public policy is a much larger one than that faced by Dworkin. Second, the rights defended by Dworkin are rooted in the standards of justice established by common law, which are usually understood to have been implemented despite the demands of utility, not because of them.

The HRA (1998) and the case of the conjoined twins

The HRA (Human Rights Act) UK (1998), which came into force in 2000, has in its first few years made an enormous practical impact upon English law. It has been woven into case law in such detail that it is now becoming a fundamental point of reference. Described by many as a constitutional landmark, the HRA is applied every day not only in such areas as family law and mental health law, but has also featured prominently in campaigns for legal reform, such as the attempt to legalise assisted suicide, and now places principles of human rights at the centre of the process of judicial review, through which the decisions of public officials and bodies can be scrutinised and challenged. This enactment was the outcome of the decision in 1997 by the British government to incorporate the 1950 European Convention into English law. This in turn had been strongly influenced by the United Nations Declaration of Human Rights (UNDHR) in 1948. The result of incorporation is an Act that protects 'basic' human rights and liberties such as the rights to life, liberty and security, the right not to be subjected to torture or degrading treatment, the right to a fair trial and to freedom of thought and expression.

While it obviously does not settle any of the philosophical questions about the status of human rights as moral phenomena, the application of the HRA does add force to the Dworkinian argument that rights that are less than absolute can be defended against rights-scepticism. Predictions by its critics and opponents in the 1990s that it would open a floodgate of trivial and dubious litigation have been confounded. This is largely because of the unwarranted assumption that individual rights and liberties would be treated by the courts as absolutes, automatically endorsing them and overriding wider group interests. This has manifestly not happened and is unlikely to in the foreseeable future. One of the reasons that it will not is that the Act is rooted in the internationalism of the late 1940s, when the drafting of the UNDHR drew as much upon Eastern communitarian values as those of Western individualism. The principles embodied in the HRA are open to continuous interpretation. The only article to have been authoritatively declared 'absolute' is the one prohibiting torture and degrading treatment. This is absolute in the sense that no exceptions will be made and no excuses heard. All verified instances of it will be declared unlawful. For each of the other articles, it seems, the rights can be balanced against factors relating to the public good.

One striking example of the problem of absolutes in relation to the HRA is provided by the first case that was heard after it came into force, the case of the conjoined twins, Jodie and Mary (*Re A (Children) Conjoined Twins: Medical Treatment (No.1)*, 2000). The case concerned two baby girls who were joined at birth in such a way that an operation to separate them would give Jodie an estimated 70 per cent chance of survival, with a serious chance of severe disability, but at the same time certainly kill Mary. Given that Mary's brain was not fully developed, that her vital organs had failed soon after birth and that she had thus become entirely dependent upon her stronger sister's heart and lungs, the only one who had any prospect of continued life was Jodie. The crucial point was that without surgical intervention both would certainly die within six months.

When the Court of Appeal was called upon to rule in advance on whether the operation would be lawful, the judges were facing several complex questions of family and criminal law. The important points in this context were that, first, the best interests of each child had to be taken into account, second, that the killing of one to save another had never been admissible as a defence under English law, and, third, that under the HRA each child had the right to life. The judges were not unanimous on the reasoning behind the judgement, but they were unanimous in declaring the operation lawful and in his ruling Lord Justice Ward declared that, although the killing of Mary would in law be 'intentional', given the certain consequences of the act, the interests of Mary had to be balanced against those of Jodie, and that although each equally had the right to life and the comparative quality of their lives was irrelevant, neither had the right to live at the expense of another. The crucial point was that while the Court recognised the universal human right to life, regardless of the quality of such life, it did not accept that this right was absolute. In a case such as this, the right of one has to give way to that of another.

The subsequent outcome of the operation was entirely successful. Mary died immediately, but Jodie lived and flourished, without any disability. It is important to note that this outcome does not vindicate the morality of the decision, but those who criticised it on the assumption that it had exposed the hollowness of the HRA almost as soon as it had come into force misunderstood the status of these rights. The claim that the right to life can in extreme circumstances be overridden does not imply that there is no right to life at all. On the contrary, it requires circumstances as extreme as these to be overridden. If Jodie's life had not been in imminent danger, the operation would not have been lawful. As we will see in Chapter 13, this ruling has potentially far-reaching implications for criminal law.

Conclusion

Despite the shift in recent decades in favour of recognising legal and moral universal rights in so many areas, there is no sign of a consensus emerging. In the current debates, the twin issues of the rights–utility conflict and the assertion or denial of absolute or basic rights remain central. These are still linked to the fundamental question of whether it is meaningful to speak of rights at all. The sceptical challenge, although it is often obscured by disputes between realists, is still prominent in philosophical and political debate. The more radical versions of rights-scepticism will be dealt with in a later chapter. For now, it is enough to note that the contemporary analysis and comparison of substantive theories of rights and justice constructed and developed by Rawls, Dworkin, Nozick and others, which differ radically in their respective emphasis on the types of rights to be regarded as genuine and fundamental, need to proceed from an understanding of how they offer distinctive responses to the sceptical challenge.

Study questions

General question: What is a right? What does it mean to claim that you have a right to something?

Further study questions: How does a legal right differ from a moral right? What does it mean to say that there is no such thing as a right? Does this apply equally to moral rights and legal rights? Critically examine the claim that a right is nothing more than the legal power to enforce one's interests. How might rights-scepticism be refuted? Are there any absolute rights? Do absolute rights have to be exceptionless? Is the recognition of rights compatible with utilitarianism? Does Dworkin's rights thesis resolve the conflict between rights and utility?

Suggestions for further reading

The classic texts for the major contemporary theories of rights are Rawls (1972), Dworkin (1977b) and Nozick (1974). Anthologies of critical essays have been edited by Daniels (1975) on Rawls, Cohen (1984) on Dworkin, and Paul (1981) on Nozick. For critical discussion of Dworkin's rights thesis, see especially MacCormick (1982: ch. 7).

Waldron (1984) contains a collection of key articles by leading rights theorists, including Dworkin, Raz, Hart, Gewirth, Lyons and Scanlon. Stewart (1983) is another valuable collection, with notable contributions from MacCormick, White and others. Among the general introductions to legal and moral rights, the most accessible are Jones (1994), Simmonds (1986), Stoljar (1984), Perry (1998) and Almond's article in Singer (1991: ch. 22). There are useful chapters in Oderberg (2000b: ch. 2), Harris (1997: ch. 14) and Riddall (1999: ch. 8). More advanced studies are found in Finnis (1980), Thomson (1990), MacCormick (1982), Raz (1994: ch. 12) and Halpin (1997).

On rights-scepticism, Waldron (1987) contains the relevant text of Bentham, with a critical reply. Other key texts are Holmes (1897), Olivecrona (1971) and Hägerström (1953). On rights and utility, the most useful is Frey's (1985) collection of essays. See also Lyons's 'Utility and Rights' in Waldron (1984). For commentaries on Hohfeld, see Halpin (1997: ch. 2), Thomson (1990: ch. 1) and Harris (1997: ch. 7).

10 Law and private morals

Only in recent times has the debate about tolerance and respect for diversity become a prominent feature of democratic societies. What is often not realised is the extent to which toleration of the right to deviate from social norms relating to personal codes of morality is at odds with the principles of democracy as majority rule. The issue at the heart of the debate about 'the enforcement of morals' is that of drawing the line between the moral and the immoral in personal behaviour. Are individuals the best judges of their own interests, or does the state, acting on behalf of society, have the right to set limits on what it regards as morally acceptable? Although the question of a right to privacy is a much wider one, the emphasis here is on sexual and sex-related practices and lifestyle. Until the 1950s, it was widely assumed that the state did have the right to criminalise homosexuality, prostitution, pornography, abortions and many other related practices. Rapid social changes over the following decades have brought about extensive revisions in the law governing this area, but it has not been a one-way process of liberalisation. On most of these matters, there is an ongoing conflict between the rights of the individual and the rights of society.

Liberalisation and the Wolfenden Report

The debate was initiated in 1957, when the Wolfenden Committee made two recommendations to the government: (1) that private prostitution should remain legal and public soliciting be outlawed; and (2) that male homosexual acts in private between consenting adults over the age of twenty-one should be legalised. What was of particular importance was the Wolfenden view of the function of the criminal law, which was stated with exceptional clarity as follows:

> The function of the criminal law, as we see it, is to preserve public order and decency, to protect the citizen from what is offensive or injurious, and to provide safeguards against exploitation and corruption of others … particularly the specially vulnerable, the young, weak and inexperienced … . It is not, in our view, the function of the law to

intervene in the private lives of citizens, or to seek to enforce any particular pattern of behaviour ... . There must remain a realm of private
morality which is, in brief and crude terms, not the law's business.

(Wolfenden Committee 1957: Cmnd 247, para. 13)

In short, Wolfenden was advocating a new spirit of tolerance. Any private
individual activities that presented no threat to other citizens, or to the
maintenance of public order and decency, should remain beyond the reach of
the criminal law. It should be noted that the emphasis of the recommendations
was firmly on the private sphere; there were no liberal implications for the
publication or public display of pornography, or any other kind of public
behaviour that might be found offensive. Also, the spirit of the Report was
morally neutral in that it passed no judgement on what was taking place in
private. It simply declared that it was none of the law's business. It was this
spirit of liberalism that also guided the subsequent legislation.

Superficially, perhaps, this sounds like a straightforward story of reasonableness and tolerance prevailing over outdated repressive and moralistic
attitudes. When we look more closely, however, we find that the relation
between the criminal law and private morality is far from simple. What
exactly, for example, does 'private' mean in this context? Does it mean 'out of
public view', or does it mean that it is the individual's own business? Are
privacy and publicness really separable? What does 'harm' or 'giving offence'
or 'causing distress' mean? These ambiguities have to be resolved.

J.S. Mill and liberty

The findings of the Wolfenden Committee were clearly based on Mill's classic
essay *On Liberty* (Mill 1972a). In one of the most influential statements in
modern political and legal philosophy, Mill had declared that:

> the sole end for which mankind is warranted, individually or collectively,
> in interfering with the liberty of action of any of their number, is *self-
> protection*. The only purpose for which power can be rightfully exercised
> over any member of a civilised community, against his will, is *to prevent
> harm to others*. His own good, either physical or moral, is not sufficient
> warrant.

(Mill 1972a: 78)

This is sometimes known as the 'harm principle', or more accurately as the
'no-harm principle'. According to this principle, there is no justification for
the use of the law (i.e. 'mankind collectively') against citizens for any purpose
other than the prevention of harm to other citizens. The law is limited in its
function to the 'self-defence' of society, and is legitimately employed if an
individual's action is threatening society in some way. The second point Mill
is making is that the law should also be limited to protecting people against

others, not against themselves. These two points are easy to conflate under the heading of a single 'no-harm' principle, but they need to be kept distinct. According to the first point, if there is no threat to others, there is no justification for legal intervention. According to the second point, if the action is only a threat to the agent, there is no such justification. The first point is an argument against legal moralism, or the enforcement of moral norms regardless of whether there is any danger. The second point is an argument against paternalism, or the interference in a person's freedom of action, when it is ostensibly for that person's own good.

One crucial exception to this principle should be noted. It applies neither to children nor to people vulnerable by virtue of mental defect or disorder such that their autonomy is seriously in doubt. In these cases, legal intervention for their own good is regarded by Mill as legitimate. Otherwise, for everyone of sufficiently mature years and sound mind, their own private behaviour – no matter how dangerous or self-destructive – is their own business.

It requires some effort of imagination to realise how bold a principle this was in Victorian England. The received wisdom about the purpose of law was that, while it included the prevention of harm to society, it was also for the protection of the moral and physical welfare of individuals affected by it, and for the general upholding of the Christian moral order. Mill's 'no-harm' principle, in both its anti-moralist and anti-paternalist aspects, was a radical challenge to the belief that the law was the proper arbiter of matters concerning morality, whether public or private. Furthermore, the temptation to regard the principle as a liberal platitude in the contemporary world, reflecting modern legal practice, vanishes with any serious attempt to think through the consequences of fully applying it. It would, for example, allow the unrestricted sale and use of heroin by adults.

The problems, of course, as Mill realised, only begin with the statement of the 'no-harm' principle. It was no less problematic than the supposedly 'very simple principle' behind his interpretation of the utilitarian philosophy, the principle of the greatest happiness for the greatest number. What he was interested in with the liberty question was establishing the 'no-harm' principle as a first base, so to speak, for theoretical negotiation. The idea was that, once accepted as basically true, the principle could be seen as establishing a dividing line, a cut-off point between the areas legitimately under the control of the individual, and the areas properly belonging to law and society. Once this distinction was accepted, it would only be a matter of thrashing out the details and defining the limits as appropriate to any particular society. The real difficulty, however, lay in having it accepted as a basic truth that there are areas in which the law should not intrude.

Mill's essay as a whole is an eloquent defence of the value to society of the recognition of the unconditional liberty of the individual in matters of conscience, expression and lifestyle. His defence of freedom of speech and liberty of action is a significant milestone in the development of democratic theory, but the most important feature of *On Liberty* concerns his claim about lifestyle that the greatest danger to the life of the individual in modern society lies in the increasing tendency towards a moral tyranny by the majority, threatening the complete elimination of private moral choices by individuals:

> And it is not difficult to show, by abundant instances, that to extend the bounds of what may be called moral police, until it encroaches on the most unquestionably legitimate liberty of the individual, is one of the most universal of all human propensities.
>
> (Mill 1972a: 216)

Mill believed – as we saw in the context of rights – that this propensity, always a danger, was actually growing rather than receding with the development of democracy and the realisation of the principle of majority rule. The idea of moral policing involved the suppression of eccentricity and peculiarity of taste, which Mill described as a latter-day Calvinism, shaping individuals in a manner reminiscent of the cutting of trees into the figures of animals.

The main point about moral policing, for Mill, is that it involves the invasion of the private space of individuals. In his examples, this space includes such forms of deviance from social norms as were widely regarded as morally degenerate – gambling, fornicating, drunkenness, uncleanliness – but it also includes any kind of behaviour that is eccentric or different in any way from that of the crowd. What Mill was condemning and resisting was the growing tendency of society and the state to seek to control every aspect of the lives of individual citizens, to enforce norms of social behaviour for their own sake, or because they believed them to be desirable and dressed these desires up as moral laws, irrespective of whether the non-conformity was actually dangerous or harmful to others.

The area in which the law should not intrude, then, is abstractly defined as the area of individual privacy, the area consisting of those actions that are of sole concern to the individual. Mill anticipated some of the problems and criticisms relating to the distinction between the private and the public. The most common objection to the idea that there is any real privacy in moral matters is the 'no man is an island' objection. Mill acknowledges the argument that there are virtually no seriously self-destructive actions that are a matter of indifference to others, to friends, family and so on. The network of social relations is such that there are repercussions and reverberations. He concedes that nothing is truly private in this sense (ibid.: 210–11); however, his reply to this objection is that it only warrants interference by the law if it leads to any breach of duty, such as the non-payment of debts. A related objection is that bad behaviour, while it may have no direct effect on others, is 'injurious by example', which may damage by corrupting or misleading others (ibid.: 211). Mill's response to this is to distinguish what he terms the merely contingent or constructive injury to society from definite damage to another or to the public. If there is no such definite damage or real risk of such, his contention is that 'the inconvenience is one which society can afford to bear, for the sake of the greater good of human freedom' (ibid.: 213).

A closely connected yet distinct set of problems relates to the *kind* of harm, damage or injury under discussion. If – according to the 'no-harm' principle – legal intervention is only justified when the issue is one of harm to others, what kind of harm are we talking about? Is it restricted to real tangible damage of the type that can be measured, or does 'giving offence' or 'causing distress' count as harm? Mill's treatment of this question is vague and inadequate; it will, as we shall soon see, become one of the most important questions in the modern debates on legal moralism.

A most important general feature of Mill's defence of the liberty of the individual in matters of private morality is that it is rooted, not in a general theory of rights, but in the doctrine of utility. He is not arguing that there are individual rights which create an inconvenience for society, but which must be tolerated out of respect for these rights. What he is in fact arguing is an empirical historical thesis about the conditions of a healthy society. It is, he insists, in the long-term interests of society as a whole to encourage the flourishing of the individual. Society should refrain from using the law to repress either criticism or non-conformity, because individual freedom of expression and lifestyle, and the conflict that these engender, are the real sources of dynamic development in any society. Without them, society withers and dies. This is a utilitarian argument, because he is basing the claims to liberty on the general welfare. Society strengthens itself when it gives ground to the individual.

Devlin's critique of the Wolfenden Report

There was little doubt about the intentions of the authors of the Wolfenden Report when it was published in 1957. They had been commissioned by the government to investigate the state of the law on the two issues of prostitution and homosexuality. Their recommendations were that both were to be permissible in private, with public soliciting subject to prosecution. In their view, Mill's 'no-harm' principle was paramount. Private consensual activities between adults that did not directly harm anybody else should be beyond the reach of the criminal law. There was a great deal less certainty in the reactions to the Report. The government accepted the proposals on prostitution and rejected the proposal on homosexuality, which was to remain illegal until 1967.

More interesting was the response by Patrick Devlin, a senior judge who had given evidence in favour of legal reform. Although he was not opposed to legalisation, he delivered a lecture in 1958 in which he attacked the thinking behind the findings of the Wolfenden Report. In this lecture, which was the opening shot in what was to become a very long debate, Devlin argued forcefully against the Wolfenden interpretation of how the law should be used against behaviour regarded as immoral. This apparent contradiction between his support for legalisation and his rejection of the liberal thinking behind it is explained by his recommendation that there should be tolerance of unconventional sexual practices solely on humane grounds, without the state conceding any rights.

Devlin bluntly rejected the assertion of Wolfenden that there is a realm of private morality and immorality that is not the law's business. As Devlin saw it, 'there can be no theoretical limits to legislation against immorality' (Devlin 1965: 14). Accordingly, he also rejected the separation of morality into a private and public sphere, a distinction that he regarded as no more intelligible than 'carving up the highway into public and private areas' (ibid.: 16). What this amounted to was a complete rejection of Mill's 'no-harm' principle, according to which the harmfulness of an action is a necessary condition for using the law against it. If there are no limits to the reach of the law, and hence no recognition of privacy, it cannot be conceded that there is an area of activity – however apparently harmless to the public – that the law cannot touch.

Devlin's argument for this strong and provocative conclusion is developed in three stages, and takes its point of departure from the fundamental principles of English law as it currently existed. First, he argues that the function of law is to enforce morality – 'the moral order' – as well as to promote public order and the smooth running of society. That is to say, the real function of law is wider and includes the one advocated by the authors of the Wolfenden Report. Second, he argues that this is how it should be, that it would be dangerous to relinquish such a fundamental principle, because a serious offence against morality constitutes an attack on society, which should retain the right to use the law to protect its own interests. Third, he argues that the law should be used sparingly and with maximum toleration to enforce morality.

At an early stage in the lecture, Devlin accepts that the authority of the law can no longer depend on Christian doctrine, because in contemporary society the civil right to disbelieve is beyond dispute. In the search for a secular alternative, however, he insists that society must retain the right to pass moral judgement, to approve or condemn from the standpoint of a clear-cut distinction between good and evil. It is precisely this right that he accuses the Wolfenden authors of undermining. What they were saying, he reminds us, is that although we retain the right to disapprove, we should relinquish the right to enforce this disapproval. Once an area of privacy in matters of morality and immorality is conceded, Devlin argues, the right to approve or to condemn has been implicitly given up. Without such a right, even a murderer will only be apprehended and punished for purposes of public order; the immorality of such offences will be irrelevant because we will have relinquished our right even to find the act morally repellent.

How do legislators tune in to this collective moral judgement? How do they know they are not speaking for themselves and a relatively small group of like-minded people? Devlin is on very difficult ground here, and his forthright answer is highly controversial. Legislators are to refer to the standard of 'the right-minded man', 'the man in the Clapham omnibus', or the conclusion that 'any twelve men or women drawn at random' would be expected to reach unanimously. It is the mass of experience embodied in 'the morality of common sense'. Most importantly, he distinguishes the reasonableness of these people from their rationality. The reasonable man 'is not expected to reason about anything and his judgement may be largely a matter of feeling' (Devlin 1965: 15). One problem here is that the assumption of unanimity in this context can scarcely make sense, given that we are talking about matters on which there is an unknown but presumably sizeable number standing out against the supposed consensus. Deeper problems, as we shall see, arise from the explicit abandonment of rationality in favour of feeling as the basis of moral judgements.

In the course of reaffirming the wider function of the criminal law, Devlin makes two telling points about the consequences of adopting the narrower Wolfenden conception of this function, as derived from Mill's 'no-harm' principle. First, it would overturn the established principle that consent by the victim is no defence in English law to any form of assault or murder. Such offences with consent can be committed without any threat or harm to the wider community. The reason a victim may not either consent beforehand or forgive afterwards is that a criminal assault is an offence, not merely against an individual, but against society. Second, if there is to be consistency, many other specific acts would have to be allowed:

> Euthanasia or the killing of another at his own request, suicide, attempted suicide and suicide pacts, duelling, abortion, incest between brother and sister, are all acts which can be done in private and without offence to others and need not involve the corruption or exploitation of others.
>
> (ibid.: 7)

His argument here is that if consent between prostitutes and their clients, and between adult homosexuals, is made the basis of their legality, then consistency will demand that all of these other acts are legalised as well.

Devlin's main concern in this lecture was to argue for the continuing right of society to pass moral judgement on the behaviour of its citizens, and the right to use the law to enforce this judgement. His central argument for these rights is by his own description a conceptual one, which can be established *a priori*. In short, the argument is that a society is entitled to pass judgement on any of the activities (public or private) of the individuals of which it is composed, because a society is, by definition, a community of political and moral ideas. This is what makes a society more than an aggregate of individuals living on the same territory. Being thus defined as a community of common ideas or beliefs, it follows that those who are out of step with these beliefs are threatening the continued existence of society:

> Society means a community of ideas; without shared ideas on politics, morals and ethics, no society can exist ... . if men and women try to create a society in which there is no fundamental agreement about good and evil, they will fail; if, having based it on common agreement, the agreement goes, society will disintegrate.
>
> (ibid.: 10)

For Devlin, then, passing moral judgement and enforcing it with the sanctions of law is analogous to political judgement and suppression of sedition and rebellion; both are justified by the right of society to protect itself. This is his central argument for legal moralism, for the use of the law for the enforcement of moral norms. One point that should be noted is that this argument seeks to establish a conclusion diametrically opposed to that of Mill. Where Mill argued that there was an empirical link between a healthy and enduring society and allowance of maximum freedom to individuals in choice of moral principles and lifestyle, Devlin argues that it is a necessary truth that, without individual conformity with the consensus, society will collapse. He softens the authoritarian tone of his argument with his urging of legal restraint in the prosecution of immorality, but this makes no essential difference. The most he is conceding is that there is sometimes a case for tolerating moral 'depravity'; he is equally clear that this tolerance can be withdrawn whenever society feels sufficiently threatened.

Devlin's setting of the limits of such tolerance brings us back to the instinctive moral reactions of 'the reasonable man'. At which point can this reasonable tolerance of offensive behaviour be withdrawn? Devlin's central argument here is that, while toleration should be stretched well beyond the point at which most people feel moderate dislike and disgust, the limit is reached when the acts in question are perceived to represent a real danger to society. He argues that what must be present to justify depriving individuals of freedom of choice is a genuine and deeply felt 'intolerance, indignation and disgust'. Comparing sexual offences with cruelty to animals and sadism, he argues that the limits cannot be set by rational argument, but must depend on feelings of real abhorrence (ibid.: 17). This is the most notorious of Devlin's arguments, but it should be remembered that what he is actually arguing for here is maximum toleration. He is not, as is frequently assumed, arguing that anything that makes people sick should be criminalised. It is nevertheless a vague and highly subjective standard that he is proposing, which opens the door to the perpetuation of popular prejudice as the guiding force behind the use of the criminal law.

Hart's reply to Devlin

In 1963, H.L.A. Hart published the text of three lectures as *Law, Liberty, and Morality*, in which he developed a qualified defence of Mill's liberalism, supporting the recommendations of the Wolfenden Committee and countering Devlin's critique of both. His main purpose was to clarify the issues at stake, and in so doing to argue that the use of the criminal law to enforce morals was deeply misguided. Much more in step than Devlin with the liberalising spirit of the early 1960s, Hart set out to undermine moral conservatism and to defend the Wolfenden contention that there is an area of private behaviour that should be no business of the criminal law.

Mindful at the outset of the vulnerability of Mill's libertarian position to a criticism of its dangerous implications, Hart took care to distinguish between coercion for the sake of enforcing society's moral norms, and coercion for the agent's own good. According to the version of liberalism that Hart was developing in these lectures, it is only the latter form of state coercion that is to some extent defensible. Society does have the right to prevent its members from harming themselves as much as from harming others, but it does not have the right to enforce conformity with collective moral standards. The particular example he has in mind here is the prohibition of the sale and use of hard drugs, which is justified on paternalistic grounds. In the name of liberty, Mill had opposed any state interference into such activities, but Hart sets a new limit to the 'no-harm' principle, which is in fact a more literal interpretation of this phrase. What he argues is that the proper reach of the criminal law stops at the point of tangible harm as such – to self or others – whereas for Mill it stops only at the point of harm to others. What Hart endorses in Mill is his defence of the right to follow one's own lifestyle; what he rejects is his insistence that this right has no internal limits.

With this modified version of Mill's defence of individual liberty to hand, Hart was able to confront Devlin's arguments on more solid ground. One of his main complaints about Devlin's case against liberty is that he blurs the distinction between paternalist law and what Hart now labels 'legal moralism'. This is the distinction between laws for the protection of people against themselves and laws that merely seek to enforce moral standards. It is easy to see how this distinction can be blurred and the issue confused. If behaviour deemed to be immoral is widely regarded as by definition harmful and self-destructive, laws prohibiting it will be seen as paternalistic and defensible. With this distinction now drawn clearly, however, it becomes a question of whether – as Devlin argues – society does in fact have the right to condemn actions as inherently immoral and to punish them solely as such, irrespective of their effects on others.

The question of whether society has such a right is a normative one. For Hart, employing Bentham's distinction, it is a question of critical rather than positive morality, and of normative rather than descriptive jurisprudence. It is not a question of determining whether this right already exists in common law; it is a moral question behind the campaign for legislative amendment to the law. Hart argues that there is a strong and unwarranted presumption in Devlin and other legal conservatives that the current state of the law is justified, by virtue of its natural evolution. Hart argues that if society is indeed, as Devlin believes, a community of political and moral ideas, it is a contingent matter whether these ideas will stand up to critical moral scrutiny. Devlin in particular wrongly assumes that any society has the automatic right to protect itself when its morals are threatened, regardless of how defective or misguided these might be. In the past, the moral conventions of the day have justified slavery and the persecution of witches. Hart questions Devlin's assumption, even to the point of denying that a morally defective society is automatically justified in preserving its own existence, if it is grossly unjust in substance or if the steps taken to preserve it are abhorrent. If society does have the right to pass moral judgements on its citizens and to use the law to enforce these judgements, it is not by virtue of Devlin's conceptual argument from the positive morality of that society.

Perhaps the most important of Hart's criticisms is the distinction, which he dwells on only briefly, between the core morality of a society and its sexual morals. This is in fact the crucial point, because the limitations of the English language have always produced a tendency to conflate these two senses of morality and immorality. In the core sense of the word, 'immoral' simply means 'wrong'; the core morality as enforced by virtually any legal system worthy of the name includes all the central prohibitions against violence, theft and other antisocial behaviour. In the more specific sense of the word, 'immoral' refers to deviations from conventional norms governing sexual and sex-related matters. Hart's criticism of Devlin is that his implicit merging of these two senses of the words establishes an underlying assumption, quite unwarranted, that:

> all morality – sexual morality together with the morality that forbids acts injurious to others such as killing, stealing and dishonesty – forms a single seamless web, so that those who deviate from any part are likely or perhaps bound to deviate from the whole.
>
> (Hart 1963: 50–1)

When we are dealing with moral 'crimes', which do not actually affect or harm anyone else, the implication of this 'seamless web' assumption is that if these private offences are allowed to proliferate without threat or sanction by the law, then the core morality of society will also suffer.

This assumption that morality constitutes a seamless whole, with every aspect meshing together to form a unified model of personal integrity, is also related to Hart's distinction between what he sees as extreme and moderate versions of legal moralism. The extreme version he attributes to James Fitzjames Stephen, the nineteenth-century judge who had published a critique of Mill's *On Liberty* from a utilitarian standpoint, emphatically rejecting Mill's proposal for an area of privacy. Stephen's arguments for the punishment of all forms of 'vice' rested on his claim that it was the function of the criminal law to punish wrongdoing as such, regardless of whether it had any harmful effects. Stephen rejected Mill's 'no-harm' principle because it would remove this essential part of the function of the criminal law, the duty to condemn vice. One of Stephen's main arguments for punishing purely 'moral' offences was based on the practice of judicial sentencing in a case that actually does involve harm. In such cases, he argued, judges invariably take into account not only the degree of harm or damage, but also the odiousness of the crime and its perpetrator. Variations in sentence reflect malice, responsibility and degree of temptation, over and above the actual nature and extent of the injury caused. Moral judgement and condemnation are inescapable. The implication is that the 'surfeit' part of the sentence is purely to reflect the moral revulsion felt by the judge, speaking for society; the conclusion is that the prosecution of vice solely because it is immoral is a function and duty of the law quite independently of whether any harm has been caused (Stephen 1874).

This argument is clearly invalid, because it trades on different senses of immorality and moral revulsion. What is condemned in a case of, say, aggravated burglary is quite different from what is condemned in unconventional sexual activity. Also, the immoral 'component' of the crime would not be punishable in isolation from the criminal act. Hart's refutation of the argument is less important than his use of it to draw a contrast with what he sees as Devlin's moderate version of legal moralism. The extreme thesis is that the state's right to punish wrongdoing is derived solely from its wrongness and excitement of public revulsion. The moderate thesis is that the state's right to punish wrongdoing is derived from its social dangers, that if it is allowed to go unpunished the society whose morals it is flouting will, by definition, begin to fall apart.

Hart's rejection of this supposedly moderate social disintegration thesis is based largely on his observation that it is expressed by Devlin as a conceptual truth, based on his definition of society as a community of ideas and moral values. If this were the case, any permitted deviation from these ideas and values would constitute not so much a threat as a *de facto* disintegration of this society or body of values. Apart from Hart's criticisms, already noted, that it is wrong to assume that every society is worth defending or that any measures taken to defend it are justified, he argues that the assumption in the first place that a society is simply identical with every aspect of its positive morality is highly dubious. There is no reason to suppose that societies cannot evolve morally, allowing more personal liberty and diversity of values, without losing the core morality that sustains them or without losing their essential identity.

Dworkin's critique of Devlin

Defending liberalism and toleration from a different angle, Dworkin's arguments against Devlin focused on the question of the foundations of the moral judgements made by or on behalf of the community as a whole (Dworkin 1977b: ch. 10; 1989). Against Devlin's feeling-centred ethics, Dworkin argued that the minimal requirement for even granting an opinion the status of 'moral position' or 'moral principle' is that it is based on reasons and satisfies demands for consistency. The important feature of the argument is his contention that some 'reasons' must be discounted if the moral case for legal intervention is to be taken seriously. To be excluded are prejudices posturing as judgements, personal emotional reactions, false propositions of fact and parroting the beliefs of others. If genuine reasons are produced, and they can be shown to be applied consistently, then there will at least be a moral case to be answered. Devlin's attempt to show that the legislator is obliged to act on behalf of the deeply held moral beliefs of the majority is undermined by his identification of 'the reasonable man' as the barometer for public opinion, because there is nothing reasonable about the criteria of 'intolerance, indignation and disgust'. These are precisely the kind of reasons that are ruled out in any other context for determining a sound moral judgement, so they should be ruled out in the context of personal morals as well. The mere fact of a moral consensus, if it is not based on reasons that will stand up to scrutiny, does not for Dworkin make it morally legitimate.

One common objection to Dworkin's argument is that it would also disqualify vast numbers of ordinary moral judgements on acts of gratuitous cruelty, which an average jury member will condemn primarily on the basis of angry indignation and disgust. Many statutes embody prohibitions originally based on this kind of popular revulsion. This is a mistaken objection, because most people in this position, jury members or legislators, would be able to give non-prejudiced reasons to support the emotional reaction, to explain why such acts should not be allowed.

The other key feature of Dworkin's critique of Devlin is his rejection of the democratic majoritarian argument for the right of a community to impose the moral views of one section – even if it is a very large majority – on the rest of the community. Drawing an analogy between 'the ethical environment' and the economic environment, he argues that just as the majority does not have the right to gather all economic resources to itself and leave the rest to starve, it does not have the right to dominate the ethical environment in such a way that the minority is completely deprived of the right to make its own impact on this environment. The majority in turn has no rights solely by virtue of being the majority; its rights to mould the ethical environment exist only in proportion to its numbers. This is defended by Dworkin as a democratic principle that works against and in tension with the democratic principle of majority rule.

Conclusion

Forty years on from the Hart–Devlin debate, various social factors in both Britain and the USA might seem to have changed the original issues beyond recognition. While one can say that there has been a decisive shift of opinion towards tolerance in private matters of sexuality, such that it is difficult to imagine the 1960s legislation being reversed, the controversy about the state of the law on these and related matters, and the rights of the community to enforce its moral norms, has continued to evolve in ways not countenanced by the early protagonists. Nevertheless, the wrangle between Devlin and his critics created the framework in which the political and philosophical differences have continued.

Study questions

General question: To what extent, if any, should the criminal law be used to regulate private behaviour that does not conform with the moral norms of society?

Further study questions: Was the Wolfenden Report correct in its insistence that 'there must remain a realm of private morality which is, in brief and crude terms, not the law's business'? Do Mill's arguments in defence of liberty show that there is never any justification for laws that are aimed at protecting people from themselves? Is Devlin right to insist that there can be no theoretical limits to the authority of the state over the individual? Is Hart's defence of paternalism consistent with his criticism of Devlin's legal moralism? Is Dworkin right in claiming that Devlin does not have a 'moral position'?

Suggestions for further reading

The most important primary texts for this topic are Mill's *On Liberty* (Mill 1972a), originally published in 1859, the Report of the Wolfenden Committee (1957), Patrick Devlin's *Enforcement of Morals* (Devlin 1965) and Hart's *Law, Liberty, and Morality* (Hart 1963). Other important contributions include Dworkin (1977b: ch. 10; and 1989), Mitchell (1970) and Hughes's 'Morals and the Criminal Law', in Summers (1968).

Of the collections of relevant material, Wasserstrom (1971) is the established text. Kipnis (1977: §2) contains several important items. The discussion in Gavison (1987: pt 3) of toleration and the harm principle is particularly useful. The articles collected in G. Dworkin (1994) address this and a wider range of issues relating to liberty. Other useful commentaries and critical surveys of the Hart–Devlin debate and related issues can be found in Bix (2015: ch. 15), Leiser (1973, 1981), Lyons (1984: 178–93), Golding (1975: ch.3), Feinberg (1973: chs 1–3), Dias (1985: ch. 6), Harris (1997: ch. 10) and Riddall (1999: ch. 21). For a close analysis of the problems of harm and distress, see Thomson (1990: chs 9–10). For specialist books on Mill's defence of liberty, see Ten (1980), J. Gray (1996) and J. Gray and Smith (1991).

11 Radical critiques of liberal theories of law

The questions and problems relating to authority, rights and liberty as we have encountered them over the last three chapters arise from differing interpretations of the proper reach and limits of the law in the modern world. For the radical critics who conceptualise and attack 'modernity' as a whole, however, the real problem lies in the complete absence of justification or grounding to give the law and its declared rights any authority at all. From this point of view, any attempt within the theoretical framework of modernity to define the reach and limits of the law in terms of authority and rights is no more than an exercise in power. In this chapter, we will be looking at the themes that have been most prominent in the radical writings in recent decades and how they relate to the origins of modernity, and we will be considering the responses in defence of mainstream jurisprudence and its philosophical basis.

The liberal concept of the individual

Right at the centre of these debates, we find the concept of the individual. The very purpose of modern liberalism at its inception was to affirm the value of the human individual against the despotisms of the premodern world and to make the protection of its interests paramount. The important point concerns the way in which the individual has been conceptualised. The specifically liberal conception took shape in the classic accounts of the social contract and the state of nature in the seventeenth century, and was later given a more complete formulation in the following century in Kant's moral and political philosophy. According to the modern contract theories, the assumption had to be made that the contracting parties were free and equal, fully conscious and rational agents. Similarly, the emerging theories of natural rights were based on the assumption that it was the autonomous, reasoning individual who was the bearer of natural rights. In more recent times, the defence of the liberty of the individual against the state in all matters of private morality presupposes sufficient autonomy and rationality to make reasoned decisions on one's own behalf. The ideal that took hold of the Enlightenment imagination, then, was of the individual with more or less perfect self-control, equal in standing to any other, able to make responsible judgements and act upon them without reference to authority, consenting to obey laws that he himself has (at least in theory) rationally affirmed. The fundamental moral right that flows from this is the universal right to be treated as an end in oneself, and the fundamental duty is to treat others with reciprocal respect. What was radically new about this was that the only ground for it was the reason possessed in equal measure by every individual.

Critiques of the liberal concept of the individual

This liberal conception of the individual has come under fire from many different directions, both from within and without what is usually seen as 'modernity'. The most influential critique – that this conception was both abstract and skewed to favour one type of individual – came from Western democracy's most trenchant critic, Karl Marx, and was developed not only by the ideology of Soviet Marxism, but also by a wide range of critical social theories in the West. Critiques of liberal individualism, however, are by no means confined to the political left. Communitarians of all political colours reject the basis of individualism, on the grounds that it destroys the communal ties that are fundamental to a cohesive society. Radical feminists who reject the traditional liberal attempts to extend the recognition of equality of basic political and civil rights to women tend to do so because they regard the liberal conception of the individual as inherently distorted and deeply biased towards masculinity. Critical race theorists have also developed critiques of the liberal conception as carrying cultural assumptions specific to the white societies of modern Europe and North America, thus facilitating the exclusion of black African slaves from the category of humanity. Postmodernists from various points on the political spectrum generally regard the liberal concept of the individual as the cornerstone of the 'grand narrative' of the progressive liberation promised by modernity, and thus as eminent a candidate for deconstruction as can be imagined. As an invention or a 'construct' that comes to seem natural, as the only way in which to conceptualise a human being, the liberal conception can supposedly be unmasked as a complete fiction and thus as a very poor foundation or grounding for human rights.

We can see how this scepticism gains a firm foothold by considering the problems surrounding the concept of the human individual. When liberals speak of the value and autonomy of the individual, who exactly is it they are talking about, and what is it individuated *from*? The fundamental point that has to be remembered through all the philosophical debate is that what the analysis always has to come back to is the flesh-and-blood human beings of both sexes and all races and creeds, thinking, feeling, acting and generally experiencing the world in an infinite variety of ways. So which of these individuals are they talking about? Clearly, what is at least consciously intended today is that 'the' individual refers to none of these in particular, nor to one particular type, but to each and every living human individual. 'The individual' is the human individual in the abstract, the outcome of deliberately setting aside idiosyncrasies and abstracting the characteristics common to all of them. In other words, it refers to the essential humanity in each individual, the qualities whereby each is a member of the species.

Liberal humanism and the individual

When the philosophers of the Enlightenment and the French Revolution's Declaration of the Rights of Man were articulating their humanistic defences of the freedom and equality of 'Man' (as opposed to 'men' and/or 'women'), it was this essential being who was conceptualised as being in possession of reason and universal natural rights. At the same time as creating a liberating and at the time shocking vision of fundamental human equality, confronting the old social hierarchies with the demand for their own dissolution, they were launching what would soon be criticised as an abstract humanism, divorced from the reality not only of society as a whole but also of any of the real individuals that comprised it. In truth, the concept of the individual was arrived at by abstracting from a limited range of real individuals, not from the full spectrum of humanity. The idealised conception of Man nevertheless took root as the inspiration for the continuing political struggles for liberal democracy. The political value of proclaiming basic rights to be natural and universal is too obvious to require explanation, and the idealised nature of the concepts deployed to justify such proclamations is not necessarily a fatal defect. The point was that however defective its actual manifestation might appear in retrospect, the principle of universality had been established. The proclaimed rights were at least potentially open to all.

The point of the postmodernist attacks on this humanism of the early modern period is to draw out what they see as the repressive character of the specifically modern version of humanism. This is based on their perception of the distinction between the theoretical 'subject' of the liberal conception of the individual and the really existing empirical self. The idea of individual subjective selves with the right of ownership over their own minds and bodies was in fact a philosophical creation of the seventeenth century, quite unknown to premodern thought, as critics of modernity are never slow to point out. What these postmodern critics emphasise is the artificiality of this newly created 'individual subject' and the way in which it was immediately passed off as part of a natural state of affairs, as the only way it could be. The essence of the political revolution at this time was the transfer of power from the old hierarchy to this sovereign individual, who became the source of legal authority and the bearer of fundamental rights, which were now portentously declared to be universal, when it was plain for all to see that they were born out of a historically specific political struggle, and natural, when these rights along with their fictitious 'owner' were manifestly artificial constructs.

The contextualisation of universal rights

The key word in the line of criticism of Enlightenment humanism and universal rights that has persisted throughout the modern period is 'context'. Taking words or actions out of context and thereby distorting their meaning is one of the most familiar features of everyday disputes and verbal skulduggery. Keeping or placing them within context is generally seen as a precondition of understanding. It is not so much, though, merely a question of placing them within their proper context as *weaving* them in. This is the etymological root of the word. Linguistic context is often interpreted as analogous to a closely woven fabric. The insistence upon the contextualisation of anything – words, ideas, theories – can be understood as the demand that they be woven into any 'fabric' or background to which they are said to apply. This is the main thrust of the type of criticism of universalism and natural rights that complains of their lack of context-sensitivity. From this point of view, the proclamation of universal rights is not merely worthless but positively dangerous if the rights are not rooted in the specific historical and cultural context to which they are supposed to apply. In its postmodernist versions, this idea of contextualisation is expressed in terms of positionality, embeddedness or situatedness, all of which emphasise the particularity of the social conditions at any point in history. The general idea here is that one cannot rise above history and impose moral truths upon society from a universalist standpoint outside of it.

This contextualist strain of criticism has a complex modern history in political and legal thought. It is associated as much with progressive as conservative and reactionary thought. Although the most famous instance of it is Edmund Burke's (1729–97) attack on the natural rights of the French Revolution, its influence has pervaded the critiques of the Enlightenment up to the present day. It has been particularly strong in English jurisprudence and was a motivating force in the 1990s resistance to the campaign for a Bill of Rights and the passing of the UK 1998 HRA (Human Rights Act), which was thought by many to be alien to the tradition of English common law. This was one of Burke's original complaints, and it has been echoed ever since.

The idea behind this resistance depends upon an organicist conception of society. In opposition to the dominant mechanistic paradigm of modern scientific thought, the analogy between society and a living organism assumes that a society is composed of mutually dependent elements, which, taken together, grow naturally and spontaneously, rather than through any conscious overall design. This natural evolution involves the gradual transformation of custom into law and the emergence of *de facto* rights and duties. Laws or rights that have thus emerged from the ground of local custom are felt to be solidly rooted in the indigenous social and legal culture.

It follows that if laws or rights that have no pedigrees within that culture are abruptly introduced from outside, they will not take root and will probably be violently rejected. This was the essence of Burke's critique of natural rights universalism. Laws that are claimed to embody universal rights, derived solely from reason (which in its Enlightenment sense is by definition ahistorical), are precisely the kind of alien rights that can only be imposed by force. If a right is natural and universal, it emanates from nowhere in particular and therefore does not belong anywhere in particular. It might be added that universal rights can be seen to suffer from the same defect as rigidly applied general legal rules, which do not take into account the uniqueness of every set of facts in each unrepeatable case. Genuine rights – if such are possible – have to be such that they are adaptable to local diversity and can be genuinely instantiated.

This kind of response to the universalism of modern natural rights has always had a very wide appeal, not least because of the natural suspicion that such universalism is intrinsically linked with an arrogant cultural imperialism, as the Western liberal democracies expand their influence throughout the world and impose their own standards of justice and rights on cultures that have not evolved through the same channels of 'enlightenment'. The dispute between the cultural relativism that this criticism embraces, and the moral objectivism of those who believe that there are transcultural moral standards to be defended, is in its twentieth-century form a heritage of Western colonialism and long predates the contemporary disputes between the modern and post-modern. There are many dimensions to this general moral question, but it is not resolved by simplistically declaring each culture to be as morally sound as any other. It should be remembered that one of the main implications of a strict adherence to the principles of cultural relativism, and to the kind of organicist theory of society that supports it, is that in the case of extremes it becomes impossible to criticise societies that have deeply embedded traditions of slavery and other racist institutions that are anathema to the standpoint of universal natural rights. Even with less extreme injustices, strict cultural relativism also deadens criticism if the standpoint of natural justice is ruled out.

Abstractness and irrelevance

The criticism that is often thought to strike at the heart of modern natural rights is that they are 'abstract' in the sense that they are merely formal. Connected with this is the complaint that charters and bills of universal rights are irrelevant to the real needs of actual concrete individuals, especially those who are living in conditions of severe deprivation. What is the good of guaranteeing the right to liberty under the rule of law to somebody dying of starvation? What is the practical value of the right to life for the victims of ethnic cleansing? To the people in such situations, all the rights proclaimed over the last few centuries are nothing but empty documents.

This kind of criticism is well founded, but we have to be clear what it is a criticism of. The gap between the vision of a just society governed by Kantian principles of mutual respect for the dignity of every individual, and the reality that often falls a long way short of such a vision, certainly provides grounds for moral and political criticism or even condemnation of the existing institutions that create or allow this gap. The confusion sets in, however, when this criticism is translated into a wholesale rejection of rights on the grounds that they are empty because they are merely formal. This is based on a misunderstanding of what 'formal' means. This will become clear in the light of the following critical theories.

Marx and Marxism

Many of the doctrines of Marxism that evolved with the political conflicts of the twentieth century are relevant to the disputes between radical and mainstream jurisprudence. As a general theory of law, it can be seen from one angle as a radical and somewhat narrower version of the command theory developed by English positivism, as it strips away the moral rhetoric to reveal the mechanics of political power, and reduces legal doctrines to expressions of the interests of the ruling class. As such, the law is regarded as one of the main arenas of class struggle. As a wider theory of history, Marxism depicts social development as a morally progressive spiralling upward ascent. Marx himself saw history as an epic 'human journey' from the natural primitive communism of early hunter-gatherers, through a succession of civilisations, empires, wars and revolutions, towards the final goal of a complete realisation of human potential in a 'return' to the original communist state, built upon the experience and knowledge acquired along the way. The belief that in the modern world the human race was about to enter the last phase of struggle towards this collective destiny lay behind the politics of Marx's revolutionary socialism. The postmodernist rejection of this vision of the future, unmasking it as a 'grand narrative', placed it in the same category as the liberal dreams of complete enlightenment and universal peace between fully rational and autonomous individuals. Marxism was increasingly seen as part of the same Enlightenment project of an impossible liberation of humanity from all its imperfections. At the same time, however, Marx developed a theoretical perspective on the question of the rights of the individual in society that has had an immeasurable positive influence on the critical theories well beyond the confines of socialist politics, including those of postmodernist critics.

Marx's critique of liberal rights

Marx's own hostility to rights is well known, but not always clearly understood. In the political tradition that he inspired, the scepticism and even contempt for the individual rights valued by liberalism are notorious. The Soviet Marxist justification for downplaying human rights was based on the claim that collective socioeconomic rights – such as the rights to basic shelter, healthcare and education – were more important to the welfare of individuals as a collective than respect for the more typically liberal negative rights of each and every individual was to those who suffered persecution.

Marx himself was certainly no liberal, but this played no part in his argument against rights. In his criticisms of the natural rights of the French Revolution he was, as is often pointed out, attempting to expose them as mere abstractions masking the true nature of these rights, which were in practice to be extended only to the free activity of the rising bourgeois class, the members of which would have the means to take advantage of them, at the expense of the propertyless majority. More importantly, though, this critique of rights can be linked with his doctrine of commodity fetishism. The fetishism of commodities is for Marx the crucial transformation that occurs in the capitalist economic system when things of different quality are produced for exchange rather than use. In this process, the stamp of equal value on heterogeneous products creates the illusion of homogeneity, such that unequal objects appear as equal.

This 'veil of equality' idea was applied critically to the language of universal rights, such that the main thrust of Marx's criticism of liberal (bourgeois) natural rights was that they were hopelessly irrelevant, because they treated individual people who were in fact different and unequal in their particular characteristics and powers as 'universally equal', thus imposing a veil of generality upon a social world that has to be understood in all its vast array of particularities. In short, what he was criticising was the liberal conception of the individual as a theoretical abstraction in sharp contrast to the reality of concrete individuals. For Marx, the thinking of the supposedly radical liberals was dominated by a conception of the individual that he described as 'monadic', as a self-enclosed entity walled in and separated from its social environment, but most importantly with the social side of its own nature carefully eliminated. This monad is pure egoistic man, which became the model for all the human sciences, from economics to psychology. What Marx was proposing as an alternative model was a concrete conception of humanity, a 'subject' more in tune with the real constitution of human individuals in both their individuated and socialised dimensions. The liberal-bourgeois subject with its natural rights tried to step outside of history to adopt a universal standpoint from which it could confront the injustice and inequality of the premodern world, but the new subject that would carry the revolution forward was rooted in the real historical process of class struggle. There was no talk of rights in this conflict – only a struggle for power and social justice. The important concept that was to exercise so much influence on later social theory was that of egoistic man, the falsely individuated subject of liberal theory. This is the conception presupposed by liberalism from Hobbes's egotistical man to the subject of Rawls's rational contract.

Feminist jurisprudence and the rights of women

Given that women make up roughly one half of the human race, the impact of the wider social phenomenon of feminism upon mainstream jurisprudence is potentially greater than that of any of the other critical perspectives. Over the past forty years feminism has diversified into a richly complex field of theories and research programmes, reflecting many different political positions. Within the confines of legal theory, there has been much overlap and interaction with CLS (critical legal studies), critical race studies and socialist and Marxist theories. The pattern of development has been, in very broad terms, the transition first from the traditional campaigns for equality to more radical forms of feminism in the decades following the upheaval of the 1960s, then somewhat belatedly in the late 1980s to the more confusing world of postmodernist criticism. The original setting in which feminism as a struggle for the rights of women took shape, however, was the liberal tradition of the Enlightenment. The problems confronted and the variety of positions adopted by contemporary feminists writing about law should be seen in the light of their reactions to this liberal tradition.

The subordination of women and the liberal campaigns for equality

Behind the diversity, the one premise upon which all feminists in jurisprudence as elsewhere are agreed is that the fundamental experience of women in society is one of subordination to males. It is in their interpretation of the nature and explanation of this subordination and how to develop a constructive response that there is disagreement. The traditional response, from Mary Wollstonecraft's (1759–97) *Vindication of the Rights of Women* (1792) to the present day, has been to confront the male-dominated liberal establishment with its own ideals, demanding that they be extended to all, male and female alike. If the ideals of the Enlightenment are genuinely universal, it was argued, then the recognition of individual autonomy and equal status, or of the right to be treated with reciprocal respect as an end in oneself, could not be restricted to one sex. The much-proclaimed 'rights of man' had, by virtue of their own supreme value of reason and rational consistency, to be applied to women as well. Individual women who argued in this way were at the time almost universally regarded as eccentric and atypical of their sex, which was generally seen as lacking in the quality of rationality essential to the possession of liberal rights. From the standpoint of the overwhelming majority of the male revolutionaries, the explanation of women's subordination lay in nature rather than in the oppression of women by men. For a typical male liberal of the time, there was no inconsistency in denying equal rights to irrational women.

The solid point of reference and platform for women's equality is the long history of campaigning for the public recognition of the inferior position of women in society and under the law, and the legislative and case-law milestones that were a mark of progress in terms of this recognition. The achievement in Britain of universal suffrage in stages by 1928, the gradual breakdown of exclusion from holding public office, from entry into the universities and professions (Sex (Removal of Disqualification) Act, 1919), were fundamental to the cause of basic equal rights. The Equal Pay Act (1970) and the Sex Discrimination Act (1975) are the best known, but among equally far-reaching specific reforms have been those on the rights of married women to own property (Married Women's Property Act, 1882), the equalisation of custody rights over children (Guardianship of Minors Act, 1971), the right of any woman to take out a mortgage without a male guarantor (1975), the gradual legal recognition of domestic violence and the outlawing of marital rape (1994). These are only the most notable examples of what has been achieved in recent times by relentless campaigning and it is undeniable that they have all been established against deeply ingrained hostility and resistance. These reforms have nevertheless been achieved and have gradually changed the relative status in society of males and females beyond recognition over the past century, a point frequently emphasised by liberal feminists against those who disparage these legal changes as 'merely formal'.

The feminist critical engagement with liberalism

Contemporary feminist reactions to this long slow history of reform has been mixed. Many legal scholars continue to regard it as the main focus for feminist jurisprudence, concentrating their research on specific issues of injustice and inequality. Others, however, have been more sceptical of the value of establishing legal rights, arguing for a more fundamental and thoroughgoing critical analysis of legal theory and practice. In particular, some have argued that the formalities of legal rights are insufficient in the face of the realities of male domination and violence that lie beyond the reach of the law, leaving deeply embedded discrimination and injustice untouched. The universalism of natural rights is said to make no contact with the real lives of individual women, because they are decontextualised and devoid of real content. Beyond this, it has been argued that the achievement of such rights can be not only inadequate but also counterproductive in as far as they create the illusion of a substantive equality that has only been formally recognised. From this point of view, legal rights are seen as a positive obstruction to advancing the cause of equality and justice.

The main objection to feminist liberalism, with its focus on the struggle for recognition of the subordinate position of women, for equal opportunities and full citizen's rights, is the argument that this strategy falls into the trap of demanding parity on terms that have been defined by males, demanding all the same rights, which are typically 'male' rights. The rights as formulated were, it is said, constructed specifically for males. On the face of it, this is a puzzling objection to rights successfully secured, such as those relating to political participation, the right to hold public office, and so on. The implication would seem to be that they allow the male domination in these areas to continue unchallenged. The objection, however, runs deeper than this. The claim on which it rests is that gender bias is built into all the political and legal institutions, and that it permeates the language of politics and especially law so thoroughly that all its fundamental concepts, standards and methods of reasoning are deeply biased against women. The masculine presuppositions embedded in all the legal concepts are said to be so deep-rooted that they are like the air we breathe. So the general idea here is that gender bias is concealed or subliminal, and it is at this deeper level that it has to be confronted.

Compare this with the kind of masculine bias in law that is overt and visible to everyone on a moment's reflection. The explicit exclusion in the past of women from legal training or higher appointments on the grounds of inherent unsuitability was at the time relatively uncontroversial. Justifications included claims that women had the wrong kind of brains and cognitive abilities, or the wrong pitch of voice to speak in the appropriate tone. Explicit prejudices like these have been dying out, but the language of the law is still regularly criticised for its overt gender bias. One of the common law principles of natural justice states that no 'man' is to be judge in 'his' own cause. The most common example is the standard of 'the reasonable man' as the measure of the kind of behaviour that can be expected by the law. Such expressions, of course, have run right the way through the English language, not just the law. These are relatively superficial grammatical biases, creating an atmosphere of masculinity in the law, which has prompted their recent correction to gender-neutral terminology, such as 'the reasonable person'.

The point of the radical argument is to emphasise bias that is more subliminal than this. The concealment is effected, it is said, by the male judicial 'pretence' of neutrality and objectivity in legal reasoning, in resolving matters of law. The question of whether this pretence is conscious or unconscious is secondary. The claim is that every appearance of neutrality can be maintained while applying rules and standards that have built-in masculine assumptions, standards that favour male over female plaintiffs or defendants. To take the most general example, the real concealment is found in the concepts of reason or rationality within the concept of the reasonable man. It is not the overt masculinity of the reasonable 'man', but the covert masculinity of the 'reasonable' man that remains when the term is changed to 'reasonable person'. The deep gender bias lies in the Enlightenment ideal of reason and the rational individual (supposedly of either sex). The radicals argue that the liberal feminists who aim for parity of legal rights have been setting themselves the aspiration of achieving equality by conforming with male standards of rationality and individualism, accepting the male definition of reason and individuality as the standard point of reference. Adapting Marx's critique of liberalism, radical feminists argue that the fictitious 'individual' of liberalism is an idealised male who exhibits all the characteristics culturally associated with masculinity and suppresses all those associated with femininity. The individual who constitutes the legal subject or person displays the qualities that a patriarchal society values and rewards more highly than the constructed feminine qualities. The characteristics of manliness, virility, strength and independence (exhibiting the male entrepreneurial spirit) are typical of the liberal 'autonomous individual', whereas the virtues of womanliness, patience, gentle submissiveness, care and nurture are marginalised. The ideal is framed in such a way that it is easier for males to conform with it or aspire to it. Females can only realise their rights by imitating male patterns of behaviour.

The most significant implication of this argument is that the great ideal of liberal feminists, the pursuit of equal opportunities, is only meaningful and realisable for women who can demonstrate masculine abilities, in particular the male conception of rationality, which embodies a particular set of cognitive abilities. Thus, the liberal reformers are on the wrong road, as they submit to the ongoing male-dominated structure of society by accepting the male rules of the game. Against this, the radical feminists are arguing that it is this underlying structure that has to be questioned and challenged.

Difference and sameness

Over the past few centuries, the principal justification of the privileged position of males has been expressed in terms of women's supposed general inferiority and their specific differences from men. The subordination is seen not as oppressive and unjust, but as an inevitable imbalance of rights arising naturally from these biological differences. Resistance to specific legal reforms in areas such as education and employment are linked to the questioning of specific abilities and capacities, such as natural mathematical ability or physical strength. The history of this argument is well known. Directly confronting the arguments for the justifiability of discrimination, feminists generally have argued for male–female identity in the areas relevant to the legislation, and have concentrated on exposing assumptions about female disabilities as male prejudice.

From the more radical point of view that emerged in the 1970s, these liberals were making the mistake of saying 'we are just the same as you'. The result of the shift in emphasis from the overt to the subliminal gender bias in radical feminist thinking was the reshaping of the debate about difference and sameness. If mere conformity with male standards of reasonableness led only to oppression in another guise, it was perhaps necessary to reconceptualise the basis of the demands for change. It was argued that it should not only be accepted but also emphasised that women are different from men, that they have special characteristics that men do not have, and that this should be the basis for a relationship of mutual respect and concrete rights that related to the individuality of women. 'Cultural feminism', in particular, tried to break the grip of the assumption that made women the 'equals' of men in a sense that threatened their own identity and sidelined their own inherent character and qualities. This line of thought provoked a strong reaction from those who saw it as playing into the hands of male domination. Males have to be contested on their own ground. The abandonment of the insistence on sameness invites misinterpretation and a reinforcement of traditional attitudes of paternalistic protection of 'the weaker sex'.

This debate about difference and sameness has continued, especially in the light of child developmental research, some of which has indicated different patterns of cognitive ability and distinctive approaches to moral reasoning in girls and boys (Gilligan 1982). It has also been partly instrumental in the emergence of the distinctive radicalism of 'dominance feminism', which rejects the debate on difference and sameness as an irrelevant distraction from the main issue of male dominance. According to Catherine MacKinnon, the difference between men and women is that 'men have power and women do not' (MacKinnon 1987: 51). In the radical feminist writings of MacKinnon and Andrea Dworkin there is a strong emphasis on physical male violence against women, both in public and in the 'privacy' of the home, as the fundamental fact of women's experience and as the root of the problem.

Feminism and postmodernism

The influence of postmodernist thinking on feminism has been mixed. Its obvious potential for deconstructing and destabilising all the assumptions and norms of what radical feminists see as the central locus of male power in modernity is counterbalanced by the threat it represents to the coherence and stability of their own theories. It is in the nature of postmodernist analysis to be disrespectful of all established 'truths'. Nevertheless, the typical motifs of postmodernist thought appeared in feminist theory as elsewhere some time before it was consciously applied. The influence of Foucault's 'discourses' and analysis of localised power, his histories of the marginalised and oppressed, had obvious resonance for the feminist projects of exposing the hidden ways in which male dominance was perpetuated. Similarly, Derrida's methods of deconstruction, identifying binary oppositions and the privileging of one term over the other, had obvious application to the male–female, reason–emotion, mental–physical distinctions. In more general terms, 1970s feminists tended to fall in with a widespread and rather uncritical absorption of the new 'anti-metaphysics' dogmas, in particular the assumption that foundationalism in epistemology was dead, with all the sceptical and perspectivist conclusions that in postmodernist hands this led to.

When postmodernism was adopted by some as an explicit feminist strategy, it was not only addressed to the problems of articulating women's experiences of oppression, but was also directed at the earlier feminist schools of thought, all of which were seen as trapped within the theoretical framework of modernity, with all its 'grand concepts' and 'grand narratives'. Not only traditional liberals, but also the culture-difference feminists and radical-dominance theories came under the critical spotlight for remaining under the spell of essentialism, the crucial modernist assumption that there is a common core to the experience of being a woman, regardless of her position in society, her relative power or powerlessness, her colour or ethnic background, or her sexual orientation. Postmodernists have sought to place the excluded and marginalised at the centre of theory, emphasising the diversity of the experiences of real individual women in real situations, so they have used the deconstructive techniques to express the reality of particularised and detailed experiences of oppression, which are thought to be as effectively smothered by the generality of the feminist concepts as they are by conventional jurisprudence. The concepts of 'woman' and 'gender' are as much the objects of deconstruction as any other.

Feminist jurisprudence as a whole, however, has been poised uncertainly between the values of Enlightenment modernity and a full embrace of the contemporary postmodernist culture. In the first place, the destabilisation that it brings threatens to disintegrate their own conceptual schemes. 'Feminists should be wary of the siren call to abandon gender as an organising concept' (Barnett 1998: 199). In more general terms, the postmodernist perspectivism, which makes of every truth-claim an ideological construct, undermines the critical feminist positions as effectively as it does the dominant male doctrines. Most importantly, perhaps, there has been a growing recognition that the traditional struggle for equality under the law within a liberal framework established at the very least a solid platform or springboard from which to work for substantive as well as formal equality. The scepticism towards the 'masculine' rights promoted by the Enlightenment, on the grounds that these were designed for the enhancement of male power, has its limits.

Rights in relation to class, sex and race

The main force of the criticisms of liberal thinking on rights, from feminists, Marxists and CLS, lies in their universality and supposed emptiness. These criticisms, while they contain many insights and expose weaknesses in liberal assumptions, are at their most damaging when they go beyond the claim of irrelevance to real problems and criticise the enactment of rights as constituting a positive obstruction to the promotion or defence of the real interests of those whose rights are ostensibly being protected. This is a long-standing theme in the Marxist criticisms of the liberal rule of law and, as we have just seen, it appears in radical feminist theories. It is also a prominent theme in the writings of the critical legal scholars, who have adapted Marx's critique of liberal rights and his concept of the 'monadic' bourgeois individual to a critique of individualist human rights in contemporary law. A strong motif in CLS criticism in the 1980s was the argument that rights as they are understood by liberals in the modern world actually have the effect of deepening the individualistic structure of society, because the preoccupation with legal rights and protections sets up barriers around artificially isolated individuals, denying their essentially social nature and breaking down local relations of community.

This argument has been developed separately by some feminists, but vigorously resisted by others who see the danger in undervaluing what has proved to be the main instrument for the advancement of the cause of gender equality. It may be that the much maligned 'rights culture' does create, among its other effects, divisions and greater distance between individuals, but this is surely not one of its most unwelcome effects. Many people's interests and desires are not served by closer integration with others. The balance between the individual and his or her community is a delicate one. This is a point emphasised by critical race theorists against the radical tendency to disparage individual rights. Patricia Williams, for example, criticises those feminist and critical scholars who are sceptical of rights on the grounds that they seem oblivious to the importance of legal formalities within the world (male and female alike) of black resistance to discrimination and oppression (P. Williams 1991). She and others have persuasively argued that the attainment of formal equality in law has been the necessary condition for achieving substantive equality. She also sets women's oppression within the different historical context of slave-ownership and the more recent struggles for civil rights, emphasising the different position in which black people find themselves under the formal protection of the law today. This argument can be generalised beyond the contexts of sex and race. Among their many other functions, legal rights serve primarily the purpose of the legitimate protection of vulnerable individuals.

Conclusion

The Enlightenment ideal of the autonomous individual, equal in standing with others and capable of making responsible judgements, is essentially the image of the legally responsible individual with which we are still familiar today. This essentially Kantian conception of the subject has at most been the dominant force within modern ways of thinking; it does not constitute it, as so many undiscriminating critics of 'modernity' seem to believe. It has survived as the dominant way of thinking, despite the relentless assault upon it over the past two centuries by Marxist economic determinism, reducing subjects to the status of bearers of ideology, with their consciousness determined solely by their material existence; by theories of the unconscious – Freudian and post-Freudian – which threaten to undermine conscious agency completely; by radical mechanistic and behaviourist theories that 'abolish' the conscious subject; and by decentring theories of language that displace the rational subject and represent us as prisoners of the structures of language. The survival of the modern liberal conception of the subject in the popular mind can be seen either as impressive evidence in its favour, or as an indication of the pervasiveness of its ideological power.

Study questions

General question: To what extent are the radical critiques of the modern concept of the individual justified?

Further study questions: Assess the impact of these critiques on mainstream theories of rights. How do they differ from mainstream rights-scepticism? Does the emphasis on context-sensitivity effectively undermine the idea of universal rights? Compare the rights-scepticism of the critics of modernity with the rule-scepticism of the legal realists. Explain and evaluate Marx's critique of liberal rights and the monadic concept of the individual. Compare the liberal feminist approach to legal rights with the radical feminist critiques of rights. Are the feminist critiques of the individual and the concept of reason in law justified? Do the postmodernist arguments help or hinder the feminist goal of equality under the law?

Suggestions for further reading

For general reading on the values of liberalism and the Enlightenment, and their postmodernist critics, see the references at the end of Chapter 7.

Sarat and Kearns (1996) and the Oxford Amnesty Lectures in Shute and Hurley (1993) are collections that include a range of critical theories of rights. On Burke's rights-scepticism, see Waldron (1987: ch. 4). On Marx and Marxist theories of law and rights, see Cain and Hunt (1979), Patterson (1996a: ch. 23) and Morrison (1997: ch. 10). 'On the Jewish Question', one of the rare occasions on which Marx spoke explicitly about rights, is reprinted with a commentary in Waldron (1987). McLellan (1973) is a classic introduction to the life and thought of Marx. On Marx's critique of possessive individualism and rights, see MacPherson (1962).

On the CLS (critical legal studies) criticisms of rights, see Morrison (1997: ch. 16), Douzinas (2000), Patterson (1996a: ch. 7). On critical race theory and rights, see P. Williams (1991), Morrison (1997: ch. 16) and M. Davies (1994: ch. 6.4)

On the range of feminist theories and their impact on law and jurisprudence, Barnett (1998) and M. Davies (1994: ch. 6) are recommended. Also useful are Morrison (1997: ch. 17), Patterson (1996a: ch. 19), Richardson and Sandland (2000), Graycar (1990), Graycar and Morgan (2002), Frug (1992) and Kramer (1995).

Part III

Criminal responsibility and punishment

12 Guilty minds
Recklessness, manslaughter and murder

Criminal responsibility and the *mens rea* doctrine in English common law

Criminal law is concerned with the kind of conduct that is subject to state punishment. The wrongful acts and omissions that it covers have to be distinguished from torts on the one hand, wrongs which are subject only to civil law, and morally wrongful acts on the other hand, which are subject only to social disapproval, unless and until they are criminalised. Criminal law, however, is concerned not only with acts and omissions, but also with the states of mind accompanying them. In most common law jurisdictions, a defendant on a criminal charge normally has to be found guilty in mind as well as in deed. The guilty act is known as the *actus reus*. The guilty mind is called the *mens rea*. To be held guilty in mind, the defendant has to have known what she was doing, to have done it intentionally and to have carried it out of her own free will. This is the norm, and there is a strong presumption in its favour.

There is nevertheless an important exception to the principle that such *mens rea* has to be proved, when the offence has been declared by the government to be one of strict liability. With such offences, the prosecution has only to prove that the act was committed, not that it was done in any particular state of mind. Factory owners who pollute rivers with dangerous chemicals, dog-owners whose dogs are dangerously out of control in public, cannot be heard to argue that it was through no fault of their own that these things happened. This is what strict liability means. If the *actus reus* is proved, the defendant is guilty. Such offences, which are justified on the grounds of public health and safety, usually lead to heavy fines, rather than to prison sentences. For the great majority of criminal offences, however, the burden of proof is on the prosecution to show that there was indeed the necessary *mens rea* in the committing of the offence.

Intention and mens rea

As a fundamental component of *mens rea* intention is one of the most important concepts in criminal law. When it can be proved that a serious criminal offence has been committed with clear malicious intent, there is normally no difficulty in attributing *mens rea* and justifying the use of criminal law and state punishment. It is with the grey-area cases in which intention is in doubt that a problem arises. The difficulty lies in determining what counts as actual intention, and distinguishing lack of such intention from culpable lack of care, shading into openly reckless disregard for the safety of others.

Negligence and recklessness

Since the nineteenth century, a complex of laws on negligence has evolved largely through common law, with landmark cases establishing standards of care. Since 1931, there has been in law what is called *a general duty of care.* This established a standard that must be adhered to by anyone engaging in the kind of activities that it is reasonable to assume might impact directly upon the health or safety of others. In the historic ruling on *Donoghue* v. *Stevenson,* in which a manufacturer was found liable for injury caused to a consumer of his product, Lord Atkin declared that a 'neighbour principle' was observed by English law, requiring everyone to take reasonable care to avoid acts or omissions that they can reasonably foresee would be likely to injure their neighbour. This standard of what can reasonably be foreseen means that everyone must be alert to the dangers that they might be creating for others. The crucial point here is that this applies to acts or omissions that are culpably but inadvertently harmful, with no suggestion of intention or recklessness. Those who fail to reach this standard will be liable in civil law for damages. The distinction between this standard negligence and criminal recklessness is of the greatest importance. Those found guilty of the latter face gaol sentences, rather than merely financial penalties. The traditional distinction between negligence and recklessness, then, can be expressed clearly in terms of the agent's attitude towards risk-taking, thus:

> *Negligence* = the inadvertent taking of a risk through lack of reasonable care.
> *Recklessness* = the deliberate and knowing taking of an unjustifiable risk.

In a standard case of negligence, it has to be shown that there was a loss (injury, damage, harm), that there was a duty, that this duty had been breached and this breach was the cause of the loss. Typical cases include the failing to make a facility open to the public safe, when it is reasonably foreseeable that injury may occur. They do not include the deliberate and malicious exposure of people to risk. Negligence always constitutes inadvertent lack of appropriate care. This is what distinguishes it from criminal recklessness. To be charged with the latter, actual awareness of the risk and the decision to proceed regardless has to be established.

Gross negligence

One factor that complicates the distinction between civil negligence and criminal recklessness is the category of gross negligence, which is criminal and in effect equivalent to recklessness, despite the inadvertence. These are cases in which the degree and type of negligence are so extreme as failures to take due care, that they are made subject to criminal law. In the case of *R.* v. *Adomako* (1995) for example, in which an anaesthetist failed to see that an oxygen tube was disconnected, despite all the signs being visible, resulting in the patient's death, it was ruled by Lord Mackay that the omission was so serious that it had been right to leave it to the jury to decide whether the appellant's conduct was so bad as to amount to a criminal omission and conviction for man-slaughter. What this and other similar cases show is that the law takes the view that when an instance of inadvertent negligence is so extreme, it will be treated as an exception to the rule that criminality requires the kind of con-scious and deliberate carelessness or risk-taking associated with recklessness. Gross negligence is sufficient to secure the same legal outcome.

Recklessness defined subjectively

The definition of recklessness and the dispute over the kind of test that should be used by the courts to determine whether a particular act is reckless or not, has been under way for well over a century. What was to become almost a default position can be found in the case of *R.* v. *Faulkner* (1877), in which a sailor on a British Navy ship, while engaged in the illicit act of stealing rum from the spirit room, accidentally ignited the rum, starting a fire which quickly engulfed and destroyed the ship. Initially convicted of arson, he was cleared by the Court of Appeal, where it was argued that there was no evidence that the accused believed or supposed that the stealing of the rum would be attended with a result so accidental and so dangerous to himself. The appeal revolved around the defendant's state of mind at the time of the offence. Whether or not his actions were objectively dangerous was beside the point. The emphasis in this judgement is on the *actual* state of mind, what he actually believed about what he was doing. It was a question of whether malice (in the sense of actual intention or recklessness) was proved. As neither manifestation of malice had been proved, it was held that there was no guilty mind. Others have queried this. Yes, they say, it was plainly an accident, but should he really be cleared of recklessness when he must have known the dangers involved in bringing the oil lamp into close proximity with such a combustible spirit? The fact that he was thereby placing himself in such danger *should* be seen as irrelevant. People behaving recklessly often put such dangers out of mind – for example by driving too fast in the fog. Whatever reservations one may feel about this case, though, the important point that was established was that the focus of the judge's and jury's attention had to be on the actual state of mind of the defendant. It was in this sense a 'subjective' test for recklessness.

In a very different case a few years later, *R.* v. *Martin* (1881), the defendant was convicted of malicious wounding after having caused multiple injuries at a theatre by barring an escape door and turning out the lights as the audience was leaving, in order to cause panic. His defence was that it was motivated by mere mischief, rather than malice. One ruling by the Court of Appeal was that malice included mischief, so this was no defence. There was malice, they said, because there was actual intention to cause the chaos and recklessness as to the outcome. In this case, in sharp contrast to *Faulkner*, the judges are declaring Martin's actual state of mind to be irrelevant. While it was true that he intentionally caused the chaos, it was not necessary to prove that he was subjectively reckless in his actions, or that he actually foresaw the high risk of injuries. It was only necessary to show how objectively likely such injuries were. In retrospect, it is quite clear that Martin was more at fault than Faulkner, but the point to note here is that the judges were applying a different standard to establish the defendant's guilt. This was an 'objective' test for recklessness, not a subjective one.

In the course of his definition of malice in 1902, stressing the difference between the legal concept and the common understanding of 'wickedness in general', the legal authority C.S. Kenny stipulated that recklessness as to whether harm occurs or not means that 'the accused has foreseen that the particular kind of harm might be done and yet has gone on to take the risk of it' (C. Kenny 1902). It is the actual foresight that is crucial here: the danger and injuries have to be foreseen, not merely foreseeable. Kenny's principle was reaffirmed in the landmark case of *R. v. Cunningham* in 1957, when the Court of Appeal overturned a conviction for recklessly endangering life.

In this case, the defendant had inadvertently fractured a gas pipe while breaking into the cash-box to which it was attached, leading to serious injury to a person sleeping in the next room. At the appeal, the defence argued that for *mens rea* to be satisfied, the appellant must have intended to do the particular kind of harm that was done, or that he must have foreseen that that harm may occur, yet continue recklessly. This, they said, was thoroughly implausible, given that he was quite unaware of there being anyone sleeping next door. The Appeal judges ruled that the trial judge had misdirected the jury by equating malice with wickedness, thus obscuring the legal definition of recklessness. They also commented that they could not know how the jury would have decided on the defendant's actual guilt on the charge of endangering life, had they been free to consider it. The definition endorsed by this ruling is the subjective definition of recklessness, because it relates to the actual state of mind of the defendant at the time of the offence. What it means is that it is for the jury to decide what this actual state of mind was, rather than to determine what state of awareness a responsible person *should have* displayed. They have to be satisfied from all the evidence that they believe the defendant to have been subjectively guilty, rather than just behaving in an objectively dangerous manner.

The move towards objective recklessness

Not everyone in the legal profession was happy with this state of affairs. In the later twentieth century, growing dissatisfaction with the subjective

Kenny–Cunningham definition culminated in the establishment of a new test for recklessness, in the rulings on *MPC (Metropolitan Police Commissioner)* v. *Caldwell* and *R.* v. *Lawrence*, both in 1982. In *Caldwell*, an ex-employee of a hotel who believed himself to have been unfairly dismissed sought his revenge, after drinking heavily, by breaking windows and starting a fire on the carpet at night, while ten guests were asleep upstairs. He was charged with criminal damage and recklessly endangering life. Caldwell's defence to the latter charge was that in his inebriated state he did not contemplate the dangers to life. This was rejected on appeal against his conviction, on the grounds that for offences of basic intent (recklessness) there was no need to prove intention. The ruling by the majority amounted to an expansion of the test for recklessness. The subsequent shift in the law was reinforced by a ruling on the same day on another case, *R.* v. *Lawrence* (1982), in which a motorcyclist had killed a pedestrian allegedly through reckless driving. The new test for recklessness that emerged from both rulings has often since been called 'Caldwell–Lawrence' recklessness. What was common to both was Lord Diplock's reference to 'the ordinary prudent individual' as the yardstick by which to judge the defendant.

The outcome of these two cases was that there were now two legal tests for recklessness alongside each other. The broader scope of *Caldwell–Lawrence*, however, soon made *Cunningham* irrelevant:

- According to the old subjective test (Cunningham reckless), the defendant who sees the risk and proceeds regardless is guilty of a reckless act.
- According to the new objective test, the defendant *either* sees the risk and proceeds regardless, *or* does an act which creates an obvious risk, but gives no thought to the possibility of such risk and proceeds to act in a dangerous manner.

These are described as the two 'limbs' of the Caldwell test, which are conceived in such a way that one or the other can be applied to cover every eventuality, or any case in which recklessness should properly be attributed to defendants.

The Caldwell lacuna

It soon became clear, however, that the Caldwell test did not cover every eventuality. The wording of the two limbs, dividing the test into subjective and objective alternatives, in fact allowed a wide loophole or 'lacuna' to open up, such that there were many cases of apparent recklessness which could not be subsumed under either limb. It was then unclear whether such anomalies should be categorised as a third type of recklessness, or as a legitimate defence. The essential point was that there were many cases in which the defendant had seen the risk, then taken great care to avoid causing harm or injury, but failed to avoid it. This could not be classed as recklessness under either the subjective limb, which ruled out the taking of care, or the objective limb, which stipulated that they had not seen the risk, but should have done. The problem is that such cases can still look like recklessness, because they should not have been engaged in such risks in the first place.

Criticisms of the objective test

For just over twenty years – 1982–2003 – the Caldwell test was applied to cases of recklessness, thus allowing the objective test alongside the old subjective test, such that juries who failed to find defendants guilty according to their actual state of mind could fall back on the grounds of what a reasonable and prudent individual would understand about the risks they were running. Although this was gradually reined in, to apply to offences against property but not to offences against the person, it was constantly problematic in many ways. The main problem in addition to that of the lacuna was the attribution of the ideal standard of 'the reasonable person' to each and every individual, regardless of age, mental capacity or any other deviation from the norm presupposed by this standard. There were a number of publicised injustices against defendants with learning difficulties and those with mental illness. Beyond this, however, it was thought by critics to be deeply unjust to apply a fictitious standard which took no account of individual idiosyncrasies. The crucial criticism was that what the objective test amounted to was the suspension of the *mens rea* requirement. Connected with this was the criticism that in some cases it amounted to criminalising negligence. In 2003, the Law Lords finally overturned *Caldwell*, declaring it to be bad law in their ruling on *R. v. G. and another* (2003) (known as *R. v. Gemmel and Richards*) and restored the subjective Cunningham test.

Intentional killing and murder

Murder and manslaughter: the basic distinction

> Murder is when a man of sound memory, and of the age of discretion, unlawfully killeth within any county of the realm any reasonable creature *in rerum natura* under the king's peace, with malice aforethought, either expressed by the party or implied by law, so as the party wounded or hurt die of the wound or hurt within a year and a day after the same.
>
> (Sir Edward Coke, *Institutes of the Lawes of England*, 1797,
> 3 Inst. 47, in Smith 2002: 353)

As this quote indicates, the *mens rea* for murder has long been malice aforethought. This is what one guilty of murder has, and one guilty of manslaughter lacks. In addition to the *actus reus*, the malice aforethought must also be present. Great care should be taken with this expression, however, as it does not mean what it does in everyday language. In law, it does not mean malicious in the sense of being vindictive – which it may or may not be – and it does not require any feeling of ill-will towards anyone. Furthermore, 'afore-thought' does not mean premeditated, in the normal sense of being planned. It means only that the intention must be formed in advance of carrying out the act, and there is no minimum time requirement. One can decide to kill and do so a split second later without any further reflection and still be convicted of murder. This particular point is often misunderstood when defences are run, claiming the act to be spontaneous rather than premeditated. Such defences are always rejected under English law if the relevant *mens rea* conditions are satisfied. Our starting point here, then, is this distinction:

Murder = the unlawful premeditated killing of person or persons by another with malice aforethought.

Manslaughter = the unlawful killing of person or persons by another without malice aforethought.

Involuntary manslaughter

The first qualification to this distinction is that there are forms of voluntary manslaughter in which the *mens rea* for murder is satisfied, but for special reasons the charge is reduced to the lesser one. These reasons we will be dealing with in the chapter on insanity. For present purposes, by far the most common and the most important is the involuntary form of manslaughter. What this means is that although the defendant is guilty of committing an unlawful act causing a death, the complete absence of intention clears him or her of the charge of murder. In legal terms there is no malice aforethought, but they are guilty of manslaughter through *either*

• an unlawful or dangerous act, *or*
• gross negligence or recklessness.

Involuntary manslaughter involves substantial culpability but no actual intention to cause harm or death, and no awareness that one is likely to cause a death. The act may be unlawful and dangerous, which is to say a highly risky criminal action, or involve gross negligence, behaving with excessive lack of care in an exceptionally foolish way, or it might involve the reckless taking of unnecessary risks with people's lives and safety, but what holds it on this side of the line from murder is the absence of malicious intention towards those who have died. It should be noted that this is sometimes quite a fine line to draw.

The main conceptual problem with manslaughter is to establish its upper and lower boundaries. It has to be distinguished from murder on the one hand and accidental death on the other. In a typical case, the defendant in *R.* v. *Goodfellow* (1986) conspired with his wife to get his family rehoused by the Local Authority by setting fire to his house and staging a rescue of the occupants, including another woman and three children. One child and the two women died in the fire, as it spread more quickly than anticipated. His appeal against his conviction for manslaughter was rejected, as was his argument that the act was not directed at the victims and the deaths were an unpredictable accident. The act clearly qualified as unlawful and dangerous, and might equally have been held to constitute manslaughter through recklessness. The act also falls decidedly short of murder, because nobody thought that he actually intended any personal harm and certainly not anyone's death. In other words, there was no malice aforethought. The specific intention or malice was directed at property, which he aimed to destroy, not at persons.

Types of malice aforethought

Malice in law comes in different forms. In the past, there were three categories of malice, each of which could lead to a conviction for murder. The first and most obvious was 'express malice', which means that there was an actual explicit intention to kill the victim. The second category is known as 'implied malice', and has been deeply controversial in modern times. The intention in such cases is not actually to kill, but rather to inflict grievous bodily harm (really serious injury) on the victim, who then dies from the injury. This kind of malice was said by Coke to be 'implied by law' (see above), by which he means that it is simply stipulated by common law that acts with such intentions and outcomes will be considered murder. The idea behind this is that if a man renders another unconscious by violent means, aiming only to inflict this injury, the probability of the victim dying as a result of the attack is high enough to justify a conviction for murder if death does ensue. As we shall see shortly, there are serious problems with this category of malice.

The third category is that of 'constructive malice'. This was not included in Coke's definition; it evolved in common law over the following centuries, and was even more controversial. This is sometimes called 'felony murder', as it is the *mens rea* for the felony that is all that has to be proved. If someone inadvertently causes a death while committing a felony, there is no need to prove intention to kill or wound. The death can even be a complete accident, if it is the result of the intended felony. In modern times, this was thought to be such dubious law that it was in practice downplayed by judges as early as the late nineteenth century. The tendency was to restrict it to the context of violent crimes when the circumstances were particularly damning for the felon. When the move to abolish this category of malice by statute came in 1957, parliament was only endorsing a long-held negative view of it. Today, there are similar formulations in various jurisdictions around the world, but in the UK, constructive malice has been consigned to the past. The manner of its abolition, however, inadvertently created a problem. The wording of the statute was ambiguous enough to allow some interpreters to read it as if it had done away with implied malice as well.

Intending to kill and intending harm

The dispute over intended malice is between those who believe that the charge of murder should be reserved for those whose acts show express malice, and those who think many cases in which this explicit intention is absent are sufficiently serious to class as murder, because what they actually did intend was not far short, and in effect equally culpable. The 1957 Homicide Act (s. 1) explicitly abolished constructive malice for murder. It did not, however, abolish implied malice. There is no dispute over whether constructive malice was abolished. It was gone, and there has been no attempt to restore it. There has, however, been a great deal of confusion on this question, because of conflicting interpretations. The Court of Appeal in the case of *R*. v. *Vickers* in 1957, immediately following the Act, interpreted the relevant section as retaining the extension of murder to cases in which the victim died, but only grievous bodily harm was intended (i.e. implied malice). The defendant broke into a shop intending to steal. He was seen and recognised by the occupant of the living quarters above the shop, an elderly woman of seventy-two, who attempted to raise the alarm. The defendant ascended the stairs, attacked her and struck her many blows and kicked her repeatedly in the face until she was unconscious. She died soon afterwards in hospital from the injuries inflicted. Vickers was convicted of murder and sentenced to death. He appealed.

Vickers's defence relied on the new Homicide Act and on his behalf it was argued that there was no specific intention to kill, that he only intended limited harm, hence there was no express malice aforethought. This was rejected by the Court of Appeal. The judge ruled that although 'perhaps only intending to render her unconscious ... he is guilty of murder because he has killed a person with the necessary malice aforethought being implied from the fact that he intended to do grievous bodily harm' (Allen and Cooper 2010: 448). This was a crucial ruling, reinforcing the long-standing common law principle that the intention to commit grievous bodily harm does indeed satisfy the *mens rea* for murder.

Proposals for reform

More recently, there has been much controversy over this issue. Is it really appropriate, it is asked, to class as murder an act in which the agent had no intention to kill at all? Surely it is just a misfortune when a victim dies as a result of an act by an agent who had no such intention? Should this not be manslaughter through unlawful and dangerous act? In line with this thinking, the Law Commission in 2002 proposed that:

A person is guilty of murder if he causes the death of another –
(a)   intending to cause death; OR

(b)   intending to cause serious personal harm and *being aware that* he may cause death.

… a person acts 'intentionally' with respect to … a result when he acts either in order to bring it about or *being aware that* it will occur in the ordinary course of things.

(Smith 2002: 362, also in Allen 2001: 88; italics mine)

This minor adjustment would sensibly rule out a person who, despite his intention to cause serious harm, did not foresee the risk of death. Such an act would be one of manslaughter, rather than murder. The point is that this category (implied malice) as it stands is too blunt an instrument for distinguishing properly between the two charges. The law needs to separate those who have the required malicious intent – hence the malice aforethought – from those who do not. So *being aware* that death might occur should be a minimal condition of a conviction for murder. With this amendment, defendants like Vickers would still be convicted; others less reprehensible, in cases where it is clear that the death was the result of bad luck rather than malice, would not be: for example, a death unexpectedly following a street brawl, when there was an intention to harm but not to kill and no awareness of the danger of death. Maintaining this distinction, however, allowing implied malice more carefully defined, is essential for upholding the credibility of the law.

Contemplating the death

In the premodern era, one of the strongest indicators of a guilty mind with respect to murder was evidence that the accused had contemplated the death of his or her victim. This idea was seen as a prominent component of the *mens rea* for murder. This was a broad concept, intended to embrace several aspects of the state of mind. It meant not simply thinking about, or reflecting upon a course of action, but also taking steps to bring about the death. It also meant that they intended the death, but it covered two senses of intending: (1) bringing about the death as the purpose behind the action, which is a very explicit form of intention; and (2) intending it in the wider sense that they carry out an act with a different purpose, knowing full well that it is also going to bring about a death. The idea, then, was that if they contemplated the death of their victim in either of these ways, they were guilty of murder. If they did not contemplate it at all, they were not. It was the vagueness of this concept, allowing multiple interpretations, which prompted the modern attempt to make it more precise by analysing the meaning of intention. This traditional test for murder of whether the accused had contemplated the death was the background to Bentham's attempt to reform the common law on this point. He thought the concept of contemplating the death was too vague and ambiguous and allowed inconsistent results and convictions in the courts.

Direct and oblique intention

The distinction that stands right at the centre of this debate is drawn between direct intention and indirect (or oblique) intention. It is easy to misinterpret the purpose of this distinction if it is taken as the demarcation line between murder and manslaughter. It is nothing of the sort, and it was never meant to be. Bentham drew this distinction in order to extend the category of murder to include those who were plainly guilty of contemplating a death, yet might argue that their intentions were quite different, and thus guilty only of manslaughter. Direct and oblique intention are proposed as just that, two kinds of intention, either of which justifies classifying the act as one of murder.

The distinction thus extends the category of murder to those whose main purpose was not to kill, nor to harm in any way, yet their actions were such that they were fully aware that they would or might result in death. A directly intended consequence is the agent's demonstrable purpose. An obliquely intended consequence is one which is closely tied up with this intended consequence, though not itself intended or wanted for its own sake.

Over time, there have been three tests devised for the drawing of the direct–oblique distinction. The first is the causal link test, which was Bentham's own explanation of it. A consequence is obliquely intended if the prospect of bringing it about played no causal part in the formation of the agent's intention to commit the act. If it was indeed causally linked, the intention was to be taken as direct. Either way, the act is one of murder. It is only manslaughter if the death was not intended in either sense, so that it is neither direct nor oblique. In other words, it is not sufficient to argue that the death played no part in one's deliberations or calculations prior to the act. It is still murder.

There are problems, however, with this causal link test. By phrasing it in a negative way, by specifying the kind of defence to be ruled out, it states what cannot be counted as unintentional, but it does nothing to clarify the class of acts that should be seen as falling *outside* the category of murder. In other words: 'No causal link = obliquely intended'. This formula can add confusion rather than removing it, because 'no causal link' can also mean 'not intended at all'.

A second test – which has come to be known as the failure test – was articulated later, to throw light upon the meaning and implications of the direct–oblique distinction. According to this test, a consequence is obliquely intended if the agent's main enterprise would have been counted a success even if the fatal consequence failed to occur. It means that the death would have been thought of as an irrelevance. If it would have been counted a failure, the act was directly intended. If not, it was still obliquely intended. It would still be murder. The point is that it is not sufficient to reduce the offence to manslaughter to argue that the death was not the main purpose.

This only added to the confusion left by the causal test. It seems to suggest that oblique intention is less reprehensible than direct intention, yet the very point of it is to insist that they are both sufficiently bad to count as murder. Also, again, this test does nothing to clarify which acts should be seen as falling outside the circle of acts of murder. What it seems to do is open up the category of murder to many acts that one would otherwise have seen as manslaughter, in any case in which death occurred without being the main purpose of the act (unlawful killing without malice aforethought, through 'unlawful and dangerous act' or 'reckless' actions). It would seem to confirm that these are obliquely intended, therefore to count as murder, which is quite wrong. It would only be right if they knew perfectly well that somebody would very likely die as a result of their actions.

In short, the problem is this. There is no doubt at all that directly intended acts are plain cases of murder. That is true by definition. However, the fact that obliquely intended acts span the categories of murder and manslaughter is systematically concealed by the direct–oblique distinction. The advantage of the distinction interpreted thus is that it rightly removes a class of acts from the category of manslaughter, those which should be classed as murder (those in which they know perfectly well that their acts are likely to cause a death). The disadvantage is that it threatens to undermine the distinction between murder and manslaughter altogether.

Now consider the more recent interpretation of this distinction from the 1980s (which is generally applied today). The so-called 'corner of the eye' test was devised by Glanville Williams:

> Direct intention is where the consequence is what you are aiming at. Oblique intention is something *you see clearly, but out of the corner of your eye*. The consequence is not in the straight line of your purpose, but a side-effect that you accept as an inevitable accompaniment of your direct intent. There are twin consequences of the act, *x* and *y*; the doer wants *x*, and is *prepared to accept its unwanted twin* y. Oblique intent is, in other words, a kind of knowledge or realisation.
>
> (G. Williams 1987: 421; italics mine)

On this definition a consequence is obliquely intended (and thus still fully reprehensible) if it was foreseen clearly, but from the corner of the eye, outside of the straight line of one's purpose. This is the important emphasis: the consequence is *actually foreseen clearly* – on the other two tests, this is not explicitly required. If you see the consequence (the death) and accept it as inevitable, then you are guilty of murder.

This interpretation has not been universally popular. If you saw it clearly, some critics think, then it must have been fully within the field of your conscious awareness, not somewhere around the edges, in which case it is as good as direct. Whatever the truth of this objection, this test has the advantage over the other two that it at least gives guidance on how to distinguish, not only the two classes of direct and oblique intention, but also the obliquely intended from the third class of entirely unintentional causing of death without malice aforethought, in other words keeping the manslaughter option distinct. These are the acts that you did not foresee, even from the corner of the eye. You had no idea that you might be causing death. So on this model, manslaughter is when you do not foresee it, even from the corner of the eye.

One case often used to illustrate these distinctions is that of *R. v. Desmond, Barrett and Others* (1868). The defendants were members of the Fenian Brotherhood, whose objectives were to establish an independent Irish Republic. In an unsuccessful attempt to rescue two of their members from Clerkenwell Gaol they detonated a barrel of gunpowder outside the prison wall. The aim was to blow a hole in the wall during the prisoners' exercise period. The subsequent explosion was larger than they expected, and the victims included a woman in an adjacent house, who was killed outright, and another woman and three young children playing nearby, who were seriously injured in the blast. Four men were charged with murder. Barrett, who had lit the fuse, was found guilty and was sentenced to death. The others were found not guilty. Regarding the direct–oblique intention distinction, Lord Chief Justice Coleridge stated that it is murder 'if a man did an act not with the purpose of taking life but with the knowledge or belief that life was likely to be sacrificed by it'. (A. Kenny 1978: 31).

Should this have been murder or manslaughter? It was certainly 'an unlawful and dangerous act', and maybe it was reckless, but was there malice aforethought? Applying Bentham's causal test, the intention to kill was certainly not direct. The prospect of the death that occurred played no part in the forming of their intention to facilitate the escape by blowing up the wall. Barrett may have been indifferent to this danger, but it was no part of his plan to kill anyone. On the second 'failure' test, if nobody had died – as was quite possible – and had the escape been successful, they would not have regarded the enterprise as a failure. Each of these tests point to the conclusion that there was an oblique intention to kill, but the truth is that there may have been no intention to kill at all. What these tests taken in themselves imply is that even if the defendants did not intend or foresee the deaths, they were still guilty of murder – which has to be wrong. What the tests fail to distinguish between is those acts which do obliquely intend death, and those which do not intend it in either sense. This is the source of confusion in many writers who have advocated the outright abolition of oblique intention and the restriction of the *mens rea* for murder to direct intention.

A more acceptable approach would be based on the corner of the eye test, asking whether or not the defendants did actually clearly foresee – albeit from the corner of the eye – the probability of death. If they did, they obliquely intended it and are guilty of murder. If they did not, they did not intend it in either sense and are guilty of manslaughter through an unlawful and dangerous act. It is this either/or that the court has to remain open to. It is only murder if they did clearly see that they might well kill somebody, yet still went ahead. Given the proximity of potential victims, it does look in this case as though Barrett, who lit the fuse, did see this, so if the corner of the eye test had been applied, it may well have been sufficient to convict him. It is this question, however, that has to be left to the jury after closely considering all the evidence. Does it, however, qualify as murder anyway on the grounds of constructive malice, given that the death occurred in the course of a felony? If this was, as some have suggested, the sole basis for Barrett's conviction, it would imply that this and cases like it should be classed as manslaughter if the jury accepts that the death was neither directly intended nor actually foreseen at all. It would only be murder if the death was the price he was prepared to pay for the success of the enterprise.

Inseparable and separable consequences

The corner of the eye test has also been criticised for creating a very high standard of predictability of death for the act to be counted as murder. The unwanted side-effect – the death – is seen as 'the inevitable accompaniment' of what is directly intended, and is described as an 'unwanted twin' that the agent is prepared to accept as the price s/he is prepared to pay for the success of the enterprise. This line of thought binds together very closely the main purpose with the side-effects, so that what is required for oblique intent, hence murder rather than manslaughter, is a virtual certainty that the unintended deaths will occur. It seems that anything less than this 'preparation to accept the death as a price' would lead to a conviction for the lesser offence of manslaughter through recklessness. If the foresight is described as 'a kind of knowledge or realisation', rather than merely an awareness of the danger one is placing people in, then there are varying degrees of probability – from very high to very low, fading to mere possibility – which would lead to manslaughter rather than murder.

A prime example commonly used to illustrate the point about inseparable consequences – where the certainty of death is brought about by an act with an oblique intention – is that of a saboteur placing a bomb on an airplane with the aim of destroying the cargo. While the bomber does not actually intend the deaths of the people on board, he knows that these are virtually certain consequences – indeed, as certain as it is ever possible to be about anything. In such cases, the agent is plainly to be held fully responsible for the deaths, whatever the explicit intentions. The intention is oblique because there is no causal link between the prospect of the deaths and the decision to commit the act, and the enterprise of destroying the cargo would have been counted successful without the deaths. According to Williams' new legal distinction – the corner of the eye test – such 'side-effects' are obliquely intended, which is just as culpable as being fully intended. Not all cases of unintentional homicide, however, result in consequences so closely bound up with the act. With dangerous acts in general, there are degrees of likelihood that fatal consequences will occur, ranging from virtual certainty through degrees of probability to remote possibility. In Barrett's case, it seems from the evidence that the likelihood of death was very high, but one could not call this inseparable consequences, as all the victims might well have survived. All one could say is that it was certainly not surprising that someone was killed. On Williams' definition, then, Barrett would probably have been found not guilty of murder. In grey areas like these, it is much harder than in clear-cut cases such as the bombed plane to decide whether or not the defendant is guilty of murder, as we shall see in the cases that follow.

The subjective–objective controversy

The key question for determining the extent of responsibility for secondary side-effects of one's actions relates to the kind of test that is applied by the courts to establish the *mens rea* requirement of malice aforethought for murder. The main issue here is whether the test is a subjective one, in the sense of whether it is a matter of determining what the defendant actually foresaw and believed about the circumstances in which the death was caused, or an objective one, in the sense that it is a matter of determining what was reasonably foreseeable and believable about those circumstances. We have already seen earlier in this chapter how this has been disputed in the context of recklessness. The law on murder, however, is quite different and more complex, but there are some similarities. As with the law on recklessness, the law on murder also deviated for a short period from the long-established *mens rea* norm that the test was subjective.

If the test for the *mens rea* is subjective, it means that the jury has to reach a conclusion from the evidence about the defendant's actual state of mind at the time of the offence. What consequences did they anticipate or foresee? How likely did they believe them to be? What did they actually intend when they proceeded with the act? If, alternatively, the test is objective, they do not have to ask these questions at all. It means that it is sufficient for the court to establish what it would have been reasonable to believe in the position of the defendant. What consequences would a reasonable person have foreseen? How likely in fact were they? What can the defendant be taken to have intended, given the actual foreseeability and likelihood of these consequences? These are very different questions, and they assume the existence of 'a reasonable person'.

This issue became acutely controversial during the 'capital murder' period following the 1957 Homicide Act. In the case of *DPP* v. *Smith* (1961) a man trying to drive away in a car containing stolen scaffolding clips caused the death of a police officer who was clinging to the door of the car. By wildly zigzagging, he succeeded in throwing him off, but the constable fell into the path of an oncoming car. Smith returned a few minutes later, to discover that the policeman was dead, and was horrified by what he had done. He denied having had any intention to cause serious harm or to kill him.

Smith was charged with murder, convicted and sentenced to death. The jury had been directed to decide whether he should have realised that at least grievous bodily harm was the likely outcome of his action. At the Court of Criminal Appeal, the defence argued that the judge had misdirected the jury by applying the test of the reasonable man, when the test should have been whether he actually intended to cause serious harm or death. The Court substituted a conviction for manslaughter and a ten-year prison sentence. They ruled that the relevant test was not 'reasonable foreseeability', but the outcome he actually contemplated (or actually foresaw). The *mens rea* was the straightforward one of whether or not he meant to kill.

When the appeal by the Crown went to the Lords, the argument between defence and prosecution revolved around the issue of the appropriate test for *mens rea*. Counsel for the prosecution argued that the law made a presumption that a man intends the natural and probable consequences of his acts. From that, an intent to cause serious harm or death can be inferred. Any reasonable man would have seen such harm or death as the natural consequence of driving in this manner. Smith was a reasonable man in the sense that he was neither insane nor incapable of forming an intention. Therefore, Smith must have intended serious injury or death. It was no defence to say that he did not actually foresee these consequences.

The case for the defence was that a murder conviction could only be upheld if the intention to cause serious harm or death was actually in the mind of the accused. This, they insisted, is what it comes down to. A central point was their argument that the presumption of intent (of natural and probable consequences) should be regarded as disprovable by the specific circumstances of the case, in this instance the claim that the defendant was driven by fear and panic. They added that if the reasonable man test is to be used, it must be that of the reasonable man in the position of the defendant, rather than in the position of reflecting on the facts from outside, after the event.

Faced with these alternatives, the Lords came to the unanimous decision that Smith had been properly convicted of murder, and that it was indeed appropriate to apply the reasonable man test and make the presumption of intent. In rejecting what they called 'the purely subjective approach', they declared that it was self-evidently wrong because it would oblige the jury to take the word of the defendant and acquit him, and that the subjective test would constitute a serious departure from all previous law. We can see from our vantage point today that this was a highly inaccurate assessment of all previous law, and it was backed up, oddly enough, by reference to the authority of Oliver Wendell Holmes Jr, who had written in 1881 that the law would not inquire whether the offender did actually foresee the consequences or not. For Holmes, the test of foresight was not what this very criminal foresaw, but what a man of reasonable prudence would have foreseen (Hart 1968). This was a strange authority to cite as representative of 'all previous law', because Holmes was well known to be out of step with prevailing legal opinion on objective liability. It is also highly questionable to argue that the subjective test obliges juries to take the word of the defendant. Nearly all defendants deny intention to kill, but it is the crucial role of the jury to assess their credibility and they have always been free to reject such declarations of innocence, as they often do.

What makes it unclear whether this judgement does or does not conform with the principles of the *mens rea* for murder as malice aforethought, is the studied ambiguity in the supposed presumption that he intended the natural and probable consequences of his act, as to whether this presumption means that, as a sane and sober man, he must actually have done so, or that if, as a reasonable man acting unreasonably, he did not intend them, then so much the worse for him. This ambiguity pervades the judgement. Even on the former interpretation that Smith must in fact have intended the death, it means that the determination of actual intent is taken out of the hands of the jury. They are simply instructed to make the connection without reference to the defendant's own account of his actions. Smith's ultimate fate was that he was reprieved by the Home Secretary and served a prison sentence for murder.

Whatever the perceived rights and wrongs of this decision, it was not long before Parliament – under the influence of recommendations from the Law Commission – intervened to restore the subjective test by statute in the 1967 Criminal Justice Act, section 8. This section implicitly rejected the reasonable man test by laying down that courts or juries were to determine whether a person was guilty, not by inferring intent or foresight of results of his actions solely from their natural and probable consequences, but by deciding whether he did intend or foresee them by reference to all the evidence as appears proper in the circumstances. It was this contrast between the presumption of intent and reference to 'all the evidence' that was vital. The totality of evidence included what the presumption was designed to exclude; the defendant's own account of his actions, however apparently unreasonable, are indispensable to the jury's consideration of whether or not there was actual intent to do serious harm or to kill. This meant, not that the natural and probable consequences were to be disregarded, but that there was to be no *presumption* that they were intended. As for the suggestion that with the subjective test in place, juries would be obliged to believe the defendant and acquit him, this is simply a misreading of what the subjective test requires, that they take the *mens rea* requirement of proving malice aforethought seriously, not that they display credulity towards any story a defendant cares to invent.

In short, the jury must be satisfied that there was actual intention to kill or at least actual intention to cause grievous bodily harm, otherwise it is manslaughter. At the same time, however, it was stated that the jury is entitled to use the objective 'reasonable person' test as part of the total evidence, provided that they explicitly draw the inference from this to the conclusion that the defendant was actually subjectively guilty. This has been described as a compromise between the two tests, allowing both their place, but in effect it means that the jury must in the end be satisfied that there was actual subjective intention to kill or actual intention to cause grievous bodily harm, otherwise it is manslaughter. That is the essence of how the law still stands on this matter today. It is not a purely subjective test, but the attempt in the ruling on *Smith* to replace it with an objective test was decisively rejected. This compromise is widely regarded as having struck the right balance.

The crucial point is that actual intent always has to be proved. The conditions for establishing the *mens rea* for murder by clarifying what malice aforethought means, is absolutely essential, but they do not point one way or the other to the guilt or innocence of any of these defendants. The crux of the matter is that real actual intention – whether to kill, to inflict serious injury, or to expose to deadly danger – is a necessary condition for convicting a defendant of murder. In the words of Lord Lane, ruling on a later case:

> a jury simply has to decide whether the defendant intended to kill or do serious bodily harm. In order to reach that decision, the jury must pay regard to all the relevant circumstances, including what the defendant himself said and did.
>
> (Allen 2001: 90)

Probability and foresight

The law on the question of the *mens rea* requirement for murder was clarified further and ostensibly settled in the mid-1980s, but not without further complications. In the case of *DPP* v. *Hyam* (1975), in which a woman motivated by jealousy set fire to her rival's house, killing two children sleeping there, her conviction for murder was upheld by the Law Lords who argued that deliberate exposure of people to deadly risk satisfied *mens rea*. There was much dispute over whether this was another attempt to turn the law back in the direction of objectivism, but it has been convincingly argued that this did not contradict the law on combining the subjective and objective tests.

Regarding probability, there are two connected problems to look at here. First, in the phrase 'natural and probable consequences of an act', does 'natural' mean the same as 'probable'? Second, is the intending of these consequences the same thing as foreseeing them? For any natural course of events, which can take one turn or another, there are estimates of probability and virtual certainty of possible outcomes of acts. For any dangerous act, such as the firing of a gun, there is usually more than one possible sequence of natural consequences that might occur. If the one sequence realised in the actual world involves the death of someone in the line of fire, this outcome will be seen in retrospect as the natural – and perhaps inevitable – outcome of the act. If, however, another quite different sequence were to be realised, such as the unexpected harmless deflection of the bullet, it would be seen in retrospect as an equally natural – if unlikely – turn of events and outcome of the act. The point is that a process is natural regardless of whether it is seen in advance as virtually certain, as fairly probable, or as a remote possibility. Whatever the prediction, a complete chain of cause and effect will still be traceable after the event.

In any of the cases discussed in the last few sections, it seems reasonable to suppose that the degree of probability or certainty of the outcome that did in fact occur should play a vital role in arguments about the evidence for the actual intent. Consider some slight variations on the facts of the cases. If the constable had died as a result of being thrown back immediately from the car as it took off, rather than when it had already reached a dangerous speed, the much lower likelihood of death would have counted heavily in favour of the defendant. If Hyam's fire had caused death only by spreading to neighbouring houses because of an unexpected change of wind, the evidence of actual intent to kill would have been very much weaker. The assessment of likelihood, then, in the mind of the defendant and in the judgement of the jury, is an indispensable part of the evidence for intent. In the case of *R.* v. *Moloney* (1985), the defendant denied intent when on trial for shooting his stepfather dead in what he claimed was a friendly gun-loading contest under the influence of drink. The judge's instruction that the jury should find him guilty if they were satisfied that death was the 'probable' outcome of this reckless contest, led to a verdict of murder, and was interpreted by the Court of Appeal as in effect an attempt to restore the objective test. They ruled that such probabilities had to be 'little short of overwhelming' to establish murder. That was an innovation which was to stick.

Just as the probability of the consequences of an act is relevant as evidence for intent to kill, so also is the foresight of these consequences. If it is found that the defendant saw that a certain outcome would probably happen, or was virtually certain to occur, the strength of evidence here would increase in proportion to the level of probability foreseen. The point here is that foresight is evidence of actual intent; it does not actually constitute intent. The existence of intent is inferred from the fact of foresight. It is not in itself sufficient to prove that the defendant foresaw an outcome, whatever the degree of probability or certainty. This proof is a preliminary to drawing the inference from foresight to intent, which is left to the jury.

Conclusion

These are some of the key themes in the question of what determines responsibility, the details of which are regularly disputed in the appeal courts. If the doctrine of *mens rea* is broadly speaking a just one, both its basic principles and the ways in which it is converted into just decisions, have to remain under scrutiny. Being subject to evolution in the common law, pronouncements and adjustments to the application of the doctrine by Parliament and the Law Lords have been guided by a concern for precedent and continuity with earlier interpretations, but such adjustment always involves clarification and thereby a new interpretation of what is supposedly already implicit in the law. What should be clear from the small sample of cases given in this chapter is that there is a permanent tension within the concept of criminal justice, between the principles of justice as recognised by the *mens rea* doctrine and the perceived requirements of public policy.

Study questions

General question: Critically assess the application of the *mens rea* doctrine to the offences of recklessness and murder in English criminal law.

Further study questions: How does recklessness differ from negligence? What is it that turns mere negligence into a criminal act? Should the test for recklessness be subjective or objective? Explain the problems with both. Should those cases which fall into the Caldwell lacuna be excused criminal conviction? How does the *mens rea* for murder differ from that of lesser criminal offences? How is murder distinguished from manslaughter? Should implied malice be sufficient to convict for murder? Explain the idea of contemplating the death of another as the condition for convicting a defendant of murder. Did the distinction between direct and oblique intention solve the problems raised by this condition? Is the clear foresight of a death that is not intended sufficient for murder? How high does the probability of death have to be? Overall, does the doctrine of *mens rea* require that death must have been actually intended or objectively likely?

Suggestions for further reading

The basic legal details and cases for negligence, recklessness and murder can be found in the relevant chapters of *Smith and Hogan's Criminal Law* (14th edn, Ormerod and Laird 2015), or *Elliott and Wood's Cases and Materials on Criminal Law* (11th edn, Allen and Cooper 2013). The latest editions of these sources should be used if possible. Also useful in this respect is Nicola Padfield's *Criminal Law* (9th edn, 2014) and Jonathan Herring's *Criminal Law* (7th edn, 2016).

Major contributions to the analysis of criminal responsibility and the philosophy of action include Hart (1968), A. Kenny (1978), Duff (1990), Norrie (2014), Katz (1987), M. Moore (1993) and Gardner (2007).

On negligence and recklessness, more extensive analysis can be found in Duff (1990: ch. 7) and Norrie (2014: ch. 4).

On strict liability and negligence, see Hart (1968: ch. 6), Jacobs (1971: chs 4, 5), A. Kenny (1978: chs 1, 3) and Ten (1987: ch. 5), and also Hart's 'Legal Responsibility and Excuses' and Wasserstrom's 'Strict Liability in the Criminal Law', both in Kipnis (1977). See also the selections on 'Negligence, Recklessness, and Strict Liability' in Morris (1961: ch. 5).

On murder and manslaughter see Bentham (1970: ch. 8), Hart (1968: ch. 5), Duff (1982, 1990), Gavison (1987: ch. 6), Kenny's 'Intention and *Mens Rea* in Murder' in Hacker and Raz (1977), Glover (1977: ch. 6) and Norrie (2014: ch. 3). See also the selections on 'intention and motive' in Morris (1961: ch. 4).

13 Unlawful killing
The defences of necessity and duress

According to the doctrine of *mens rea*, as we have seen, the law requires that the defendant be guilty in mind as well as in deed. The three conditions to be satisfied are that the criminal act was carried out intentionally, knowingly and of the defendant's own free will. It is the last of these conditions that is now coming under scrutiny, and it is in many ways the most problematic of the three. The defences of necessity and duress are both complete defences, which if successful lead to acquittal. In such cases, they admit to the *actus reus*, but deny the *mens rea*. In both of them, the question of how free their action was is central to the deliberations on their guilt or innocence. We will consider the defence of duress first.

The defence of duress

There are ways of putting pressure upon people without using overt physical force, such as moral pressure, blackmail or economic strangleholds, such that the victim's freedom of manoeuvre is severely limited. The only kind of pressure allowed by law as constituting duress is that of threats of physical harm or death to the victims or to others if they fail to comply. For legal purposes, this is what acting under duress means – this is usually expressed as 'succumbing to the threats of others'. The defence has been allowed in English law for a multitude of offences, such as shoplifting, receiving stolen goods, criminal damage, drugs offences or arson. It has always been excluded for murder and nearly always for closely related offences such as attempted murder, or aiding and abetting. Around the rest of the common law world, we find a similar situation, with much variation in details.

When the defence of duress is run, there are strict conditions and high standards of proof. The threat must be immediate and credible, it must be of a very serious nature, involving personal injury or death to oneself or others. Other forms of coercion, such as blackmail or financial pressure, are deemed irrelevant. It must not be self-induced, by voluntary association with those making the threats. The burden of proof lies with the defendant, not with the state. These conditions may sound harsh and limiting, but it is clear enough why the law imposes tight conditions. As is often pointed out by critics, this

214 Criminal responsibility and punishment

defence is easy to fake or exploit. The upshot is that someone who can prove that they genuinely were under serious duress can – subject to the limitation excluding murder already noted – be acquitted of the offence completely.

One of the most famous examples of duress of threats was, ironically, a case in which the defendant did not opt to avail himself of this defence, because he mistakenly believed that the defence was not available for a charge of treason. In *R.* v. *Steane* (1947), a film actor who had found himself in Germany at the outbreak of war in 1939 had been immediately taken into custody by the Gestapo, because they saw the propaganda potential in recruiting a British citizen to work in their film industry. Faced with beatings and threats to transfer him along with his wife and children – who were also in custody – to concentration camps, Steane succumbed and agreed to work on Nazi film production, which he did until the end of the war. On his return to Britain, he was charged with carrying out 'acts likely to assist the enemy with intent to assist the enemy'. His only defence was that there was no such intent, that he intended to save himself and his wife and children from almost certain death. After the judge had inexplicably directed the jury to ignore the circumstances under which the defendant agreed to cooperate with the enemy, Steane was convicted and sentenced to three years prison with hard labour. On appeal, the conviction and sentence were quashed and he was released. The ruling at the Court of Appeal by Lord Chief Justice Goddard was an important one, because it made clear that in his view at least duress should have been considered, even on a matter as serious as this. In Goddard's view, the jury should have been left to decide whether it was true in this case that it was a genuine instance of duress.

Excuse and justification

As it stands, duress is taken to be a complete rather than partial defence, but as an excuse it is not equivalent to justification. For an act to be justified, it must by definition be the right thing to do. Stealing from a shop, for example, cannot possibly be defended as such, but it can be excused if the alternative was to face a severe beating from a shoplifting gang applying the duress. If an act is justified, no wrong and therefore no offence has been committed. Self-defence, for example, is justified despite the harm inflicted on the attacker. A harm is not necessarily a wrong. When, by contrast, excusing conditions are cited, the argument is that the act was wrong but understandable in the circumstances. When justifications are argued for, there is no such ambivalence: it was simply the right thing to do.

Aristotle on necessity and duress

One of the key sources for the development of these doctrines in English common law was Aristotle's *Nicomachean Ethics*. One of the aims of this work was to provide guidelines for the Athenian courts. What is especially useful to any analysis of these defences is an understanding of his basic classification of acts, which revolved around the extent to which they should be seen as voluntary or involuntary. These are broken down into:

1   Voluntary acts, which are entirely internal to the agent. They originate from within and are the result of choices. There is full responsibility and blame.
2   Involuntary or compulsive acts, originating entirely from outside. The agent contributes nothing. Example: a sea voyager blown off course by wind, taking him to the wrong port. No choices, no blame.
3   'Mixed acts', with a voluntary and involuntary component, but closer to the former than the latter. Examples: a tyrant holding a man's family hostage and forcing him into criminal acts; a sailor jettisoning cargo in a storm to save the vessel. Both involve reluctant choices.

Crucially, Aristotle subdivides the mixed acts into three types:

3a   those which 'though not commended are pardoned', because 'the alternative is too much for human nature, and nobody could endure it'.
3b   those which are actually praised as the taking of decisive action.
3c   those which are ruled out completely: 'There are some things such that a man must sooner die than do, though he suffer the most dreadful fate.' The example given here is an extreme one of matricide, taken from a Euripides tragedy (Aristotle 1985: 3.1).

Types (3a) and (3b) correspond closely with what today we call excuse and justification. For Aristotle, as for modern common law, both are presented as grounds for a defence, the first for duress, the second for necessity. Most importantly, what this analysis shows is the importance he attaches to the narrowing down of choices by external forces, and the idea that some choices are unendurable and should be dealt with leniently. Probably the most influential and hotly disputed of these categories, however, is (3c). Although he leaves the content of this proscription vague, it has been widely argued that he meant that, no matter how great the duress or danger, the line should be drawn at the murder of the innocent. Whatever Aristotle's meaning, this was how it was to be interpreted by English common law.

Murder and the Hale authority

Lord Chief Justice Matthew Hale was one of the most famous common law judges of the early modern period (see Chapter 1). In the following declaration he directly addressed the issue of duress in connection with murder:

> If a man be desperately assaulted, and in peril of death, and cannot otherwise escape, unless to satisfy his assailant's fury he will kill an

innocent person then present, the fear and actual force will not acquit him of the crime and punishment of murder, if he commit the fact; for he ought rather to die himself, than kill an innocent.

(Hale 1972 [1680]: 51)

This stark statement – hereafter the Hale authority – has presented a formidable obstacle to those trying to legitimise the defence of duress for all offences. For over three centuries it has been repeated and endorsed throughout the common law world. This was undoubtedly influenced by Aristotle's stipulation that there are acts 'such that a man must sooner die than do' (see above, i.e. class (3c)). The Hale authority was reaffirmed by Blackstone a century later, by Lord Chief Justice Coleridge a century after that, and by various legal authorities around the world. Those were the origins, but why did Hale's assertion command such authority? This has not been a matter of unthinking judicial subservience to a venerable principle, as some have suggested. The unconditional prohibition of the killing of the innocent and its condemnation as murder is not just an important detail of criminal law, it is the basic moral principle upon which the law rests.

DPP *v.* Lynch *(1975)*

Reports of the facts of this case have been subject to much variation. It seems from the original statement given by the defendant, from submissions to the Lords by counsel for the defence and prosecution, that Lynch's participation in an IRA murder of a police officer was quite extensive and to some extent voluntary, in as far as he made no attempt – despite at least one clear opportunity – to escape from the men responsible. For reasons not entirely clear he was drawn into the enterprise against his will, as he was neither a member nor a supporter of the IRA. He was first a passive participant in the hijacking of a civilian car at gunpoint, after which he was allowed to return home. Some hours later, he responded to another summons by the leader of the unit, and drove the stolen car to a garage where the policeman was working on his own car. Three hooded gunmen jumped out of their car and shot him dead. Lynch then drove them away and the car was abandoned. That was the extent of his participation. On his own account, he was too overcome with fear of the armed men to refuse to obey or to attempt to escape.

Lynch was initially convicted because the judge directed the jury that duress was not admissible in such cases. When his appeal reached the Lords, counsel for the defence stressed the state of fear Lynch was in at the time of the offence. Anyone else in this situation, they maintained, would have responded in the same way. They argued that Lynch's only direct intention was to save his life, and that the intention to commit the crime was at best oblique. They maintained that the law was seriously unsettled on this question, that the classic authority Justice Hale had himself been mistaken in law when he ruled out duress as a defence to murder, because there were other precedents allowing the jury to consider duress in at least one case of high treason. They concluded by arguing that most views that the law ruled out duress for murder were of antique origin, and that the issue had not been tested in a modern court. They added that there is nothing repugnant to public policy in duress being a defence to murder. Throughout the submission, they repeatedly asserted that such serious duress renders the act in question both lawful and justifiable.

The response from prosecuting counsel rejected all of these submissions and reasserted the authority of Hale, additionally listing many others from Justices East and Blackstone to Smith and Hogan today. While accepting that there were no recent court decisions on this issue, they pointed out that there are many *obiter dicta* (judicial remarks in passing) made in recent times in UK and other common law courts, ruling out duress as a defence for murder in any degree. Furthermore, there is no valid argument for separating murder from aiding and abetting murder. They disputed the claim that direct threats of death had been applied in this case, and pointed out that Lynch had not availed himself of at least one clear chance of escape. He also seemed to have voluntarily associated with the gunmen who he knew in advance to be IRA members. So the standard conditions for arguing duress in lesser offences were not even satisfied. They might have added that if successful, it should be on the grounds of excuse, not lawful and justified act, as the defence had maintained.

By a decision of three to two, the Law Lords nevertheless found in favour of Lynch and quashed the conviction, ordering a retrial on the grounds that the jury should have been allowed to consider the duress he was under. In reaching this decision, two of the majority judges (Morris and Wilberforce) insisted that they were not creating new law in apparently overturning the authorities of Hale and others, but rather they were drawing out the principles of the law as a whole. Morris argued that the words of Hale excluding duress were inappropriately extended to cases in which the defendant played a role but was not the actual killer. Wilberforce argued that there was no convincing principle justifying the withdrawal of the defence from the most serious crimes connected with murder. They also pointed to logical anomalies and inconsistencies in the law, whereby, for example, duress might be available on a charge of assault or attempted murder, then suddenly be withdrawn when the victim dies and the charge becomes one of murder.

The overall purpose of these arguments was to establish the principle that each case be treated on its own merits and the defence of duress put to the jury, regardless of the seriousness of the charge. It is another matter, of course, whether the defence will be successful. At the retrial, Lynch was again convicted, having failed to convince another jury that it was a genuine case of duress. It should also be emphasised that this outcome does not decisively affect the arguments either way. They were concerned solely with the justice or injustice of disallowing the defence of duress from being heard. Lynch's second conviction might even strengthen the arguments on the liberal side, on the grounds that justice was now seen to be done, having given him every chance to explain the circumstances. On the other side, it will always be argued that those accused of murder or assisting murder should not have the chance of persuading a jury to acquit them on these grounds.

English law on these matters then entered a period of some confusion and uncertainty, during which time it was unclear whether or not duress was available as a defence to murder as well as the closely related offences, such as attempted murder, aiding and abetting, and accessory after the fact. The situation was resolved twelve years after *Lynch,* in 1987, when the Law Lords took the unusual step of overruling their own earlier decision, declaring *Lynch* to be unsound law and restoring the *status quo ante.* The authorities of Hale and Blackstone *et al.* were now firmly reasserted.

On the question of principle, Hailsham argued that it was the fundamental purpose of law to protect the innocent and set clear standards of behaviour. It had never been accepted in English law that one could take the lives of others to save one's own, and it never should be. In all such cases there was a clear duty to follow the words of Hale and find another way to save one's life than by killing the innocent, and if necessary to die oneself in the attempt. Morally speaking this might sound highly demanding, but in recent history – Hailsham pointed out – there have been countless examples of people making this sacrifice. A particularly telling analogy had been drawn earlier by Lord Simon, who argued that it was inconsistent to allow the defence of duress in criminal courts when it had not been allowed to the defendants on war crime charges at Nuremberg in 1945–9 when they tried to argue either duress or obeying superior orders.

Against this, others have voiced the opinion that many of the Nuremberg procedures were actually quite unfair, and that those genuinely under great duress – as opposed to being instigators of the crimes and massacres – should indeed have had the defence. It should be added that the Hailsham position outlined here was not helped by his unfortunate choice of words in describing those who succumb to threats as 'cowards and poltroons', which seemed to indicate a narrow-minded assumption that all such defendants were only trying to save their own skins, when the truth of it is that many of these victims of duress have been responding to credible threats to hostages. These potential victims of violent death are also innocent. The law's spokesman who callously dismisses people who find themselves in this intolerable dilemma as cowards is seriously lacking either in imagination or empathy. This does not mean we should swing the other way on this question. Hailsham's insistence that the law must not withdraw its primary protection from the innocent still stands (Allen and Cooper 2010: 193). These arguments prevailed and to date, while the defence of duress is still allowed for nearly every other offence, the English legal system has continued to resist pressure from the Law Commission to allow unrestricted use of the defence of duress.

The defence of necessity

Like duress, defendants who plead necessity are arguing that they had no alternative, that although their actions were *prima facie* criminal, there were no acceptable choices to be made. Although the formulations of the two defences have interacted in the legal mind, they have evolved separately in common law and each needs to be evaluated in its own right. Unlike duress there is no question of 'succumbing to threats'. With cases of necessity, the danger to life and limb typically comes from natural forces, rather than the malice of others. When extreme measures have to be taken to save life, for example, by committing a serious criminal offence, the defence is that there was no alternative but to choose the lesser of two evils. In sharp contrast to duress, this is not usually presented as an excuse for wrongdoing; on the contrary it is argued to be a wholly justified response to an emergency or a natural disaster in which health or lives are jeopardised, such as an emergency operation or the facilitation of an escape from a life-threatening natural disaster. The most controversial cases are those that arise in the wake of disasters such as earthquakes or storms at sea, when survivors are scrambling for their lives. So those who take the defence tend to be arguing for justification rather than forgiveness – they look for endorsement of their claim that it was the right thing to do.

The classic cases

In the famous case of *R. v. Dudley and Stephens* (1884), two of the survivors of a shipwrecked yacht – the *Mignonette* – in the South Atlantic were convicted in London of the murder of a young cabin boy called Richard Parker. Adrift in an open dinghy for twenty days, exposed to the elements and desperately short of provisions, which had run out after ten days, all four were slowly dying of thirst and hunger. Hopes of rescue were fading when the two defendants outvoted the third adult, Brooke, and decided to kill the cabin boy in order to keep themselves alive by cannibalising him. The boy was the sickest of the four and the argument was that he was going to die soon anyway. There seemed no alternative for them but to die themselves. So Dudley, with Stephens's collusion, cut the boy's throat and they lived on the blood and flesh until their rescue. Four days after the killing, they were picked up by a German boat en route to England.

The question is, having deliberately killed one of their number for the purposes of their own survival, are these two men guilty of murder? It was certainly a premeditated and fully conscious act, but does the deadly danger they were undoubtedly in give them a legal defence? A number of points should be noted immediately. The first feature of this case that should be set aside is the 'survival cannibalism'. Eating human flesh is in itself not a major offence, and there have been numerous examples in the age of exploration, especially in remote regions in the Antarctic and the Andes, in the wake of disasters when the only food is the flesh of dead bodies. No prosecutions have ever been brought for such practices, no matter how distasteful, and the only act that is under scrutiny in this case is that of the killing. There was no suggestion at the trial that the cannibalism should be considered an aggravating feature of the murder.

Secondly, their selection of the weakest and youngest seemed to count most heavily against them, even if he was likely to be the first to die. If he really was so close to death, why not wait until he died? If he was not, there was no justification in selecting him over one of the adults. The third point is that although Dudley and Stephens quietly discussed the possibility, there was no attempt to draw lots, and they justified the selection of Parker on the dubious grounds that he did not have dependants. A fourth point is that there was some evidence that their mental health had declined, after many days of hunger, but an insanity defence was not seriously considered, on the grounds that Dudley had said a prayer while committing the murder, showing that he was still in a reasonable state of mind. Finally, the fact that he in particular was quite unrepentant and seemingly proud of his actions, did not help their case.

At the trial, the court took the unusual step of constraining the jury to find only on matters of fact, with the verdict being left to the bench, because the issue was regarded as a matter of fundamental importance and the law on necessity was – at least in its details – relatively unexplored. This was largely because the traditions of the sea had rarely been interfered with by the laws of the land. The jury concluded from the evidence that the three adults would have died without the action taken, that Parker would probably have died first, but also that there was no greater necessity for killing him rather than one of themselves.

Giving his verdict and sentence, Lord Chief Justice Coleridge ruled that the Hale authority applied as much to necessity as to duress. Killing the innocent to save oneself was not an option. He ruled that necessity could not be a common law defence to murder, either on the grounds of precedent or moral argument. Sanctioning such acts by the law, he said, would amount to 'the casting away of morality'. Dudley and Stephens were both convicted and sentenced to death. At the same time, however, Coleridge expressed the view that nobody should forget how terrible was the temptation to do such things in extreme circumstances and in pronouncing the mandatory death sentence for murder, he added a recommendation for mercy. This was promptly exercised by the Crown on the advice of the Home Office and the sentence was commuted to six months imprisonment. The outcome, then, was an ambiguous one, with the state declaring that the criminal law must be upheld in the face of defences of necessity to murder, but also making a significant concession in the direction of leniency. This mixed message has coloured the debates about the rights and wrongs of this defence ever since, as well as the many attempts to bring about legal reform in this area.

Well over a century later, *Dudley and Stephens* still stands as the main modern precedent for the principle that intentionally taking human life without recognised lawful excuse will always be treated as murder in an English court. This case is often linked with an American judgement forty years earlier in *US* v. *Holmes* (1842). The disputed factual description of the events is too complex to record in full here, but the essential facts seem to be as follows. The *William Brown* was an immigrant ship sailing from Liverpool to

Philadelphia with a crew of seventeen (including captain and officers) and sixty-four passengers. When the ship struck an iceberg, the only disciplined procedure that followed openly prioritised the safety of the crew. The fact that the final tally of survivors was all seventeen crew members, and just seventeen out of the original sixty-four passengers, speaks for itself. Seriously under-equipped with lifeboats – one longboat and a small jolly boat – the passengers below decks were falsely assured that there was no danger while the captain and crew were already lowering and occupying the lifeboats.

After the scramble that followed, a number of passengers managed to force their way into the longboat, while thirty of them, the majority of whom were children, went down with the sinking ship. The two surviving boats separated, with the captain and half the crew in the uncrowded jolly boat, and a total of forty-one passengers and crew in the seriously overcrowded longboat. The captain refused to transfer any to the jolly boat and sailed it away, leaving the first mate in command of the longboat. After making it through the first night and following day, in the course of which the passengers were vigorously helping to bail out the water from the leaking boat, the officer in charge instructed the crew to 'set to work' and start removing male passengers. Despite protests and sporadic resistance, during the course of this second night fourteen men and two women were picked off one after another and violently pitched into the icy waters by four of the crew. The last two men were dispatched in the same manner the next morning, when the danger had clearly passed. Holmes was the most prominent seaman out of the four involved in all of these kill-ings. Just thirty minutes after the last one, the survivors were picked up by a passing American ship. The longboat had been well-equipped with navigation instruments and provisions sufficient for many days sailing.

When reports of this incident reached the public and the authorities, there were at first mixed reactions, until it became clear that all the victims were defenceless passengers. This prompted expressions of strong condemnation in the Washington press. When the authorities decided to act, Holmes was the only perpetrator who could be found, so he was the sole defendant at the trial, at which murder charges were dropped in favour of 'wilful manslaughter on the high seas'. Necessity was no more a defence to homicide in American common law than it was in Britain, but the arguments on Holmes's behalf were heard, in great detail.

Compared to *Dudley and Stephens*, the victims were far more numerous and fully conscious, and none of them were sick. Until the attacks started, everyone had an equal chance of survival. The selection criteria were thoroughly unfair – it came down to a question of physical power. The only excuse offered for this selection was that the crew were needed to sail the boat to safety, but it certainly did not need all of them. So it is hard to deny that the crew were merely imposing their will on the weaker passengers.

We nevertheless need to ask whether these actions might be thought wholly justified by the overall outcome, which is to say, whether it is a genuine case of Aristotle's category (3b). In other words, was this decisive action the right thing to do in these perilous circumstances? Given that more lives were saved than lost from the longboat, did the ends justify the means? A certain kind of blunt utilitarianism, which asserts that the right thing to do is always measured in terms of the greatest good for the greatest number, would probably endorse these actions as the right thing to do. Modern utilitarians, however, usually have various side-constraints upon the kind of means that can be used to bring these ends about, and would be much less likely to endorse these actions. It can also be objected, of course, that 'the greatest number' was calculated only in relation to the crew, with the passengers apparently not counting at all.

Alternatively, if we interpret these actions as relatively unfree – with their hands 'forced by necessity' so to speak – might they be seen as excusable, hence not liable to punishment (Aristotle's category (3a))? That is to say, was it the wrong thing to do, but understandable in the circumstances? The idea is that anyone would do it out of desperation, forcing whoever they could out of the boat, because the only alternative was 'too much for human nature to bear'. Or was it absolutely wrong to kill these people? Does it fall under Aristotle's category (3c) of an act which 'a man must sooner die than do', as echoed by the Hale authority? These were in effect the three choices facing the court.

Arguments for and against necessity as a defence to murder

The following are the important moral arguments for not punishing people who genuinely act out of necessity, even when they kill. First, following from the above, the net gain in life justifies it and negates the criminality. Some see this as self-evident, but it is highly questionable. If adopted as a general moral principle it would justify all manner of atrocities – for example, killing the wounded on a battlefield or survivors of a disaster to save food and medicine for the others. Secondly, it is argued that it was not murder because there was no malice aforethought. Their intention was not to kill, but to save as many lives as possible. This disavowal of intention is dubious. As we have seen in the discussion of duress, the acts may be either enthusiastic or reluctant, but still intended as the means to desired ends.

A third argument is that sacrificing oneself in this situation requires an unrealistic degree of moral heroism, which is too much to ask. Ordinary people should only be expected to display reasonable fortitude. This is a tacit admission that it was wrong, but at the same time a plea for empathy, which is to say an excuse rather than a justification. One weakness of this argument is that it too readily assumes that most people are willing to commit murder in situations of danger and hence that refraining from this 'temptation' is heroic. Remember that the outvoted sailor in the *Dudley* case, Brooke, refused to agree to the killing. A fourth argument is that everyone has much stronger natural inclinations to prioritise the interests of themselves and their families and friends over those of strangers. This is certainly true, but the idea that it is normal for a sense of justice to be completely abandoned in situations such as these, is unrealistic as well.

The lawyer speaking for Holmes at his trial made great play of 'the state of nature' argument. The strongest legal point was his claim that the whole incident was beyond the jurisdiction of the court in Philadelphia. This was not because of its physical distance, nor because the law of the sea was different from the law of the land. In normal circumstances, a ship's company falls under the jurisdiction of the country in which the ship was registered. It was because they claimed that in situations of natural disaster, such as the sinking of a ship, everyone involved moves into a Hobbesian state of nature, a state in which there is no law. In this respect, it is equivalent to a return to the original state of nature, in which everyone has the natural liberty to do anything to preserve their own lives (see Chapter 8). Killing in this situation should be seen as self-preservation and self-defence. 'In such peril', said Holmes's advocate, 'a man makes his own law with his own right arm' (Learmonth and Tabakoff 2013: 228). This argument has been subjected to a great deal of critical discussion, on such questions as how and when it can be proved that the protagonists have at some point entered this state. The best argument against it, however, is that the state of nature is regarded by most today as simply a myth, designed and interpreted to support a variety of political positions. What it amounts to in this context is a bare assertion that 'might is right' when there is no law at hand to protect anyone. It was always unlikely that such a doctrine would be accepted by an American court in the 1840s.

A short summary of the arguments against the defence will suffice here. Its general availability would, in Coleridge's words, lower the value of human life, because it is impossible to weigh the value of one life against another. The Hale authority, according to which it is never justified to take an innocent life to protect another's, self-evidently applies as much to necessity as to duress. The state of nature argument is irrelevant, because it is the purpose of law to civilise, not to endorse natural survival ethics. According to US Supreme Court Justice Cardozo, 'there is no rule of human jettison. Who shall choose in such an hour between the victims and the saved? Who shall know when masts and sails of rescue may emerge out of the fog?' (Cardozo 1931: 39).

The judge presiding at the trial of Holmes took a hard line against Holmes's defence that everyone in the boat was in an equal position. Justice Baldwin emphasised the question of the relative status in terms of rights and duties of the passengers and the crew. Against the defence's insistence that all were on the same level in the state of nature, Baldwin declared that the duty of the crew to the passengers was fundamental and does not diminish in times of emergency, and they had a duty to make sacrifices from their own number if they were to have a defence. This did, of course, tacitly accept the possibility of their having a necessity defence, which was ruled out in English and many other jurisdictions, but it was still a highly demanding condition.

These 'classic cases' were not isolated or particularly exceptional, as has so often been claimed. For various reasons, *Dudley and Stephens* was the only such case that came before an English court, and relatively few cases anything like *Holmes* have been tried in American courts. There was nevertheless an abundance of examples in the age of maritime exploration and commerce, involving lifeboats from wrecks of ships from many different nations. Famous instances included the wreckage of a French ship, the so-called *Raft of the Medusa* in 1816, involving extensive cannibalism and throwing of people overboard. On the British ship *Granicus* in 1829 there was evidence of cannibalism. On the American whaling ship *The Essex* (1820) and the Norwegian ship *The Thekla* (1893), cannibalism by lottery was practised. None of these cases were tested in the courts.

Should the Hale authority allow any exceptions?

The central problem, which is often obscured by a false alternative – either Hale is upheld as an exceptionless principle, or unrestricted defences should be allowed – is how the law should distinguish between unacceptable acts of homicidal necessity and acts involving killing the innocent which should be accepted as justified. In other words, it is arguable that while the Hale authority in nearly all circumstances should be upheld, there are cases which should count as exceptions and the rule excluding the killing of the innocent relaxed.

Consider four examples of this type of case:

HMAS Westralia (1994). When a fire broke out in the engine room of an Australian warship, four sailors were immediately engaged in attempts to extinguish it. As the fire intensified and spread, the captain saw the threat to the ship, which contained 20,000 tonnes of flammable fuel. The ship with its crew of over 100 was in imminent danger of destruction. Strenuous efforts were made to rescue the trapped sailors, but when the crisis point was reached, Captain Dietrich ordered the room to be sealed off, simultaneously stifling the fire and killing all those trapped inside. At the inquiry, he was cleared of any wrongdoing, and it was commented that if anything he had left the action longer than was safe. Four lives – 3 men and 1 woman – were sacrificed to save over 100.

The Herald of Free Enterprise (1989). When a large ferry capsized in the English Channel off Zeebrugge, causing many deaths, a group of over thirty survivors found themselves trapped in an air pocket underwater. The only means of escape was via a rope-ladder to one narrow exit. The first person to attempt it lost his nerve and froze in fear on the ladder, preventing anyone else from escaping. After five minutes of frantic attempts to encourage him to go forward or come back, an off-duty naval officer ordered those at the front to pull him off the ladder and push him out of the way. They promptly did so and all thirty passengers made their escape. At the inquest, the coroner raised the possibility of charges of murder, but recommended that no further action be taken. The outcome here is that one life had – deliberately, it seems – been taken, to save over thirty lives.

The Model Penal Code mountaineer. This is a variation on the fictitious example devised by the American Model Penal Code. After a mountaineering fall, two climbers are suspended in space, with their connecting rope snagged around a bush which is slowly breaking under the weight. A third climber arrives and seeing their predicament immediately goes to their aid and cuts the rope while hauling the conscious survivor to safety, allowing the one who is unconscious and out of reach to fall to his death. One life is saved rather than none.

The conjoined twins (2000). Doctors at a hospital in Manchester sought permission from the High Court to separate by operation two baby girls whose bodies were fused at the spine (see Chapter 9). Only one could be saved, and without any intervention, both would die very soon. The High Court's permission to operate was reinforced by the Court of Appeal's unanimous approval. One life was saved rather than none.

As with the classic cases, these also are only the tip of the iceberg. Numerous examples of such situations – especially the naval ones – are found in modern literature and true accounts of disasters in war and peacetime. A further important point is that two of these 'acts of necessity' are carried out by private citizens, while the other two are officially sanctioned. Nevertheless, similar moral dilemmas are raised in each of the four cases.

A veil of ignorance test

How, then, do we distinguish potentially legitimate cases such as these from those classic cases in which the perpetrators should be charged with murder? One way to do it might be found by applying a Rawlsian analysis of the dilemma, by asking what any rational agent 'behind the veil of ignorance' – see Chapter 8 – would agree to in each of these circumstances. Along these lines, what we need to ask is what would anyone in the group agree to, solely on the basis of self-interest, as the right course of action in the event of just such a disaster, if they did not know which of the persons in the case they were going to be?

If they did not know whether they were going to be the captain or one of the officers, crew or passengers – given the relative numbers of each on the *William Brown* – they would certainly not agree with the course of action that was taken. There would be much too strong a chance of their being one of the victims. From behind the veil, it would be seen for what it was, as the stronger asserting their power over the weaker and committing premeditated murder. This would be less clear-cut in the case of *Dudley*, but would a rational agent looking out for their own interests really endorse the course of action that arbitrarily selects one out of four for killing and eating for the sake of survival, when it is by no means certain who is going to die first?

In the second type of case, the agents behind the veil would be much more inclined to endorse the course of action taken. In the case of the *Herald,* this would be overwhelming. What rational agent behind the veil would condemn as murder a course of action aimed at saving such a number by killing one whose very short-lived survival threatens their own long-term survival so directly? This would be quickly agreed, regardless of which passenger they imagined themselves to be. On the *Westralia*, this would be less certain. Behind the veil, they would not know whether they would be the captain taking the decision, one of the trapped members of the fire-fighting team or one of the much larger number of crew. With the full facts, they would probably assent to the deadly action. Imagine, though, that they were asked whether they would agree on a policy that the majority should always be saved at the expense of the minority, such that if a situation arose in which there were forty rather than four sailors trapped in the engine room, the air would be cut off. Would they still agree? What would be the rational decision? They might decide that when the numbers were over a certain limit the ship's officers should take the chance on continuing to fight the fire and hope that they come through the crisis without an explosion. Where the cut-off point comes is very uncertain. These cases, of course, do not always involve large numbers. It seems, nevertheless, that in those in which it is one life against another, the decision would be easier. Would the two mountaineers behind the veil not agree quickly that the action taken by the third climber was the right one, given that they will both die without it?

Three criteria for distinguishing the cases

Overall, one really cannot equate these two types of case of apparent necessity. Such an equivalence would either justify the murders in the first type or unfairly condemn people as murderers in the second type. What we need now is a set of criteria to apply to all the cases, to evaluate the merits of the arguments for and against considering a defence of necessity.

The first obvious one is the numbers factor. As with lesser offences, the good to be achieved must outweigh the evil of the death or deaths involved. This, however, does not settle it, because the numbers can vary enormously, from a 100:1 ratio to a simple 1:1. It would nevertheless – as we have seen – be quite wrong to exclude cases like the twins or Model Penal Code mountaineer on the grounds that it was just one life against another. Does this necessarily exclude cases one could easily imagine involving the saving of one life out of four or five? What if, for example, it had been a team of four climbers tied together, with only one in a position to be rescued? There seems to be no reason to stipulate that this would be unlawful, solely on the grounds of numbers.

A more decisive criterion is provided by the selection factor. The victims in most of these cases are either self-selected or selected by fate, not by human agents. In the two classic cases this was the main problem. The selection was arbitrary. In addition to this, where there was a selection problem, this selection was based on superior strength and as such thoroughly unfair. So it is possible to argue that when there is a selection problem, a fair procedure – at least an attempt to apply sortition – to decide who should live and die would justify it. This does seem dubious, as any procedure chosen would be open to dispute and criticism. As a minimum, though, we can say that where there is no selection problem, the presumption must be that they do at least have a defence.

A third factor that pervades these cases is that of time running out and the prospect of imminent death. This was most prominent in the twins case, as the health of the stronger baby was rapidly deteriorating every day. If it was going to be done, it would have to be done quickly. In each case, there is a different angle on this factor. With the *Westralia*, time was absolutely crucial; indeed it was the careful timing of it that was essential to the captain's defence. Too early and he might be court-martialled; too late and they would all be dead. Different again is the time factor in the case of the *Herald*, but it was no less critical. With the water rapidly rising, this was what we might call a closed time-frame. It was only a matter of minutes before they would have all drowned, along with the victim, who would die as well. With the two classic cases, this was not so at all. While it is true that in *Holmes* it was repeatedly insisted that time was running out, nobody could say how long they had before the lifeboat sank. It was a much more open time-frame. On the *Mignonette* it was even more open, as there was no danger of sinking, even though there was a limit to how much longer they could survive without provisions. The common factor was that there was an absence of certainty in these cases as to when the end would come. In fact, in both cases the survivors were picked up by passing ships only days or minutes (in *Holmes*) after the killings. On the *Herald,* underwater in a shrinking space, the certainty that time was running out was an absolute. This clearly counts much more strongly in the group's favour, as does the fact that they did all they could to help the trapped passenger before forcibly removing him from the ladder.

Intention and necessity

Intention is the central requirement for establishing malice aforethought. So did the doctors intend to kill Mary? Did the captain intend to kill the fire-fighting team? Did the *Herald* passengers intend to kill the trapped man? Did the mountaineer intend to kill the unconscious man? The undoubted fact that none of them *wanted* to kill has no bearing on this question. In all of these cases, their intention is a grey area. In the classic cases, by contrast, the answers are plain. Dudley intended to kill the cabin boy as he cut his throat. Holmes and the other sailors intended to kill the passengers. Only their deaths would achieve their purpose. There is no way in which these acts can be interpreted as unintended. With the grey-area cases, these are terrible things that cannot be avoided without suffering an even worse loss. This, however, is the way the others will justify their killings. In terms of their intentions, why are they different? One difference is that we know that in the grey-area cases, they did everything possible to avoid the killing. Most moral intuitions support the taking of life in these circumstances, but recoil from what looks like cold-blooded murder in the classic cases.

In one sense, in all six cases, they intended to kill. They all knew what they were doing and decided to proceed, being perfectly aware that the victims would die. The question is whether some of them can be exceptions to the rule that an intentional killing is sufficient for a conviction for murder. Another way of looking at it is to ask whether we have to show that those who should be exonerated are those who did not really intend to kill, because what they intended was something else.

There are two relevant senses of intention here. In the narrow sense, what is intended is what the agent explicitly aims to achieve. The wider sense also takes in what the agent knows the effects of the act will be, in addition to what s/he wants to achieve. Now consider how this applies to these cases. The mountaineer does not aim to achieve the end of the unconscious climber falling to her death, but knows that she certainly will. In the wider sense, then, he intends her death. In the narrow sense, he does not. He does not use her death as the means to the end of saving her companion. It is a highly unfortunate side-effect of his act of cutting the rope, an act which is aimed at a praiseworthy end. Those who forcibly removed the man from the ladder in the *Herald* aimed to clear the escape hatch. They did not actually kill the man, but knew that it was very unlikely he would survive being pushed away into the water in such circumstances. So were these deaths the price these defendants were prepared to pay for their own survival? If so, should these acts then be classified as oblique intention, thus under Bentham's definition of intention, murder, on the same level of culpability as an arsonist who obliquely kills? Intuitively, this cannot be right. Apart from the fact that these defendants were not already engaged in unlawful acts, the key difference seems to be that the victims were fated to die whatever the course of action.

The main conceptual difficulty is this. If we take intention in the narrow sense as the appropriate concept in this legal context, then the defendants do not need the necessity defence. They have every chance of acquittal without it, by simply arguing that they had no such intention and if the court accepts this the *mens rea* for murder is not satisfied. If we take intention in the wider sense and extend it to include the cognitive factors, we ought to conclude that an act of necessity is sometimes justified even when there is intention to kill. Then the necessity defence is the only one that might succeed – were it not excluded by the law. In the classic cases, there is no conceptual problem. Whether the defendants are cutting a boy's throat or pitching passengers into icy waters, the intention to kill is as direct as it could be, so there could be no sensible debate about whether or not they intended the death. The deaths of the victims are the means to the ends of their own survival. In stark contrast, it is in the grey-area cases that there is always a problem with intention.

Much depends on the factual evidence presented to the jury, pointing to intention or absence of intention to kill, as indicated by the behaviour of the defendants before and after the act. This is partly why the sailors in *Holmes* were damned by their own actions and behaviour. It was quite clear that they were determined to act ruthlessly and kill, even beyond the point at which they judged it to be necessary. The only reason Dudley and Stephens were arrested in Portsmouth and charged with murder was that Dudley had been bragging in public about what he had done. They had no regrets and regarded the murder as justifiable. It is also why the passengers on the *Herald* tend to elicit a more sympathetic response, given that they made every attempt to avoid the act of killing, which they saw as highly regrettable. The only criticism of the captain of the *Westralia* was that objectively speaking he should have acted sooner, and had taken an unnecessary risk in his attempt to avoid causing the deaths of his crew. Such information is crucial to determining whether or not various defendants had 'murderous intent'.

Conclusion

In the context of the arguments for legal reform, there is a clear need for defining carefully the circumstances in which it is thought there might be a defence to murder when the intentional taking of innocent human life seems justifiable. In doing so, the greatest care must be taken to distinguish genuine cases from the 'might is right' examples, which are properly treated as murder. This requires a central focus on the selection factor. The existing proposals for legal reform, recommending the extension of necessity and duress without qualification to all offences, would be very dangerous. The possibility, however, of formulating a new defence of necessity, akin to but distinct from that of self-defence, is a real one. In the meantime, the law will continue along its uneasy path of exercising discretion not to prosecute in hard cases of duress and necessity, and to hear cases of medical necessity on a one-by-one basis.

Study questions

General question: Critically assess the arguments in favour of allowing the defences of duress and necessity for all criminal offences, up to and including murder.

Further study questions: Should the defence of duress be generally available for criminal offences? Is it right that it is ruled out for murder and/or murder-related offences, such as attempted murder or aiding and abetting? When allowable, should the defence argue duress as an excuse or as a justification? In what circumstances should the defence of necessity be available? With reference to Aristotle's classification and to the Hale authority, do you think necessity should be allowed as a defence to murder? Should its exclusion be upheld in every imaginable circumstance? Look carefully at each of the cases. Can a distinction be drawn between cases of necessity in which the killing of the innocent is permissible and cases in which it is not?

Suggestions for further reading

The reading on necessity and duress is exceptionally wide and diverse in kind because of the range of circumstances in which these defences can arise. The basic texts providing the relevant legal data on the classic cases and the principles of law are: *Elliott and Wood's Cases and Materials on Criminal Law* (11th edn, Allen and Cooper 2013); *Smith and Hogan's Criminal Law* (14th edn, Ormerod and Laird 2015); and Nicola Padfield's *Criminal Law* (9th edn, 2014).

Two outstanding books on the ethics and legal implications of natural disasters are Katz (1987) and Learmonth and Tabakoff (2013). The latter is an excellent compendium of closely researched critical accounts of the most prominent disasters discussed above.

More philosophical analysis can be found in Gardner (2007), which is an outstanding careful analysis of the problems raised by the duress defence in particular. Dressler (2013) is a distinctive argument for basing the defence of necessity on excuse rather than justification. Fuller's (1949) imaginary case of 'the speluncean explorers' and Suber's (1998) extension of the same case have been highly influential in the debates on necessity. One study that provides a wealth of examples, real and imaginary, closely connected with the themes of our chapter here, is the much-discussed 'trolleyology' of David Edmonds (2014).

Other relevant texts include H.L.A. Hart, 'Legal Responsibility and Excuses', in Kipnis (1977), A. Kenny (1978: ch. 1), J.L. Mackie, 'The Grounds of Responsibility', in Hacker and Raz (1977), Norrie (2014: ch. 8), Ten (1987: ch. 5), Geddes (1973), Duff (1973), Thomson (1985) and Cohan (2006).

14 Insanity and diminished responsibility

When the criminal law is dealing with mentally disturbed or insane offenders, is it justified to any extent to hold them accountable and punish them for their criminal offences? This is the basic question to be broached here. What makes it particularly difficult is the enormously variable and problematic nature of the phenomenon of mental disturbance, the popular perception and scientific understanding of which have varied from one society and epoch to another. The practical difficulty in law has always been the articulation of a reliable and stable test for the kind of abnormality or insanity that would, if established, either absolve the defendant from responsibility, or at least reduce the degree of blame.

It is disagreement about the ways in which mental disturbance affects personal responsibility that makes the insanity defence or the plea of diminished responsibility controversial. On the one hand, liberal thinkers in this area regard it as pointless and unenlightened to punish people who, through no fault of their own, are afflicted with the kind of mental condition that leads them to commit harmful acts. Punishing them as if they were responsible agents is no more rational, it is argued, than the medieval practice of putting animals on trial for assault or murder. On the other hand, those with a more sceptical outlook argue that these defences are loopholes through which the guilty escape justice. This kind of scepticism is directed both at the defendants' pleas of insanity, and at the opinions of medical experts. In particular, it tends to involve the belief that moral choices can still be made by many classified as insane or mentally ill. From the liberal point of view, by contrast, it is assumed that it is in the very nature of mental illness that no such choices can be made. This is essentially the controversy, but there are many variations in the arguments, depending on the degree and type of mental disorder.

In this rather stark dispute, the most basic ideas about responsibility and its nullification are not usually contested. Even the most sceptical of critics are inclined to accept that it is not rational to blame anyone for what can be demonstrated to be an entirely unknowing, unintended or involuntary action. What is doubted in practice is that such demonstration is possible, or that perpetrators of evil deeds are genuinely in a mental condition that would justify such a description of their acts. This scepticism is compatible with the further assumption that serious mental disturbance – which under some classi-fications would count as insanity – does not necessarily involve the kind of cognitive impairment that would affect the ability to make moral judgements and decisions. What tends to be agreed, however, is that where impairment of these faculties is genuine, it should indeed absolve the victims of such illness from responsibility. If the mental disturbance is such that they genuinely do not know what they are doing, or believe themselves to be doing something good, or are wholly incapable of controlling their actions, it would seem impossible in all conscience to brand them as criminals.

Traditional problems with insanity

The problem of when to absolve the mentally disturbed from criminal liability has recurred and evolved throughout the history of Western legal systems. Attitudes to insanity have ranged from the relative tolerance and understanding displayed at times in European societies under the naturalistic influence of Aristotelian science and Galenic medicine, to the mystification of madness and association of it with witchcraft and demon possession in late medieval and early modern Europe. The witch-craze period between 1400 and 1700 was an age of darkness as far as the understanding of insanity was concerned. In witch trials, which were very frequently prompted by behaviour that would otherwise have been recognised as symptomatic of mental illness, the insanity defence was simply unavailable. The symptoms were regarded, not as possible grounds for exculpation, but as offering further evidence of guilt (D.N. Robinson 1996: 55).

It was the philosophical and religious problems of free will that hampered the early modern development of an understanding of insanity. The Christian doctrines of sin and redemption, requiring freedom of action as a condition for reward or damnation, evolved in such a way that the onset of mental illness was seen either as a punishment for past sins or as evidence of possession by evil spirits. Either way, the misfortune was regarded as the responsibility of the victim, who was assumed to have voluntarily consorted with the devil.

The general process of intellectual enlightenment, initiated by Descartes and his contemporaries, and culminating in the eighteenth-century Age of Enlightenment, steadily eroded this entire world view. With the advance of natural, mechanistic explanations of human physiology, the belief in universal causation in an immanent material world led to a deterministic view of human actions in general. It was within this framework that it became possible to understand, with some semblance of scientific rigour, the various manifestations of mental illness.

One danger here is the temptation to respond to the sceptical attitude to the insanity defence by exaggerating the typical case to be regarded as deserving exculpation. In practice, there is probably no such thing as 'total insanity', or *complete* removal from reality. If the impairment were this severe, it would be difficult to imagine its victim even having the capacity to commit a crime. In ancient society and through much of the history of the common law, there was a tendency to paint insanity in black-and-white terms, with a caricatured lunatic understood to be completely devoid of reason. The standard test for insanity set by Bracton (1210–68) was the ability to count twenty shillings and name one's own parents. All this established was absolute basic rationality, and what was known as 'the wild-beast test' stipulated that, to qualify as insane, one had to have no more reason than that of such a beast. 'A madman is not able to bargain nor to do anything in the way of business for he does not understand what he has done ... such [mad]men are not greatly removed from beasts for they lack reasoning' (Biggs 1955: 82). In 1581, it was declared by Lambard that 'if a mad man or a naturall foole, or a lunatike in the time of his lunacie ... do kil a man, this is no felonious act, nor anything forfeited by it' (Biggs 1955: 84). Only complete 'lunacy' and total absence of knowledge of good and evil were regarded as grounds for exculpation. It was nevertheless significant that this bare minimum was established, because it meant the recognition in principle of insanity as a defence to murder, even if it applied to very few offenders.

Despite this tendency towards an all-or-nothing approach to insanity, the great common law authorities moved inexorably towards naturalistic explanation. The seventeenth-century classifications of mental disorders by Sir Edward Coke (1552–1634) and Sir Matthew Hale (1609–76) pointed towards complete secularisation of the law. What was increasingly recognised, with the growing influence of medical science, was the different kinds of 'idiocy' and 'dementia' within the category of *non compos mentis*, including the recognition of temporary insanity. Despite Hale's traditional reliance on Holy Scripture and his personal belief in witchcraft, his approach to mental illness and the legal problem of responsibility was guided by the science and medicine of his day (Hale 1972). Throughout this period, however, the test for insanity remained that of a complete deprivation of reason at the time of the offence.

The radical break with the past came in 1800 with the case of *Hadfield*, who had made an ineffective attempt on the King's life at Drury Lane Theatre. A veteran soldier who had sustained severe head wounds, Hadfield was in the grip of a delusion that he was the new messiah, commanded by God to assassinate George III. With the benefit of being defended by the famous advocate Thomas Erskine (1750–1823), and with medical testimony from one of the founders of modern psychiatry, Sir Alexander Crichton, Hadfield was acquitted on the grounds of insanity. Using Crichton's testimony to maximum effect, Erskine succeeded in persuading the court that, in the light of the new science, the traditional law on insanity – requiring total deprivation of reason – was hopelessly outdated. Despite his brain injuries, which had also led him to attempt to kill his own child, Hadfield was in many respects sane and rational. The legal turning point here was that this partial rationality was readily conceded by the defence, who argued that it should not count against the case for insanity. This was because, or so they argued, legal insanity was no longer to be determined by the wild-beast test, but the test of *delusion*. If it could be proved that the defendant was suffering from a specific delusionary belief that caused him to commit the offence, then – notwithstanding his being in other respects sane and reasonable – he was not responsible for the act. What this meant was that partial insanity, in the sense of being judged insane without being completely devoid of reason, was to be recognised by the law for the first time.

The case of Daniel M'Naghten

The case that led to the settling of English law on insanity for more than a century was that of *M'Naghten* (1843). Daniel M'Naghten, charged with the murder of Edward Drummond, secretary to the Prime Minister, Sir Robert Peel, pleaded insanity. It was undisputed that his real target was Peel himself. The defence for M'Naghten was that he was in the grip of an insane delusion that the local Tory Party in his native Edinburgh was conspiring to kill him. Even when he attempted to escape to France, he believed that he was pursued by Tory agents disguised as Jesuit priests. Convinced that Peel, as leader of the party, was personally responsible, he decided that he could only stop the persecution by killing him. The unanimous opinion of the doctors who examined M'Naghten was that this delusion was and remained quite genuine.

The prosecution argued that Erskine (in *Hadfield*) had been wrong to maintain that delusion was sufficient for the insanity defence, when the accused knew the difference between good and evil, as M'Naghten in this case surely did. This argument, however, was overwhelmed by another dazzling display of advocacy in conjunction with the new medical science. For the defence, Alexander Cockburn – the future Lord Chief Justice – quoted extensively from Dr Isaac Ray to discredit all the tests and assumptions of the pre-scientific age. Crucially, he persuaded the court that the new scientific psychiatry proved beyond all doubt that a man could be 'the victim of the most fearful delusions, the slave of uncontrollable impulses' (D.N. Robinson 1996: 168), while still able to function normally in other respects. With regard to M'Naghten, he persuaded the court that M'Naghten had acted under the influence of such a delusion, believing it to be a reasonable act of self-defence. Faced with one-sided medical evidence for the defendant, the judge stopped the trial and gave the jury what amounted to a direction to acquit on the grounds of insanity.

The furore that followed this acquittal was largely due to the belief that M'Naghten – like others before him – was simply a political assassin trying to escape justice by taking the insanity defence. Given that the 1840s was a time of growing unrest and revolutionary agitation, this was not entirely implausible. In response to this controversy, Queen Victoria – herself a victim of three assassination attempts – intervened by demanding from the House of Lords a clarification of the law on insanity. Five questions on the test for criminal responsibility in cases of insanity were then put by the Lords to the sixteen most senior judges. The answers delivered on behalf of the majority by Lord Chief Justice Tindal became the text known subsequently as 'the M'Naghten Rules'.

The M'Naghten Rules and their critics

Over the years since the Hadfield decision, the law had dealt with insanity cases in an *ad hoc* manner, with various cases decided on apparently contradictory principles. What the authors of the M'Naghten Rules now sought to lay down was a clear guideline on how the law stood and on how juries were to be instructed. The meaning of the text that emerged from their deliberations on the history of common law on the subject was not entirely clear. The main difficulties arose from the abandonment of the clear-cut rationality tests of Bracton and Hale, the intrusion into law of medical science and the problem of understanding partial insanity and delusion. In other words, the conceptual difficulties started when the law began to take mental disorders seriously and to formulate general principles to guide the legal response to these disorders. Bearing this in mind, it is hardly surprising that the rules that were laid down in these circumstances were not a model of clarity.

The main preoccupation of the questions and answers was to clarify the law on cases of partial delusion, in which offenders 'are not in other respects insane' (Allen 2001: 216). Three main issues arose from the judges' answers to questions about the criminal responsibility of such offenders:

- the offender's knowledge of the nature and quality of the act;
- the offender's knowledge of right and wrong, moral and legal;
- the excusability of the act that the offender believed himself to be committing.

The central point in the Rules is the judges' opinion that the insanity defence can only succeed if it is proved that:

> at the time of committing the act, the accused was labouring under such a defect of reason, from disease of the mind, as not to know the nature and quality of the act he was doing, *or*, if he did know it, that he did not know he was doing what was wrong.
>
> (Allen 2001: 216)

What they appear to mean here is that he must either not know what he is doing, in the sense that he does not understand that he is killing, or he does not know that this act of killing is wrong.

On the matter of knowing right from wrong, the answers are ambiguous. On the one hand, the judges reply that a partly deluded offender is punishable 'if he knew at the time of committing such crime that he was acting contrary to law'. On the other hand, switching to the language of moral value, they concede that the offender is punishable if 'conscious that the act was one that he ought not to do', if this coincides with violation of the law.

The most important point here concerns the distinction between the offender having general awareness of the difference between right and wrong – which indicates no more than the antiquated rationality test – and, more specifically, his 'knowledge of right and wrong, in respect to the very act with which he is charged'. In other words, he might have complete moral integrity without understanding that his own act is wrong, because of the nature of his delusion. M'Naghten and Hadfield, like many others, knew perfectly well that murder was wrong, but did not regard their own acts as murder. If the offender has the more specific understanding, the judges decided, then he is punishable. The question of knowing the law of the land, which virtually all offenders will be aware prohibits murder, obscures this issue of specific understanding.

The third point is the most difficult. The fourth question had asked whether a person committing an offence as a consequence of an insane delusion as to existing facts is thereby excused. The judges replied by dividing possible cases of delusion into two categories, those in which the imagined facts would have excused the act, and those in which they would not. 'We think he must be considered in the same situation as to responsibility as if the facts with respect to which the delusion exists were real' (Allen 2001: 217). Had the situation actually been as he in his deluded state imagined it, the criminal liability that would then have obtained is applied to the situation in which he now finds himself. The example given in the Rules is that if he believes himself to be responding legitimately to a deadly threat, he will not be held liable. If, on the other hand, he believes himself to be avenging an injury to his character or fortune, he will be held liable. This is how it would be if there were no delusion. In place of the plea of self-defence, those in the position of M'Naghten, for example, can plead insanity. Those who imagine themselves to be avenging an insult cannot.

Criticisms of the M'Naghten Rules

Despite the resilience and longevity of these Rules as the legal test for the insanity defence, they have been subjected to relentless criticism since their adoption in the 1840s. There are several types of criticism, coming from different directions.

The most general criticism is that, due to the ambiguity and vagueness of the language, especially on the legal–moral distinction, they are open to multiple interpretation that undermines their credentials as a clear and reliable guideline. Coupled with this is the criticism that they fail to provide general principles adequate to the task of dealing with the variety of particular cases that the courts have to face. The vagueness especially applies to the concept of *knowing*. 'Knowing' the nature and quality of the act can be taken to indicate a literal understanding that, for example, guns are potentially lethal; or it can be taken in the more complex sense of appreciating the implications of the act of firing a gun. If the usage of the word is such that it can be taken either way, interpretation can be either factual or normative. This applies also to the phrase 'nature and quality'. This is interpreted by some to mean simply that the agent understands what he is doing, the two words being taken as near-synonyms. By others, it is interpreted as meaning an understanding of the nature of an act as what it factually *is*, and seeing the *moral* quality of the act. This confusion of factual and normative, it is commonly suggested, will inevitably lead to inconsistent interpretations of what the Rules require.

A more specific criticism relates to the coherence of the delusion test. The division of delusion into two categories – those in which the act would be justified if the imagined facts were real, and those that would not – is initially plausible, but on closer analysis is not entirely clear. One aspect of this criticism is that this rule is based on an artificial compartmentalisation of beliefs, implying the kind of distinctions that only an unimpaired rational mind can draw. With the partially insane, the ability to distinguish between life-threatening situations and relatively harmless ones is precisely what is said to have been lost or at least impaired. If someone commits murder in the belief that it is an appropriate response to an imagined insult, would this really be any less insane a delusion than that of one who believes himself to be defending his life? With all such delusions, the ability to make rational discriminations is at least seriously impaired. There is, furthermore, a deeper problem here. Is it really intelligible to instruct sane members of a jury to assess the excusability of an act carried out in the deluded belief that, for example, the defendant is the new messiah commanded by God to sacrifice himself, or that his victim is an agent of Satan, as if these 'facts' were *real*?

Historically, the most significant criticism of the Rules is that, in their tests for liability, they are narrowly and exclusively cognitive. They are said to be narrowly cognitive in the sense that they treat the state of knowing in a very restricted way, ruling out any emotional component of knowledge. It is therefore sufficient that defendants have formal knowledge of the nature and quality of the act, without needing full realisation and understanding. The Rules are said to be exclusively cognitive in that they focus solely on the cognitive, to the exclusion of other aspects of the defendant's state of mind, in particular, the volitional.

As we saw in the last chapter, one of the basic conditions for *mens rea* is that, at the time of the offence, there is an unconstrained will. If this freedom of will is absent or severely constrained, it is assumed to be an injustice to hold the agent responsible for the act. We also saw, however, that this was deeply problematic in the context of the defences of necessity and duress. It is no less so with the insanity defence. Most critics of the M'Naghten Rules have focused their fire on the absence of the volitional condition, which is simply ignored in the Rules, thereby – the critics argue – opening up a wide gap for unjust convictions.

It is undeniable that the sole concern of the Rules is with what the agents believe and understand about what they are doing and about the rights and wrongs of it. There is no provision for offenders whose mental disturbance consists in their inability to prevent themselves from committing offences that they fully understand to be criminal and morally wrong. The criticism has been based on the claim that a large proportion of those who should be excused on grounds of insanity can be shown to be suffering from this kind of inability, rather than a demonstrable cognitive impairment. They might know perfectly well how bad the act is, but be unable to control themselves. For such offenders, treatment is said to be more appropriate than punishment. The most prominent demand of the campaign for the amendment of the Rules has accordingly been the inclusion of an 'irresistible impulse' clause, whereby those who are demonstrably incapable of resisting criminal impulses are also treated as insane.

Before we consider the problems with the irresistible impulse argument, it should be noted that this was not a post-M'Naghten innovation or an expression of an ultra-liberal interpretation of mental illness based on modern psychiatry. It was a response that arose immediately in Britain and the USA to the M'Naghten tightening up of the legal definition of insanity. In fact, it does no more than hark back to the original challenge to the anachronistic rationality test in Erskine's speech in 1800 and Cockburn's advocacy for M'Naghten in 1843. Each of these – rightly or wrongly – understood the new medical science to have demonstrated a close link between 'fearful delusions' and 'slaves of uncontrollable impulses' (D.N. Robinson 1996: 168). A volitional insanity defence, then, should have arisen naturally from the admissibility of partial insanity as a defence. Instead, the M'Naghten Rules closed the door on it.

Defences of the M'Naghten Rules

Defences of the Rules have been aimed in two directions: at those who regard them as too broad and liberal, allowing the insanity defence to offenders who do not merit it; and at those who see them as too restricted and illiberal, unjustly condemning as criminal and often executing too many mentally ill offenders.

The charge of ambiguity and vagueness can come from either direction. It can be argued by critics that this looseness of language allows too much discretion for the judicial direction of juries, allowing judges to exercise their own bias for or against those taking the insanity defence. Or it can be argued that this indeterminacy results in unreliable general principles, inevitably leading to inconsistency and injustice. Against either of these criticisms, defenders of the Rules have seen this indeterminacy as the virtue of flexibility, rather than as the vice of ambiguity. It enables the court to deal with the unique facts of each individual concrete case appropriately.

As far as the charge of incoherence is concerned, there is no real answer other than to deny it and reassert the validity of the delusion test. If it is true that the Rules do not make good sense, it would seem that there is no convincing answer to the case for replacing them. A very general reply to this is that the Rules have provided a legal definition of insanity, rather than a medical one. As such, they are concerned not with a definitive distinction between the sane and the insane, but rather with a delicate balancing act between the requirements of justice and the need to protect the public from the criminally insane. What this involves is a practical decision within the legal profession on who is to be held criminally responsible and who is not. Bearing this in mind, it is said to be impossible to formulate general principles that are perfectly coherent.

Within the English legal system, resistance to the century-long campaign for an irresistible impulse amendment to the M'Naghten Rules has been implacable. A parliamentary bill in 1923, proposing the addition of a clause that it be proved that the defendant was capable of conforming his action with the law, was defeated in the House of Lords. Several recommendations in later years were also emphatically rejected. The reasoning behind this peculiarly English scepticism towards the idea of impulses that cannot be controlled is very complex, but there are three main types of argument.

The first and most obvious objection, frequently voiced in Parliament, is that the admission of irresistible impulse would have the effect of increasing the number of insanity defences beyond an acceptable level. In one sense, this implies that too many sane and cunning people would be capable of exploiting this defence; in another sense, it implies that the defence itself would be suspect, because even people genuinely subject to irresistible impulse should not be excused; everyone should be responsible for their own impulses – especially when the impulses are murderous – irresistible or otherwise.

A second type of argument questions the intelligibility of the concept of irresistible impulse. Kenny, for example, has argued that an impulse is by definition something that can be resisted (A. Kenny 1978). He argued further that, if there really is such a thing as the kind of compulsive behaviour that would remove criminal responsibility, it would have to be a literally unstoppable causal force. The test he suggests for such a force is that the agent would be compelled to perform these irresistible acts even if a policeman was standing next to him. People who display enough cunning to avoid the attention of the law cannot be deemed to be out of control of their own actions.

This scepticism was also voiced by Barbara Wootton (Wootton 1981), arguing from a quite different point of view that all criminals should be treated rather than punished. Her influential argument in this context was that one should not be too ready to infer from the fact that an impulse *has* not been resisted, to the conclusion that it *could* not have been resisted. The assumptions she challenged were that impulses are always overwhelming, rather than mere temptation; that the more evil the impulse, the more difficult it must be to resist.

In Britain, sceptical arguments such as these against the introduction of irresistible impulse as a defence have prevailed. The significance of this issue, however, was radically altered by two pieces of legislation, the 1957 Homicide Act and the abolition of capital punishment in 1965.

Diminished responsibility and the 1957 Homicide Act

Instead of any amendment to or clarification of the M'Naghten Rules, a new special defence of diminished responsibility, adapted from Scottish law, was introduced into English law in 1957. This was partly a response to the long-standing dissatisfaction with the Rules, designed as it was to cover cases that do not involve the kind of cognitive impairment required for the full insanity defence. Insanity was and remains a complete defence – under the same Rules – which if successful leads to acquittal and confinement for life in a psychiatric hospital. In such cases, there is no responsibility. With the plea of diminished responsibility, the defendant is pleading not guilty to murder, but guilty to manslaughter on the grounds that he is less than fully responsible for his action. It is this reduction, this partial responsibility, that constitutes the important innovation. The defendant is held to be less than fully culpable, by virtue of what is now called 'abnormality of mind', in place of the much more specific 'defect of reason' in the M'Naghten Rules.

This plea has largely replaced that of insanity, because it leads to a definite prison sentence, rather than an indefinite confinement under the 1959 Mental Health Act. Until the abolition of capital punishment in 1965, defendants successful in either defence avoided the death sentence.

According to section 2 of the 1957 Homicide Act, any person accused of killing or being a party to killing:

> shall not be convicted of murder if he was suffering from such abnormality of mind – whether arising from a condition of arrested or retarded development of mind or any inherent causes or induced by disease or injury – as substantially impaired his mental responsibility for his acts and omissions in doing or being a party to the killing.
>
> (Allen 2001: 528)

The key points here are abnormality of mind and substantial impairment of responsibility. What a jury is called upon to decide is, first, whether there is such abnormality, and, second, whether this has led to sufficient impairment of the defendant's responsibility to merit a reduction of the verdict from murder to manslaughter. At the same time, it must be found that there is sufficient respon-sibility – it is diminished, not negated – to merit a sentence appropriate for manslaughter. In reaching these decisions, the jury is expected to take into account the evidence of medical experts only as one component of the evidence as a whole, including all witness statements and the demeanour of the defendant.

The 1957 Act, then, has replaced the 'insanity or nothing' situation with an alternative flexible enough to counter many of the criticisms of the M'Naghten Rules. The criterion of mental abnormality, replacing the strictly cognitive test, is deliberately phrased in such a way that juries are free to interpret it as emotional instability or constrained will, if they believe that this is enough to prove sub-stantial impairment of responsibility. When a judge in 1961 attempted to exclude these non-cognitive factors, he was overruled on appeal (Bavidge 1989: 26). It was also through the 1957 Act that irresistible impulse was tacitly admitted, as acknowledged in the ruling on *R.* v. *Byrne* (1960), in which it was accepted that the 'inability to exercise will power to control physical acts', providing this inability results from the kind of mental abnormality specified in the Act, is allowable as a defence to murder (Allen 2001: 533).

Conclusion

What this reform of the law has amounted to in practice is a recognition that both mental disturbance and responsibility are a matter of degree, and a belief that the borders of insanity are grey areas in which the good sense of the jury, with the benefit of all evidence available, is the most reliable method for determining the presence of abnormality and the degree of responsibility. Historically speaking, this is a long way from the wild-beast test. Neither the 1957 Act nor the M'Naghten Rules require the defendant to be entirely devoid of rationality. The tension between liberal and sceptical responses to mentally disturbed offenders persists, but the test for criminal liability remains distinctively legal.

Study questions

General question: Is there a coherent and fair rationale behind the current excusing conditions for insane and mentally disturbed offenders?

Further study questions: Are the M'Naghten Rules consistent with the doctrine of *mens rea*? Is the delusion test a reasonable one? Is the criticism that the Rules are narrowly and exclusively cognitive justifiable? Was the exclusion of the volitional clause of *mens rea* from the insanity defence justifiable? Should an 'irresistible impulse' defence excuse an offender from criminal responsibility? Has the introduction of the concept of diminished responsibility solved all the problems raised by the M'Naghten Rules?

Suggestions for further reading

Recommended general works on insanity and the law are D.N. Robinson (1996), Reznek (1997), Fingarette (1972), Fingarette and Hasse (1979), Bavidge (1989) and Schopp (1991). There are also important analyses in Hart (1968: chs 8, 9), Jacobs (1971: ch. 2), Ten (1987: ch. 6), Norrie (2014: ch. 9), J. Murphy (1979: chs 9–11) and A. Kenny (1978: ch. 4). Porter (1987) and (2002) are excellent short histories of insanity.

For further information and analysis of the M'Naghten trial and Rules, see D.N. Robinson (1996: ch. 5), Keeton (1961), West and Walk (1977) and Biggs (1955: ch. 4). See also the selections on 'legal insanity' in Morris (1961: ch. 8). The M'Naghten Rules are reprinted in numerous anthologies, including Morris (1961: 395).

15 Theories of punishment

The institution of state punishment is so widespread in the contemporary world that the question of justifying its very existence does not often arise. This is partly because the answer seems so obvious. Without any structure of positive sanctions in place, it is assumed, normal social transactions could not be governed by law. Without any mechanism for coercion or enforcement of legal norms, we could hardly speak of a legal system at all. Close analysis of the justification of punishment, however, reveals serious tensions, not only between competing theoretical perspectives but also between conflicting practical attitudes on questions about what kinds of punishment are morally acceptable. Various defences of the existing systems offer inconsistent accounts of the principles underlying punishment. They also collide with proposals for penal reform and even with frankly abolitionist arguments. What philosophical analysis over the last few centuries has aimed at is a clear examination of the principles in conflict here.

The problem of justification

We need first to remember why state punishment requires justification. Like many other common practices, punishment is at least *prima facie* problematic because it involves the kind of treatment that in any other context would be morally indefensible. As is well known, the history of the practice of punishment has spanned the full range, from the mildest of penalties to the most cruel and inhumane treatment imaginable. Even in an age when we like to think that most state punishment is relatively humane, policies such as the death penalty or imprisonment, involving the deprivation of life or liberty, clearly stand in need of justification.

It has often been found instructive to compare this question about justifying punishment with other, non-punitive instances of state coercion, which are also in their very nature morally problematic. Any state action or policy that involves the apparent violation of individual rights requires a special justification. Emergency measures in times of national crisis, the introduction of military conscription or national service, the Prevention of Terrorism Act (2005) and other suspensions of specific civil liberties are generally agreed to be subject to special justification. Non-punitive coercion also includes practices such as the rationing of scarce resources, the requisitioning of property or internment of enemy citizens in wartime, compulsory purchase and the enforced quarantine of blameless victims of contagious diseases. None of these examples normally involve punishment or penalisation; nevertheless all of them are, to say the least, morally questionable and need to be justified.

Apart from the obvious consideration that the question of whether such measures can be justified will depend on the specific circumstances in each case, it at first seems that there is only one type of justification available, that of reference to ends and the invocation of 'necessary evil'. The greater the danger to be averted or the greater the good to come out of the action – in terms of public safety, public health or national security – implies that the ends are desirable enough to outweigh the distress or inconvenience involved in the means. The assumption, then, is that the only justification available for such 'harsh measures' is based on an instrumental, means–ends type of reasoning.

Does it follow that the practice of state punishment is of the same order as these other questionable practices and that justification must follow the same instrumental route? Some philosophers have certainly thought so. Surely, it might be argued, the victims of such policies are blameless and, if such treatment can be justified, then the punishment of the guilty can *a fortiori* be justified along the same lines.

To show that this argument is too peremptory, we need to look more closely at the claim that all morally questionable acts can only be justified by instrumental reason. Is it possible to justify such an act without any reference at all to the good that will come out of it? One way to argue this would be to deny that the act was in fact morally questionable, or 'an evil' in itself. To argue that an activity is 'perfectly justified' is often to claim that there is nothing wrong with it, that those who disapprove are entirely mistaken. In a wider context, this is frequently said in defence of 'victimless' crimes, where no harm has been done. Another way, however, is to accept that in normal circumstances the act would be indefensible, but that in these unusual circumstances it is justified in itself as a response to another act. Thus, one might argue that 'a justified outburst' or 'justified anger' at an unwarranted attack on oneself or another is a morally appropriate response to provocation and contemplated without any view to the future. This could, of course, be represented as covertly instrumental, in that the justification is derived from the intention to defend one's interests, character or reputation. The ends again justify the means. This tendency, however, to reduce all justifications to forward-looking ones, with reference only to goals or objectives, obscures an important normative distinction.

Punishment justified by its effects

Given that state punishment can involve extremely harsh treatment, which in normal circumstances (which is to say, without good cause) would be regarded with horror, philosophers who adopt the instrumentalist outlook insist that the only justification for such drastic measures must lie in the compensating benefits that will come out of it. The standard practice of imposing long periods of imprisonment for serious crime, for example, can only be justified if this practice as a whole is at least partly instrumental in the reduction or control of crime. If it cannot be justified with reference to these or some other social goals, then punishment inflicted for its own sake would be seen as nothing more than pointless cruelty, and hence manifestly unjustified. The basic requirement of justification is that the punishment has some definite purpose. What this purpose might be varies enormously. To define it as the reduction of crime is the most general statement of the purpose of punishment, thus understood. For this reason, this perspective is often referred to as 'reductivism' (Walker 1991). This objective is in turn justified in terms of more general moral aims, such as the need for personal security and the opportunity to fulfil human potential. This in turn is justified until we reach a goal – such as the utilitarian standard of the general happiness – that does not need to be justified in any other terms. That is to say, we reach a goal that has non-instrumental value.

The reductivist aim is itself broken down into many specific penal strategies, with widely varying moral implications. The most obvious preventive strategy is the use of temporary or permanent confinement – either in prison or psychiatric hospital – to neutralise or incapacitate dangerous offenders. Consequently, the most basic justification of punishment is the need to remove offenders from society. Taken in isolation, this justification is morally equivalent to the enforced quarantine of carriers of deadly diseases. Another of the central reductivist strategies is the threat or the implementation of punitive sanctions in order to discourage or pre-empt the need for punishment. What this involves is the use of punishment as a deterrent, in a specific form to deter its recipient from reoffending, and in a general form to discourage others from committing the same kind of offence.

In addition to the goals of prevention and deterrence, reductivist strategies have included various attempts to adjust the behaviour of persistent offenders. The ideal aim here is to achieve the rehabilitation or reintegration of the offender into society. This rehabilitative ideal takes us beyond the scope of the standard consequentialist theories of punishment, primarily based on prevention and deterrence, because it ranges from the kind of moral education and reform strategies that see punishment itself as the agent of such effects, to approaches that regard the adjustment of the offender's behaviour as a preferable alternative to punishment. The latter includes the belief that offenders can be 'cured' of their criminal tendencies by various kinds of aversion therapy. Overall, though, this general goal of rehabilitation still exemplifies a broadly instrumental approach to the problem of justification, in that it rests on the assumption that this is the only way to justify either openly punitive practices or compulsory reformative alternatives.

The instrumental justification of punishment requires that at least one of these strategies lies behind its practice. The condition of its justification is that the evil of punishing is outweighed by one or more of these compensating benefits.

Justifying punishment retrospectively

For those who look exclusively to the present and the past for justification, the good that may come out of the practice of state punishment is contingent or incidental to the justification. Whether or not there exists a right to punish depends on what has already happened. The various social and individual benefits of the practice – the prevention and reduction of crime, the creation of greater peace and security, the effects on the offenders and their victims – are recognised as important considerations in themselves, but also as outcomes to be encouraged quite independently of the legitimacy of punishing. The right, in other words, precedes the good. The right to punish is derived from the offender's breaking of the law, or from his or her violation of the rights of others. How exactly the right to punish is derived from these past events rather than from projections into the future is, for the retrospectivist, the crux of the justification problem.

The main issue for retrospectivists, then, is how far they succeed in fixing a strictly non-consequential horizon. In its purest versions, the committing of a crime is both necessary and sufficient for the justification of punishment. The crime in some sense calls for or demands a punitive response. The classic statement of this claim was made by Hegel (1770–1831), who represented both crime and punishment in terms of the negation or annulment of its opposite. Punishment is justified because it nullifies or makes nothing of the crime; it negates it both legally and morally. This is why, morally speaking, it can be done, and why it has to be done; the state has both the right and the duty to punish.

This was one version of what is known as retributivism. Although the literal meaning of 'retribution' concerns the idea of the duty of repayment or reparation for wrongs committed, the connotations attaching to this ancient term are much wider. The core concept of the traditional theories of retribution is that of desert, indicating the principle that punishment should be given to people according to what they justly deserve, rather than to what we may feel is necessary for purposes of deterrence or rehabilitation.

Most of the other key retributive concepts revolve around this one. The right to retaliate with equivalent force against intentional violations of the moral code as enforced by the law is intrinsically linked with the idea that wrongdoing deserves punishment of the same level of seriousness as the offence. The general idea that retributive justice is the proper goal of punishment, rather than consequentialist calculations of outcomes, is also based on the idea of just deserts. Desert lies behind the retributive belief that the suffering inflicted by the punishment on the guilty is not an intrinsic evil to be regretted, but on the contrary a desirable state of affairs. This can only be so if those who have inflicted suffering on others can be said to deserve to suffer themselves. Each of these elements of the retributive justification is essentially backward-looking; the repayment, the retaliation, the deserved sufferings for past wrongs, all seem to be purely retrospective in their frame of reference.

Several other elements combine to produce the standard retributive justification. One of the more prominent is the Kantian insistence that the precondition of just punishment is that it treats offenders with respect for their dignity and capacity for free choice. Treating offenders as ends in themselves is the positive requirement here, but what is perhaps more important is what this prescription rules out, the use of others 'merely as a means' for greater social objectives.

Criticisms of the traditional theories

The most general and fundamental criticism of the forward-looking, instrumental approach is the claim that it is unjustifiably lenient in its implications for penal policy, that it releases the state from its obligation to punish crime in accordance with desert. Retributivists argue that, if desert is removed from the justification, nothing is left to prevent inappropriately light sentencing for serious crime. The role played by desert in this respect cannot be taken over by deterrence, because it is precisely the restriction of the goal of punishment to this unpredictable factor that destabilises the entire institution of state punishment.

It may at first seem paradoxical that the other main type of criticism focuses on the personal dignity and rights of those who are liable to be punished by consequentialists. The first aspect of this line of criticism is the belief that we – or the state – owe it to the offenders themselves to punish them as if they were free reasoning agents. If offenders are punished in accordance with factors extraneous to the fact and nature of their crime, or their degree of culpability, the implication is that they are being treated – contrary to the Kantian dictum – merely as a means to an end, rather than as responsible human agents. This idea that it is morally repugnant to regard people merely as objects for manipulation is applied generally to the practice of punishment, but it is thought especially relevant to the forcible re-educative and 'curative' rehabilitation programmes favoured by some consequentialists. A typically retributive view is that even the most severe punishment is less dehumanising than this kind of 'treatment'.

The second aspect of this line of criticism is that there is an irresistible logic whereby the unrestricted pursuit of utility leads to outright injustice. This is a criticism applied much more broadly to utilitarianism as a moral theory, but it becomes particularly focused in the philosophy of punishment. The danger in this respect is quite clear. If the administration of punishment, especially in sentencing, were to be guided solely by considerations of social policy and expediency, calculating the best probable consequences for society as a whole, there would be no limit to the potential injustice suffered by individuals or minority groups for the sake of the general good. There would be no restraint on favouritism or victimisation, or on the nature of the punishment. Even the complete absence of guilt would provide no good reason for not punishing, if the occasional scapegoating of the innocent could be shown to be in the public interest. This, it is often said, is the logical conclusion of making the justification of punishment purely forward-looking. The overall criticism is that, when the core requirements of guilt and desert are removed, there remains no steadiness of purpose or stability in the philosophy of punishment. Every policy is subject to variation and experimentation.

It is in their attack on this inherent lack of control or limitation on the instrumentalist approach that retributivists score most heavily. Their insistence that prospective benefits – even the prospect of the complete elimination of a particularly threatening crime – do not give the state the right to punish, that this can only be derived from the prior fact and nature of the crime and what the criminal thereby deserves, puts them in a position to make the retributivist case persuasive by virtue of its focus on the injustice of punishing the innocent, which makes an almost universal appeal to moral intuition.

Weaknesses of retributivism

The weaknesses found in traditional retributivism fall under three headings: (1) doubts about its status as a moral justification; (2) problems with intelligibility; and (3) problems of rationality. Overall, it has been argued by critics that retributivism is morally dubious, that its key concepts are incorrigibly vague or ambiguous, and that it is based on feeling rather than reason. It will become clear that these sets of problems are interconnected, but it is important first to isolate them as distinct weaknesses.

The moral-status problem

This is seen by many consequentialist critics as the basic and decisive one. Retributivism, it is said, does not really qualify as a moral theory of justification at all, because it is based on the premoral instincts to retaliate and take revenge. What this sanctions is the taking of sadistic pleasure in the self-righteous infliction of suffering. The point of constructing a modern moral theory is to civilise our instincts, not to give them free rein by institutionalising them.

Traditional retributivists hold that the state draws not only the right but also the duty to punish exclusively from the fact and nature of the crime, rather than from any benefits the punishment might produce. The duty as well as the right to punish is strictly backward-looking. This is the source of the most damaging criticisms of the retributive case. If the duty arises solely from what cannot be undone, it is argued, the state has no moral alternative but to exact retribution, regardless of the good or evil that may come out of it, even if a non-punitive response would be manifestly preferable. In this respect, it is argued, they are saddled with an outdated superstition, that every crime must be paid for, regardless of exonerating circumstances. On this line of reasoning, the logical conclusion of retributivism is a completely irrational and vindictive insistence on punishment for its own sake.

The retaliatory character of the retributivist justification is central to Kant's philosophy of punishment and is rooted in the ancient biblical doctrine of *lex talionis*. A standard line of defence against the criticism that retributivism is rooted in an Old Testament morality of vengeance, from which we should long since have distanced ourselves, is that even in the original sources these maxims were intended to civilise rather than to urge vengeance. The idea is that the 'eye for an eye' maxim was a judicial rule aimed at limiting revenge to inflicting equivalent harm – that is, to take no more than an eye – rather than insisting that justice demands the taking of revenge. It has to be said that there is little support for this interpretation in the relevant passages, which do seem to insist upon responding punitively, rather than urging restraint in the response. It is quite possible, of course, that both meanings can be intended simultaneously. Even on the softer interpretation, however, the question of whether the returning of 'like for like' is really a moral response remains unresolved.

Although appeals to intuition are frequent in this debate, they do not seem to take us much further, because there is a deep intuitive conflict on this matter. While some find it self-evident that a serious offence intrinsically merits an equally serious punishment, others find it intuitively obvious that punishment for the sole purpose of retribution is pointless, that it serves no useful or civilised purpose. The retributive reply that the point of punishment is that it serves the purpose of criminal justice is met by the response that this is a particular, outdated and severe conception of justice that is inappropriate to a modern humane society.

Problems with intelligibility

In addition to the claim that the retributive attitude is morally reactionary, the second major weakness identified by critics is that all attempts to develop a systematic elucidation of its key concepts have led only to deeper mystification. What does it really mean, for example, to say that a criminal 'deserves' to suffer or be penalised for the crime? Does it mean any more than that we believe they ought to suffer for it? If so, how does this 'ought' mysteriously arise from the fact or nature of the crime? Why should it not be derived from, for example, the need to prevent and deter other such crimes?

The retributivist reply to this is complex. On the face of it, one might imagine, it is easy to argue that desert, like acknowledgement or gratitude, is an essentially retrospective concept and is intuitively intelligible as such. The difficulty that remains, however, is that of showing that it makes sense to say that either a moral right or an obligation to punish can be generated by the simple reflection that we commonly use this retrospective concept.

More specifically, what is the reasoning behind the retributive claim that the punishment should 'fit' or 'match' the crime? In the context of the death sentence for murder – 'a life for a life' – it is conceded by critics that this is at least intelligible; however, what would the matching sentence be for fraud, for treason, for rape? The idea of even a rough correspondence in this sense between a crime and its punishment is said to be of little practical value. Ultimately, it is argued, the retributive language of desert is mere rhetoric to mask the absence of an intelligible justification.

The standard retributivist reply to this criticism as a whole is that the intelligibility of desert as a justification is exhibited in the principle of proportionality, the violation of which – handing out disproportionate punishment – is a clear injustice. To punish a minor theft, for example, more severely than an armed robbery is manifestly unjust. Starting from such examples, it is easy to construct parallel scales of seriousness in criminal offences, on the one hand, and penalties or sentences, on the other. That one should match the other is a requirement of desert, not of any consequentialist calculation.

There are basically two problems with this. The first is that any ranking of criminal offences according to desert is controversial. Which is the more serious, meriting more serious punishment: robbery with violence, or a non-violent crime such as fraud, the illicit proceeds of which are much greater? Second, even if a scale of desert is settled, this only solves the problem of the relative severity of the punishment. It does not fix the level of the mean, which in practice is relative to the standards of a particular society. Nor does it fix the range (minimum and maximum) or the spread (ratio of one offence to another) of the scale. A retributivist might well reply that the very recognition of these problems amounts to a tacit admission that desert is the appropriate basis for justification. The consequentialist can in turn reply that the principle of proportionality gives us at most a justification for treating some offences as more serious than others; the scale might as easily be applied to the appropriate degree of disapproval or reprimand, as to the institution of punishment. What this demonstrates, however, is that the justification is difficult, not that the idea of desert as justification is unintelligible.

The most notoriously vague aspect of the retributivist account originates in Hegel's theory that the punishment constitutes an annulment of the crime. The idea at the heart of this theory is that the act of punishment constitutes a denial of the legitimacy of the criminal act, in Hegel's dialectical terms, a rightful negation of the criminal negation, leading to a moral reaffirmation of the legitimacy of the rightful order. Although this perhaps comes the closest to a purely retributive justification, problems of intelligibility have frequently been voiced. How can punitive action nullify or 'make nothing of' an offence in which death or permanent injury has been caused? How can the situation prior to the crime be restored? These objections, however, rest upon a misinterpretation of the sense of negation intended by Hegel. It is not the offence itself that is annulled or 'cancelled out', it is the implicit claim to a morally and legally invalid legitimacy that is 'made nothing of'. For Hegel, the dialectical process of crime and punishment is a struggle for the recognition of the validity of the moral order that has been challenged. The justification of punishment is purely retrospective because it is drawn solely from the challenge to the moral and legal authority of the state.

Problems of rationality

In addition to doubts about moral soundness and intelligibility, the third type of weakness commonly attributed to the retributive approaches is the absence of a rational basis for the justification of punishment. The problem here is that, even if we can make it clear what is required for a retributive justification and give an intelligible account of the state's right and duty to punish without reference to consequences, we cannot give any good reasons for preferring this justification, without such reference. The best that can be done is to clarify by example the intuition that the guilty deserve 'to be brought to justice'. The problem here is that most phrases that seem to capture the elusive meaning of the retributive justification are highly emotive ones. The general charge in terms of rationality is that retributivism is entirely dependent on intuition and the negative emotions of anger, resentment and hatred. An important accompanying criticism is that attempts at elucidation depend too much on symbol and metaphor, not enough on reasoned argument.

There are essentially two ways in which retributivists can reply to this. They can either accept that retributivism is not rational, but argue that it is nevertheless morally defensible, or they can reject the instrumentalist model of rationality and argue that a rational account of retributivism can be given. With the first approach, it can be argued that the retributive emotions, properly controlled and channelled by law, express a wholly legitimate response to crime and that this in itself constitutes a justification. The reason for preferring the retributive justification is that it is held to be psychologically and morally realistic, in that it conforms with the sentiments of disapproval or abhorrence that most people feel in response to serious crime. This approach questions the assumption that justification as such has to be rational (Mackie 1985: ch. 15).

The second way is more difficult. It is insufficient – though quite correct – to point out that retributivists do not lack reasoned arguments; the question is about the basis of these arguments. What has to be shown here is that a strictly non-consequential justification can sensibly be called a rational one. If 'rationality' simply means 'thinking in terms of consequences', any non-consequential thinking becomes irrational by definition. If, on the other hand, its meaning is wider than this, including retrospectivist thinking in terms of pre-existent rights and the duty to respect them for their own sake, then the constraints on the application of the narrower rationality will themselves be seen as an integral part of rationality, rather than as emotive constraints.

Modifications and compromises

It should be clear from the discussion to this point why, unless one side gives way on an important point of principle, the two positions cannot be simply combined into a unified theory of punishment. There have nevertheless been numerous attempts, especially in the second half of the twentieth century, to modify the theories in such a way that they might complement one another. The idea behind the 'mixed theory' is to search for a common ground on which some of the opposing elements can be synthesised into a coherent theory that will either reflect the reality of existing legal practices or provide the basis for realistic proposals to reform the current system. From this standpoint, neither the instrumental justification nor the retributive one in their pure and intransigent versions are seen as realistic in either sense.

There are three important possible structures for the mixed theory to adopt. It can be (1) retributive in its basic justification, making concessions to the demands of social policy; (2) instrumentalist in its basic justification, making concessions to one or more of the retributive principles; or (3) more radically innovative in that the basis of justification is extended across both areas, so that both retributive justice and social value are necessary conditions, but neither alone is sufficient.

Strong and weak retributivism

The first option has been a very popular one. What the moderation of retributivism involves is the distinction between a maximum version, insisting on both the right and the duty of the state to punish, and a minimum version that relinquishes the duty, insisting only on the prior right to punish and the forfeiture by the criminal of the right not to be punished. The main advantage of this is that it avoids the range of criticisms relating to its moral status. On the minimum interpretation, the state only exercises its right when there actually is a non-retributive point, which is to say that it takes a flexible approach to prosecution and sentencing, allowing that consequential considerations can override the *prima facie* duty to punish.

The maximum interpretation is clearly indicated by the traditional versions of retributivism. Kant's insistence on the solemn duty to execute every last murderer (Kant 1887: 194–201) is the paradigm case of strong retributivism. Hegel's theory of annulment also implies the inseparability of the duty and the right to punish; the theory is an explanation of why the state is morally obliged as well as entitled to invalidate the crime. It cannot let the offence stand. The case for minimalism, however, has been defended by modern retributivists such as W.D. Ross (1930), Armstrong (1961) and Mundle (1954).

There is certainly some plausibility in arguing that the minimal thesis is more in line with actual practices; the commuting of sentences and reprieves, the royal prerogative of mercy, the powers of the Home Secretary, judicial discretion and mitigation of severity of sentence have played a prominent role in the history of the English legal system, and also many prosecutions are not held to be in the public interest. In short, the right to punish is not always exercised. Against this, however, some sentences have been mandatory and many offences are not regarded as subject to discretion.

The relevant question here, however, is about the kind of principles in operation. Flexibility and mitigation of sentence tend to be desert-based – focusing on degrees of responsibility – rather than consequentialist. To the extent that this is true, the mixed theory is not a concession to consequentialism at all. If, on the other hand, the theory were to accept the principle that consequentialist considerations should govern sentencing as a proposal for systematic reform, it would be making so many radical concessions that it would be difficult to see it as retaining any more than a formal commitment to retributivism. Either way, the minimal version, abandoning the duty to punish, does not seem to provide a basis for a real compromise. The dilemma we are left with is that, while the Kantian strong version is too strong, the weak version either makes no real concessions or virtually dissolves as a retributive theory.

Lex talionis *and unfair advantage*

A different kind of attempt to modify the retaliatory character of retributivism is represented by theories that shift the justification from the doctrine of *lex talionis* to the idea that desert is based, not on the right of the state to retaliate against offenders, but on the right and duty to remove the advantage unfairly gained by the offender's refusal to play by the rules. The duty is towards those who have not taken similar advantage, those on behalf of whom the state acts, and the focus is on the injustice towards the law-abiding. Offenders deserve to suffer in a measure equivalent to their offence, not by virtue of an ancient moral law commanding such equivalence, but because the failure to cancel the advantage is an injustice.

This line of thought is aimed at defusing the criticism that retributivism is based solely on the vengeful emotions. The idea that the suppression of unfair advantage is morally mandatory is aimed, not at changing the substance of the theory, but at providing it with rational rather than emotional backing and thereby making it more intelligible.

Consequentialist compromises

There are a number of important theories that are explicitly instrumentalist in their basic assumptions, but that are designed specifically for the purpose of reconciling this kind of justification with retributivism. The two most influential were developed by Rawls (1955) and H.L.A. Hart in 1959 (Hart 1968).

The essential feature common to each of these theories was the claim that the problem of justification in punishment theory cannot be expressed by one question – such as 'How is punishment justified?' – but must address a more discriminating set of questions, the answers to which are different in kind. It is the difference between these answers that is supposed to create the ground for a compromise, or for a combined theory of punishment.

Rawls's opening distinction is between (1) any practice or system of rules, such as a game, a governing assembly or the institution of punishment, and

(2) a particular action falling under these rules, such as a move in a game, a parliamentary enactment or a judicial decision, any one of which is governed by the relevant system of rules. Justifying a practice, Rawls argued, is quite different from justifying any of its instances. With the practice of punishment, what we are determining is the initial purpose of setting up the institution and punishing anybody at all. This, he claimed, can only be justified in utilitarian terms, as furthering in some way the interests of society. Nobody, he believed, would want to argue that the very *purpose* of punishment was to match wrongdoing with suffering. With a particular instance of punishment, by contrast, the conviction and sentencing of an individual lawbreaker can only be justified in terms of that individual's guilt, or the fact that he has broken the rules of the practice.

What Rawls was arguing was that it would be inappropriate to try to justify any such punitive action in forward-looking, consequentialist terms. While the legislator laying down the law looks to the future, the judge applying the law looks to the past. In this way, Rawls argued that utilitarians and retributivists both have a legitimate point, and that the two perspectives can be combined by recognising this distinction.

Hart's starting point is similar to that of Rawls, in that he distinguishes between a 'general justifying aim' behind punishment as a whole, and the specific principles of justice guiding and restricting the application of punishment. He then rejects retribution as the general aim and argues that it is legitimately to be found in the principles constraining the operation of utility. This he describes as 'retribution in distribution', which he finds morally defensible. The main feature of this distributive justice is the requirement that guilt is a necessary condition of punishment. Punishment as a whole is justified in the first place – as it had been in Rawls's version – by the general justifying aim of its beneficial consequences, primarily crime reduction. What Hart was seeking, in his own words, was 'the middle way between a purely forward-looking scheme of social hygiene and theories which treat retribution as a general justifying aim' (Hart 1968: 233). One of Hart's central themes was the need to untangle the conceptual confusion caused by utilitarians and retributivists alike in failing to see the distinction between the general justifying aim and the principled constraints upon it.

Both Rawls and Hart worked on the assumption that, if the implications of these distinctions could be made clear, only the most intransigent of old-fashioned retributivists could fail to see that the justifying aim must be consequentialist, especially given the recognition of the real place of the retributivist principles in the practice of punishment. The implication that they both attached great importance to, that the problem of punishing the innocent could be avoided by combining the utilitarian general aim with 'retribution in distribution', was thought to be decisive. That these assumptions were unduly optimistic was to be clearly demonstrated by the retributivist revival in the 1970s. The main practical concern in this revival was to reinstate the priority of desert over deterrence as the fundamental justification.

Punishment as communication: Nozick and Hampton

The theme of expression and communication implicitly runs through all the literature on punishment. Even where it is not explicit, the idea of a negative value judgement embodied in or accompanying the punishment is present in any attempt to justify it. In recent times, the close attention given to the communicative aspect of punishment as its inner meaning has been developed in order to find the source of the conflict between the different perspectives on justification.

Communicative theories have been predominantly but not exclusively retributivist. The idea that the inherent meaning of punishment is to convey a message of emphatic denunciation, whether to the offender, the victim of the crime, or the society in whose name the state punishes, can as easily be interpreted as having an instrumental function (as serving the ends of crime prevention or moral education) as being an end in itself. This kind of theory has nevertheless been associated mainly with the retributivist revival since the early 1970s, with attempts to clarify, reinforce or amend the traditional versions of retributivism. The commitment of many of the new retributivists to theories of communication should be seen partly as an attempt to move the debate forward, partly as a continuation of the old project of defending the moral respectability and rational intelligibility of punishment as retribution.

Robert Nozick: connecting with correct values

Robert Nozick's retributive theory is an attempt to do both, to illuminate the old tradition within the framework of a distinctive communicative theory. For Nozick, 'retributive punishment is an act of communicative behaviour' that communicates the unwelcome message to the offender, 'this is how wrong what you did was' (Nozick 1981: 370).

Taking as a guiding structure the simple formula $r \times H$ (degree of responsibility, multiplied by actual harm done), Nozick argues that retributive punishment is justified to the extent that a wrongdoer intentionally causes harm. The retributivist claim that the intentional committing of the crime is sufficient justification is expressed by Nozick in his central argument that the unwelcome message of wrongness forcefully delivered by punishment constitutes a reconnection with correct values of those who have flouted them through criminally harmful acts, thereby disconnecting themselves from these values.

Recognising the retributivist need to detach the justification from any hint of instrumental objectives, Nozick contrasts his own version with what he calls teleological retributivism, which looks primarily for a positive effect on and a response from the offender. Despite the forward-looking aspect and the reformative implications, this is still retributive because it is a message of condemnation merited by the wrongdoing. On his own version of reconnection, however, the retribution is justified even if the message is entirely unsuccessful. All that is required is that the message be sent and received. In cases where the message has no effect, the connection is still imposed via punishment. 'The act of retributive punishment itself effects this connection' (Nozick 1981: 374). To be punished is to be connected. Like most previous retributivists, Nozick regards a positive response by the offender to the message as a valuable bonus, but unlike them he describes this as an *intensification* of what is already achieved without it.

The difficulty many have found with this lies in the highly teleological flavour of the phrase 'reconnection with correct values', which sounds as though it must depend on a project of moral improvement. Despite his denials that any reformative goals, successful or otherwise, are necessary for this justification, Nozick's purely non-teleological retributivism remains difficult to interpret.

What he seems to mean by this is that, right from the outset, the imposition of punishment is an involuntary connection with correct values of those who have broken and resisted this connection, thus 'flouting' correct values. This enforced connection is already justified solely in terms of connecting even if the offender subsequently comes nowhere near to understanding or responding to the message and is determined to reoffend as soon as released. If the offender does show signs of internalising the correct values, exhibiting understanding and remorse, what is happening is not something qualitatively different, it is the connection – already in place – beginning to work.

One thing Nozick is trying to defuse is the standard criticism that punishment without beneficial results is pointless. What he is implicitly denying in his insistence on the continuity of the communicative behaviour of the punisher is the radical breach between intrinsic and instrumental value and justification. As he sees it, the latter might or might not emerge from the former.

Jean Hampton: defeating the wrongdoer

The retributive emphasis on rights is of particular importance to the attempts to interpret the tradition in the light of the idea of punishment as communication. The pressure from instrumentalist criticism is resisted by viewing retributive punishment as the legitimate sending of a message that responds to criminal violations or infringements of the rights of others. The justification originates in the criminally coercive invasion of rights, rather than in the instrumental value of the denunciatory message.

Jean Hampton places the issue of rights violation at the centre of her communicative theory. Following up Nozick's theory of connection or 'linkage' to correct values, she is less concerned with detaching the justification from moral reform or other penal policies than with explaining punishment as an inherently justified response to the rights-violating message sent out by the offender, and to explain why the state is at fault if it fails to respond with the appropriate message. Her essays rest on Kantian ideas about respect and human value; they offer a modern interpretation of the *lex talionis* and of the Hegelian theory of annulment (J. Murphy and Hampton 1988).

Hampton's central idea is that of 'inflicting a defeat' on the wrongdoer, whose violation of the rights of others is seen as sending out an objectively demeaning message of domination or mastery over the victim. The reason tough punishment, inflicting suffering in equal measure to the seriousness of the violation, is essential to the communication of the message is that the defeat must be a real one, rather than a merely symbolic denunciation. When society fails to deliver the appropriate punitive action, we allow ourselves as a whole, and the victim in particular, to be demeaned and defeated.

The message conveyed by the wrongdoer who invades the rights of another is that the other is of less personal worth than he or she actually is. At the same time as it expresses a diminishment of the worth of the other, the wrongdoer's message lays false claim to his or her own superior worth. It is the rightful correction of this false representation of their relative worth that justifies the punishment. The purpose of retributive punishment is to bring down the exaggerated claims about the offender's worth, while at the same time, through the same act, reasserting and restoring the worth of the victim. If the state fails to administer punishment sufficiently serious to bring about this defeat, it implicitly endorses the false representation of the relative worth of the rights of invader and victim.

Hampton calls this representation of relative worth 'false evidence of mastery'. It is this evidence, she argues, that is the proper object of Hegelian annulment. The negation of the evidence for a distorted representation of the relative worth of offender and victim restores the true picture in the same way that a scientific disproof of misleading evidence uncovers the true picture of a natural reality. It does not make the evidence disappear; it simply discredits it and shows that it does not prove what it appears to prove. This 'refutation' can only be achieved through punishment, because this is the only practical demonstration of the invalidity of the evidence and vindication of the victim's true worth. To punish is to force the would-be master to suffer defeat at the hands of the victim or the victim's agent. No amount of verbal or symbolic denunciation can inflict this defeat.

The point of Kant's insistence that the failure to punish every murderer implicates the entire community in the crimes left unpunished is explained by Hampton as a general insight into the significance of the message conveyed by punishment. In terms of her theory of false evidence, she argues that, when we abandon the retributive goal of punishment, we condone the false evidence for the inferior worth of the victim, because it stands undefeated. In allowing it to stand, we 'acquiesce in the message it sent about the victim's inferiority'.

Her reinterpretation of *lex talionis* is that this is a formula demanding that the wrongdoer suffer a defeat on a similar scale to the one he or she has inflicted. Hampton argues that this should be restricted to the principle of proportionality, whereby the greater the offence the greater the defeat needed to reassert the victim's value. What she claims can be removed from the traditional doctrine is the severity of the 'eye for an eye' demand for equivalence, for the punishment to match the crime. The retributive punishment designed to nullify the demeaning message can be constrained by upper limits determined by the Kantian demand for the respect for the humanity of the wrongdoer, even when the wrongdoer has not shown similar respect for the humanity of others. She argues that this demand for respect imposes a ceiling on the severity of punishment, the function of which is to defeat without dehumanising and degrading. By rooting her demand for these humane upper limits to punishment within her own theoretical framework, rather than in *ad hoc* consequential reasoning, she seeks to avoid the old criticisms that retributivism is by its own logic necessarily barbaric.

Hampton's account as a whole certainly throws light on how the Kantian and Hegelian theories can be plausibly interpreted in line with contemporary penal policies, and it has radical implications both for minimum and maximum sentences. The idea that only punishment and the actual 'lowering' of the offender can deliver a real defeat of the criminal offence is perhaps more convincing than earlier retributivist accounts; it probably comes closer than most theories to bridging the gap between the rational case for denunciation of wrongdoing and the case for hard penal treatment.

There are, however, several serious problems. It is dubious that the restriction of *lex talionis* to proportional punishment, relinquishing the idea of it 'matching the crime', counts as a retaliatory principle at all. It is not even clear why it is distinctively retributive, as we shall see in the next section. There is also a stronger than usual emphasis here on personal worth and the lowering of personal value. This kind of account is at its most convincing in the context of offences against the person. When the emphasis is on crimes with victims who suffer irreversible physical or psychological damage, it is easier to find this justification plausible. It is more difficult to extend it to the full range of crime. Is it really plausible to interpret ordinary offences of theft as attempts by criminals to elevate themselves above their real moral status and to demean their victims? How does it fit impersonal crime, in which the victims are anonymous? The unfair advantage explanation seems more appropriate to such cases.

Instrumentalist censure and reprobation

For instrumentalists, the important question about the message communicated by punishment is how this expression of disapproval or condemnation can be most effectively used. Thus, Walker and Padfield (1996: 116) describe it as one sentencing strategy among others, aimed specifically at increasing disapproval of the offence and increasing respect for the law. Braithwaite and Pettit (1990: 160–4) regard the censure or reprobation of the offender as an integral part of punishment, but only for the purpose of what it can achieve in terms of reducing crime and protecting people's freedom. They reject what they term the 'intrinsic reprobationism' of Nozick, von Hirsch and others, all of whom promote the idea that reprobation is a good in itself. In particular, they argue that the need for effective denunciation or reprobation does not support the retributive insistence on some degree of hard treatment, on the grounds that this can only be justified as a last resort, when prevention and public safety demand it.

Desert and deterrence in sentencing

One of the intractable difficulties that seems to have defeated the retributivist imagination is the problem of devising a method to determine the general level of what is deserved. It is much easier to find consensus on the question of relative desert, on which kinds of offender and offence deserve greater or less punishment than others, than it is to set the average level, reflecting the initial equivalence between the punishment and the crime. How do we determine, for example, whether the respective punishments for burglary and armed robbery should be five years and ten years imprisonment, or five months and ten months? This 'absolute' question is sometimes obscured by the arguments for proportionality in sentencing.

More recent theories of desert have focused on the question of how deterrence-based sentencing stands in relation to the desert requirements in terms of both equivalence and proportionality. Given that deterrence is the central factor in the attempts to control or reduce crime, the crucial question concerns the compatibility between this goal and the pursuit of justice in the sense of adhering to both of these principles. It should be noted that the orthodox judicial opinion in Britain and the USA today is that this requires a delicate balance between rights and social policy, and that this balance is largely achieved.

For some theorists, it is a question of which way the balance should be tilted, towards maximising crime reduction or safeguarding justice. For others, this balance is wholly fictitious, concealing the reality that in many areas of crime hard decisions have to be made, seriously compromising either the reductivist strategy or the demands of justice. Alan Goldman (in Simmons *et al.* 1995) has argued that a paradox or dilemma presents itself as soon as we compare the requirements of deterrence and desert. Given that the rate of apprehension and conviction for any type of crime is always less than perfect and often very low, those who in fact are caught and punished have to pay the price for the low rate of conviction, by serving sentences that are always greater than the crime would otherwise merit in terms of the principle of equivalence. The paradox is that, while the resulting injustice, which is tantamount to punishing the innocent, is quite intolerable, the relaxation of this policy, allowing a massive increase in the criminal violations of the rights of innocent victims, would be equally intolerable. Goldman's conclusion is the unremarkable one that the only appropriate response is to increase levels of detection and attack the socioeconomic roots of crime.

He deals with three possible objections to this account of sentencing practices. The 'exceptive clause' argument, that the excessive punishments are justified by the harms greatly outweighing the rights, is rejected on the grounds that there is nothing exceptional about them. The 'fair warning' objection, that if excessively harsh penalties are well-advertised, then the criminal has only himself or herself to blame for ignoring the warning, is rejected on the grounds that this would justify any degree of punishment, however extreme, which would clearly be an unacceptable consequence. The 'lynch mob' objection, that the criminals are themselves being protected from angry public reaction by excessive punishment, is rejected on the grounds that such reactions would justify punishing the vigilantes rather than the criminals.

Given the premises of the argument, these replies sound persuasive. The assumptions Goldman is making, however, are certainly questionable. We have to ask whether effective deterrence in general really requires more punishment than is deserved. The more usual retributive objection to deterrence is not that it is inherently excessive but that it has a destabilising effect on justice, in that it fluctuates according to current social circumstances and type of crime rather than according to equitable criteria. The retributivist conclusion is that lower sentences than desert demands are as common as sentences in excess of desert. With unusual crimes that are unlikely to be emulated, the need for deterrence is negligible, but the retributivist still insists that there must be an equivalence between harm intentionally caused and the punishment. With exceptionally long sentences, such as the 'life tariff', it is quite plain that desert outlives the need for deterrence. What Goldman's argument assumes is that the general level of desert is actually very low, relative to current sentencing practices, such that it will always be less than what is needed for deterrence. The mistake behind this is the assumption that the imperfect rate of detection and conviction is the only factor governing the operation of deterrence. It is, however, often applied quite independently of such considerations, for example to discourage the spread of a new kind of fraud, which would have nothing to do with making people suffer additionally for those who have not been caught.

Another argument that works against the Goldman paradox is found in the influential 'desert-band' theory put forward by Norval Morris (Duff and Garland 1994). This takes the edge off the equivalence problem by introducing flexibility into the determination of how much punishment any particular crime merits. If the attempt to determine the level of punishment deserved is not burdened with the assumption that there must be a precise equivalent, a range can be established, within which the punishment is morally acceptable in terms of desert. Desert is seen as a limiting principle, setting 'the outer limits of leniency and severity which should not be exceeded'. Thus one might argue that, for example, a particular kind of serious assault merits at least 6 months, at most 2 years imprisonment, rather than fixing it at exactly 200 days. With a rigid equivalence principle such as Hegel's, one day too many or too few would be an injustice. Morris's intention is to promote a sentencing practice whereby there is room for manoeuvre or 'fine tuning' within this desert band, applying lower or higher sentences for purposes of incapacitation and deterrence. This, for Morris, is the model upon which discretionary sentencing should operate.

How does this work against the Goldman paradox? The overall point of Morris's argument is that retributive justice does not have to clash with the pragmatic goals of crime reduction, which can be accommodated within the spectrum of desert. It means that increasing the sentence within the minimum–maximum range solely for purposes of deterrence does not constitute an injustice. It does not mean that the tension is eliminated, because there is still an upper cut-off point beyond which deterrence strategies should not go, and a basic minimum that should not be ignored. Thoroughgoing consequentialists will still reject this as an obstacle to rational social policy. It has the potential, however, to reduce the tension between desert and deterrence.

Morris's desert-band theory has greater appeal, in that it offers both an explanation and a kind of justification of common sentencing practices, but it faces serious objections, the most obvious of which is that it merely shifts the problem of determining equivalence from an exact point to a range. Why, for example, should the range itself be fixed at 2 to 4 years, rather than 4 to 8? Why, indeed, should it be a prison term at all? Why not a 10-to-20-minute severe reprimand?

Even if one accepts that the substitution of a range for a precise point facilitates the intuitive setting of equivalence, Morris's theory faces other objections from a retributivist position. There is, for example, nothing to prevent the range of deserved punishment from being manipulated and over-stretched to accommodate grossly unjust sentences. It also explicitly sanctions inequality in sentencing and violates the principle of proportionality. Morris defends his rejection of the principle that 'like cases should be treated alike' on the grounds that equality in law is at most a guiding principle, to be balanced against other values and suspended whenever outweighed.

This was exactly the point that was rejected by von Hirsch (1993) in his defence of the 'commensurate desert' principle, which links the idea of just deserts with the principle of proportionality and 'commonsense notions of equity', ruling out disparate sentences for identical offences. Norval Morris's desert-band theory is unacceptable, he argues, because it holds the principle of equal treatment to embody merely one value among others, to be dispensed with whenever desirable on utilitarian grounds. Von Hirsch, by contrast, insists that there should be a presumption in favour of the principle of commen-surate deserts, that it should have *prima facie* controlling effect on sentencing, only giving way in exceptional circumstances.

Conclusion

The intention throughout this examination of the justifications has been to dispel some of the misconceptions surrounding the debates on punishment, in particular the one that sees two well-defined camps in stark opposition. At the same time, I have tried to show that there are nevertheless two very different modes of moral thinking about punishment, as there is with war and other instances of serious state coercion. Any well-informed reflection on the theory and practice of sentencing reveals a permanent tension between these two ways of thinking.

The search for a coherent link between these two approaches will certainly continue, but what most contemporary philosophers are anxious to avoid is a repetition of past mistakes, the most obvious of which is a simplistic endorsement of the uneasy compromise embodied in the contemporary institutions of punishment, combining the goal of controlling and reducing crime with retributive 'elements' in sentencing. The search continues, not so much for a 'mixed theory' that tries to establish a compromise between incompatibles, but rather for the articulation of a unified theory that combines the two sides, if not into a single position, at least into a framework in which genuine dialogue is possible. What is sought is a realistic theory that tries to root the justification in the kind of punishment which is the least ineffective, holding out some prospect of actually working towards the achievement of its basic goals, which in themselves neither exclude the proper concern with blame and desert, nor set up the kind of institutional framework that will systematically violate any of the principles of justice highlighted by the retributivists.

Study questions

General question: Can punishment be justified? If so, how?

Further study questions: Compare the merits and defects of forward-looking and backward-looking justifications of punishment. Is it possible to synthesise them into a single theory of punishment? What place should the concept of desert have in a theory of punishment? Might it be possible to base a theory of punishment solely on deterrence? Should levels of sentencing be fixed according to desert or deterrence? Does Nozick's communicative theory make better or worse sense of retribution? Is the Hegelian theory that punishment annuls the crime intelligible? Evaluate Hampton's version of annulment theory.

Suggestions for further reading

Outstanding general books on the philosophy of punishment include Honderich (1976), Hart (1968), Lacey (1988) and Ten (1987). More introductory accounts can be found in Lyons (1984: ch. 5), Harris (1997: ch. 5) and J. Murphy and Coleman (1990: ch. 3).

Very useful anthologies of influential traditional writings and modern essays include Grupp (1971), Acton (1969) and Duff (1993). Two anthologies are particularly useful for the more recent developments in this area, the Duff and Garland reader (Duff and Garland 1994) and the *Philosophy and Public Affairs Reader* (Simmons *et al.* 1995).

Any attempt to attain a comprehensive view of twentieth-century and contemporary philosophy of punishment should begin with the hard core of influential arguments contained in these anthologies. The key passages from the classics are in Kant (1887: 194–201), Hegel (1942: 68–73) and Bentham (1970: 158–73).

In the early to mid-twentieth century, the most significant writings were those of the mixed theorists Ewing (1929), Rawls (1955) and Hart (1968); and the defences of retributivism by Mabbott, Mundle and Armstrong (Acton 1969).

As a representative sample of late twentieth-century writings, one should read J. Murphy (1979, 1987), Andenaes (1974), Kleinig (1973), Cottingham (1979), Mackie (1985: ch. 15), Primoratz (1989), Nozick (1981: ch. 4), Hampton (1984), J. Murphy and Hampton (1988), Walker (1991), Braithwaite and Pettit (1990) and von Hirsch (1993). On particular problems relating to sentencing, see Walker and Padfield (1996), Gross and von Hirsch (1981) and Duff (1993: pt 4).

16 Radical perspectives on crime and punishment

Scandals in criminal justice in the Western liberal democracies today tend to be linked not only with high-profile miscarriages of justice, with outspoken comments by eccentric or controversial judges, with false convictions and the imprisonment or execution of the innocent, but also with standing abuses such as the inappropriate judicial treatment of the mentally ill, or the unfair aspects of standard trial procedures, when they are said to be inherently biased or discriminatory against women or ethnic minorities. Such problems are serious, but the agenda of the theories critical of modernity in criminal law is more probing than this. It is not just that the idealised theory of equal justice for all sometimes comes into conflict with the practice in the criminal courts. Radical critics claim that even in theory the system of criminal justice in modern legal systems does not stand up to examination, because it rests on internally inconsistent foundations and flatly contradictory attitudes towards justice. This constitutes a fundamental challenge to the principles of criminal justice as discussed over the last three chapters. In this final chapter, I will critically assess this challenge.

Enlightenment liberalism and its critics

What exactly is under attack here? The first point is that the general framework of the principles of criminal law today is provided by the doctrine of *mens rea* that emerged from the liberal individualism deeply associated with the Enlightenment, and from the English common law tradition. In accordance with the Enlightenment ideal of the rational, autonomous individual, the fundamental liberal assumption behind the *mens rea* doctrine is that every individual who is subject to the sanctions of the legal system is a free, rational agent, self-aware and consciously deliberating and acting on choices, hence presumed to be fully responsible unless proven otherwise. The free rationality of this agent is of special significance to criminal law, because the praise and blame that come with it generate specific conceptions and doctrines of fault and punishment, and it is the absence of this rationality that governs the law on insanity. The second point, as was made clear by the cases considered (Chapters 13–14), is that there is always a tension between the recognition of *mens rea* as vital to a

just legal system, on the one hand, and the judicial and governmental perceptions of the needs of public policy in terms of public health and safety, on
the other. The doctrine of *mens rea*, then, is only one component of the
system of criminal justice. Some see it as the idealised component, the feature
that gives the system its character as an essentially just one, comprising a set
of ideals that can be aspired to but not always wholly achieved.

The range of radical criticism

The range of radical criticism of this picture of criminal law as a precarious
balance between individual justice and the protection of the public is very
broad. Critics have attacked both its general principles and their application
in great detail. The criticism ranges from Marxist and CLS (critical legal
studies) historical analysis of criminal law as essentially an instrument of class
oppression, designed primarily for the protection of private property, to feminist
critiques of the masculine assumptions behind its theory and practice, to
postmodernist deconstructions of all the doctrines, theories and concepts that
sustain criminal law. As with legal theory in general, a critical approach to the
concept of the individual as the 'legal subject' is prominent. Deconstructing
this subject involves an analysis of privileging and marginalisation. Questions
of power are again central, revealing in particular the influence of Marx,
Nietzsche and Foucault. Understanding the philosophy of crime and punishment
purely in terms of power means not only the unmasking of ulterior motives
and drives behind the institutions and ideologies associated with them, but
also the reduction of the language of rights, justice and justification to
expressions of the hierarchical relations of power in contemporary society. It
means that all the liberal assumptions about the courts judging whether or
not defendants are responsible for their actions, or juries determining whether
or not defendants are sane according to law, or the general defensibility of the
rationale behind sentencing, while not exactly meaningless, are at best to be
regarded as indications of self-deception, and at worst as the cynical manipulation of public opinion. So let us see how this critical perspective on the
criminal law is built up.

The individual and society

For most of the critical theories, the autonomous rational individual presupposed by liberalism is a myth designed to legitimise the state and the legal
system. Marx's critique of liberalism and its 'monadic' individual, abstracted
from its social relations, is the single most influential idea in modern critical
theory. This individual is said to be a relatively recent creation, an artificial
construct, projecting the idea of a self-contained, isolated individual person
who plays, among other roles, that of the central subject of the criminal law.
As a rational, deliberating individual, seeking only his own interest, he can
choose to conform his behaviour to the moral law and the law of the land, or

face the punitive consequences. This 'person', it cannot be emphasised enough, is a fiction. The real individual, by contrast, is a concrete person, embedded in a social context of family, environment and social class, exhibiting a unique combination of individuated and socialised characteristics. According to its critics, it is the almost universal tendency of modernity (or, for Marxists, bourgeois ideology) to superimpose this fictitious conception of the individual upon the vast diversity of concrete individuals and thus to arrive at a 'subject' suitable for the purposes of criminal law.

Intention and determinism

One of the central lines of criticism by the critical legal scholars of recent times is largely derived from this contrast between the real and fictitious conception of the individual or the person. One prominent criticism is that there is a contradiction at the heart of liberal legal ideology on the question of free will and determinism, as it applies to human action in society. The question concerns the contexts in which people have real choices and those in which they do not. In criminal law, this age-old metaphysical problem comes into sharp focus. The reasonable assumption is that blame and criminal liability are completely dependent upon the presence or absence of these choices, but it is often not clear how to draw this distinction. A prominent CLS criticism is that liberal legal reasoning on these matters is completely confused, to such an extent that it makes criminal law, like every other area of law, radically indeterminate.

There are several versions of this criticism, but Mark Kelman's is representative and has been influential (Kelman 1987). His argument is essentially that in liberal society nearly everyone tends to oscillate between the two poles of 'intentionalist discourse' and 'determinist discourse'. His distinctive thesis is that most people, including lawyers, are drawn simultaneously to both descriptive accounts of the same course of events and find themselves compelled to accept one and suppress the other, while always remaining aware of what has been suppressed. Only at the outer extremes do we find philosophers or lawyers fixing exclusively on one pole or the other, either asserting universal responsibility and blame for all acts, regardless of pressure of circumstance, duress, illness, etc., or at the other extreme denying blame entirely by asserting universal determinism and negating personal agency.

Despite the implausibility of these extremes, what the criminal law is said to do is privilege the intentionalist discourse over the determinist, the latter being subordinated and arbitrarily confined to particular acceptable areas, so that the standing presumption is always one of a perfectly free agent. The fictitious 'monadic' self is imposed when it is thought necessary to uphold an intentionalist discourse, in order to show that free choices could have been made. When such choices are assumed, offenders are legitimately punishable. A version of the alternative socialised self is substituted when excuses are thought appropriate – so that the self is seen as helplessly caught up in a causal chain of events beyond its control. In the modern liberal mind, there is an uncomfortable oscillation between these two discourses, as if everyone were aware of the arbitrary nature of the division of human action into these two domains. The result is a deep indeterminacy in criminal law as practised in the liberal democracies. This allows the criminal law to become a political battleground between leftist judges who interpret human actions as literally 'products' of their circumstances, thus excusable, and more conservative judges interpreting the same actions as outcomes of the unconstrained individual will.

Nevertheless, beneath the surface of this political conflict, we find agreement on the basic liberal commitment to the idea of the substantiality of the self as a metaphysical entity, a fixity that is only in specified circumstances 'causally dissolved' by the pressures of social life. The realistic alternative obscured by these abstractions, according to Kelman, is to see the self as a 'crossroads, a locus where things occur, a place in which action is just one result of past actions, known and unknown' (Kelman 1987: 112), a concrete view of the self that is supposed to be neither determinist nor intentionalist, at least in the usual senses of these terms. What we need to consider now is the extent to which this critique can be upheld in relation to the central problems with the doctrine of *mens rea* (as laid out and discussed in Chapter 12).

Free agency, criminal intention and mens rea

According to the critical scholars, then, the main body of criminal law rests upon the assumption of a mythical legal subject, a typical self-sufficient individual who from his position of isolation is able to engage morally with the world beyond his island. He is capable of perfect self-control, is morally equal in standing with all others and in full possession of all his rational faculties. From the standpoint of mainstream jurisprudence, this picture of the legal subject is a caricatured exaggeration of what is a wholly reasonable and necessary normative framework in which to develop general and specific principles of criminal justice. Without such assumptions about individual autonomy and rationality, it would be impossible to justify a system of punishment that respects the rights of the individual. Such assumptions are built into the very idea of criminal justice. For the critical theorist, however, this response misses the point not only about what concrete individuals are really like, but also about the naturalisation of a conception that is really historically specific and relative. The assumptions embodied in the essentially fictitious picture of the individual in society today, far from being natural and inevitable, are said by the critics to be anachronistically rooted in the age in which liberal ideology was born, an age of laissez-faire capitalism, colonialism and extreme individualism, in which property owners constituted a small minority, slavery was still legal and flourishing, starvation wages were paid to legally free labourers and women of all races had virtually no rights. The new conception of the individual was an idealised character drawn from the educated, privileged elite. This was the age in which the principles of liberal justice took shape and it has left a lasting mark upon them (Norrie 2001).

The function of the *mens rea* doctrine stipulating conditions of responsibility is to distinguish those who are to be blamed for their harmful and criminal acts from those who are not. In the case of mental illness, it also distinguishes the fully from the partially responsible, or those who are less than fully culpable. Generally speaking, the defendant is required to have acted freely, knowingly and intentionally. On the specific question of freedom and unconstrained action, it is in the context of the defences of necessity and duress that the central tensions in the attitudes of the law come into sharp focus. In the classic case of *R. v. Dudley and Stephens* (1884), the 'freely' chosen actions of the starving sailors who murder the cabin boy are both condemned and mitigated. There was and remains a deep ambivalence about their guilt or blamelessness and about whether a private defence of necessity should be available at all. In such cases, there is usually a conflict between sympathetic public opinion and the harsh rulings of the courts, but there are also divisions within legal opinion. In a more recent incident, a decision not to prosecute survivors of the *Herald of Free Enterprise* (1987), when there was evidence that a man inadvertently obstructing their exit had been deliberately killed in the scramble to escape the sinking ship, seems to have been prompted by the realisation that under existing law they would have no defence to a charge of murder, and that this would be widely regarded as unacceptable (Smith 2002: 273), given the circumstances that many lives had been saved at the expense of one, who was going to die anyway. As noted in Chapter 13, the recent ruling (*Re A*, 2000) on the case of the conjoined twins indicates that the law might be shifting in a direction more in line with public opinion.

For the CLS critics, this legal uncertainty is symptomatic of the deep confusion and incoherence of the criminal law (Norrie 2014: ch. 8). Situations of extreme necessity or duress – as in the case of *DPP v. Lynch* (1975), in which the defendant was forced at gunpoint to assist in a murder – are said to explode the myth of the rational, autonomous subject, but at the same time the courts are more disposed to find them guilty than not guilty, for reasons of expediency. The idea that people in such extreme situations of need or danger can be viewed in terms of the Enlightenment ideal as autonomous agents in full possession of their rational capacities, making carefully reasoned decisions, is seen as completely unrealistic. Such agents, the critics say, do not exist anywhere outside of the philosophical and legal imagination, let alone in the middle of an emergency. In Kelman's terms, the courts and lawmakers have readily at their disposal the discourses of intentionalism or determinism, so that the actions of the defendants can be set within the framework of either voluntaristic decisions or of a chain of events beyond the agent's control, according to the inclination of the judges or drafters of the law.

Intention and *mens rea*

Intention and motive

With this kind of critical approach, all the elements of the *mens rea* doctrine fall under scrutiny. The concept of intention in particular is deconstructed to show how it has developed to serve particular political objectives. According to Norrie, the artificial distinction between intention and motive was originally drawn in such a way that any aspect of poverty could be eliminated as a defence, no matter how extreme the circumstances of cold or hunger, so that the threat to property would be defused, leaving the common law with a distinction that would be applied indiscriminately (Norrie 2014: ch. 3), from relatively trivial offences such as criminal trespass, to the most serious such as treason and murder. With the separation of intention and motive, the most relevant aspect of a defence to criminality is said to be removed, resulting in a prominent principle of law that flatly contradicts its own proclaimed concern for individual justice. In excluding motive as a defence, the criminal law divests itself of the only element that could make coherent moral sense of criminal justice.

Intention and recklessness

CLS critiques of the common law tests for recklessness tend to focus on the unsettling of criminal law in recent decades on the question of whether the test should be subjective or objective for all offences. To reiterate, if the test is subjective, the prosecution has to prove that the defendant was actually aware of the risk implicit in the action that caused the harm. The 'subjectivity' is relative to the actual state of mind. If the test is objective, the prosecution only has to prove that the defendant ran an obvious risk that should have been apparent to any reasonable man/person. According to the subjective Cunningham test (*R.* v. *Cunningham*, 1957), the jury had to be satisfied that the defendant had actually seen the risk and proceeded regardless. With the establishment of the Caldwell test (*MPC (Metropolitan Police Commissioner)* v. *Caldwell*, 1982), the stringency of this requirement was relaxed for offences against property, so that the jury had to be satisfied that either the defendant saw the risk or the risk was of such a nature that as a rational agent he should have seen it. The implication was that if he closed his eyes to the obvious risk, he was as guilty of acting recklessly as if he had actually seen it. Finally, the so-called 'Caldwell lacuna' or loophole concerns cases that neither the subjective nor the objective test seem to cover. When the defendant does see the risk of, for example, pulling the trigger of an apparently unloaded gun, but then disregards the risk for what he erroneously believes to be good reasons and proceeds to run the risk, it cannot be proved with either test that he is guilty of recklessness.

The controversy that the *Caldwell* ruling caused has had several dimensions. Many have seen it as an application of common sense to an area of law that had been long overdue for reform. Given the difficulty of seeing into the defendant's mind, especially to determine such an intangible and passing state of mind as recklessness, rather than the more enduring intentions that leave marks on the person's behaviour, the serviceability of the reasonableness standard was obviously an attraction. The plain fact that this would make it easier to get convictions, though, counted both in favour of the new test and against it. It was argued by critics that it would open the door to unlimited injustice in obtaining automatic convictions regardless of the subjective qualities of the defendants in each case, given that the reasonableness test was applied to young people and schizophrenics to whom it was completely inappropriate. It also raised some odd anomalies, such as the implication that personal injury would be easier to raise a defence against than criminal damage. If *A* recklessly takes out *B*'s eye with an air rifle and damages *B*'s spectacles in the process, the application of the Caldwell test would result in the conviction of *A* for the damage but not for the injury, thus raising a fundamental doubt about the distinction. Some have responded to this by arguing that Caldwell should be universalised and applied to all offences, a suggestion that has so far been wisely resisted. Its introduction in the first place was also criticised at the time for pre-empting the authority of Parliament, which it was claimed had ruled out such a test. It was also criticised for blurring the distinction between recklessness and what was traditionally seen as the less culpable category of inadvertent negligence.

The wrangle over these two tests, which matches quite closely the similar dispute over the tests for the *mens rea* for murder, has been criticised by CLS scholars on numerous grounds. The main point in Norrie's historical analysis (Norrie 2014: ch. 4) is his argument that the Cunningham and Caldwell versions of recklessness rest upon concepts of subjectivity and objectivity that are juxtaposed against each other rather than synthesised (thus allowing space for the Caldwell lacuna to appear), and that they are limited and distorted conceptions, the inadequacies of which can be explained by the nineteenth-century attempts to positivise the criminal law by eliminating the moralistic language of the common law, which had made it increasingly difficult for juries to determine guilt. The heritage for modern criminal law is an overrestricted concept of subjectivity and an overbroad concept of objectivity. The concept of subjectivity as embodied in C.S. Kenny's (1902) definition of malice and the *Cunningham* ruling is too narrow because it excludes what should properly be seen as subjective (such as the failure to take proper care by an agent who is well capable of it, even if he gave it no thought), rather than being shifted to the realm of objective negligence or recklessness. In Duff's colourful example, the bridegroom who 'genuinely' forgets to attend his own wedding is subjectively guilty; there is no need in such cases to resort to the imaginary 'reasonable man'. This narrowness in turn provokes the overextended concept of objectivity, counting as 'objectively' culpable what really could have been avoided. The result is a depth of conceptual confusion in the law that cannot be untangled by for-mulating ever more refined tests for recklessness. What is required is a genuine synthesis in a unitary understanding of recklessness in relation to intention, within the context of a social consensus on the kinds of risks that it is justifiable to take. Without such a consensus, there is no possibility of such a synthesis.

The decision in *R. v. G. and another* (2003) (see Chapter 12), overruling *Caldwell* for cases of criminal damage, was at least in part a response to the relentless criticism by 'subjectivists' that it had opened the door to ever-increasing complexity on the law on recklessness, and to serious injustice to young offenders and the mentally unsound. This reinstatement of the subjective test without any revision or readjustment, however, will almost certainly perpetuate the problems in the more typical cases featuring adults of sound mind who claim never to have seen an obvious risk in their behaviour. The switch from the objective to the subjective does nothing to counter the criticisms that either test taken in isolation is inevitably defective.

Intention and foresight

As is well known, the *mens rea* for murder, resting on tests to distinguish it from manslaughter, underwent regular reassessment and adjustment in the second half of the twentieth century. At the heart of the problem in this area lay a collision of views on how the guilty mind in cases of homicide should be established, in terms of what was intended and what the defendant foresaw. The eventual, more or less stable outcome of the disputes and reversals on this question was a test for murder that incorporated both the subjective and the objective test, in as far as it retained the fundamental *mens rea* principle that the actual state of mind in terms of intention and foresight had to be proved, but also allowed the jury to infer actual intention (to cause at least grievous bodily harm) from what was objectively foreseeable by 'the reasonable man', along with the rest of the evidence.

There have been many detailed criticisms of this and subsequent minor adjustments to the law on this issue. CLS criticisms have been mixed, but the general tenor of the criticism is that the uncertainty and wavering are symptomatic of a deeper malaise in the law, that they point to an indeterminacy that opens the law to political manipulation. Norrie's argument (Norrie 2014: 64–71) is that the perpetual narrowing and broadening of the definitions of intention and foresight have served the purpose of enabling the judiciary to switch almost at will between the requirements of individual justice and the interests of state policy and social control. The elaborate pretence of following legal logic is designed to bridge the gap between legal ideology and the social reality, given that the facts of all the cases of homicide under consideration over these years are so radically different.

Critical perspectives on criminal law and insanity

In mainstream jurisprudence, the orthodox framework for the law relating to insanity is, as its critics point out, predominantly rationalistic. The fundamental idea governing legal thinking in this area is that individuals beyond the age of majority who lack reason (the great Enlightenment virtue) are not legally responsible – they are legally insane. This, it should be remembered, does not necessarily mean that they are medically insane, or that all those found medically insane are legally insane. Insanity is defined as a distinct legal category. It is a question of what the law is to regard as the kind of mental impairment that will be accepted as negating responsibility. It was partly the recognition of the unrealistically strict dichotomy between the presence and absence of the faculty of reason that led to the 1957 introduction of the distinct defence of diminished responsibility through impairment of the mind, thus allowing a gradation of insanity and responsibility. Nevertheless the concepts of the reason and rationality of the individual remain at the centre of legal thinking in this area.

Twentieth-century medical research and psychiatric theorising on sanity and madness underwent transformations more far-reaching than at any earlier time, but it occupies a domain quite distinct from that of the law. In general cultural terms, the impact of modern theories of the unconscious on the understanding of madness has still not been fully absorbed. More radical anti-establishment theories derived from existentialism and existential psychoanalysis (such as the anti-psychiatry movement), or the philosophies of Nietzsche and Foucault, have deeply influenced criticisms of the social and legal treatment of the insane. Scientifically and medically, however, there is no real consensus on even the most basic features and causes of mental disorders. There is no common thread running through the radical critiques of the modern treatment of insanity, but a number of features are prominent. Most are united in the claim that the medical heritage of the Enlightenment is anything but humane and 'enlightened'. On the contrary, it is seen as the increasingly repressive and dehumanising exercise of institutional power for the sake of social control, rather than the well-being of the patient. One of the basic beliefs behind many of these critiques is that the rationalistic language of the law on insanity and responsibility carries all the uninterrogated assumptions of modernity. From this point of view, the labelling of some people by others as 'insane' is the focal point of a power struggle, through which the self-designated 'sane' dominate and exclude others. 'Sanity' itself is as much a construct as 'insanity', identified as its assertion is with the excessively rationalistic mind. Madness is seen as a holistic condition, which cannot be diagnosed or treated as a malfunction in one isolated aspect of the whole person, such as the capacity to reason.

Some of the CLS writers have drawn extensively upon these sources to present a picture of English and US law on insanity that is sharply at odds with the mainstream interpretation. The most cogent of these accounts is developed by Norrie, who focuses on the concepts of rationality and power. Citing Foucault's histories of the early modern transitions in the treatment of madness (Foucault 1967) and the new practice of confinement of the insane, in conjunction with the rise of psychiatric science, Norrie identifies the struggle for power between the psychiatric and legal professions as the key to understanding contemporary law on insanity. The real struggle, he says, is seen in the advance of scientific psychiatry invading the domain of lawyers, whose professional interest lies in retaining control over the definition of insanity. Historically, the conflict developed in the nineteenth century when the focus on moral education and reform of the asylum inmates gave way to the emergence of scientific medical expertise in theories of underlying organic causes behind the various types of mental illness. Although the two professions were united in their interests as agents of social control in their own respective domains, they came into inevitable collision over their fundamentally opposed approaches to insanity. If, for a scientific psychiatrist, insanity is a matter of physiological causation in the brain, the medical evidence takes the matter out of the hands of the court (as was evident as early as the cases of *Hadfield* (1800) and *M'Naghten* (1843)).

Furthermore, the organic causes could attack the will or the emotions as much as the cognitive abilities, thus potentially rendering the legal rationality tests virtually irrelevant. This is why in Britain the legal profession has resisted encroachment by psychiatry upon the law on insanity. The causal physiology is seen as a threat to the liberal conception of the rule of law, with its presumption of the liberty of the individual, which was increasingly regarded as an object of scientific control and manipulation. It is also seen as having implications throughout the criminal law, in as far as 'sickness' models of crime were applied, negating the very idea of individual responsibility and retributive punishment. In the USA, by contrast, psychiatry has made greater inroads into the legal domain, since the Durham ruling in 1954 (*Durham* v. *United States*), creating the 'product test' for insanity, according to which the defence has only to prove that the criminal conduct was caused or produced by the mental disorder. Irresistible impulse has also been incorporated as a complete defence, in the USA and elsewhere, rather than as a mitigating defence, as in Britain.

The overall point of this account is that, if the current state of the law on insanity is shaped by this professional power struggle, the official version of the function of the law, in terms of individual justice and public safety, is nothing but a legitimating ideology. Norrie illustrates this by linking insanity and mental illness in general with social and economic status. It is not so much that its distribution is directly caused by factors of class, sex and race as that there is a deliberate and explicit legal strategy to decontextualise all forms of madness by focusing exclusively on the question of presence or absence of rationality in the individual, removed from the environment in which the condition developed. As in every other area of law, individuals are regarded by liberalism as self-enclosed 'monads', in abstraction from the social relations within which they have their true meaning.

Feminist criticisms of criminal law

One of the most obvious facts about crime is that most of it is committed by males. There is therefore insufficient evidence for the comparison of treatment of male and female defendants in the criminal courts to substantiate any strong conclusions about the fairness or unfairness of this treatment. Feminist research in this area focuses more on the general experience of the criminal law by women, who are of course no less the victims of crimes than males. The research has revolved around male sexual violence against women, in particular domestic violence and rape. Apart from this focus on issues of special significance and concern to women, however, feminist jurisprudence also extends to critical analysis of the general concepts and principles upon which the criminal law rests, including the doctrine of *mens rea* and the principles behind the legal defences.

As in other areas of law, the question of judicial impartiality and even-handedness features prominently in the feminist criticisms. Almost the defining characteristic of the liberal ideal of justice is the principle that it is unfair to apply different rules to different classes of people, whether this involves gender, social class, race or any other irrelevant feature. The principle of applying the same rules to males and females is seen as a question of basic equality and justice. It would be unfair, for example, for the *mens rea* for murder or the test for recklessness to be different according to the sex of the offender. The problem for feminist critics is their perception that this apparent balance does not lead to fairness at all. On the contrary, it is argued, this formal equality, if uncritically and rigidly applied, can reinforce the substantive unfairness that is already present in criminal law, embedded in the legal concepts. In real life, a difference between a typical woman's options and those of a typical man can make the operation of legal principles completely unfair. This argument can be illustrated with the two central examples, domestic violence and rape.

As a social problem, violence against women in the home has traditionally been treated as a domestic issue, reinforced by the private–public distinction in law. Criticism of this distinction is the basis of the feminist analysis of this problem. Wives and partners of violent males have had very little substantial protection from the criminal law. The main criticism lies in the disparity between the low levels of prosecution of male perpetrators of violence and the treatment of women who react violently against it. In cases of murder in response to long-term domestic violence, one point at issue concerns the possible defences, which include the complete defence of self-defence (leading to acquittal) and the partial defences of provocation or diminished responsibility, which are the two 'mitigating' defences leading to reduction of the charge of murder to a conviction for manslaughter. Self-defence is defined so narrowly, in particular with the stipulation that it must be a response to an immediate threat to one's life that it is almost impossible to run as a defence, especially given the relative physical power of the average male and female. The alternative defences, provocation or diminished responsibility, are regarded as inadequate because they only mitigate the offence, and are inherently biased against women by virtue of the standards of reasonableness that they rest upon.

The main criticism, though, addresses the distinction between intention and motive, which we have already seen criticised by the critical legal scholars. The feminist arguments against the exclusion of motive from the defences in criminal law are that it works against female defendants because it deprives them of any reasonable line of defence to the kind of crime that is almost exclusive to women. In cases of murder in response to long-term abuse and violence, the conceptual separation of intention and motive is said to be unfair, because it abstracts one discrete mental state (whether they meant to kill) from the other, morally crucial one, of why they formed the intention, or what drove them to it. The law is designed to exclude motivation by despair, which is the most common female reaction to such a situation.

The law on rape is one of the most contentious issues, because feminists argue that it is here that all the gender bias, both overt and covert, comes sharply into focus. As is well known, cultural prejudices about female sexual behaviour and norms of femininity colour the atmosphere of rape trials. Attempts at character assassination are commonplace and there is an imbalance between attitudes towards male and female sexual histories. In short, the much-reported experience of rape victims is that it is they, rather than the accused, who are on trial. In the feminist critical writings on the law on rape, the problem of consent in relation to *mens rea* has been central. This problem has several dimensions, but there are two important points to concentrate on here. Part of the definition of rape is sex with one of the parties withholding consent. It was ruled in *R.* v. *Olugboja* (1982), a case in which two women were terrorised into submission, that consent was no defence to rape. This was a clarification of the law that meant in effect that it was actual consent under duress of threats that was no defence, that submission did not imply consent and that the prosecution did not have to prove that the victim physically resisted. On the question of whether the defendant 'believed' that the woman was consenting when she clearly was not, however, recent law has been much more problematic.

In an earlier case (*DPP* v. *Morgan*, 1976) Lord Hailsham notoriously ruled that a man who genuinely but mistakenly believed that a woman was consenting to sex was not guilty of an offence. His argument that the principles of *mens rea* had to be applied evenly regardless of gender sounded entirely fair and reasonable. As in other non-sex-related cases involving males or females, the subjective test of recklessness had to establish the actual state of mind of the defendant at the time of the offence, rather than the objective test of what it was reasonable to believe. Thus, it had to be established that a man charged with rape did actually believe or realise that the woman was not consenting, regardless of how unreasonable this belief might be. The objective standard, he said, would undermine the presumption of innocence. Among the numerous feminist criticisms of this ruling, some have focused on the sudden readiness of a male judge to abandon the cherished standard of the reasonable man in a context in which its application would favour female victims (Barnett 1998: 277). Others have argued that existing law did not in fact dictate the selection of the subjective test for this type of offence, and that the underlying principles would equally have allowed the imposition of the objective test. Each of these interpretations is questionable, given the state of the law at that time on recklessness, but the imposition of the objective test was, of course, exactly what was done a few years later (*Caldwell*, 1982) for a specified class of offences against property, with considerations of social policy overriding the subjective test. Apart from the question of the perceived importance for social policy of the problem of rape in comparison to the security of property, this raises all the problems laid out by Norrie (see above) in relation to the excessive narrowness of the subjective test for recklessness. In the context of rape, does it really make sense to allow a defendant who, against however much evidence to the contrary, has chosen to believe that a woman is actually consenting, is 'subjectively' guilty of no offence? The conceptual problems with defining recklessness unambiguously are accentuated here, but the core of the feminist argument, that the bias in favour of males can be concealed by the appearance of judicial impartiality, does seem to be vindicated. It was not until the Sexual Offences Act (2003), which stipulated that a jury must be convinced that a man's belief that a woman was consenting was a reasonable one, that this particular injustice was eliminated.

It is the way in which this concept of reasonableness operates in criminal law, however, that remains one of the principal targets of feminist criticism. It features prominently in all the defences. In judging guilt and innocence, or degrees of responsibility and grounds for mitigation of sentence, the standard of behaviour is what can be expected of a reasonable man or person. With necessity and duress, it is a question of what could be expected of a person of 'reasonable fortitude'. With self-defence, it is a question of what constitutes 'reasonable force', and of what a reasonable person would have done in the circumstances. In cases of provocation, it is a question of the kind of provocative acts that might induce a reasonable person to suddenly and temporarily lose self-control. According to the feminist criticisms, all of these are defined in such a way that they implicitly refer to male standards of reasonableness, making one assumption after another about the substantive equality of power between males and females, when the opposite is manifestly the case.

An assessment of the critical theories

As noted at the outset of this chapter, the real force of the radical criticisms lies in their charge that even at a deep theoretical level the modern systems of criminal justice are defective, and that it is not just a failure of putting sound principles into practice that leads to tangible injustices in the courts. We have to ask now whether this is borne out by the arguments and examples given by the radical critiques, and if so, whether or not it is fatal to the credibility of a liberal theory of criminal justice. A plausible answer is that to an extent it is borne out, that one can concede many of the insights into the problems and inconsistencies in the presuppositions made within mainstream criminal law and jurisprudence, but without allowing the conclusion that, for example, the rule of law is an empty ideology or that the criminal law is nothing but an instrument of oppression rather than of justice.

On each of the specific criticisms of the principles and operation of the *mens rea* doctrine, a common feature is that problems and dilemmas are exposed without a positive solution being proposed. Let us consider again the essential points in each area. On the question of agency in the defences of necessity and duress, it may well be that cases such as these raise intractable dilemmas that have to be dealt with pragmatically by the courts. It is widely agreed that the state of law on these defences is inconsistent and overdue for radical overhaul. Norrie and Kelman, among others, have highlighted some of the conceptual problems effectively, but the basic moral problem is a deep one. The question of the value of human life and of the justifiability of killing the innocent creates a deep moral schism in contemporary society and poses dilemmas that cannot be resolved by utilitarian numerical calculations. These dilemmas are arguably not created by particular societies, by the ascendancy of an economic class or by male domination. They are the inevitable outcome of serious moral reflection in any pluralist liberal society that does not impose uniformity on moral thinking.

The problems relating to *mens rea* and intention also run deep. Both CLS and feminist critics have criticised the separation of intention and motive as morally counter-intuitive and as an expedient for the protection of property and/or male domination, by expelling from the main trial process the one factor that could lead to acquittal. The separation of the process of determining guilt or innocence from the secondary process of sentencing in the light of mitigating factors, however, does have a purpose, which cannot be reduced to these charges of expediency and cynicism. The admission of blameless motive as a substantial defence, which if successful would lead to acquittal, would almost certainly create more problems than it solved. Would it really be satisfactory to allow a standard defence to offences against the person, based upon honourable or blameless motive, given that the intention was to harm? Norrie's argument that the present state of the law makes a cold-blooded contract killing morally equivalent to a mercy killing motivated by compassion (Norrie 2014: 46) only illustrates the problems with the mandatory life sentence for murder, which could be reformed with lower minimum sentences for euthanasia and possibly other forms of homicide. The case for root-and-branch reform of the intention–motive distinction has simply not been made.

The problems and inconsistencies in the law on intention in relation to recklessness are undeniable. Many contradictory stands have been taken by judges and legal writers in recent years on questions of criminal liability in relation to the thorny problem of how and where to set the boundaries of intentionality in relation to, for example, drunkenness, dangerous driving or the use of firearms. The distinction between criminal negligence and recklessness has been particularly problematic. It can be argued against the CLS critiques, however, that this difference of opinion and lack of certainty is an inevitable feature of any society and its legal system, rather than specifically of the modern liberal legal systems. The tension may in part be the consequence of attempting an almost impossible balancing act between assumptions about autonomy and responsibility, on the one hand, and the need for consideration of public safety, on the other, and this tension may in certain respects be more acute at some times and in some systems than others, due to specific social conditions, but this does not vindicate the CLS thesis that the law is entirely incoherent or radically indeterminate.

Similar problems appear in any critical assessment of the radical critics of the law on insanity. In mainstream criminal jurisprudence the evolution of the law on insanity has to be understood in terms of the *mens rea* doctrine, but as any examination of this history will reveal, the standard *mens rea* requirements of cognitive and volitional competence are constantly balanced against consideration for public safety, even where this is not explicit. One of the problems with the critical theories is that genuine concern for public safety is systematically interpreted as social control, as if there were no concern for justice within the legal system or for humane and beneficial treatment within the psychiatric profession at all. The argument that because legal reasoning conceals relations of power and struggles between vested interests, then there are only relations of power and no real values at stake is invalid. The whole of human affairs and human interaction can be described in terms of power, if one is determined to do so, but this is only one description from one particular angle. There is more to it than this.

Conclusion: Enlightenment values and the rule of law

Resistance to the sweeping criticisms of the systems of criminal justice in the liberal democracies has revolved around a defence of the independent value of the rule of law, regardless of its origins. It is certainly arguable that the development of procedural rights in the eighteenth century was intrinsically linked with the interests of the privileged few in their battle against the old order, but this does not undermine their real value to real individuals. The security of the individual citizen from arbitrary arrest, imprisonment and torture has an impact on the realities of criminal law in a liberal society, quite independently of how fictitiously liberals conceptualise 'the individual'. An illuminating example of this can be seen in one of the milestones in the struggle for women's rights. In the case of *R.* v. *Jackson* (1891) a woman estranged from her husband had been abducted and imprisoned by him. The remedy at law was for her relatives to apply to the court for *habeas corpus*, legally compelling the husband to release her. This unprecedented action established the common law principle that such imprisonment of married women was not legal, an outcome that was only made possible by the liberal rule of law. It may be objected that such legal remedies were only in practice available to the educated elite, but it can hardly be denied that such developments constituted a real advance in the cause of women's equality.

In assessing the values of the Enlightenment it is also necessary to separate them from the political and social conditions with which they were contemporaneous. While it is true that there were glaring contradictions between the grand universalism in the proclamations of human rights and the practical, and in some senses legal, denial of those rights to the lower classes, to women and to black slaves, there were at the same time liberal reform movements to change these social and economic conditions. The 'empty' ideal of universality was an essential presupposition behind these reforming ideals. The concept of the autonomous reasoning individual, although formulated in abstract terms, was also indispensable as a general formulation, as was the idea that each of these autonomous individuals was equal in standing, even while this flatly contradicted the social reality of differences in social status.

The principle of autonomy has, as we have seen in the critical writings, given rise to numerous problems, but one of the most general of these in criminal law – not just in critical legal scholarship – is that the obvious truth that autonomy as the capacity for self-governance is a matter of degree, that people vary enormously in the type and quality of their rationality, is frequently overridden by the assumption that one either has this capacity or one does not. The generally unexamined assumption is that there is an implicit standard of sufficient degree of autonomy (rationality, specific cognitive skills, ability to choose, etc.) for the ascription of responsibility. As we have seen repeatedly, the traditional standard of the reasonable man is notoriously implausible for assuming a general norm to which everyone and no one conforms. However, when suitably adjusted to 'the reasonable person', it seems hard to avoid the conclusion that, despite the problems highlighted by feminist critics, some such generality is inescapable when formulating a standard that everyone is presumed capable of. The liberal ideal of the autonomous self may be a fiction, but it is also an inescapable one. It is undisputed that a new conception of the self emerged in the early seventeenth century, a new dimension of inwardness and individuality, which had momentous political and philosophical consequences. It was linked with, among other things, the growing awareness throughout the following centuries of individual human rights. What is not generally agreed is that this new idea of 'the individual' was simply the ideological product of the capitalist mode of production, or the latest strategy to perpetuate male domination.

Study questions

General question: Are the radical critics of modernity justified in their attack on mainstream criminal law theory?

Further study questions: Explain the role of the rational, autonomous individual as the subject of criminal law and assess the critics' arguments that it leads to incoherence and radical indeterminacy. Does the *mens rea* doctrine stand up to the scrutiny of the radical critics? Does the deconstruction of intention and the intention–motive distinction undermine the assumptions behind the *mens rea* doctrine? Do the CLS critiques of the tests for recklessness resolve the problems surrounding the subjective–objective wrangle? Are the radical criticisms of the law on insanity convincing? Explain the distinction between overt and covert gender bias. How justified are the feminist critiques of the legal concepts of reasonableness and rationality in the context of domestic violence and rape?

Suggestions for further reading

For general reading on the values of liberalism and the Enlightenment, and their postmodernist critics, see the references at the end of Chapter 7.

The essential background in criminal law is provided by the cases, critical discussions and proposals for reform in *Elliott and Wood's Cases and Materials on Criminal Law* (11th edn, Allen and Cooper 2013), and the Smith and Hogan textbook on criminal law (14th edn, Ormerod and Laird 2015). Elliott and Quinn (1996), *Criminal Law* is also useful.

The most relevant Marxist and CLS (critical legal studies) writings on criminal law referred to in this chapter are Norrie (2014) and Kelman (1987: ch. 3).

The most useful examples of feminist perspectives on criminal law are Lacey *et al.* (2003), Graycar and Morgan (2002) and Nicolson and Bibbings (2000). See also Barnett (1998: chs 11 and 12) on criminal law in relation to domestic violence and rape.

On the radical critiques of the modern treatment of insanity in general, the most influential writings are found in Foucault (1967), Szasz (1960) and Laing (1965). For critical discussions of insanity in relation to criminal law, see Reznek (1997) and Norrie (2014). These should be compared with the more orthodox accounts referred to in Chapter 14.

Appendix

Cases

Brown v. *Board of Education* (1954) 347 US
Donoghue v. *Stevenson* (1932) AC 562; House of Lords
DPP v. *Hyam* (1975) AC 55; House of Lords
DPP v. *Lynch* (1975) AC 653; House of Lords
DPP v. *Morgan* (1976) AC 182, House of Lords
DPP v. *Smith* (1961) AC 290; 3 WLR 546; 3 All ER 161
Durham v. *United States* (1954) 214 F2d 862; US Court of Appeals DC Cir.
Hadfield (1800) 40, George III, Howell's State Trials, vol. 27, 1281–1356
Henningsen v. *Bloomfield Motors Inc.* (1960) 32, NJ 358, 161 A2d 69
M'Naghten (1843) 10 C and F 200; 8 ER 718
Owens v. *Owens* (1888) 100 NC 240; Supreme Court of North Carolina
R. v. *Adomako* (1995) 1 AC 171; 3 WLR 288
R. v. *Byrne* (1960) 2 QB 396; 3 WLR 440
MPC (Metropolitan Police Commissioner) v. *Caldwell* (1982) AC 341; House of Lords
R. v. *Cunningham* (1957) 2 QB 396, CCA
R. v. *Desmond, Barrett and Others* (1868) 11 Cox CC 146, CCC
R. v. *Dudley and Stephens* (1884) 14, QBD 273
R. v. *Faulkner* (1877) 13 Cox CC 550; IRCCC
R. v. *G. and another* (2003) UK HL 50; 3 WLR 1060; 4 All ER 765 (known as *R.* v. *Gemmel and Richards* in the Court of Appeal)
R. v. *Goodfellow* (1986) 83 Cr. App. R 23
R. v. *Jackson* (1891) 1 QB 671
R. v. *Lawrence (Stephen)* (1982) A 510; House of Lords
R. v. *Martin* (1881) 8 QBD 54
R. v. *Moloney* (1985) AC 905
R. v. *Olugboja* (1982) QB 320
R. v. *Steane* (1947) KB 997; 61 LJR 969
R. v. *Vickers* (1957) 2 QB 664
Re A (Children) (Conjoined Twins: Medical Treatment) (No. 1) (2000) 4 All ER 961

Riggs v. *Palmer* (1889) 115 NY 506; 22 NE 188
US v. *Holmes* (1842) 25 Fed. Cas. 3

Statutes

Married Women's Property Act (1882)
Sex (Removal of Disqualification) Act (1919)
Rent Restriction Act (1920)
United Nations Declaration of Human Rights (1948)
European Convention (1950)
Homicide Act (1957)
Mental Health Act (1959)
Criminal Justice Act (1967)
Equal Pay Act (1970)
Guardianship of Minors Act (1971)
Sex Discrimination Act (1975)
Human Rights Act (1998)
Sexual Offences Act (2003)
Prevention of Terrorism Act (2005)

Glossary

command theory Most notably the theory of John Austin, that the law is essentially a set of commands laid down by a sovereign, enforced by sanctions.

common law The system of law developed in Britain and followed by numerous countries, primarily in the English-speaking world, which combines the precedent of case law in the courts with statute law as laid down by government.

consequentialism (act and rule) Act-consequentialism is the moral philosophy which holds that all acts are to be judged solely in terms of the value of their consequences. Rule-consequentialism holds that the more appropriate way of judging our behaviour is in terms of adherence to moral rules which experience has shown to have the best consequences.

critical legal studies A loose-knit group of legal scholars, which emerged in the 1970s, with a radical agenda for legal studies. It includes Marxist, socialist, feminist, critical race theories and many other radical perspectives.

deontological ethics An approach to moral philosophy which emphasises duties and rights, morally evaluating acts according to principle, rather than their consequences.

emotivism A subjectivist moral philosophy which denies the existence of moral truth and places subjective feelings at the centre of evaluating human acts. Moral judgements are thought to be no more than expressions of approval or disapproval.

epistemology One of the central branches of philosophy, dealing with questions about knowledge, belief and truth. It concerns the perennial dispute about what qualifies as knowledge rather than mere opinion.

habeas corpus The name given to one of the most far-reaching instruments devised by English common law in the interests of liberty. Literally, it means 'produce the body', and it has the force of law in compelling individuals or government institutions to bring an imprisoned or detained person before a judge or a court to determine whether there is lawful cause for depriving them of their liberty.

intrinsicalism A moral philosophy which recognizes the intrinsic value of an act in itself, for its own moral worth, rather than because of its outcomes. Compare with 'consequentialism'.

legal formalism   A long-standing theory in common law countries, according to which lawyers and judges should apply authoritative rules to the facts of every case, using deductive logical methods to arrive at the one certain answer. Reaching its peak at the turn of the nineteenth century, under the influence of Langdell, it was derided by American legal realists as mechanical jurisprudence.

legal positivism   An evolving legal theory, originating in Bentham's philosophy, which insists on the separation of legal from moral issues and questions. The chief opponent of natural law, it later evolved into the predominant legal theory in the common law world. More recently it includes a variety of hard and soft versions, most of them allowing for more judicial discretion to resolve hard cases.

legal realism   American legal realism ran from the late 1890s to the 1930s and challenged the formalist legal establishment on a multitude of connected issues. Essentially, they urged that the teaching of law be brought into line with the realities of the law in and around the courts, to be open to concerns about social policy and to dispense with the idealised jurisprudence taught at that time.

metaphysics   A central area of philosophy dealing with fundamental questions about the world or reality as a whole, which go beyond the questions that can be investigated by natural science.

natural law   An ancient legal philosophy which sees law as deeply rooted in moral values. Its central claims relate to the question of how law stands in relation to justice, and it sees a necessary connection between law and morality more generally. Its principal exponent was Aquinas. Modern defenders include Jacques Maritain, Lon Fuller and John Finnis.

normativity   Relating to rules or norms of any sort governing human behaviour, concerning ethics, morality, aesthetics, social science or anything else involving values. Normative statements concern the way things ought and ought not to be.

obiter dictum   (Literally, 'said in passing'.) These are remarks made by judges in addition to the *ratio decidendi* (see below) of the judgement. *Obiter dicta* are 'persuasive' but not binding, and are often cited by judges in support of later decisions.

obligation   Moral obligation concerns the duties we have towards each other. Legal obligation concerns the duties we have with respect to the law. Political obligation is the duty to obey the law solely because it is the law.

Ockham's razor   A principle derived from William of Ockham (alternative spelling Occam), which urges us not to multiply entities beyond necessity. When choosing between two explanations of apparently equal merit, one should always opt for the one which posits the fewest entities.

ontology   The area of philosophy relating to the existence or non-existence of things.

pragmatism   Originally an American philosophy initiated by C.S. Peirce, now a much wider philosophy, whose main feature is its linking of philosophical questions about meaning and truth with the way they are answered in real life. Its effects on legal theory were mostly its relinquishing of the quest for certainty and its focus on the real processes of thinking and reasoning.

ratio decidendi   (Literally, 'reason for the decision'.) The reason given by the judge to justify the decision in any given case. Unlike *obiter dicta* (see above), the *ratio* is binding on later judges.

rule of law   A many-faceted concept, which essentially means that adherence to the law by everyone, including the lawmakers, is a fundamental political virtue, any major departure from which can be challenged as unlawful.

rule of recognition   Hart's term for the fundamental rule at the apex of the legal system, which confers legal validity on all the other rules in the system.

stare decisis   (Literally, 'to stand on the decision'.) A common law doctrine, according to which precedent from earlier cases must be followed by courts of the same or lower status.

utilitarianism   As the original template for consequentialism, a major moral philosophy initiated in modern times by Jeremy Bentham. The defining principle is that acts are to be morally judged according to how much utility they promote or maximize for the greatest number of people affected by them.

virtue ethics   A twentieth-century revival of Aristotelian ethics, which promotes a shift of attention from assessing the moral qualities of acts to the moral character of agents.

virtue jurisprudence   A relatively recent theoretical enterprise, which applies the philosophy of virtue ethics to jurisprudence.

Bibliography

Acton, H.B. (ed.) (1969) *The Philosophy of Punishment*, London: Macmillan.

Adams, D.M. (ed.) (1992) *Philosophical Problems in the Law*, Belmont, CA: Wadsworth.

Allen, M.J. (2001) *Elliott and Wood's Casebook on Criminal Law*, 8th edn, London: Sweet & Maxwell.

Allen, M.J. and Cooper, S. (2010) *Elliott and Wood's Cases and Materials on Criminal Law*, 10th edn, London: Sweet & Maxwell.

Allen, M.J. and Cooper, S. (2013) *Elliott and Wood's Cases and Materials on Criminal Law*, 11th edn, London: Sweet & Maxwell.

Altman, A. (1986) 'Legal Realism, Critical Legal Studies, and Dworkin', *Philosophy & Public Affairs* 15: 205–235.

Andenaes, J. (1974) *Punishment and Deterrence*, Ann Arbor, MI: University of Michigan Press.

Aquinas, St Thomas (1948) *Selected Political Writings*, ed. A.P. D'Entreves, trans. J.G. Dawson, Oxford: Blackwell.

Aquinas, St Thomas (1988a) *On Law, Morality and Politics*, ed. R.J. Regan and W.P. Baumgarth, Cambridge: Avatar Books.

Aquinas, St Thomas (1988b) *On Politics and Ethics*, ed. and trans. P.E. Sigmund, New York and London: W.W. Norton.

Aristotle (1924) *Rhetorica*, trans. W.R. Roberts, in W.D. Ross (ed.) *The Works of Aristotle*, vol. 11, Oxford: Clarendon Press.

Aristotle (1948) *Politics*, trans. E. Barker, Oxford: Clarendon Press.

Aristotle (1985) *Nicomachean Ethics*, trans. T. Irwin, Indianapolis: Hackett.

Armstrong, K.G. (1961) 'The Retributivist Hits Back', in H.B. Acton (ed.), *The Philosophy of Punishment*, London: Macmillan, 1969.

Atiyah, P.S. (1983) *Law and Modern Society*, Oxford and New York: Oxford University Press.

Atiyah, P.S. and Summers, R.S. (1987) *Form and Substance in Anglo-American Law: A Comparative Study of Legal Reasoning, Legal Theory and Legal Institutions*, Oxford: Clarendon.

Augustine, St (1958) *City of God*, trans. G. Walsh, D. Zema, G. Monahan and D. Honan, New York: Image Books, Doubleday.

Austin, J. (1995 [1832]) *The Province of Jurisprudence Determined*, Cambridge: Cambridge University Press.

Baker, C.D. (1991) *Tort*, 5th edn, London: Sweet & Maxwell.

Baker, J.H. (1990) *An Introduction to English Legal History*, London: Butterworths.

Baraz, Y. (2012) *A Written Republic: Cicero's Philosophical Politics*, Princeton, NJ: Princeton University Press.

Barnett, H. (1998) *Introduction to Feminist Jurisprudence*, London and Sydney: Cavendish.

Barry, B. (1973) *The Liberal Theory of Justice*, Oxford: Clarendon Press.

Bavidge, M. (1989) *Mad or Bad?* Bristol: Bristol Classical Press.

Bechtler, T.W. (1978) 'American Legal Realism Revaluated', in T.W. Bechtler, *Law in a Social Context: Liber Americorum Honouring Professor Lon Fuller*, Dordrecht: Kluwer.

Bedau, H. (ed.) (1969) *Civil Disobedience: Theory and Practice*, New York: Pegasus.

Bedau, H. (ed.) (1991) *Civil Disobedience in Focus*, London and New York: Routledge.

Benditt, T.M. (1978) *Law as Rule and Principle: Problems of Legal Philosophy*, Brighton: Harvester Press.

Bentham, J. (1970 [1789]) *An Introduction to the Principles of Morals and Legislation*, ed. J.H. Burns and H.L.A. Hart, London: Athlone Press.

Bentham, J. (1987 [1843]) 'Anarchical Fallacies', in J. Waldron, *Nonsense upon Stilts: Bentham, Burke and Marx on the Rights of Man*, London: Methuen.

Beran, H. (1987) *The Consent Theory of Political Obligation*, Beckenham, Kent: Croom Helm.

Bertens, H. and Natoli, J. (eds) (2002) *Postmodernism: The Key Figures*, Malden, MA, and Oxford: Blackwell.

Beyleveld, D. and Brownsword, R. (1986) *Law as a Moral Judgement*, London: Sweet & Maxwell.

Biggs, J., Jr (1955) *The Guilty Mind: Psychiatry and the Law of Homicide*, Baltimore, MD: Johns Hopkins University Press.

Bix, B. (1993) *Law, Language and Legal Determinacy*, Oxford: Clarendon.

Bix, B. (1996) *Jurisprudence: Theory and Context*, London: Sweet & Maxwell.

Bix, B. (2011) *Radbruch's Formula and Conceptual Analysis*, Legal Studies Research Paper Series, nos.12–13, Minneapolis, MI: University of Minnesota Law School.

Bix, B. (2015) *Jurisprudence: Theory and Context*, 7th edn, London: Sweet & Maxwell.

Blackstone, W. (1829 [1765]) *Commentaries on the Laws of England*, vols 1–4, London: Sweet & Maxwell.

Bobbio, N. (1990) *The Age of Rights*, trans. A. Cameron, Oxford: Polity Press.

Boucher, D. and Kelly, P. (eds) (1994) *The Social Contract from Hobbes to Rawls*, London: Routledge.

Braithwaite, J. and Pettit, P. (1990) *Not Just Deserts: A Republican Theory of Criminal Justice*, Oxford: Clarendon.

Brown, J.M. (1977) *Gandhi and Civil Disobedience*, Cambridge: Cambridge University Press.

Burke, S. (1998) *The Death and Return of the Author: Criticism and Subjectivity in Barthes, Foucault and Derrida*, Edinburgh: Edinburgh University Press.

Burns, T. (1998) 'Aristotle and Natural Law', *History of Political Thought* 19: 142–166.

Cahoone, L.E. (ed.) (1996) *From Modernism to Postmodernism: An Anthology*, Cambridge, MA, and Oxford: Blackwell.

Cain, M. and Hunt, A. (1979) *Marx and Engels on Law*, London: Academic Press.

Campbell, J. (2001) *The Liar's Tale: A History of Falsehood*, New York and London: W.W. Norton & Co.

Campbell, T. (1988) *Justice*, London: Macmillan.

Campbell, T. (2006) *Rights: A Critical Introduction*, Abingdon and New York: Routledge.

Cardozo, B.N. (1931) *Law and Literature and Other Essays and Addresses*, London: William S. Hein & Co.

Cicero (1928 [54–52 BCE]) *De Republica and De Legibus*, trans. C.W. Keyes, London: Heinemann.

Clark, M. (1990) *Nietzsche on Truth and Philosophy*, Cambridge: Cambridge University Press.

Cohan, J.A. (2006) 'Homicide by Necessity', *Chapman Law Review* 10(119): 119–186.

Cohen, M. (ed.) (1984) *Ronald Dworkin and Contemporary Jurisprudence*, London: Duckworth.

Coleman, J. and Paul, E.F. (1987) *Philosophy and Law*, Oxford: Blackwell.

Connor, S. (ed.) (2004) *The Cambridge Companion to Postmodernism*, Cambridge: Cambridge University Press.

Cornell, D., Rosenfeld, M. and Carlson, D. (1992) *Deconstruction and the Possibility of Justice*, New York and London: Routledge.

Cotterell, R. (1989) *The Politics of Jurisprudence: A Critical Introduction to Legal Philosophy*, London and Edinburgh: Butterworths.

Cottingham, J.G. (1979) 'Varieties of Retribution', *Philosophical Quarterly* 29 (July): 238–246.

Cottingham, J.G. (1987) 'Just Punishment', *Proceedings of the Aristotelian Society* (Supplement), 1987: 41–55.

Cottingham, J.G. (ed.) (1996) *Western Philosophy: An Anthology*, Oxford: Blackwell.

Critchley, S. (2001) *Continental Philosophy: A Very Short Introduction*, Oxford and New York: Oxford University Press.

Cross, R. and Harris, J.W. (1991) *Precedent in English Law*, Oxford: Clarendon.

Daniels, N. (ed.) (1975) *Reading Rawls*, Oxford: Blackwell.

Davies, H. and Holdcroft, D. (1991) *Jurisprudence: Texts and Commentary*, London: Butterworths.

Davies, M. (1994) *Asking the Law Question*, Sydney: Sweet & Maxwell.

Deflem, M. (ed.) (1996) *Habermas, Modernity and Law*, London: Sage Publications.

D'Entreves, A.P. (1951) *Natural Law: An Introduction to Legal Philosophy*, 2nd edn, London: Hutchinson, 1970.

Devlin, P. (1965) *The Enforcement of Morals*, Oxford: Oxford University Press.

Dews, P. (1987) *Logics of Disintegration: Post-structuralist Thought and the Claims of Critical Theory*, London and New York: Verso.

Dias, R.W.M. (1985) *Jurisprudence*, London: Butterworths.

Dinwiddy, J. (1989) *Bentham*, Oxford: Oxford University Press.

Douzinas, C. (2000) *The End of Human Rights: Critical Legal Thought at the Turn of the Century*, Oxford and Portland, OR: Hart Publishing.

Douzinas, C. and Warrington, R. (1994) *Justice Miscarried: Ethics, Aesthetics and the Law*, New York and London: Harvester Wheatsheaf.

Dressler, J. (2013) 'Reflections on *Dudley and Stephens* and Killing the Innocent: Taking a Wrong Conceptual Path', in D.J. Baker and J. Horder (eds), *The Sanctity of Life and the Criminal Law: The Legacy of Glanville Williams*, Cambridge: Cambridge University Press.

Duff, R.A. (1973) 'Intentionally Killing the Innocent', *Analysis* 34(1): 16–19.

Duff, R.A. (1982) 'Intentions, Responsibility and Double Effect', *Philosophical Quarterly* 32(126) (January): 1–16.

Duff, R.A. (1990) *Intention, Agency and Criminal Liability: Philosophy of Action and the Criminal Law*, Oxford: Blackwell.

Duff, R.A. (ed.) (1993) *Punishment*, Brookfield, VT, and Aldershot: Dartmouth Publishing Co.

Duff, R.A. and Garland, D. (eds) (1994) *A Reader on Punishment*, Oxford: Oxford University Press.

Dworkin, G. (ed.) (1994) *Morality, Harm and the Law*, San Francisco and Oxford: Westview Press.

Dworkin, R. (ed.) (1977a) *The Philosophy of Law*, Oxford: Oxford University Press.

Dworkin, R. (1977b) *Taking Rights Seriously*, London: Duckworth.

Dworkin, R. (1986) *Law's Empire*, London: Fontana.

Dworkin, R. (1989) 'Liberal Community', *California Law Review* 77(3) (May): 479–487; repr. in G. Dworkin (ed.), *Morality, Harm and the Law*, San Francisco and Oxford: Westview Press, 1994.

Dworkin, R. (2000) *Sovereign Virtue: The Theory and Practice of Equality*, Cambridge, MA, and London: Harvard University Press.

Dworkin, R. (2006) *Justice in Robes*, Cambridge, MA, and London: Harvard University Press.

Dworkin, R. (2011) *Justice for Hedgehogs*, Cambridge, MA, and London: Harvard University Press.

Dyzenhaus, D. (ed.) (1999) *Recrafting the Rule of Law: The Limits of Legal Order*, Oxford and Portland, OR: Hart Publishing.

Edmonds, D. (2014) *Would You Kill the Fat Man? The Trolley Problem and What Your Answer Tells Us about Right and Wrong*, Princeton, NJ: Princeton University Press.

Edmundson, W.A. (2004) *An Introduction to Rights*, Cambridge: Cambridge University Press.

Elliott, E. and Quinn, F. (1996) *Criminal Law*, Harlow, Essex and New York: Addison-Wesley Longman.

Ewing, A.C. (1929) *The Morality of Punishment*, London: Kegan Paul.

Feinberg, J. (1973) *Social Philosophy*, Englewood Cliffs, NJ: Prentice-Hall.

Fingarette, H. (1972) *The Meaning of Criminal Insanity*, Berkeley: University of California Press.

Fingarette, H. and Hasse, A.F. (1979) *Mental Disabilities and Criminal Responsibility*, Berkeley: University of California Press.

Finnis, J. (1980) *Natural Law and Natural Rights*, Oxford: Oxford University Press.

Finnis, J. (ed.) (1991) *Natural Law*, vols 1 and 2, Brookfield, VT, and Aldershot: Dartmouth Publishing Co.

Finnis, J. (1998) *Aquinas: Moral, Political and Legal Theory*, Oxford and New York: Oxford University Press.

Fish, S. (1994) *There's No Such Thing as Free Speech and It's a Good Thing Too*, New York and Oxford: Oxford University Press.

Fitzpatrick, P. (1992) *The Mythology of Modern Law*, London and New York: Routledge.

Fitzpatrick, P. and Hunt, A. (eds) (1987) *Critical Legal Studies*, Oxford: Blackwell.

Flathman, R.E. (1973) *Political Obligation*, London: Croom Helm.

Fleming, J. (1994) *Barbarism to Verdict: A History of the Common Law*, Sydney: HarperCollins.

Fletcher, G.P. (1996) *Basic Concepts of Legal Thought*, New York and Oxford: Oxford University Press.

Fogelson, S. (1990) 'The Nuremberg Legacy: An Unfulfilled Promise', *Southern California Law Review* 63: 858–867.

Foucault, M. (1967) *Madness and Civilisation: A History of Insanity in the Age of Reason*, trans. R. Howard, London and New York: Tavistock; republ. by Routledge, 1989.

Foucault, M. (1977) *Discipline and Punish: The Birth of the Prison*, trans. A. Sheridan, London: Allen Lane.

Frank, J. (1949 [1930]) *Law and the Modern Mind*, New York: Coward McCann; London: Stevens & Sons.

Frey, R.G. (ed.) (1985) *Utility and Rights*, Oxford: Blackwell.

Friedmann, W. (1944) *Legal Theory*, London: Stevens & Sons.

Frug, M.J. (1992) *Postmodern Legal Feminism*, New York and London: Routledge.

Fuller, L.L. (1949) 'The Case of the Speluncean Explorers', *Harvard Law Review* 62(4): 616–645.

Fuller, L.L. (1969 [1964]) *The Morality of Law*, rev. edn, New Haven, CT, and London: Yale University Press.

Gabardi, W. (2001) *Negotiating Postmodernism*, Minneapolis and London: University of Minnesota Press.

Gardner, J. (2007) *Offences and Defences*, Oxford: Oxford University Press.

Gavison, R. (ed.) (1987) *Issues in Contemporary Legal Philosophy: The Influence of H.L.A. Hart*, Oxford: Clarendon.

Geddes, L. (1973) 'On The Intrinsic Wrongness of Killing Innocent People', *Analysis* 33(3): 93–97.

George, R.P. (ed.) (1992) *Natural Law Theory: Contemporary Essays*, Oxford: Clarendon.

George, R.P. (ed.) (1996) *The Autonomy of Law: Essays on Legal Positivism*, Oxford: Clarendon.

Gilligan, C. (1982) *In a Different Voice: Psychological Theory and Women's Development*, Cambridge, MA: Harvard University Press.

Glover, J. (1977) *Causing Death and Saving Lives*, London: Penguin.

Golding, M.P. (1975) *The Philosophy of Law*, London and Englewood Cliffs, NJ: Prentice-Hall.

Golding, M.P. (1984) *Legal Reasoning*, New York: Borzoi Books.

Golding, M.P. and Edmundson, W. (2005) *The Blackwell Guide to the Philosophy of Law and Legal Theory*, Oxford: Blackwell.

Goldman, A.H. (1979) 'The Paradox of Punishment', *Philosophy & Public Affairs* 9(1) (Fall); repr. in A.J. Simmons, M. Cohen, J. Cohen, and C.R. Beitz (eds), *Punishment: A Philosophy and Public Affairs Reader*, Princeton, NJ: Princeton University Press, 1995.

Gould, C.G. (2003) *Constructivism and Practice: Towards a Historical Epistemology*, Lanham, MD: Rowman & Littlefield.

Gray, J. (1996 [1983]) *Mill on Liberty: A Defence*, London: Routledge.

Gray, J. and Smith, G.W. (eds) (1991) *J.S. Mill 'On Liberty' in Focus*, London: Routledge.

Gray, J.C. (1921 [1909]) *The Nature and Sources of the Law*, New York: Columbia University Press.

Graycar, R. (ed.) (1990) *Dissenting Opinions: Feminist Explorations in Law and Society*, Sydney: Allen & Unwin.

Graycar, R. and Morgan, J. (2002) *The Hidden Gender of Law*, 2nd edn, Sydney: Federation Press.

Greenawalt, K. (1987) *Conflicts of Law and Morality*, Oxford and New York: Oxford University Press.

Gross, H. and von Hirsch, A. (eds) (1981) *Sentencing*, Oxford and New York: Oxford University Press.

Grupp, S.E. (ed.) (1971) *Theories of Punishment*, Bloomington, IN: Indiana University Press.

Guest, S. (1992) *Ronald Dworkin*, Edinburgh: Edinburgh University Press.

Gutting, G. (ed.) (1994) *The Cambridge Companion to Foucault*, Cambridge and New York: Cambridge University Press.

Haack, S. (1998) *Manifesto of a Passionate Moderate*, Chicago and London: University of Chicago Press.

Hacker, P. and Raz, J. (eds) (1977) *Law, Morality and Society*, Oxford: Clarendon.

Hägerström, A. (1953) *Inquiries into the Nature of Law and Morals*, ed. K. Olivecrona, trans. C.D. Broad, Stockholm: Almqvist & Wiksell. [Edited essays 1916–1939.]

Hale, M. (1972 [1680]) *History of the Pleas of the Crown*, London: Professional Books.

Hall, J. (1938) *Readings in Jurisprudence*, Indianapolis: Bobbs-Merrill Co.

Halpin, A. (1997) *Rights and Law: Analysis and Theory*, Oxford: Hart Publishing.

Hampton, J. (1984) 'The Moral Education Theory of Punishment', *Philosophy & Public Affairs* 13(3) (Summer): 208–238.

Hampton, J. (1986) *Hobbes and the Social Contract Tradition*, Cambridge and New York: Cambridge University Press.

Hampton, J. (1997) *Political Philosophy*, Boulder, CO, and Oxford: Westview Press.

Harding, A. (1966) *A Social History of English Law*, London: Pelican.

Harris, J.W. (1997) *Legal Philosophies*, 2nd edn, London, Edinburgh and Dublin: Butterworths.

Hart, H.L.A. (1961) *The Concept of Law*, Oxford: Clarendon; rev. edns 1994, 2012.

Hart, H.L.A. (1963) *Law, Liberty, and Morality*, London: Oxford University Press.

Hart, H.L.A. (1968) *Punishment and Responsibility*, Oxford: Clarendon.

Hart, H.L.A. (1982) *Essays on Bentham*, Oxford: Oxford University Press.

Hart, H.L.A. (1983) *Essays in Jurisprudence and Philosophy*, Oxford: Clarendon.

Hart, H.L.A. (1994 [1961]) *The Concept of Law*, 2nd edn, Oxford: Oxford University Press.

Hart, H.L.A. (2012 [1961]) *The Concept of Law*, 3rd edn, Oxford: Oxford University Press.

Hawkes, T. (1977) *Structuralism and Semiotics*, London: Methuen.

Hegel, G.W.F. (1942 [1821]) *The Philosophy of Right*, trans. T.M. Knox, Oxford: Clarendon.

Henberg, M. (1990) *Retribution: Evil for Evil in Ethics, Law and Literature*, Philadelphia, PA: Temple University Press.

Hobbes, T. (1962 [1651]) *Leviathan*, London: Collins.

Hohfeld, W.N. (1919) *Fundamental Legal Conceptions: As Applied in Judicial Reasoning*, ed. W.W. Cook, New Haven, CT, and London: Yale University Press.

Holmes, O.W. (1897) 'The Path of the Law', *Harvard Law Review* 10: 457–478; repr. in D.M. Adams (ed.), *Philosophical Problems in the Law*, Belmont, CA: Wadsworth, 1992.

Holmes, O.W. (1968 [1881]) *Common Law*, London and Melbourne: Macmillan.

Honderich, T. (1976) *Punishment: The Supposed Justifications*, London: Penguin.

Hook, S. (ed.) (1964) *Law and Philosophy: A Symposium*, New York: New York University Press.

Horton, J. (1992) *Political Obligation*, London: Macmillan.

Hume, D. (1972 [1738–1740]) *A Treatise of Human Nature*, London: Fontana.

Hunt, A. (ed.) (1992) *Reading Dworkin Critically*, New York and Oxford: Berg.

Hunt, L. (1991) *Nietzsche and the Origin of Virtue*, London and New York: Routledge.

Husak, D. (2008) *Overcriminalization: The Limits of the Criminal Law*, Oxford: Oxford University Press.

Hutcheson, J. (1929) 'The Judgment Intuitive', *Cornell Law Quarterly* 14: 274–278; repr. in D.M. Adams (ed.), *Philosophical Problems in the Law*, Belmont, CA: Wadsworth, 1992.

Ishay, M.R. (2004) *The History of Human Rights: From Ancient Times to the Globalization Era*, Berkeley and London: University of California Press.

Israel, J.I. (2001) *Radical Enlightenment: Philosophy and the Making of Modernity 1650–1750*, Oxford: Oxford University Press.

Jacobs, F.G. (1971) *Criminal Responsibility*, London: Weidenfeld & Nicolson.

Jameson, F. (1972) *The Prison-House of Language*, Princeton, NJ: Princeton University Press.

Jones, P. (1994) *Rights*, London: Macmillan.

Kant, I. (1887 [1796]) *The Philosophy of Law*, trans. W. Hastie, Edinburgh: Clark.

Katz, L. (1987) *Bad Acts and Guilty Minds: Conundrums of the Criminal Law*, Chicago and London: University of Chicago Press.

Keeton, G.W. (1961) *Guilty but Insane: Four Trials for Murder*, London: Macdonald.

Kelley, P.J. (2002) 'Holmes, Langdell and Formalism', *Ratio Juris* 15: 26–51.

Kellogg, F.R. (2007) *Oliver Wendell Holmes, Jr, Legal Theory, and Judicial Restraint*, Cambridge: Cambridge University Press

Kelly, E. (2009) 'Criminal Justice without Retribution,' *Journal of Philosophy* 106: 440–446.

Kelly, J.M. (1992) *A Short History of Western Legal Theory*, Oxford: Clarendon.

Kelman, M. (1987) *A Guide to Critical Legal Studies*, Cambridge, MA, and London: Harvard University Press.

Kelsen, H. (1957) *What Is Justice?* London: University of California Press.

Kelsen, H. (1970 [1934]) *Pure Theory of Law*, trans. M. Knight, Berkeley: University of California Press.

Kelsen, H. (1973) *Essays in Legal and Moral Philosophy*, ed. O. Weinberger, trans. P. Heath, Dordrecht and Boston: Reidel.

Kennedy, D. (1976) 'Form and Substance in Private Law Adjudication', *Harvard Law Review* 89: 1685–1778.

Kenny, A. (1978) *Free Will and Responsibility*, London: Routledge.

Kenny, C.S. (1902) *Outlines of Criminal Law*, ed. J.W.C. Turner, 19th edn, Cambridge: Cambridge University Press, 1966.

Keown, J. and George, R.P. (2015) *Reason, Morality and Law: The Philosophy of John Finnis*, Oxford: Oxford University Press.

Kipnis, K. (ed.) (1977) *Philosophical Issues in Law*, Englewood Cliffs, NJ: Prentice-Hall.

Kleinig, J. (1973) *Punishment and Desert*, The Hague: Martinus Nijhoff.

Kolakowski, L. (1968) *Positivist Philosophy: From Hume to the Vienna Circle*, Harmondsworth: Pelican Books.

Kramer, M. (1991) *Legal Theory, Political Theory, and Deconstruction: Against Rhadamanthus*, Bloomington, IN: Indiana University Press.

Kramer, M. (1995) *Critical Legal Theory and the Challenge of Feminism: A Philosophical Reconception*, Lanham, MD: Rowman & Littlefield.

Kramer, M. (1999) *In Defence of Legal Positivism: Law without Trimmings*, Oxford: Oxford University Press.

Lacey, N. (1988) *State Punishment: Political Principles and Community Values*, London and New York: Routledge.

Lacey, N. (2004) *A Life of H.L.A. Hart: The Nightmare and the Noble Dream*, Oxford: Oxford University Press.

Lacey, N., Wells, C. and Quick, O. (2003) *Reconstructing Criminal Law: Text and Materials*, London: LexisNexis UK.

Laing, R.D. (1965) *The Divided Self*, Harmondsworth: Penguin.

Learmonth, E. and Tabakoff, J. (2013) *No Mercy: True Stories of Disaster, Survival and Brutality*, Melbourne: Text Publishing Co.

Lee, K. (1989) *The Positivist Science of Law*, Aldershot: Avebury.

Leiser, B.M. (1973) *Liberty, Justice and Morals: Contemporary Value Conflicts*, New York and London: Macmillan.

Leiser, B.M. (1981) *Values in Conflict: Life, Liberty and the Rule of Law*, New York: Macmillan.

Lessnoff, M. (1990) *Social Contract Theory*, Oxford: Blackwell.

Levin, D. (1999) *The Philosopher's Gaze: Modernity in the Shadows of Enlightenment*, Berkeley: University of California Press.

Leyden, W. von (1981) *Hobbes and Locke: The Politics of Freedom and Obligation*, London: Macmillan.

Llewellyn, K. (1930) *The Bramble Bush*, New York: Oceana Publications, 1960.

Lloyd, D. (1964) *The Idea of Law*, London: Penguin.

Locke, J. (1924 [1690]) *Two Treatises of Civil Government*, London: Everyman.

Lyons, D. (1984) *Ethics and the Rule of Law*, Cambridge: Cambridge University Press.

Lyons, D. (1993) *Moral Aspects of Legal Theory: Essays on Law, Justice and Political Responsibility*, Cambridge: Cambridge University Press.

Lyotard, Jean-François (1984) *The Postmodern Condition: A Report on Knowledge*, Manchester: Manchester University Press.

MacCormick, N. (1978) *Legal Reasoning and Legal Theory*, Oxford: Clarendon.

MacCormick, N. (1981) *H.L.A. Hart*, London: Edward Arnold.

MacCormick, N. (1982) *Legal Right and Social Democracy*, Oxford: Clarendon.

MacCormick, N. and Weinberger, O. (1986) *An Institutional Theory of Law: New Approaches to Legal Positivism*, Dordrecht: Kluwer.

McCoubrey, H. (1987) *The Development of Naturalist Legal Theory*, New York: Croom Helm.

MacIntyre, A. (1981) *After Virtue: A Study in Moral Theory*, London: Duckworth.

Mackie, J.L. (1977a) *Ethics: Inventing Right and Wrong*, London: Penguin.

Mackie, J.L. (1977b) 'The Third Theory of Law', *Philosophy & Public Affairs* 7(1) (Fall): 3–16; repr. in J.L. Mackie, *Persons and Values*, Oxford: Clarendon, 1985.

Mackie, J.L. (1985) *Persons and Values*, Oxford: Clarendon.

MacKinnon, C. (1987) *Feminism Unmodified*, Cambridge, MA: Harvard University Press.

McLellan, D. (1973) *Karl Marx: His Life and Thought*, London and Basingstoke: Macmillan.

McLeod, I. (1999) *Legal Theory*, Basingstoke and London: Macmillan.

MacPherson, C.B. (1962) *The Political Theory of Possessive Individualism*, London and New York: Oxford University Press.

McWilliams, P. (1996) *Ain't Nobody's Business If You Do: The Absurdity of Consensual Crimes in Our Free Country*, Los Angeles: Prelude Press.

Mansell, W., Meteyard, B. and Thomson, A. (2004) *A Critical Introduction to Law*, 3rd edn, London, Sydney and Portland, OR: Cavendish.

Marmor, A. (1997) *Law and Interpretation: Essays in Legal Philosophy*, Oxford and New York: Oxford University Press.

Mertens, T. (2005) 'Darker Legacies of Law in Europe: The Shadow of National Socialism and Fascism over Europe and Its Legal Traditions', *Ratio Juris* 18: 285–291.

Meyerson, Denise (2007) *Understanding Jurisprudence*, Abingdon: Routledge.

Midgley, M. (2004) *The Myths We Live By*, London and New York: Routledge.

Mill, J.S. (1972a [1859]) *On Liberty*, London: Everyman.

Mill, J.S. (1972b [1861]) *Utilitarianism*, London: Everyman.

Mitchell, B. (1970) *Law, Morality and Religion in a Secular Society*, London: Oxford University Press.

Montefiore, A. (ed.) (1975) *Neutrality and Impartiality*, New York and London: Cambridge University Press.

Moore, M.S. (1993) *Act and Crime: The Philosophy of Action and Its Implications for Criminal Law*, Oxford: Clarendon.

Moore, R. (1978) *Legal Norms and Legal Science: A Critical Study of Kelsen's Pure Theory of Law*, Honolulu: University Press of Hawaii.

Morris, H. (ed.) (1961) *Freedom and Responsibility: Readings in Philosophy of Law*, Stanford, CA: Stanford University Press.

Morrison, W. (1997) *Jurisprudence: From the Greeks to Postmodernism*, London: Cavendish.

Mulhall, S. and Swift, A. (1996) *Liberals and Communitarians*, 2nd edn, Oxford: Blackwell.

Mundle, C.W.K. (1954) 'Punishment and Desert', in H.B. Acton (ed.), *The Philosophy of Punishment*, London: Macmillan, 1969.

Murdoch, I. (1992) *Metaphysics as a Guide to Morals*, London: Chatto & Windus.

Murphy, J.G. (ed.) (1971) *Civil Disobedience and Violence*, Belmont, CA: Wadsworth.

Murphy, J.G. (1979) *Retribution, Justice and Therapy: Essays in the Philosophy of Law*, Dordrecht and London: Reidel.

Murphy, J.G. (1987) 'Mercy and Legal Justice', in J. Coleman and E.F. Paul, *Philosophy and Law*, Oxford: Blackwell.

Murphy, J.G. and Coleman, J.L. (1990) *Philosophy of Law: An Introduction to Jurisprudence*, San Francisco and London: Westview Press.

Murphy, J.G. and Hampton, J. (1988) *Forgiveness and Mercy*, Cambridge: Cambridge University Press.

Murphy, M. (2007) *Philosophy of Law: The Fundamentals*, Malden, MA, and Oxford: Blackwell.

Nickel, J. (1987) *Making Sense of Human Rights: Philosophical Reflections on the Universal Declaration of Human Rights*, Berkeley: University of California Press.

Nicolson, D. and Bibbings, L. (eds) (2000) *Feminist Perspectives on Criminal Law*, London: Cavendish.

Norrie, A. (1993) *Crime, Reason and History: A Critical Introduction to Criminal Law*, London: Weidenfeld & Nicolson.

Norrie, A. (2001) *Crime, Reason and History: A Critical Introduction to Criminal Law*, 2nd edn, London: Butterworths.

Norrie, A. (2014) *Crime, Reason and History: A Critical Introduction to Criminal Law*, 3rd edn, Cambridge: Cambridge University Press.

Novick, S.M. (1989) *Honourable Justice: The Life of Oliver Wendell Holmes*, New York: Dell.

Nozick, R. (1974) *Anarchy, State and Utopia*, Oxford: Blackwell.

Nozick, R. (1981) *Philosophical Explanations*, Oxford: Clarendon.

Oderberg, D.S. (2000a) *Applied Ethics: A Non-consequentialist Approach*, Oxford: Blackwell.

Oderberg, D.S. (2000b) *Moral Theory: A Non-consequentialist Approach*, Oxford: Blackwell.

Olivecrona, K. (1971 [1939]) *Law as Fact*, London: Stevens & Sons.

Ormerod, D. and Laird, K. (2015) *Smith and Hogan's Criminal Law*, 14th edn, Oxford: Oxford University Press.

Owen, D. (1994) *Maturity and Modernity: Nietzsche, Weber, Foucault and the Ambivalence of Reason*, London & New York: Routledge.

Pateman, C. (1979) *The Problem of Political Obligation: A Critical Analysis of Liberal Theory*, Chichester and New York: John Wiley & Sons.

Patterson, D. (ed.) (1996a) *A Companion to Philosophy of Law and Legal Theory*, Oxford: Blackwell.

Patterson, D. (1996b) *Law and Truth*, New York and Oxford: Oxford University Press.

Patterson, D. (ed.) (2003) *Philosophy of Law and Legal Theory: An Anthology*, Oxford: Blackwell.

Paul, J. (ed.) (1981) *Reading Nozick: Essays on Anarchy, State and Utopia*, Oxford: Blackwell.

Perry, M.J. (1998) *The Idea of Human Rights: Four Inquiries*, Oxford: Oxford University Press.

Porter, R. (1987) *A Social History of Madness: Stories of the Insane*, London: Weidenfeld & Nicolson and Phoenix.

Porter, R. (2000) *Enlightenment: Britain and the Creation of the Modern World*, London and New York: Allen Lane.

Porter, R. (2002) *Madness: A Brief History*, Oxford and New York: Oxford University Press.

Porter, R. (2003) *Flesh in the Age of Reason*, London and New York: Allen Lane.

Poser, N.S. (2013) *Lord Mansfield: Justice in the Age of Reason*, Montreal and London: McGill-Queen's University Press.

Posner, R.A. (1988) *Law and Literature: A Misunderstood Relation*, Cambridge, MA, and London: Harvard University Press.

Posner, R.A. (1990) *The Problems of Jurisprudence*, Cambridge, MA, and London: Harvard University Press.

Postema, G.J. (1986) *Bentham and the Common Law Tradition*, Oxford: Clarendon.

Pound, R. (1969 [1924]) *Law and Morals: The McNair Lectures 1923, Delivered at the University of North Carolina*, New York: Augustus M. Kelly.

Powell, J.G.F. and North, J.A. (eds) (2001) *Cicero's* Republic, London: Institute of Classical Studies.

Primoratz, I. (1989) *Justifying Legal Punishment*, Atlantic Highlands, NJ, and London: Humanities Press.

Raban, O. (2003) *Modern Legal Theory and Judicial Impartiality*, London: GlassHouse.

Radbruch, G. (2006) 'Statutory Lawlessness and Supra-statutory Law', *Oxford Journal of Legal Studies* 26(1): 1–11.

Rawls, J. (1955) 'Two Concepts of Rules', *Philosophical Review* 64 (January): 3–32; repr. in H.B. Acton (ed.), *The Philosophy of Punishment*, London: Macmillan, 1969.

Rawls, J. (1972) *A Theory of Justice*, London: Oxford University Press.

Rawls, J. (1993) *Political Liberalism*, New York: Columbia University Press.

Raz, J. (1970) *The Concept of a Legal System: An Introduction to the Theory of Legal Systems*, Oxford: Clarendon.

Raz, J. (1975) *Practical Reason and Norms*, London: Hutchinson.

Raz, J. (1979) *The Authority of Law: Essays on Law and Morality*, Oxford: Clarendon.

Raz, J. (1986) *The Morality of Freedom*, Oxford: Clarendon.

Raz, J. (1994) *Ethics in the Public Domain*, Oxford: Clarendon.

Reznek, L. (1997) *Evil or Ill? Justifying the Insanity Defence*, London and New York: Routledge.

Richardson, J. and Sandland, R. (eds) (2000) *Feminist Perspectives on Law and Theory*, London: Cavendish.

Riddall, J.G. (1999) *Jurisprudence*, 2nd edn, London: Butterworths.

Robinson, D. (1999) *Nietzsche and Postmodernism*, Cambridge: Icon Books (UK) and Totem Books (USA).

Robinson, D.N. (1996) *Wild Beasts and Idle Humours: The Insanity Defence from Antiquity to the Present*, Cambridge, MA, and London: Harvard University Press.

Rommen, H.A. (1947) *The Natural Law: A Study in Legal and Social History and Philosophy*, trans. T.R. Hanley, St Louis and London: B. Herder.

Ross, A. (1958) *On Law and Justice*, London: Stevens & Sons.

Ross, W.D. (1930) *The Right and the Good*, Oxford: Clarendon.

Royle, N. (2003) *Jacques Derrida*, London: Routledge.

Rumble, W.E., Jr (1968) *American Legal Realism: Scepticism, Reform and the Judicial Process*, Ithaca, NY: Cornell University Press.

Sarat, A. and Kearns, R. (1996) *Legal Rights: Historical and Philosophical Perspectives*, Ann Arbor, MI: University of Michigan Press.

Schauer, F. (1991) *Playing by the Rules*, Oxford: Clarendon.

Schauer, F. (2015) *The Force of Law*, Cambridge, MA, and London: Harvard University Press.

Schmidt, J. (1996) *What Is Enlightenment?* Los Angeles and London: University of California Press.

Schopp, R.F. (1991) *Automatism, Insanity and the Psychology of Criminal Responsibility: A Philosophical Inquiry*, Cambridge: Cambridge University Press.

Schroeder, D.N. (1981) 'Aristotle on Law', *Polis* 4: 17–31.

Shute, S. and Hurley, S. (1993) *On Human Rights: The Oxford Amnesty Lectures*, New York: Basic Books.

Simmonds, N.E. (1986) *Central Issues in Jurisprudence: Justice, Law and Rights*, London: Sweet & Maxwell.

Simmons, A.J., Cohen, M., Cohen, J. and Beitz, C.R. (eds) (1995) *Punishment: A Philosophy and Public Affairs Reader*, Princeton, NJ: Princeton University Press.

Singer, P. (1973) *Democracy and Disobedience*, Oxford: Clarendon Press.

Singer, P. (ed.) (1991) *A Companion to Ethics*, Oxford: Blackwell.

Singer, P. (1993) *Practical Ethics*, Cambridge: Cambridge University Press.

Smith, J.C. (1976) *Legal Obligation*, London: Athlone Press.

Smith, J.C. (2002) *Smith and Hogan: Criminal Law*, 10th edn, London: Butterworths.

Solomon, R.C. (1988) *Continental Philosophy since 1750: The Rise and Fall of the Self*, Oxford and New York: Oxford University Press.

Sorrell, T. (ed.) (1996) *The Cambridge Companion to Hobbes*, Cambridge: Cambridge University Press.

Stacy, H.M. (2001) *Postmodernism and Law: Jurisprudence in a Fragmenting World*, Brookfield, VT, and Aldershot: Dartmouth Publishing Co.

Stephen, J.F. (1874) *Liberty, Equality, Fraternity*, London: Smith Elgard & Co.

Stewart, M.A. (ed.) (1983) *Law, Morality and Rights*, Dordrecht and Boston: Reidel.

Stoljar, S. (1984) *An Analysis of Rights*, London: Macmillan.

Stump, E. (2003) *Aquinas*, London: Routledge

Sturrock, J. (1979) *Structuralism and Since: From Lévi-Strauss to Derrida*, Oxford and New York: Oxford University Press.

Suber, P. (1998) *The Case of the Speluncean Explorers*, London and New York: Routledge.

Summers, R.S. (ed.) (1968) *Essays in Legal Philosophy*, Oxford: Blackwell.

Summers, R.S. (1971) *More Essays in Legal Philosophy*, Oxford: Blackwell.

Summers, R.S. (1984) *Lon L. Fuller*, London: Edward Arnold.

Summers, R.S. (1992) *Essays on the Nature of Law and Legal Reasoning*, Berlin: Duncker & Humbolt.

Szasz, T. (1960) *The Myth of Mental Illness*, New York: Harper & Row.

Taylor, C. (1989) *Sources of the Self: The Making of the Modern Identity*, Cambridge: Cambridge University Press.

Ten, C.L. (1980) *Mill on Liberty*, Oxford: Clarendon.

Ten, C.L. (1987) *Crime, Guilt and Punishment*, Oxford: Clarendon.

Tennant, N. (1997) *The Taming of the True*, London: Cavendish.

Thayer, H.S. (ed.) (1982) *Pragmatism: The Classic Writings*, Indianapolis and Cambridge: Hackett.

Thomson, J.J. (1985) 'The Trolley Problem', *Yale Law Journal* 94(6): 1395–1415.

Thomson, J.J. (1990) *The Realm of Rights*, Cambridge, MA, and London: Harvard University Press.

Thoreau, H.D. (1983 [1849]) *Walden and Civil Disobedience*, New York and London: Penguin.

Toulmin, S. (2001) *Return to Reason*, Cambridge, MA, and London: Harvard University Press.

Tur, R. and Twining, W. (1986) *Essays on Kelsen*, Oxford: Clarendon.

Twining, W. (1973) *Karl Llewellyn and the Realist Movement*, London: Weidenfeld & Nicolson.

Twining, W. (ed.) (1986) *Legal Theory and Common Law*, Oxford: Blackwell.

Twining, W. and Miers, D. (1976) *How to Do Things with Rules: A Primer of Interpretation*, London: Weidenfeld & Nicolson.

von Hirsch, A. (1993) 'Censure and Proportionality', in R.A. Duff and D. Garland (eds), *A Reader on Punishment*, Oxford: Oxford University Press.

Waldron, J. (ed.) (1984) *Theories of Rights*, Oxford: Oxford University Press.

Waldron, J. (ed.) (1987) *Nonsense upon Stilts: Bentham, Burke and Marx on the Rights of Man*, London: Methuen.

Walker, N. (1991) *Why Punish?* Oxford: Oxford University Press.

Walker, N. and Padfield, N. (1996) *Sentencing: Theory, Law and Practice*, London: Butterworths.

Waluchow, W. and Sciaraffa, S. (2016) *The Legacy of Ronald Dworkin*, Oxford: Oxford University Press.

Wasserstrom, R.A. (ed.) (1971) *Morality and the Law*, Belmont, CA: Wadsworth.

Weinreb, L. (1987) *Natural Law and Justice*, Cambridge, MA, and London: Harvard University Press.

West, D.J. and Walk, A. (eds) (1977) *Daniel M'Naghten: His Trial and the Aftermath*, Ashford: Gaskell Books, *Br J Psychiatry*.

Williams, G. (1987) 'Oblique Intention', *California Law Journal* 46: 417–421.

Williams, P. (1991) *The Alchemy of Race and Rights: Diary of a Law Professor*, Cambridge, MA: Harvard University Press.

Wolfenden Committee (1957) *Report of the Committee on Homosexual Offences and Prostitution* (Cmnd 247) London: HMSO.

Wolin, R. (2004) *The Seduction of Unreason: The Intellectual Romance with Fascism from Nietzsche to Postmodernism*, Princeton, NJ: Princeton University Press.

Wollstonecraft, M. (1967 [1792]) *Vindication of the Rights of Women*, New York: W.W. Norton.

Woolhouse, R.S. (1988) *The Empiricists*, Oxford: Oxford University Press.

Wootton, B. (1981) *Crime and the Criminal Law*, London: Stevens & Sons.

Yang, K. (2012) 'The Rise of Legal Positivism in Germany: A Prelude to Nazi Arbitrariness?', *Western Australian Jurist* 3: 245–257.

Zetzel, J.E.G. (ed.) (1999) *Cicero: On the Commonwealth and On the Laws*, Cambridge: Cambridge University Press.

Index